THOMAS CROMWELL

THOMAS CROMWELL

The untold story of Henry VIII's most faithful servant

TRACY BORMAN

Atlantic Monthly Press
New York

First published in Great Britain in 2014 by
Hodder & Stoughton

Printed in the United States of America

ISBN 978-0-8021-2317-6
eISBN 978-0-8021-9166-3

Atlantic Monthly Press
an imprint of Grove/Atlantic, Inc.
154 West 14th Street
New York, NY 10011

Distributed by Publishers Group West

www.groveatlantic.com

15 16 17 18 19 20 10 9 8 7 6 5 4 3 2 1

Also by Tracy Borman

Witches: A tale of Sorcery, Scandal and Seduction
Matilda: Wife of the Conqueror, First Queen of England
Elizabeth's Women: The Hidden Story of the Virgin Queen
Henrietta Howard: King's Mistress, Queen's Servant

CONTENTS

To the other Thomas (Tom),
with love.

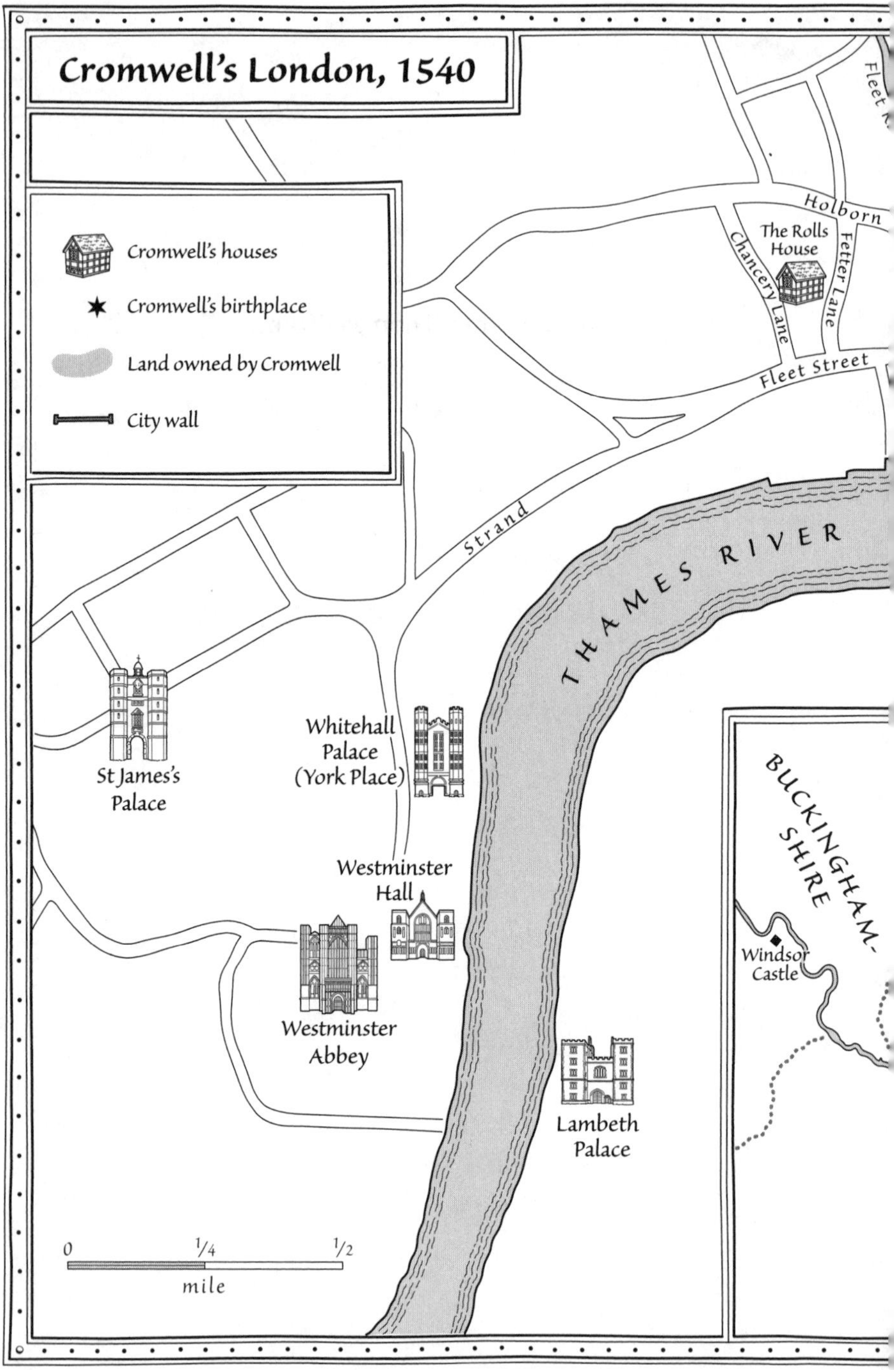
Cromwell's London, 1540
Cromwell's houses
Cromwell's birthplace
Land owned by Cromwell
City wall
Fleet
Holborn
The Rolls House
Chancery Lane
Fetter Lane
Fleet Street
Strand
THAMES RIVER
St James's Palace
Whitehall Palace (York Place)
Westminster Hall
Westminster Abbey
Lambeth Palace
BUCKINGHAM-SHIRE
Windsor Castle
0
1/4
1/2
mile

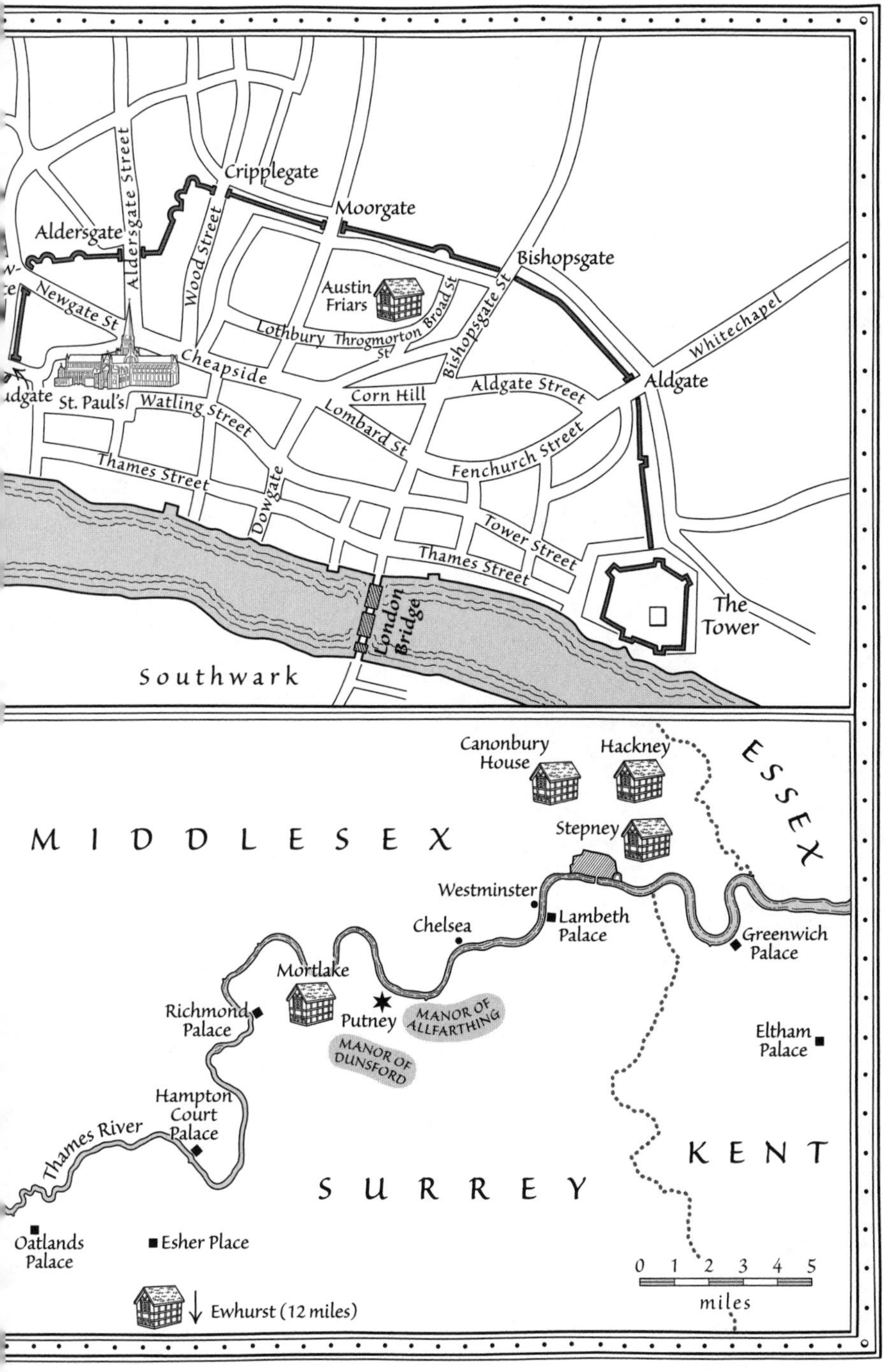
Cripplegate
Moorgate
Aldersgate
Aldersgate Street
Wood Street
Bishopsgate
Austin Friars
Newgate St
Throgmorton St
Broad St
Bishopsgate St
Whitechapel
Lothbury
Cheapside
Aldgate
St. Paul's
Watling Street
Corn Hill
Aldgate Street
Lombard St
Fenchurch Street
Thames Street
Dowgate
Tower Street
Thames Street
London Bridge
The Tower
Southwark
Canonbury House
Hackney
ESSEX
MIDDLESEX
Stepney
Westminster
Lambeth Palace
Chelsea
Greenwich Palace
Mortlake
Richmond Palace
Putney
MANOR OF ALLFARTHING
MANOR OF DUNSFORD
Eltham Palace
Hampton Court Palace
Thames River
KENT
SURREY
Oatlands Palace
Esher Place
0 1 2 3 4 5
miles
Ewhurst (12 miles)

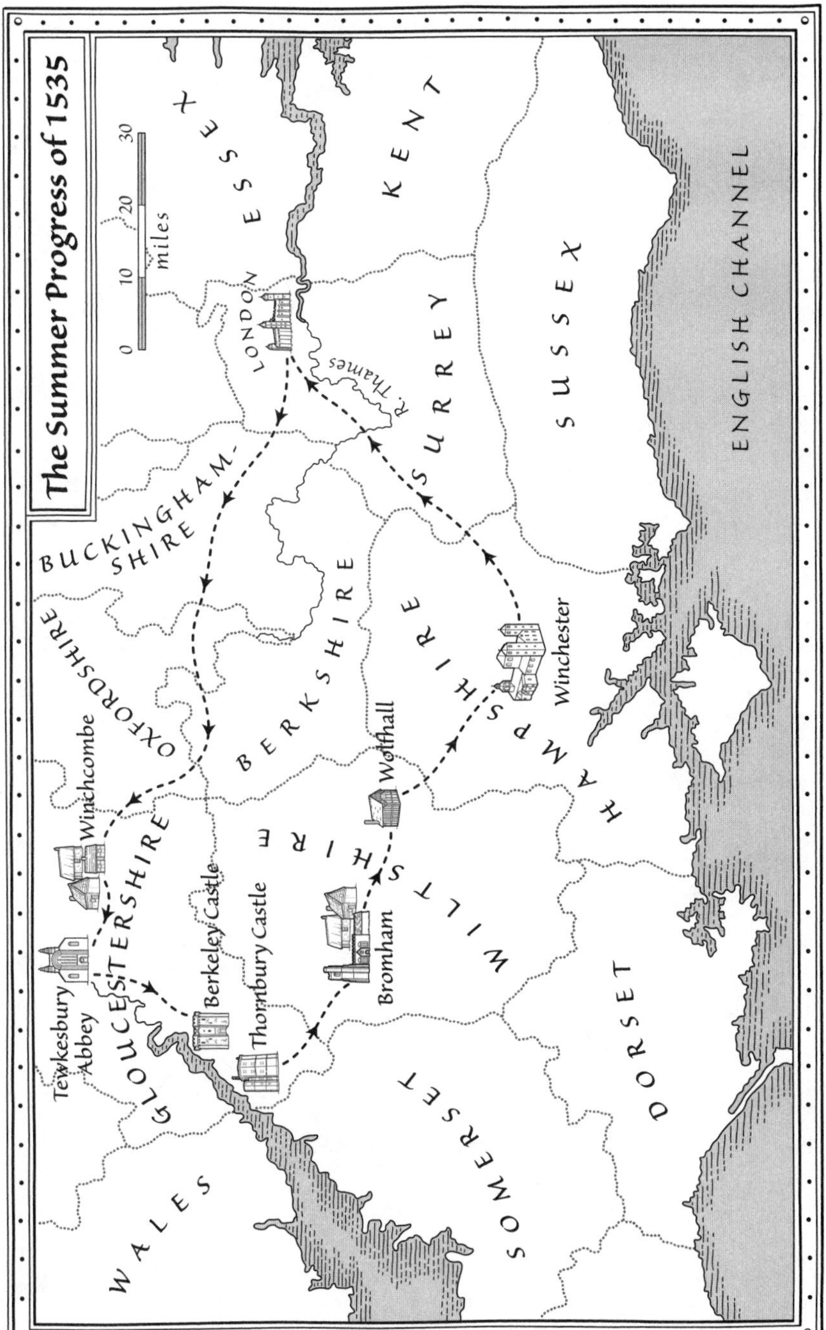
The Summer Progress of 1535
0
10
20
30
miles
ESSEX
KENT
LONDON
R. Thames
SURREY
SUSSEX
ENGLISH CHANNEL
BUCKINGHAM-SHIRE
OXFORDSHIRE
BERKSHIRE
HAMPSHIRE
Winchester
Wolfhall
WILTSHIRE
Bromham
Thornbury Castle
Berkeley Castle
Winchcombe
Tewkesbury Abbey
GLOUCESTERSHIRE
WALES
SOMERSET
DORSET

INTRODUCTION

A portrait that hangs in the Frick Collection in New York has attracted more attention in recent years than ever before. Painted by the celebrated Tudor master, Hans Holbein, it depicts a man who has divided historians as much as he did contemporaries. Reviled by many as a Machiavellian schemer who destroyed England's monasteries, ousted one queen and had another executed, and stopped at nothing in his quest for power, he has recently enjoyed a rehabilitation as an enlightened, pious and dedicated royal servant whose intelligence, wit and hospitality endeared him to friends and enemies alike. His name is Thomas Cromwell.

The publication of Hilary Mantel's *Wolf Hall* in 2009 and its sequel *Bring up the Bodies* three years later took the world by storm. They inspired a sell-out season of plays by the Royal Shakespeare Company, a major television dramatisation and two Booker Prizes for the author. Mantel's achievement has been to create a sympathetic and utterly compelling character out of one of history's most unlikely heroes. Her novels give us the private man behind the often notorious public façade. But how much can we really know about Cromwell? The accepted wisdom of historians has for many years been that his voluminous correspondence provides an appraisal only of the public man. Evidence of his private life, character, beliefs and outlook is at best fragmentary. As I discovered when researching my biography of Cromwell, this is a view at once misleading and inaccurate. By piecing together details found in the many letters, notes and accounts that were seized upon his arrest, a fascinating and very personal portrayal emerges of Henry VIII's chief minister.

It is a portrayal that was only partially captured by Holbein. By the time he painted Cromwell around 1532, the artist had won justifiable renown for his skill at bringing out the character of the sitter, not just their status. Among his most celebrated works was a full-length portrait of King Henry VIII. But his portrait of Cromwell was altogether different. It is one of the most extraordinarily revealing portraits of the Tudor age. Far from flattering the sitter, it offers a brutally honest appraisal. The first impression is of a pensive and rather grumpy bureaucrat. Cromwell has a bulky frame and appears to be of middling height, although as he is seated this is difficult to judge. Turned a little to the right, his small, prying grey eyes stare intently at something in the middle distance. His eyebrows are slightly raised in a questioning, vaguely cynical stance, and his long, thin lips are pressed together in a line. The large, bulbous nose and double chin hint at the sitter's age, as well as his portliness.

Although finely made of high-quality fabrics, Cromwell's cap and gown are hardly the attire of a fashionable courtier. Both are in sombre black, with a brown fur collar. This may have reflected Cromwell's distaste for ostentation, or it may have been a pragmatic choice. Henry VIII had laid down a strict set of guidelines to regulate dressing for court, all of which were closely tied to a person's status. The royal family alone could wear purple; dukes and marquesses could fashion the sleeves of their cloaks from gold silks; earls could wear sables; barons were entitled to a mantle of fine cloth from the Netherlands trimmed with crimson or blue velvet; and knights were permitted a shirt of damask and a collar of golden tissue. No matter how high he had risen at court by this time, Cromwell was still a man of lowly birth with none of these titles, so he was denied the privilege of wearing the rich colours and fabrics that accompanied them. He need not have chosen such plain clothes as he commonly wore, but evidence of his no-nonsense character suggests that he preferred them.

Holbein's portrait presents a compelling testament to Cromwell's brilliant mind and enormous capacity for hard work. It is as if the painter has happened upon him in his study, deep in thought on some weighty matter, his expression determined. He sits on a long panelled bench or chair, behind which is a richly decorated wall. A finely bound book sits on the desk in front of him, flanked by a cluster of letters and a quill. In his left hand, which bears two large rings, he holds another letter. The scene suggests that the minister has just received a dispatch, the contents of which have required careful thought before he decided upon the appropriate response. This is no unworldly academic, but a man of action, a shrewd and decisive pragmatist driven by a desire to succeed in all things.

If Holbein achieved a convincing, albeit unforgiving portrait of an extraordinarily active and ambitious courtier, he gives little sense of Cromwell's more endearing characteristics. His ready wit, brilliant conversation, irreverence and warmth are left to his own letters and the accounts of others to portray. According to Eustace Chapuys, ambassador of the Holy Roman Emperor Charles V, whose sprawling territories included Germany, the Netherlands, Spain and parts of Italy, Cromwell's awkward gait and dull air would suddenly be transformed when he was engaged in a conversation that interested him. His face would light up and take on a range of expressions – from intelligent and amused to cunning and thoughtful. On such occasions, he was at his most charming, entertaining everyone present with his quick wit and warm good humour. When Cromwell made a cutting or irreverent remark, the ambassador noted that he would give a roguish sideways glance to those with whom he conversed. With chameleon-like ability, he would adapt himself to his audience and his surroundings, at turns flattering or destroying his companions with a well-directed compliment or an acerbic put-down. The sixteenth-century historian John Foxe claimed that he had 'suche a dexteritie of wytt as England shal skarsly have agayne'.[1] Even Cromwell's enemies conceded that his social skills, charm and hospitality were second to none. Chapuys describes how the most seasoned courtiers could be completely disarmed by his pleasing manner, and lulled into saying things that they later regretted.

Neglecting Cromwell's personal qualities was no oversight on Holbein's part. It was as the public statesman, not the private man, that Cromwell would have wished to be remembered for posterity, and it is easy to imagine his instructing Holbein to ensure that the portrait reflected this. His practical, businesslike nature had been evident on numerous occasions by the time Holbein began his study. Cromwell's contemptuous description of how he had 'indured' his first parliament of 1523, with its long and rambling debates, only to be 'lefte wher we begann' by the end of it, is an early example of this.[2] Another is a conversation he was recorded as having with Cardinal Pole at Wolsey's house on the subject of how best to serve a prince. Pole launched into a lengthy monologue about the most effective way to enhance the honour of one's master when he was rudely interrupted by Cromwell. The latter told him to set aside the academic tomes he had been reading and take instruction from a practical new book: Machiavelli's *The Prince* – the most notorious work of political pragmatism in history, from which the phrase 'the end justifies the means' is often (mistakenly) quoted. Cromwell explained that the single most useful art of the politician was to see through the disguise that sovereigns tend to throw over their true desires, and to devise the best way to satisfy these desires without upsetting morality or religion. This was rather ironic, given the extent to which Cromwell would 'upset' the moral and religious life of England in his quest for power.

Cromwell's pragmatism enabled him to keep emotion out of his political and business affairs. His emotions were apparently strictly reserved for his personal relationships. Time and again, his actions would testify to his measured, expedient and occasionally ruthless nature. He did not flinch from sending men (and women) to their deaths if it was a matter of political necessity. Neither, it seems, did he have any qualms about determining the outcome of a trial before it had taken place. Thus, he drafted a memorandum with instructions for 'the Abbott of Redyng to be Sent Down to be tryed & excecutyd'.[3] In stark contrast to his adversary, the Duke of Norfolk, who once lost his temper and threatened to beat the king's elder daughter Mary, Cromwell never struck out in anger or passion, but in a considered way, planned and timed to perfection. As Roger Merriman, the nineteenth-century editor of his correspondence observed: 'He kept his eyes steadily fixed upon the goal; the smoothness or roughness of the road to it was of no consequence in his eyes.'[4] The recorded instances of his displaying any emotion are rare. The tears he shed upon learning of the fall of Cardinal Wolsey, chief minister of Henry VIII, were, arguably, as much for himself as for his beleaguered master.

In his personal life Cromwell was altogether different. The records provide a glimpse of a loving husband and father, a devoted friend and a tireless helper of the poor, widows and others in distress who appealed for his assistance. He was also intensely loyal to those whom he served, from his first master in Italy, Francesco Frescobaldi, to the man who launched his political career, Cardinal Wolsey, and – above all – his royal master.

But to separate Cromwell's personal and public relationships is to view the Tudor court through modern eyes. It is neither instructive nor authentic. Henry conducted as much business in the privy chamber as he did in the Privy Council. The otherwise distasteful job of groom of the stool was one of the most sought-after positions at court because of the privileged access it afforded to the king. The same blurring of domestic and official functions was evident in Cromwell's household. Service to his royal master was not something he retired from at the end of the day. His house at Austin Friars was filled with secretaries, clerks and messengers, as well as his family and domestic staff. He regularly hosted Privy Council meetings, and would discuss diplomatic affairs with the Imperial ambassador while watching his hawks circle above his back garden. The only surviving letter from Cromwell to his wife is at least as much about business as about personal concerns. Far from being problematic, this intermingling of the private and public lives of Henry VIII's chief minister is the key to understanding his character.

CHAPTER 1

'A great traveller in the world'

THE MAN WHO would one day become the most powerful in England was of such humble origins that nobody can be sure when or where he was born. In his famous account of sixteenth-century martyrs, John Foxe described Thomas Cromwell as 'a man but of a base stock and house'.[1] The likeliest date for his birth is 1485, which, if true, would be satisfyingly appropriate for it was in this year that the Tudors came to power. Henry Tudor's victory over Richard III at Bosworth Field has been hailed ever since as one of the momentous dates in history. It brought to an end the Wars of the Roses, the conflict between the rival branches of the royal House of Plantagenet (York and Lancaster), which had torn England apart for more than three decades. But, at the time, nobody could have predicted that this obscure Welshman, a Lancastrian with a dubious claim to the throne, would establish a dynasty that would dominate English and European politics, religion and society for more than a century.

Significant though it was, the dawn of a new dynasty, which took place on a remote Leicestershire field in August 1485, must have seemed a world away to the inhabitants of Putney, where Thomas Cromwell's family lived and worked. It was probably either in this small village to the west of London or in nearby Wimbledon that Cromwell was born. John Foxe noted that Cromwell was born 'of a simple Parentage, and a House obscure . . . at Putney or thereabouts'.[2] Tradition has it that his birthplace was at the top of Putney Hill, on the edge of Putney Heath – a notorious haunt of highwaymen.[3]

The Cromwells were not originally from this corner of south-west London, but from Norwell in Nottinghamshire. They were then a family of wealth and status, and John Cromwell (Thomas's grandfather) was both well-known and highly respected. By 1461, he had moved with his family and brother-in-law, William Smith, to Wimbledon, where he was granted the lease of a fulling-mill and house by the Archbishop of Canterbury.[4] His eldest son, John, moved to Lambeth and became a prosperous brewer, later securing the position of cook to the archbishop.[5] His second son, Walter, meanwhile, remained in Wimbledon and was probably apprenticed to his uncle because he took the name Smith.

The records suggest that Thomas was the youngest of three children, and the only boy, born to Walter Cromwell and his wife Katherine née Meverell. He may have been an unexpected child since he was considerably younger than his sisters. In the only recorded reference to his mother, Thomas made the unlikely claim that she was fifty-two when she bore him.[6] The only details that can be found about Katherine in the contemporary records were that she was the aunt of Nicholas Glossop of Wirksworth in Derbyshire, and that she was living in the house of a Putney attorney, John Welbeck, at the time of her marriage around 1474. The fact that Nicholas was more than thirty years older than his cousin adds weight to the theory that Thomas was the youngest of Katherine's children.

Walter Cromwell, meanwhile, was an enterprising man with a number of different but presumably complementary professions, as a blacksmith, brewer and fuller (cloth dresser). According to contemporary sources, Walter had served as a farrier in Henry Tudor's contingent at the Battle of Bosworth. As such, he would hardly have been in the thick of the battle, but the fact that he chose, or was chosen, to serve the invading army, rather than the superior force of the reigning king, Richard III, is interesting. That the Cromwells should be in the Tudors' service as soon as they landed on English soil seems very apt given the career of Walter's son.

The Cromwell family had owned a fulling mill at Putney for fifty years. Walter also owned a hostelry, called the Anchor, and a brewery, along with two virgates (sixty acres) of land. In the Close Rolls of

Henry VII's reign, he is listed as a 'bere-bruer'.[7] His success as a local tradesman was recognised by regular calls to serve as a juryman, and then his appointment as constable of Putney in 1495. He also rapidly acquired new land, and by 1500 he owned eight virgates (an amount of land that could be ploughed by two oxen). The family home and brewery were opposite the top of the appropriately named Brewhouse Lane, which today still runs the short distance from Putney Bridge Road to the River Thames. At the river's edge was a landing site for river-borne craft, and this was a common stopping place for people on their way from London to the towns and villages of west Surrey and the counties beyond. A house by the river in modern-day Putney would demand a premium, but the area was a good deal less salubrious in the sixteenth century. A fishery stood at the other end of Brewhouse Lane, so the Cromwells' home would have been constantly assaulted by the pungent smells emanating from it.

There is no record of what the house was like, but given Walter's status in the local community and his various business interests, he could probably have afforded a home with rather more comforts than most other residents of Putney. The majority of houses were built with timber and wattle and daub, rather than bricks. The timber frames were often coated with black tar to prevent them from rotting, and the walls in between were whitewashed. The predominance of wood made these houses susceptible to fire, and if Walter Cromwell's smithy was close to the family home, theirs would have been at greater risk than most. It was common for ordinary houses to have just one room, which would serve as a kitchen, bathroom, bedroom and living room. Some of the larger houses, such as the Cromwells may have owned, would have had one or two partitions to separate these functions, and an outdoor privy was usual for most dwellings. The Tudor period saw the widespread introduction of fireplaces and accompanying chimneys in more affluent households, replacing the open hearths in the centre of the room that were normally found in medieval and poorer dwellings. Even so, houses of both classes were generally cold and draughty, and many people brought their animals inside to help generate warmth in the winter months. Furniture would be sparse and simple, such as benches, stools, tables and chests. People slept on mattresses stuffed with straw and ridden with vermin of all kinds. Carpets were the luxury of the rich, and ordinary people strewed the floor of their home with rushes, reeds and sweet-smelling herbs. The herbs were required to cover a variety of unpleasant aromas, including the tallow candles and rush lights that were made from animal fat, not to mention the smell of the infrequently washed occupants.

The London that Thomas Cromwell would have known as a youth was described by Andreas Franciscius, an Italian visitor, in November 1497: 'Its position is so pleasant and delightful that it would be hard to find one more convenient and attractive,' he wrote. 'It stands on the banks of the river Thames, the biggest river in the whole island, which divides the town into two parts.' Franciscius estimated that the city itself was no more than three miles in circumference, but added: 'Its suburbs are so large that they greatly increase its circuit.' He went on to describe some of the more notable landmarks:

> It is defended by handsome walls, especially on the northern side, where they have recently been rebuilt. Within these stands a very strongly defended castle on the banks of the river [the Tower of London], where the King of England and his Queen sometimes have their residence. There are also other great buildings, and especially a beautiful and convenient bridge over the Thames, of many marble arches, which has on it many shops built of stone and mansions and even a church of considerable size. Nowhere have I seen a finer or more richly built bridge.

Unencumbered by modern flood barriers, the daily coming in of the tide was a spectacular event: 'The ocean is sixty miles from the city, but notwithstanding this, its high tide is so strong and flows up the Thames with such power that it not only stops the river's current, but even pushes it back and forces it to return upstream, which is a wonderful sight.'

Franciscius went on to describe the 'many workshops of craftsmen in all sorts of mechanical arts', including blacksmiths, like Cromwell's father. Even the food met with the visitor's approval.

> They delight in banquets and variety of meat and food, and they excel everyone in preparing them with excessive abundance. They eat very frequently, at times more than is suitable, and are particularly fond of young swans, rabbits, deer and sea birds. They often eat mutton and beef, which is generally considered to be better here than anywhere else in the world. This is due to the excellence of their pastures. They have all kinds of fish in plenty and great quantities of oysters which come from the sea-shore. The majority, not to say everyone, drink that beverage I have spoken of before [ale], and prepare it in various ways. For wine is very expensive, as the vine does not grow in this island.[8]

Not everything was to Franciscius's liking, however.

> All the streets are so badly paved that they get wet at the slightest quantity of water, and this happens very frequently owing to the large numbers of cattle carrying water, as well as on account of the rain, of which there is a great deal in this island. Then a vast amount of evil-smelling mud is formed, which does not disappear quickly but lasts a long time, in fact nearly the whole year round. The citizens, therefore, in order to remove this mud and filth from their boots, are accustomed to spread fresh rushes on the floors of all houses, on which they clean the soles of their shoes when they come in.

He was also shocked by the 'fierce tempers and wicked dispositions' of the Londoners, and abhorred the contempt and neglect they showed to their children.

Walter Cromwell seemed to conform to this stereotype, particularly in his relationship with his son Thomas. He did at least secure good marriages for his daughters, although this may have been more to consolidate his own social standing than out of concern for their happiness. The elder, Katherine, married an aspiring Welsh lawyer named Morgan Williams, whose family had moved to Putney from Glamorganshire. Morgan's brother was an important man in Putney, being the steward to John, Lord Scales of Nayland. Katherine's younger sister Elizabeth married a sheep farmer, William Wellyfed, who later joined his business to that of his father-in-law.

Despite being a man of some standing in the local community, Walter was often in trouble with the law. He was fined six pence by the manor court on no fewer than forty-eight occasions between 1475 and 1501 for 'breaches of the assizes of ale', which meant that he had been watering down the beer he sold.[9] Such offences had become increasingly common as the fifteenth century progressed, which prompted the Brewers' Company to issue a set of stringent ordinances to ensure that all those 'occupying the craft of brewing' should make 'good and hable ale, according in strength and fineness to the price of malt'. Official tasters were appointed to carry out random checks on the city's brewers, so Walter's attempts to increase his profits in this way were soon discovered.[10] It is possible that he had been assisted in this business by his wife: brewing was one of the few professions in which wives were actively encouraged to participate. The poet John Skelton created a satirical portrait of a harridan ale-wife, whose drunken antics won such women notoriety – often ill-deserved. Although there were local entrepreneurs like Walter and his wife, it was England's monastic communities that were the real centre of brewing excellence. It is ironic that the son of a brewing family would orchestrate their downfall, which in turn had a devastating impact upon the country's brewing industry.

Brewing was not the only activity that landed Walter Cromwell in trouble with the law. He was frequently reprimanded for allowing his cattle to graze too freely on public land. His most serious conviction came in 1477 when he was found guilty of assault. He had 'drawn blood' from a man named William Michell and was fined twenty pence. Walter and his father John were also regularly brought before the local court on charges of 'overburthening' the public land in Putney with their cattle, and cutting more than their share of the furze and thorns there.[11] Increasingly unpopular with the local community, Walter was finally evicted from his manorial tenancy in 1514, after 'falsely and fraudulently' altering documents concerning his tenure.[12] All his lands were forfeited, and the fact that he is mentioned no more in the records suggests that he may have died shortly afterwards.

An intriguing remark made by Walter's son Thomas many years later hints that he had inherited some of his father's less admirable traits. He would confide to Archbishop Thomas Cranmer what a 'ruffian he was in his young days'.[13] The Imperial ambassador, Eustace Chapuys, claimed that 'Cromwell was illbehaved when young, and after an imprisonment was forced to leave the country.'[14] Although there is no other evidence to corroborate this, it was possible for a father to have his son imprisoned without legal process in this period.

There are no other details of Thomas's childhood and education. Given Walter's standing in the community, and his various sources of income, it might be reasonable to assume that he had invested in some schooling for his son. But according to an account of Cromwell's life published in 1715, 'this Great Man's Father, being of so low a Vocation, was not in a Capacity to bestow much on his Son's Education.' That Cromwell was self-taught is also suggested by the Elizabethan chronicler Ralph Holinshed, who claimed that he had a 'bely of knowledge, gathered by painefull trauaile'. It was common for children to leave the family home between the ages of seven and nine in order to enter 'hard service in the houses of other people'. These apprenticeships would generally last for a further seven or nine years, 'and during that time they perform all the most menial of offices'. There is no record of Cromwell having been an apprentice, but Holinshed records that 'few are born who are exempted from this fate.'[15]

The records hint at a difficult relationship between the two male members of the Cromwell household. If Thomas was a chip off the old block, this apparently did little to endear him to his father, and it may have been a row between them that prompted his decision to leave Putney around 1503. The contemporary Italian novelist Matteo Bandello claims that Cromwell was fleeing from his father.[16]

John Foxe paints a rather rosier picture, claiming that 'in his growing years, as he shot up in age and ripeness, a great delight came into his mind to stray into forreign Countries to see the World abroad, and to learn experience.'[17]

Not content with simply escaping the family home, Thomas left England altogether. In an age when people rarely ventured beyond the boundaries of their immediate locality, and those from other counties were viewed as 'foreigners', this was an extraordinarily daring and adventurous enterprise, especially for one of his lowly status. A play written about his life and published in 1602 has the young Cromwell already dreaming of making his fortune, and telling his father: 'The time will come when I shall hold gold as trash . . . Why should my birth keep down my mounting spirit?'[18] This image of youthful ambition is seductive. It is possible that Cromwell had already secured employment abroad before he left London. The capital was full of merchants from overseas, as Franciscius describes:

> not only Venice but also Florence and Lucca, and many from Genoa and Pisa, from Spain, Germany, the Rhine valley and other countries meet here to handle business with utmost keenness, having come from the different parts of the world. But the chief exports from the island are wool and fabrics, considered the best in the world, and white lead, for the island is more freely endowed with these commodities than any other country. By sea and the Thames goods of all kinds can be brought into London and taken from the city to other destinations.[19]

Cromwell may have made contact with one of these merchants through his father's businesses.

It is not clear how he raised the money for the voyage: the notion of him as a penniless young stowaway is appealing, but he might equally have taken a job on the ship. A large vessel, such as Henry VIII's ill-fated flagship, the *Mary Rose*, could have a crew of up to 400 men. This included servants, cooks, pursers and surgeons, as well as the sailors and officers. Cromwell could have secured one of the lowlier positions. As Foxe later observed: 'Nothing was so hard which with wit and industry he could not compass.'[20]

Cromwell went first to the Netherlands, and travelled from there to France. The records provide little clue as to where precisely he lived, or how he earned money enough to survive. The first recorded mention of him is in late autumn 1503, when he joined an expedition to Italy as part of the French army. It is not clear how long he had served by this time. The fact that he would later demonstrate an unusually detailed knowledge of the French military system suggests that he may already have gained some experience by the time that he embarked for Italy. According to his future adversary, Cardinal Reginald Pole, Cromwell served as a 'gregarium militem' or 'common soldier'. Although Scottish soldiers often fought for France, it was very unusual for English ones to do so in this period. Cromwell may have been inspired by examples from the fourteenth century, when English mercenaries made their fortunes fighting in Italy. If he thought service with the French was a path to riches and glory, however, he was to be disappointed.

Since the late fifteenth century, the Italian states had been the focus of a bitter power struggle between France and Spain. The latest set of wars had begun four years earlier when the French king, Louis XII, had pressed his claim to the duchy of Milan and Naples. Until then, the French and Spanish forces had been allied in their campaign to take the latter city, but they had argued over its partition and war had broken out. The Spanish had won a crushing victory over the French at Cerignola in April 1503. Undeterred, in mid-November the French army gathered at the mouth of the Garigliano River, some sixty kilometres north of Naples. The Spanish made several attempts to cross the river, and finally succeeded during the night of 28–29 December, taking the French by surprise. Camped in marshy and unhealthy conditions, the French army was depleted by sickness and no match for the pikemen, swordsmen and arquebusiers of the Spanish infantry. Despite the heroic defence of the bridge over the Garigliano by the celebrated French knight, the Chevalier de Bayard, the French were pushed back into Gaeta and surrendered.

The defeat, and the miserable conditions that the French had endured during the weeks leading up to it, may have convinced Cromwell to abandon the military life as quickly as possible. He deserted his post soon afterwards but decided to stay in Italy, rather than return – defeated – to England. That he was living in Italy during one of the most culturally vibrant periods of its history would have a profound impact on his character, beliefs and interests. This was the age when Raphael, Bellini and Titian were crafting their masterpieces in Florence and Venice, when the Borgias were dominating the political and religious life of the Papal States, and Niccolò Machiavelli was beginning to exert his influence in the government of Florence. The Italy of the High Renaissance still retained its individualism and its society was devoted more to aesthetics than to morals. But the glories of its artistic and intellectual achievements starkly contrasted with the violence and bloodshed that the climate and native temperament made common. The beautiful piazzas to which the cultural and political elite flocked in the daytime were the scenes of brawls, stabbings and murders at night. For the young Cromwell, it would be a training-ground as brutal as it was enlightened.

Cromwell is next recorded in Florence, which was the birthplace of the Renaissance, an explosion of cultural and intellectual ideas that drew upon classical influences and transformed art, literature, philosophy, politics and religion across Europe. Such was its influence that the Renaissance is commonly viewed as the bridge between the medieval and modern world. One of its central ideas was the search for realism and human emotion in art, and the highly stylised paintings and sculptures of the medieval period were replaced by works of startlingly precise detail that brought subjects vividly to life.

Thanks in no small part to the patronage of the powerful Medici family, de facto rulers of the republic, Florence had become the most vibrant of all the Italian Renaissance cities, boasting such masters as Giotto, Fra Angelico and Botticelli. Adorned with exquisite paintings, frescos, sculptures and buildings, it was a city of incomparable beauty, famous throughout the world. The precise date of Cromwell's arrival there is not known but it would have been some time before June 1504, by which time he had entered the household of the powerful Florentine merchant banker, Francesco Frescobaldi. The Frescobaldis had been renowned financiers since the twelfth century. As well as becoming prominent in the public affairs of Florence, they had established an extremely profitable business in England, and by the end of the thirteenth century they had risen to the position of royal bankers, financing the wars of Edward I and II. Described as 'a very loyal and honourable merchant', Francesco was 'very rich' and 'carried on a great business' in trade across Europe. He lived mostly in London, although Cromwell encountered him on one of his returns to Florence. The contemporary novelist Bandello tells of how the merchant saw Cromwell ('a poor youth') begging for alms in the streets. When he stopped to speak to him, Cromwell pleaded 'for the love of God' for him to help. Observing that he was 'ill accoutred' but showed 'signs of gentle breeding in his countenance', Frescobaldi took pity on him. When he learned that the youth was from England, a country he knew and loved well, he asked who he was. 'I am called Thomas Cromwell,' he replied, 'the son of a poor clothdresser.'[21] He went on to recount how he had escaped from the Battle of Garigliano. The wealthy merchant apparently needed no further persuasion: he took Cromwell into his household, where he gave him food, clothes and shelter.

Although unauthenticated, the account is credible. Bandello's stories were based upon real-life events, and Cromwell's later history would prove his remarkable ability to win favour with members of the elite. It is corroborated by the accounts of Chapuys and Reginald Pole, both of whom knew Cromwell personally. The only inconsistency was that Bandello has Cromwell stating that his father was a shearman (a shearer of wool), rather than a blacksmith or one of his other professions. This confusion could have arisen from the fact that after Walter's death Cromwell's mother had married a wool shearer.[22]

Cromwell evidently justified Frescobaldi's faith in him and served him loyally and ably. Bandello describes him as 'a youth of exceeding high spirit, quick-witted and prompt of resolution, knowing excellent well to accommodate himself to the wishes of others, and could, whenas himseemed to the purpose, dissemble his passions better than any man in the world.'[23] These character traits, honed during his time in Italy, would serve Cromwell extremely well upon his return to England. He would also gain invaluable experience and knowledge while serving Frescobaldi. Florence was at that time a republic, and the politician, diplomat and humanist scholar Niccolò Machiavelli was an active member of its government. Credibility might just be stretched far enough to say that Cromwell learned of, and possibly admired, his methods, but the two would almost certainly never have met: Cromwell was far too lowly a resident of the republic to cross paths with such a distinguished leader.

Frescobaldi was renowned for his 'great hospitality' and lived 'very splendidly', so Cromwell enjoyed a very comfortable life in his household. It may also have inspired the future hospitality for which he himself became famous. As one of the richest and most prominent members of the Florentine nobility, Francesco employed the finest cooks, musicians and players to feed and entertain his guests. Among the family's most profitable businesses was the production of Tuscan wine, at which they had been expert since the early fourteenth century. They would later supply the court of Henry VIII himself. Frescobaldi was a great lover of art and had established a mutually beneficial arrangement with the celebrated Michelangelo, whereby he traded wine for paintings. Cromwell would therefore have been surrounded by some of the finest works of the Renaissance. Little wonder that he became such a lover of art from that time onward.

The merchant took his English protégé with him when he travelled on business in Italy, and on the last occasion he left him in the service of a Venetian merchant. There was no hint of a disagreement, however, for Frescobaldi gave Cromwell a handsome parting gift of sixteen gold ducats and a strong horse. Cardinal Pole confirms that Cromwell was subsequently employed as an accountant to a Venetian trader whom Pole knew well.[24]

Cromwell's movements after that time are not certain, but it is likely that he soon left Italy and spent some time travelling in other parts of Europe. He was certainly in the Netherlands for a time, where he worked as a cloth merchant. There were strong trading links between Venice and Antwerp, so it is possible that these prompted his travels. There could have been no better training-ground for a future English statesman than the greatest commercial capital in the world. Antwerp was a vibrant and cosmopolitan city, with thousands of businessmen from all the trading nations of Europe. Half of all the English wool and cloth exports passed through the city, and Cromwell would have experienced first-hand the economic struggle as the Merchant Adventurers, a company of London's leading overseas merchants, tried to convert these raw exports into the finished article, thus deriving the maximum possible profit. After a time, Cromwell entered the service of some merchants of the English House, and he subsequently established himself as a trader in his own right.

Many years later, a merchant named George Elyot would recall that he had enjoyed Cromwell's 'love & trew hartt . . . sensse [since] the syngsson Martt at medelborow in anno 1512'.[25] The city of Middelburg was in the south-western Netherlands and had become a powerful trading centre in the commerce between England and Flanders during the Middle Ages. The importance of English trade to the city makes it entirely plausible that Cromwell had secured employment there. His time spent in the household of one of Italy's most powerful mercantile families would have further recommended him. Cromwell may also have gained experience in the law during this time. Although untrained, he must have had a natural aptitude for this profession because he would soon become famed for his knowledge and skill in legal matters.

Cromwell probably returned to England in the late summer or early autumn of 1512. Within two years, by which time he was in his late twenties, he had become firmly established in London mercantile and legal circles. A chance reference in the official papers of Henry VIII suggests that he had almost immediately started work as a lawyer. Cromwell's signature is found on a document of around November 1512, concerning the ownership of a manor and associated lands in Great and Little Kimble, Buckinghamshire.[26] Conveyancing would be a specialism of Cromwell throughout his legal career, and during these early years many of his clients were drawn from his mercantile contacts.

But Cromwell's travelling days were not yet over. In 1514 he returned to the Netherlands and journeyed to some key centres of trade, notably Bruges and Antwerp, where he is found dealing on his own behalf that year. As well as building up experience of commerce, he also developed an important network of contacts that would prove useful in the years to come. At the same time, he gained an excellent grounding in European economic and political affairs. He learned several languages, becoming fluent in French and Italian, and competent in Spanish and possibly also German. His love of Italian would stay with him for life, and many of the letters he received from abroad were in this language. The Imperial ambassador, Eustace Chapuys, who was grudging in his praise, would later admit: 'Cromwell is eloquent in his own language, and, besides, speaks Latin, French and Italian tolerably well.'[27] Cromwell had also become well versed in the classics and was proficient in Latin and Greek – the latter being a highly unusual accomplishment. Stephen Gardiner, who would become his mortal enemy, admitted that Cromwell was often 'very stout' towards him 'for that conceat he had, what so ever he talked with me, he knewe ever as much as I, Greke or Laten and all'.[28]

Although the contemporary sources offer only the patchiest of details for this period of Cromwell's life, it seems that he also returned to Italy in 1514. The records of the English Hospice of the Most Holy Trinity and St Thomas in Rome show that he stayed there in June that year. Founded in 1362 with the stated aim of caring for 'poor, infirm, needy and wretched persons from England', by the time Cromwell was a guest the hospice had grown into the major centre for English visitors to Rome. It received many thousands of pilgrims each year, but Cromwell's visit was more likely to have been motivated by mercantile rather than spiritual matters. Documents from the archives of the Vatican City suggest that by now Cromwell was an agent for Cardinal Reginald Bainbridge and handled English ecclesiastical issues before the Papal Rota, the highest ecclesiastical court constituted by the Holy See.

Cromwell was back in England by the summer of 1514. A signature on a document dated 26 August is thought to be his. It is regarding the archbishopric of York, and is endorsed with what the editor of the volume describes as 'some lines, apparently intended as an exercise of penmanship'.[29] This offers a beguiling (though unauthenticated) image of a young Cromwell practising his signature so that it appears suitably elegant and learned. If it was indeed his penmanship, however, it presents a conundrum. How could this newly returned adventurer, virtually unknown in his native country, be involving himself in the affairs of one of the foremost ecclesiastics in the land? It suggests that Cromwell had a greater network of contacts than are revealed in the contemporary sources.

Certainly, Cromwell's years on the Continent had transformed him from a poorly educated, if precocious and streetwise 'ruffian', to a cultured, well-connected and successful merchant. It was with some justification that he later described himself as 'a great Traveller in this World'.[30] His natural intelligence had served him well, as Foxe observed: 'Neither was his capacity so good but his memory was as great in retaining whatsoever he had attained.'[31] Holinshed likewise described him as being 'of such an incomparable memorie, so bold of stomach and hardie, and could doo so well with his pen . . . that being conversant in the sight of men, he could not long continue unespied.'[32] He had experienced active military service, worked in some of the greatest trading centres in the world, witnessed first-hand the extraordinary flowering of culture and ideas during the Italian Renaissance, and had absorbed some of the radical religious ideas that were starting to take hold in northern Europe. It had been an extraordinary training-ground.

Cromwell's experience in Italy had had the most profound impact. It had fostered in him a love of art, literature, music and fine objects that would last a lifetime. His passion for the country was infectious. Many years later, Edmund Bonner, Cardinal Wolsey's chaplain, wrote to him: 'As you wished to make me a good Italian some time since, by promising to lend me the "Triumphs of Petrarch," I beg you to send it by Mr. Augustine's servant, and specially if you have it, the *Cortigiano* in Italian.'[33] One Italian author who has been credited with particular influence over Cromwell was Niccolò Machiavelli. It is possible that Cromwell acquired an early manuscript copy of his most famous work, *Il Principe* (*The Prince*). This book, which was eventually published in 1532, made Machiavelli's name synonymous with ruthless, unprincipled statecraft.[34]

Cromwell's love of all things Italian was highly unusual for a Londoner. Andreas Franciscius had been aghast to discover on his visit to the capital that its inhabitants 'not only despise the way in which Italians live, but actually curse them with uncontrolled hatred'.[35] This was corroborated by another Italian visitor of the period: 'The English are great lovers of themselves, and of everything belonging to them; they think that there are no other men than themselves, and no other world than England; and whenever they see a handsome foreigner they say that "he looks like an Englishman" . . . They have a great antipathy to foreigners, and imagine that they never come into their island, but to make themselves master of it, and to usurp their goods.'[36] How much more broad-minded was Cromwell, whose travels had given him an altogether more cultured, inquisitive and enlightened outlook than the vast majority of his countrymen. He was a true Renaissance man, in all respects.

Cromwell's years abroad had been a far cry from the apprenticeship that he would have received at his father's brewery in Putney. Armed with a knowledge of places, people and affairs that precious few monarchs, let alone ministers, would have gained in a lifetime, Cromwell was free from the usual preconceptions and prejudices of his fellow countrymen. His travels had expanded both his mind and his ambition. He had learned to question everything, defy convention and seek new ways of doing things. His experiences had taught him to trust slowly (if at all), but he had also developed a genuine interest in other people and an accessibility that few men of his profession could boast. That he had clawed his way out of obscurity and stood on the cusp of a brilliant career was entirely thanks to his own merits, as the Elizabethan chronicler Holinshed later observed. 'Notwithstanding, the basenesse of his birth and lacke of maintenance [which proved] a great hinderance for vertue to shew hir selfe . . . yet through a singular excellencie of wit joined with an industrious diligence of mind . . . hee grewe to suche a sufficient ripenesse of understanding and skill, in ordering of weightie affaires, that hee was thought apt and fitte to anye roomth or office whereunto hee should be admitted.' Holinshed was in no doubt that Cromwell's travels had been a great benefit to his future career, for he had observed 'the courses of states and gouernements as wel of his natiue countrey at home, as in foraine parties abroade'.[37]

Soon after his return to England in 1514, Cromwell married Elizabeth Williams, née Wykys. It was a sign of how far he had come that he was able to make such a good match. Elizabeth was the widow of Thomas Williams, a yeoman of the guard. Her father, Henry Wykys, was of the same profession as Cromwell's stepfather, being a shearman in Putney, and it may have been the two men who arranged the marriage – or at least introduced the couple. Henry Wykys had formerly served as a gentleman usher to Henry VII, which gave Thomas a tenuous but valuable link to the court. His father-in-law also helped him to obtain a foothold in the English cloth trade. The records suggest that Elizabeth was a woman of wealth and property, and this could have been Cromwell's chief motivation in marrying her. Certainly, his own wealth increased rapidly in the early years of their marriage – more so than it would have done as a result of his own enterprises.

Ever the polymath, as well as serving in his father-in-law's house as a wool and cloth merchant, Cromwell also established himself as a business agent, an undefined role that apparently required no formal training and may have comprised several different facets, such as money-lending. It also introduced him into English legal circles. He made the most of this entrée to pursue law as his main career. That he should so quickly prove a success at it is remarkable, given that any experience he had gained so far had been in countries with a very different legal system than England. Rather than studying at university, Cromwell may have gained his knowledge from the printed law books that were available in London, or learned from men who are not mentioned in the contemporary sources. Together with his European connections and training, he was perfectly poised for a flourishing career.

Thomas and Elizabeth had at least three children: two daughters, Anne and Grace, and a son, Gregory.[38] Their dates of birth are not recorded, but as is common throughout much of history, there is more evidence relating to the son's age than those of the daughters. He is believed to have been born around 1520.[39] The fact that Anne tends to be mentioned first in the contemporary records may suggest that she was the elder of the daughters.

The family lived in Fenchurch, on the eastern side of the City of London, and may have leased a house near the small parish church of St Gabriel. This area was frequented by numerous merchants – close by were the Clothworkers, Pewterers and Ironmongers Halls – so Cromwell would have had easy access to many of his business clients.

Although he rapidly became established back in England, Cromwell was soon on his travels again. In 1517 he received a request for assistance from an acquaintance, John Robinson, alderman of Boston in Lincolnshire. The two men may have met through Cromwell's activities in trade, Boston being part of the Hanseatic League, a powerful conglomeration of merchants that dominated trade in northern Europe. Robinson's fellow townsman, Geoffrey Chambers, was due to travel to Rome on behalf of Boston's Guild of Our Lady in St Botolph's Church (affectionately referred to by locals today as the 'Boston Stump') in order to obtain permission from the Pope to sell indulgences. This had become a lucrative business for the town, so its leaders were anxious to ensure its continuation. Robinson asked if Cromwell would accompany Chambers. The fact that Cromwell had 'no sound taste or judgement of religion' with which to impress the Pope was less of a consideration than that he was an experienced traveller who was well versed in the affairs and language of Italy.[40] Cromwell, perhaps restless for adventure, readily acquiesced. He met Chambers in Antwerp and the two men travelled to Rome together.[41] They evidently did so in some style, since the whole expedition cost a staggering £1,200 – more than £450,000 in today's money.

The Vatican City was at the height of its beauty when Cromwell and his companion visited it in 1517. Michelangelo had finished painting the ceiling of the Sistine Chapel five years earlier – a masterpiece that would have a profound impact on the progress of Western art. Another great Renaissance master, Raphael, had begun the task of decorating Pope Julius II's apartments in 1508. This lavish series of frescos adorned four reception rooms in the papal palace and was so exquisite that Julius's successor, Leo X, retained the artist and his team to complete the work when he became Pope in 1513. Work would still have been under way when Cromwell and Robertson arrived in Rome, but it is possible that they saw some of the completed frescos when they paid court to Leo.

Cromwell hatched a plan to bypass the usual long and tedious wait for an audience with the Pope. When they arrived in Rome, he found out that the pontiff was due to go on a hunting expedition, so he lay in wait for his return and surprised him with a performance of an English 'three man's song'. Knowing the Pope's weakness for 'new fangled strange delicates and dainty dishes', he then presented him with a selection of English sweetmeats and jellies 'such as Kings and Princes only, said he, in the Realm of England use to feed upon'.[42] The Pope was so impressed that he immediately granted all the guild's requests. A bull dated 24 February 1518 gave the Boston guild permission to continue its profitable sale of indulgences. Although the details of this tale are provided by John Foxe some fifty years after the event, it is certain that Cromwell worked to secure the grant and was ultimately successful. This would be the first indication of his skill and audacity in dealing with the most exalted members of society. His experience had given him a confidence that belied his humble origins, but there must have been a natural irreverence – a swagger, almost – that persuaded powerful men to do his bidding.

This episode may have had a still more significant impact. By demonstrating the ease with which the Pope could be charmed into acquiescing, Cromwell may have developed a contempt for the papacy and religious orders which would deepen into a profound antipathy during his later career. He would, as the chronicler Hall famously put it, come to harbour an intense hatred of 'the snoffyng pride of some prelates'.[43] Moreover, Foxe claims that Cromwell eased the tedium of the long journey home by learning by heart the Latin translation of the New Testament that had been recently published by Erasmus. Certainly, from that time onwards Cromwell knew the Bible exceptionally well and would retain the knowledge for the rest of his days. Becoming so intimately acquainted with the teachings of the New Testament may also have sown the seeds of Cromwell's later evangelical beliefs. This is somewhat ironic, given that it occurred during a visit to the heart of Roman Catholicism to secure a grant for the sale of indulgences – a practice that the reformists found particularly objectionable.

But for now, the story of what passed in Rome considerably enhanced Cromwell's credentials when he and Chambers returned to England in triumph. Foxe recounts that Cromwell was 'a great doer . . . in publishing and setting forth the pardons of Boston everywhere'.[44] He was determined to spread the word about his success in order to establish a reputation for dealing effectively with the mightiest potentates of the age. If the Pope could be manipulated so effectively, then so might the King of England.

CHAPTER 2

The Cardinal

CROMWELL'S VISIT TO Rome in 1517 would be his last recorded overseas journey. From that time onwards, he focused all his efforts on advancing his career in England. According to one contemporary source, he exploited his family connections as much as his business ones. His cousin Robert, son of Walter Cromwell's brother John, had become vicar of Battersea, which was under the authority of Cardinal Thomas Wolsey, Archbishop of York, Lord Chancellor of England and Henry VIII's closest adviser.

Like Cromwell, Wolsey was the son of a tavern-keeper. He was some fifteen years Cromwell's senior, having been born in Ipswich in 1470 or 1471. His father became a butcher soon afterwards, and it was this profession that inspired the jibes that the younger Wolsey would suffer in later years. No matter how high he might rise at court, he would always be derided as the 'butcher's son' by his noble adversaries.

Despite his humble origins, Wolsey was exceptionally well-educated, possibly thanks to the patronage of a rich uncle. A naturally gifted scholar, he graduated from Oxford at the age of just fifteen, earning himself the nickname of the 'boy batchelor'. He went on to study for a degree in theology at Magdalen College, which was perhaps a surprising choice for someone with ambitions in the political sphere. But for Wolsey, religion and politics were always intermingled – both in his conscience and his career. His first major breakthrough came in 1507, when he was appointed a royal chaplain. He was quick to capitalise upon his position by aligning himself with the men at court 'whome he thought to bere most rewle in the Councell and to be most in favour with the kyng'.[1] It was a lesson that Cromwell would soon exploit to the full.

Wolsey rapidly proved himself a true polymath. Far from restricting his activities to the religious sphere, he put himself at Henry VII's disposal for various diplomatic missions. He later boasted to his biographer, George Cavendish, that he had amazed the king by completing a visit to the Emperor Maximilian in Flanders in just three and a half days. Described by William Tyndale, an influential scholar and reformer, as 'a man of lust and courage and bodily strength', Wolsey had a staggering capacity for hard work.[2] His rise to power was accelerated by the accession of Henry VIII in 1509.

'For the future, the whole world will talk of him,' remarked the Venetian ambassador with remarkable foresight when Henry came to the throne at the age of just seventeen. Everyone was full of praise for this ebullient, charismatic, intelligent and handsome new king – a true Renaissance prince. 'If you could see how here all the world is rejoicing in the possession of so great a prince, how his life is all their desire, you could not contain your tears for sheer joy,' enthused the courtier Lord Mountjoy. 'The heavens laugh, the earth exults . . . Avarice is expelled from the country, extortion is put down, liberality scatters riches with a bountiful hand. Yet our King does not desire gold, gems or precious metals, but virtue, glory, immortality.'[3]

The new king literally stood head and shoulders above most of his court. At six feet two inches tall, Henry was an imposing figure – and also (until his later years) an athletic one. He excelled at sports and delighted in showing off his prowess in the jousting arena. Having inherited the good looks of his grandfather, Edward IV, he was described as 'the handsomest prince ever seen' and an 'Adonis, of fresh colour'. A Venetian diplomat who visited the English court in 1515 wrote a glowing report of the young king, whom he described as: 'the handsomest potentate I ever set eyes on; above the usual height, with an extremely fine calf to his leg, his complexion very fair and bright, with auburn hair combed straight and short, in the French fashion, and a round face so very beautiful, that it would become a pretty woman'. Thomas More was no less complimentary: 'Among a thousand noble companions, the King stands out the tallest, and his strength fits his majestic body. There is fiery power in his eyes, beauty in his face, and the colour of twin roses in his cheeks.'[4]

Henry's personality was equally attractive. The direct opposite to his dour, mean-spirited father in almost every way, he had inherited the charm and charisma of his mother's family, the House of York. Affable, quick-witted, idealistic and hugely generous, he was 'the man most full of heart' according to Erasmus. Thomas More agreed: 'The King has a way of making every man feel that he is enjoying his special favour.' The Venetian ambassador concluded that he was 'prudent, sage and free from every vice'.[5] This was not strictly true. Although at his best Henry was irresistibly charismatic, his personality had an altogether darker side. Highly strung, self-indulgent and vain, he had a terrifying and unpredictable temper which could send courtiers scattering in all directions. He was also impulsive and had a tendency suddenly to promote or demote an attendant as his fancy dictated. As yet there was no sign of the suspicious, ruthless and brutal nature that would mark his later years, but those who served him still had to beware how swiftly his favour could be lost.

The other shortcoming that would have a major impact on Henry's reign was his over-fondness for sports. He loved hunting with a passion and would regularly spend entire days out riding, setting off before dawn and returning well into the evening. This continued for many years, until the king lost his youthful vigour and was obliged to indulge in less energetic pursuits. As late as 1526 the chronicler Edward Hall wryly observed: 'Because all this Sommer the Kyng tooke his pastyme in huntyng . . . nothyng happened worthye to bee written of.'[6] Even on the days when Henry was not inclined for the chase or (more likely) the weather was not favourable, he would usually only concentrate on business matters while he heard mass in the middle of the morning, and again in the evening after supper. He had no patience for lengthy dispatches or accounts, and he himself once admitted that writing was 'to me . . . somewhat tedious and painful'.[7] The business of government would have ground to a halt had it not been for the veritable army of secretaries, attendants and councillors who carried out the minutiae of royal policy, finance and administration.

Henry's naturally pleasure-loving personality presented skilful courtiers with an opportunity, and it was one that Wolsey was quick to grasp. Perceiving the young king's proclivity for more leisurely pastimes than the affairs of state, he was said to have assured 'the kyng in Comfort that he shall not nede to spare any tyme of his pleasure for any busynes that shold necessary happen in the Councell as long as he beyng there'.[8] He used the king strategically, bringing him into play at the most advantageous moment, as the seventeenth-century Church historian John Strype observed: 'Wolsey, though he knew how to indulge the King in his pleasures, yet he reminded him sometimes of business too.'[9] The cardinal proved himself highly capable in all matters of state. The influential humanist scholar Polydore Vergil asserted that 'Wolsey, with his arrogance and ambition . . . claimed he could undertake himself almost all public duties.' As a result, he secured more and more of the king's trust and was able to assume extraordinary levels of autonomy. 'It came to such a pass,' observed an aghast contemporary, 'that the King intervened in nothing, and this Cardinal did everything.'[10]

Wolsey's favour rested upon more than his capacity for lightening the burdens of state, however. An extremely shrewd judge of character, he very quickly perceived Henry's need for unquestioning loyalty and devotion from those who surrounded him. He also knew that his route to power lay in making himself as useful as possible to his royal master. According to Cavendish, 'all his endevour was oonly to satisfie the kynges mynd knowyng rightwell that it was the very vayn and right Cours to bryng hyme to highe promocion.' Wolsey therefore 'daily attended upon the king in the Court being in his special grace and favour'. As a result, 'the king conceived such a loving fancy especially for that he was most earnest and readiest among all the council to advance the king's only will and pleasure without any respect to the case. The King therefore perceived him to be a mete instrument for the accomplishment of his devised will and pleasure [and] called him more near unto him and esteemed him so highly that his estimation and favour put all other councillors out of ther accustumed favour that they were in before.' Although no admirer of Wolsey, William Tyndale admitted that he was 'obsequious and serviceable and in all games and sports the first and next at hand'.[11]

It was a master-class in how to secure the king's favour, and one that Cromwell would learn from – with dazzling results. Wolsey's own rapid rise to power was signalled by a number of key ecclesiastical appointments, culminating in his election to the archbishopric of York in August 1514. A year later, he was made a cardinal, and it was rumoured that he had ambitions to be Pope. Contemporaries were quick to recognise where the real source of power at court lay. Erasmus, who spent some considerable time at Henry's court, described Wolsey as governing 'more really than the king himself'. The Venetian ambassador Giustiniani described Wolsey as 'the right reverend Cardinal, in all whom the whole power of the State is really lodged', and as the man 'who, for authority, may in point of fact be styled *ipse rex*'. Henry VIII himself reinforced this impression. In 1515 he instructed Pope Leo X to 'pay the same regard to what Wolsey shall say as if it proceeded from the lips of the King himself'.[12] By now, Wolsey's position as chief among Henry's councillors was fully consolidated.

Wolsey's promotion was so rapid that, for a while, his household failed to keep pace. He was therefore obliged to acquire trustworthy new servants quickly. There was no shortage of ambitious men willing to fill the places on offer, and he soon had upwards of 400 staff. At the same time, he embarked upon a series of staggeringly ambitious building projects, rivalled only by the king's. His most impressive palace was Hampton Court, an architectural masterpiece that he stuffed full of priceless works of art. Little wonder that envious courtiers began to whisper that Wolsey's magnificence was beginning to eclipse his royal master's. 'Acquiring so many offices at almost the same time, he became so proud that he began to regard himself as the equal of kings,' observed one hostile contemporary.

> Soon he began to use a golden seat, a golden cushion, a golden cloth on his table, and when he went on foot, he had his hat – the symbol of his cardinal's rank – carried before him by a servant, and raised aloft like a holy idol, and he had it put upon the very altar

> in the king's chapel during divine service. Thus Wolsey, with his arrogance and ambition aroused against himself the hatred of the whole country, and by his hostility towards the nobility and the common people, caused them the greatest irritation through his vainglory. He was, indeed, detested by everyone, because he assumed that he could undertake nearly all the offices of state by himself.

Erasmus concurred that he was 'feared by all and loved by few if any'.[13]

For now, there was no check to Wolsey's authority, and at the end of 1515 Henry confirmed his favour towards the cardinal by appointing him Lord Chancellor. It was a move that greatly angered his fellow ministers, who resented the increasing concentration of power in the hands of this 'butcher's son'. In May 1516 Thomas Alen reported 'great snarling' to his patron the Earl of Shrewsbury.[14] The new Lord Chancellor did little to ingratiate himself with his colleagues. Rather than consulting with his fellow councillors, Wolsey sought only the king's approval. His strategy was to 'first make the kyng privye of all suche matters (as shold passe thoroughe ther handes) byfore he wold procede to the fynyssheng or determynyng of the same whos mynd & pleasure he wold fullfyll & folowe to the uttermost wherwith the kyng was wonderly pleased'.[15] Dazzlingly successful in the short term, it was a strategy that would prove dangerously destructive as time went by.

The date at which Cromwell entered Wolsey's service is subject to a degree of conjecture, with some historians placing it as early as 1514 and others as late as 1525. There is however a general consensus that the two men had become acquainted by 1516.[16] Robert Cromwell may have helped his cousin to the stewardship of the archiepiscopal estate of York Place, Wolsey's magnificent London residence. But it was not until Cromwell returned from Rome in 1518 that he rose to prominence as a protégé of the cardinal. By 1519 he was a member of Wolsey's council – a move that dramatically raised his standing in society. From that time, he wore the black and tawny velvet livery that marked him out as one of the hundreds of men in the cardinal's service.

According to Eustace Chapuys, Wolsey was quick to spot Cromwell's potential. 'The Cardinal of York, seeing Cromwell's vigilance and diligence, his ability and promptitude, both in evil and good, took him into his service and employed him principally in demolishing five or six monasteries.'[17] The first part of that statement may be true, but in the second Chapuys conflated events: Cromwell did help Wolsey to dissolve certain religious houses, but not until several years after he first entered his service. That Chapuys should imply that this had been Cromwell's first task was a means of drawing attention to what he considered to be his greatest crime. John Foxe provided a more positive view of Cromwell's early service to Wolsey: 'He was fyrst brought vp in the Cardinals court, where as he did beare seueral offices, wherein he shewed suche tokens, and likelyhode of excellent wyt and fydelitie, that in short space he semed more mete for the kyng then for the Cardinall.'[18]

It is easy to see why Cromwell and Wolsey so quickly established a close confederacy. They were like two peas in a pod. Both of humble origins, they were self-made men who had used their natural wit, intelligence, shrewdness and industriousness to take the world by storm. Of course, by the time they became acquainted, Wolsey was several leagues ahead of Cromwell. But the latter saw his chance: if he could make himself indispensable to the king's chief minister, the prospect of even greater advancement lay within his grasp.

Meanwhile, Cromwell's burgeoning legal career was also drawing him ever closer to court circles. He began to act for clients in several important legal suits, and one of his first significant cases was an appeal from the Prerogative Court of Canterbury to the papal curia in October 1520. A copy of the papers was sent to Wolsey, and it included 'other information by the letters of Thomas Cromwell', in which the latter summarised the key points of the case and recommended the best way of handling it.[19] Cromwell evidently performed well, for the following year he was appointed to act for Charles Knyvett, former surveyor to Edward Stafford, third Duke of Buckingham. Knyvett had resigned from Buckingham's service shortly before the duke's execution on 17 May 1521, and proceeded to give evidence against him. He sought redress for the offices he had lost following his resignation, as well as release from bonds valued at £3,100 (equivalent to more than £1.1 million in modern money), which he had been obliged to undertake on his master's behalf.

Securing compensation for the servant of a convicted traitor was a risky commission, and one that most lawyers would have refused to touch. But Cromwell knew that the case would enable him to make connections in the highest echelons of the court, and so he accepted it with alacrity. With meticulous care, he prepared and corrected numerous petitions on behalf of his client, some of which were delivered to the king and some to Cardinal Wolsey. Although Cromwell failed to win the case for Knyvett, he achieved his objective of making a name for himself at court.

There is no record of when Cromwell first secured an audience with the king, but a description by a Venetian diplomat visiting court for the first time in 1515 gives an impression of what such an audience might have been like:

> We were conducted to the prescence [chamber], through sundry chambers all hung with most beautiful tapestry, figured in gold and silver, and in silk, passing down the ranks of the body-guard, which consists of three hundred halbediers in silver breast-plates and pikes in their hands; and, by God, they were all as big as giants, so that the display was very grand. We at length reached the King, who was under a canopy of cloth of gold, embroidered at Florence, the most costly thing I ever witnessed: he was leaning against his gilt throne, on which was a large gold brocade cushion, where the long gold sword of state lay.

Henry was lavishly dressed in white and crimson satin, and around his neck he wore a 'gold collar, from where there hung a round cut diamond, the size of the largest walnut I ever saw, and to this was suspended a most beautiful and very large round pearl . . . His fingers were one mass of jewelled rings.' To the king's right were 'eight noblemen, dressed like himself', and 'there were six men with six gold sceptres, besides ten heralds with their tabards of cloth of gold, wrought with the arms of England, and moreover a crowd of nobility, all arrayed in cloth of gold and silk.'[20] It must have been an awe-inspiring sight, even to a seasoned diplomat. Although, thanks to his travels, Cromwell was no stranger to magnificent courts, he could not fail to be impressed – and perhaps, despite his natural irreverence, a little intimidated – when he first entered the royal presence. But according to the novelist Bandello, he instantly made a good impression: 'It befell that oftentimes he [Wolsey] sent Cromwell to speak with the king of affairs of the utmost moment and the young man knew so well to ingratiate himself with the latter that he began to show him a good countenance, himseeming he was a man apt to the manage of whatsoever most important business.'[21]

After the Knyvett case, Cromwell's legal career continued to blossom. No doubt thanks to Wolsey's influence, his assignments increasingly brought him into contact with the court. Early in 1522 he represented a litigant from Bristol in a case heard by the Council in Star Chamber. Various other references to him among the official court papers suggest that his reputation as a lawyer of considerable skill and ability was growing rapidly. One of his other commissions was to act on behalf of Richard Chawfer against William Blount, Lord Mountjoy (a favourite with the king), in a case to be heard by the Bishop of London. In a letter to Cromwell written on 15 August 1522, Chawfer explained that the bishop had instructed both parties to appoint 'an indifferent person having knowledge in such reckoning', and added: 'I have chosen you, and wish to know when you will be in the city, that I may instruct you further.'[22] Neither had Cromwell neglected his business as a wool and cloth merchant, according to his correspondence from this time.[23] His English clients included goldsmiths, grocers, tailors, drapers, fishmongers and aldermen, and his contacts abroad stretched from Paris and Normandy to Augsburg and Florence. By the middle of 1522, when Cromwell had known Wolsey for about six years, he had risen in wealth and status sufficiently to be described as 'gentleman' in a power of attorney granted by the German Hanseatic League.

It was around this time that Cromwell employed an apprentice, a shrewd and enterprising young man named Ralph Sadler. Sadler had entered Cromwell's service by 1521, aged thirteen or fourteen, but it is possible that he had been raised in his household since 1514. He had probably been brought to Cromwell's notice by his father, Henry Sadler, who was a steward for Thomas Grey, second Marquess of Dorset. Cromwell was Dorset's attorney by 1522 (in itself quite a coup, given that the Greys were closely related to the king), but was apparently already acquainted with Henry Sadler by then. He was quick to spot Ralph's potential and ensured that the boy received an excellent education, which included Latin, Greek and French, as well as legal training. Ralph soon proved equal to the task, and Cromwell began to entrust him with ever greater responsibility. From the age of about nineteen, he served as secretary to his master, which gave him an invaluable grounding in all aspects of law, administration, finance and – above all – politics. Such was the trust that Cromwell placed in him that Ralph started to draft much of his voluminous correspondence. He therefore gained first-hand experience of state business and came to understand its many nuances almost as intricately as did his master. It was a position of enormous trust, and Sadler proved completely worthy of it. Before long, he was known to be so intimate with Cromwell that people began to petition him for favour.

Sadler served Cromwell with complete integrity and devotion, not only keeping pace with, but matching his ceaseless energy and industriousness. His tendency to date his letters not only by the day, but by the hour provides a fascinating insight into his gruelling work schedule, often rising by 4 a.m. and rarely retiring before midnight. It is safe to assume that his master did the same. Cromwell once complained that he had been 'so much engaged with other business that . . . he had scarcely time to take his daily meals'.[24]

A high point of Cromwell's rapid rise in society came in 1523, when he entered the House of Commons for the first time.[25] By then, parliament had evolved from an assembly of prominent subjects summoned by the king so that he could communicate his will, to an active body that could make laws, grant taxation and even – on occasion – oppose royal will. Parliament was divided between the

Lords – the foremost peers of the realm who attended by personal writ from the monarch – and the Commons, whose members gained a seat in parliament through local election.

Parliament was very much an occasional institution. Although it met irregularly, often with long gaps in between, during the Tudor period it grew considerably in significance. During his twenty-four-year reign Henry VII had summoned seven parliaments, which had sat for a total of just twenty-five weeks. By contrast, nine parliaments met during his son's thirty-seven-year reign, making a total of 183 weeks, the majority of which were concentrated in Cromwell's decade of ascendancy from 1529. Parliament became Cromwell's favourite arena for exerting his influence and that of the crown. It played to his strengths as both an orator and a lawyer.

The parliament of 1523 – the first since December 1515 – had been called to supply the money needed for Wolsey's aggressive foreign policy. Thanks to the assiduity of one of Cromwell's clerks, we have a transcript of a speech he gave, which provides a rare glimpse into the debates that raged in Henry's parliaments. Apparently unfazed by his first parliamentary appearance, Cromwell gave a memorable performance. Employing his exceptional powers of oratory, which had made him such a success as a lawyer, he ventured to cast grave doubt upon the king's long-cherished desire to assert his ancient claim to the kingdom of France. This was an extraordinarily bold move, given how fond Henry was of acting the part of the great warrior king. It also flew in the face of his new patron's strategy. But, as Cromwell reasoned, England could ill afford the huge expenditure that war with France would bring. His long speech was a masterly blend of deference and reason. Realising that, as a low-born newcomer, his opinion might be disregarded by his mighty peers, he professed: 'I reckyn myselff of all other the most unworthy to have in the awdience of so many sauge and notable persons, any manner saiyngges, especially in this weighty mattier whiche makyth me to tremble, for fere, whan I thyncke upon hyt.' He also pretended to defer to those who had 'far more assuryd Wysdom, Lernyng and experience then I'.

The arguments that Cromwell subsequently put forward drew

upon his own experience of serving in the French army because he was able to give an up-to-date appraisal of the country's military strength. This dampened the dangerously nostalgic view conjured up by the frequent references to the great English victories of Crécy and Agincourt. Cromwell concluded that the king would be better advised to concentrate on the threat posed by the Scots on England's northern border. In short, he should put his own house in order before getting carried away by delusions of grandeur overseas. He ended, as he had begun, with a show of humility: 'Thus have I here uttred my pore and symple mynde.' The real masterstroke of the speech, though, was that Cromwell had made sure to profess throughout his steadfast, passionate loyalty to the king. It was above all an intense fear for Henry's safety, he claimed, that had driven him to object to Wolsey's scheme. This was pure statecraft. Cromwell knew that every word spoken in the parliament would be meticulously recorded and presented to the king. He had therefore appreciated, and exploited to the full, his first real opportunity to flatter and impress his sovereign.[26]

This extraordinary speech was an early indication of the cautious approach to diplomacy that would be the mainstay of Cromwell's foreign policy in the years to come. Tempting though it is to ascribe his aversion to war with France to the time he had spent in that country as a youth, Cromwell was a deeply pragmatic man with a shrewd, penetrating mind. Although capable of intense loyalty to his closest associates, he never allowed personal prejudices to govern his execution of business. Besides, he would in time consistently support alliance with the Holy Roman Emperor Charles V over one with France.

It is interesting to consider whether in speaking out against the war with France, Cromwell was betraying his new master. Wolsey favoured a belligerent foreign policy, and may therefore have been aggrieved that his protégé had argued so convincingly against it. It has been suggested, though, that the ever wily cardinal put him up to it as a way of preparing the ground for a change in policy. Nonetheless, however much Wolsey believed in Cromwell's abilities, it seems unlikely that he would have risked giving such an important task to a newcomer. Besides, the tone of Cromwell's speech implies that he was sincere in his attempt to put a stop to what he felt strongly – and knew from experience – was a mistaken policy.

Despite Cromwell's persuasive arguments, the issue was not easily resolved and parliament dragged on for seventeen long weeks – almost twice the average session. Shortly after its conclusion, he complained to his friend, John Creke:

> I amongst other have endured a parliament which continued by the space of seventeen whole weeks where we communed of war, peace, strife, contention, debate, murmur, grudge, riches, poverty, penury, truth, falshood, justice, equity, deceit, oppression, magnanimity, acuity, force, moderation, treason, murder, felony, conciliation and also how a commonwealth might be edified and also continued within our Realm. Howbeit in conclusion we have done as our predecessors have been wont to do, that is to say, as well we might and left where we began.[27]

This is the earliest of Cromwell's letters to survive. Far from being intimidated by his brush with this august body of men, Cromwell was already poking fun at its shortcomings. It was a natural irreverence which was one of the hallmarks of his character. And it would win him friends and enemies in equal measure.

That Cromwell should so quickly grasp the workings of parliament is an indication both of the quickness of his mind and his suitability for a career in politics. Wolsey once told him: 'Ye [are too] depe of understanding.'[28] The Imperial ambassador, Eustace Chapuys, concurred: 'Cromwell is a man of wit, well versed in Government affairs, and reasonable enough to judge correctly of them.'[29]

Cromwell's letter to Creke also demonstrates his enormous capacity for friendship. This is not a quality commonly associated with the cunning lawyer, but the evidence is compelling. John Creke, who travelled widely on the Continent and kept Cromwell informed of affairs there, was devoted to his friend, and in July of the previous year he had sent him an extraordinarily effusive and affectionate letter. 'My love toward you resteth in no less vigour than it did at our last being together. My [hear]t mourneth for your company and Mr. Wodal's as ever it did for men . . . I never had so faithful affection to men of so short acquaintance in my life; the which affection increaseth as fire daily. God knoweth what pain I receive in departing, when I remember our gosly walking in your garden; it make me desperate to contemplate. I would write larger; my heart will not let me.' Creke ended the letter: 'To your good wife have [me] heartily commanded.'[30]

For his part, Cromwell was a faithful correspondent and showed none of the reserve that might have been expected of someone who was privy to so much confidential information. He assured Creke while the latter was resident at Bilbao that he would tell him all the latest happenings from home, 'for it is said that news refreshes the spirit of life'. He did, though, take the precaution of using coded references in some of his replies. 'All your frendes to my knowlage be in good helth and specially thay that ye wott of: ye know what I meane,' he reported in one. 'I think it best to wryt in parables because I am in dowt.'[31]

Cromwell and Creke had a number of friends in common. 'Mr Wodal' was probably John Woodall (or Uvedale), a clerk in the Signet Office and the Exchequer. Three years Cromwell's senior, he was, like him, carving out a career in government and would soon come to the notice of Cardinal Wolsey. There was a jovial camaraderie between the three men, and in one dispatch Cromwell told Creke that 'Maister Woodall is merye withowt a wyffe and commendyth hym to yow.'[32]

Another friend whom Cromwell and Creke shared was Stephen Vaughan, an English merchant and royal diplomat. He may have become acquainted with Cromwell during his time in the Netherlands and was a frequent visitor there. Vaughan hailed from a mercantile family and carried on the tradition, becoming an active member of the Merchant Adventurers. A man of similar industriousness to Cromwell, his business obliged him to be constantly on the move between the markets of the Low Countries. 'I am never at rest,' he once complained to a correspondent. 'I am now at Barrugh [Bergen op Zoom], now at Bruce [Bruges], now at Gamut [Ghent], now here now there, so that not without exceeding trouble can I satisfy to all those to whom I minister . . . as to please all if it were possible.'[33] Cromwell would have recognised and respected his dedication to his career. It paid off, for Vaughan rose rapidly through the mercantile ranks. No matter how many other demands there were upon his time, Vaughan always seemed to prioritise the requests that came from his friend in England. 'You see that I answer your instructions with all possible speed,' he once assured Cromwell, 'though it is difficult so to do, being a minister and common servant to a multitude.'[34]

Their correspondence suggests that Vaughan had known Cromwell since his youth, for most of his letters end with a wish to be remembered to Cromwell's mother.[35] Cromwell trusted Vaughan implicitly, and the two men rapidly developed a close, enduring and mutually supportive friendship. Cromwell had appointed Vaughan as his agent in the Netherlands by March 1524. He was the first of an ever widening network of contacts, agents and friends abroad who provided Cromwell with invaluable information on both foreign and domestic affairs. Vaughan, and the others in Cromwell's network, were in effect his personal spies, keeping him abreast of rumours and intelligence on economic and political events. This was a service for which Cromwell was obliged to pay significant sums, as Vaughan admitted in one dispatch: 'To know secret affairs here, one must use familiarity with those from whom they can be learnt, – which is costly, and beyond my powers.'[36] In return for his services, Cromwell helped Vaughan to secure a commission from Wolsey to 'write the evidence' for his college at Oxford in 1526.[37]

Their association extended well beyond business affairs, however. Vaughan enjoyed his patron's hospitality and the wide circle of acquaintance to whom he was introduced. Recognising him as a loyal friend, Cromwell entrusted Vaughan with the upbringing of his young servant, Thomas Avery, who was evidently a favourite with his master. Shortly before Avery's departure for the Netherlands in 1529, Cromwell had provided a generous bequest of six pounds, thirteen shillings and four pence for the young man. He asked

Vaughan to ensure that Avery was 'taught and brought up in the knowledge of things meet for his age'. His friend proved an ideal guardian and sent frequent updates on the boy's progress.[38]

Vaughan and Cromwell also shared a love of learning. The former had probably been educated at the prestigious St Paul's School in London. Aware of his friend's literary interests, Vaughan would go to great lengths to secure books for him that were not available in England. They included the *Nuremberg Chronicle*, an illustrated world history first published in 1493. A rueful Vaughan wrote to Cromwell in June 1530, having heard that his friend was impatient to receive the latest book and had offered to send him money in order to speed up the delivery: 'I say unto you, from the bottom of my heart, if you desired my coat you should have it, and also my cloak. Money I lack none to do my friend good. Less lack I for him whom above all friends I esteem.'[39] Vaughan also sent Cromwell a globe, which he assured him was 'a singular good piece of work'.[40]

The merchant was always assiduous for his friend's welfare. In March 1528, on one of his visits to London, he wrote in some alarm to notify Cromwell of a violent robbery that had taken place close to his house:

> On Thursday last, between 6 and 7 p.m., five thieves knocked at the door of Roderego, the Spaniard which dwelleth next the goldsmith against your door. Being asked who was there, they answered, 'One from the Court to speak with Roderego.' When the door was opened, three of them rushed in, and found the said Roderego sitting by the fire, accompanied with a poor woman dwelling next to Mrs. Wynsor. The other two tarried, and kept the door, and strangled the woman that she should not cry. They then took Roderego's purse, and killed him by stabbing him in the belly.

Even though the men had swiftly been arrested, Vaughan took the precaution of ordering a strong chain for Cromwell's gate so that 'no man not well known may enter'.[41] Cromwell felt just as protective towards Vaughan. The latter once thanked him for his 'friendly and rather fatherly writing'.[42]

Cromwell's other friends came from an array of different places. Some were part of his family or that of his wife, Elizabeth. Others were drawn from the more intellectual circles in which Cromwell increasingly moved. His interest in the arts and humanities, fostered during his years in Italy, led him to forge acquaintances with some of the foremost artists, writers and intellectuals of the Henrician age. They included the poet Sir Thomas Wyatt, who would later gain notoriety for his relationship with Anne Boleyn. He was said to be 'devoted' to Cromwell.[43] The leading historian and lawyer Edward Hall also became a close friend. Although they probably met in legal circles, Cromwell had a passion for history and would build up an impressive library of historical works, which included copies of ancient chronicles and charters. Edmund Bonner, Bishop of London – referred to by Foxe as 'the moste earnest champion and mainteyner of the Romyshe [Roman – i.e. papal] decrees' – set aside his distaste for Cromwell's reformist principles and raided his extensive collection of books when the opportunity arose.[44] The celebrated court painter Hans Holbein also became well acquainted with Cromwell. It was at least partly thanks to the latter's patronage that the artist gained such renown.

Cromwell's travels in Italy had coincided with the flourishing of humanism, an intellectual movement that aimed to revive classical learning. A key premise of humanist teachings was the study and translation of original texts – a principle that would gain significance for Cromwell in his later career. The movement's chief proponent was Desiderius Erasmus, whose works became widely available thanks to the advent of the printing press in 1517. As a result, they rapidly spread to England and gained currency among some of the leading members of Henry VIII's court. A particularly active proponent was Thomas Elyot, whose friendship with Cromwell began around 1519. Elyot had served his father as a clerk to the Court of Assize in its western circuit, so he had legal as well as intellectual interests in common with Cromwell. The pair may have met when Elyot came to the notice of Wolsey, who had him appointed clerk to the Privy Council. Although he and Cromwell differed in their religious beliefs, and would have several clashes in the years ahead, their friendship would endure for the rest of Cromwell's life.

One of Cromwell's closest friends was Antonio Bonvisi, a successful Genoese merchant living in London. He acted as banker for the government, transmitting money and letters to ambassadors across Europe. Thanks to his connections, he was extremely well-informed and often heard news of foreign events before it reached the court. As such, he was enormously useful to Cromwell, but their friendship went beyond a mere business connection. Bonvisi was drawn to learned men, especially those who – like Cromwell – had spent time in his native Italy. The fact that Cromwell could also speak Italian must have been a boost to their friendship. The two men lived close to each other in what is now the heart of London's financial district.

Interestingly, Bonvisi was also close friends with the man who in the future would become one of Cromwell's deadliest enemies: Thomas More. The sainted More of legend inspired eulogies and praise among Europe's elite scholars and intellectuals. He was 'a manne of singular virtue and of a cleere unspotted conscience, as witnessethe Erasmus, more pure and white than the whitest snowe, and of suche an Angelicall wytte as Englande, he sayethe, never had the lyke before nor never shall agayne.'[45] Seven years Cromwell's senior, More was trained in the law and had been admitted to Lincoln's Inn at the age of just eighteen. Like Cromwell, he was renowned for his ready wit, engaging conversation and exceptional intellect. He was also a leading proponent of humanism. As such, he came into close contact with some of the leading European intellectuals of the day, including Desiderius Erasmus, John Colet, Thomas Linacre and William Grocyn. In 1516 More published *Utopia*, an influential humanist tract that rapidly became a sensation, running into several editions. The work satirised European society for its short-sighted love of gain, and its lack of true Christian piety and charity. In so doing, it demonstrated More's own intense piety, which led him to eschew the trappings of wealth. Although a man of considerable means, he was indifferent to fine food, preferred water to wine, and was careless about his dress. This set him apart from most other members of the court, but, like Cromwell, his prowess in legal matters, coupled with his engaging personality, ensured that he rapidly rose to prominence.

More entered royal service around 1515, possibly as a protégé of Wolsey, and became a member of the Privy Council three years later. But he was always a rather reluctant courtier. His son-in-law and earliest biographer, William Roper, described him as being: 'of a pleasaunte disposition' and said that 'it pleased the kinge and Queene, after the Councell had supte, at the time of their supper, for their pleasure, comonly to call for him to be merry with them.' Henry so enjoyed More's company that 'he could not once in a moneth gett leave to goe home to his wife and children (whos company he moste desired) and to be absent from the courte two dayes together.' Roper claimed that his father-in-law resented this 'restraint of his libertie', and became increasingly sombre in the king's presence. The result was – as he no doubt intended – that he was not summoned to attend his royal master so often.[46]

Cromwell's service to Wolsey meant that his path would almost certainly have crossed with that of More. Given that they enjoyed so much common ground both personally and professionally, it is possible that they became well acquainted. But there were also notable – dangerous – differences between them. More was highly principled and pious; Cromwell was a pragmatist. More cared little for personal wealth or power; Cromwell was intent upon acquiring as much as possible of both. Little wonder that they have traditionally been cast as adversaries: the sainted More and the villainous Cromwell.

John Foxe drew an interesting comparison between the two men and Stephen Gardiner, all of whom he said had been 'brought vp together [in Wolsey's household] euen from their youthe'. As well as being roughly the same age,

> so was not their fortune also verie diuerse, although that their dispositions and studies were moste contrarie. For albeit, these thre were men in a maner of lyke learnyng and vnderstanding, and became of lyke estimation in the common wealth, and that in Moore and Winchestr there was peraduenture more learning, yet notwithstanding there was in this man [Cromwell] a more heauenly lyghte of mynde, and more prompt and ready iudge-

> ment, equal eloquence, and as it is supposed, more ready in this man, and finally in hym there was a more heroycall or pryncely disposition, borne to greater and weygtier matters.[47]

Disregarding the usual flattery that Foxe heaped upon Cromwell, he was justified in pointing out that More and Gardiner's 'learning' had benefited from an extensive education, whereas Cromwell was self-taught and had a naturally keen intellect which arguably exceeded that of his future rivals.

Bonvisi was not the only friend that More and Cromwell had in common. Cromwell became a close associate of More's brother-in-law, John Rastell, a barrister, member of parliament, printer and author. They would occasionally play bowls together and, having so many shared interests, had much to converse about. The fact that Rastell was a devout Roman Catholic would later spell trouble, but it is a testament to Cromwell's open-mindedness that some of his closest friends were poles apart from him in doctrinal and political matters.

Cromwell's rapid rise in social status prompted him to find a new residence. Some time after September 1522, he and his family moved from Fenchurch Street, which was close to the Tower of London, to Austin Friars in Broad Street. Although their new house was only a stone's throw away from where they had been living, it represented a significant uplift in their status. Austin Friars was a substantial Augustinian friary dating back to the 1260s covering about five and a half acres of land in the City of London, a short distance from what is now the Bank of England. Its founders, the Order of Augustinian Hermits, became known in England as the Augustine Friars, which was often abbreviated to Austin Friars. In his survey of London, published in 1598, the antiquarian John Stow described the magnificent church: 'Next have you the Augustine Friars Church and Churchyard; the entering thereunto by a south gate to the west porch, a large church, having a most fine spired steeple, small, high, and straight, I have not seen the like.'[48] He went on to list several eminent people who were buried in the churchyard, including the elder brother of Richard II, as well as several traitors who had been beheaded nearby at the Tower and Tower Hill, including the Duke of Buckingham in 1521.

Monastic houses in London often made a tidy profit by leasing out land within their precincts to secular tenants, and Austin Friars was no exception. Several tenements were built on the western side of the precinct, and the friary also owned a number of properties just outside the precinct, next to Throgmorton Street. The Cromwells' new dwelling was close to this, on Broad Street, and bordered the friary's churchyard to the west. They were in good company, for the other properties were occupied by some distinguished tenants – including the renowned humanist scholar Desiderius Erasmus, who had left without paying his bill. Their immediate neighbour (to the north) was John Cavalcanti, a wealthy Italian merchant. Although it

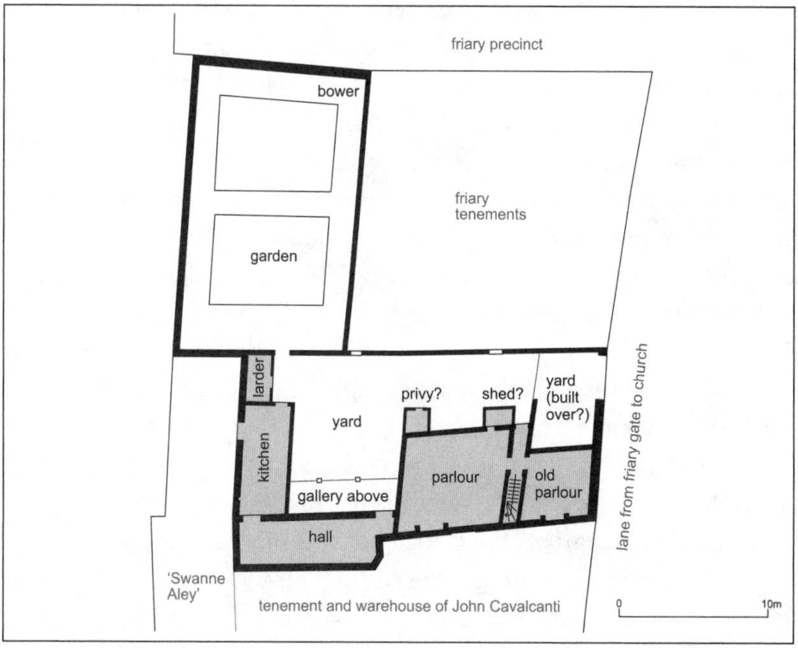

Thomas Cromwell's first house in Austin Friars (scale 1:400)

perfectly reflected Cromwell's new status, his choice of residence in the grounds of Austin Friars was deeply ironic, given that he would later become the monastic orders' greatest enemy.

According to contemporary records, Cromwell's house was a

substantial three-storey property, with no fewer than fourteen rooms arranged in three wings, and a garden attached. Although it is not clear exactly when he and his family moved there, it may have been as early as 1522. In December that year, Cromwell attended a meeting of the Broad Street ward, apparently as a resident of the area.[49] He was certainly there by the end of the following year, when he was elected as a senior officer, probably secretary, in the inquest set up by the court of the Broad Street ward, which involved the compilation of an annual report on the ward for its alderman. This was another indication of Cromwell's rapidly growing profile, for it was usually necessary to hold several less distinguished offices in a ward before being promoted to the senior role.

The sources provide few other clues about Cromwell's domestic life at this time. His wife Elizabeth was certainly living at Austin Friars in 1525. Her mother, Mercy Pryor, and her second husband came to live with them soon after. They were very well provided for, each being appointed a comfortable and richly furnished chamber, and the sources imply that Mercy lived out her days there. She was certainly still there in 1532, when an acquaintance of Cromwell reported that she was in good health.[50] That Cromwell later made a generous bequest to his mother-in-law suggests that he held her in some esteem.

What patchy evidence there is of Elizabeth's life at Austin Friars gives the impression that it combined domestic duties with supporting her husband's career. On 29 November 1525 Cromwell wrote to her from Kent, where he was dealing with the suppression of Bayham (or 'Begham') Abbey. He sent her a doe that he had killed on a hunt nearby. His covering note is brief and rather perfunctory. 'Elyzabeth I commend me unto you and have sente you by this berer a fatt doo, the one half whereof I pray you may be delyvered unto my gossyp mastres Smyth, and the rest to use your pleasure.' The remainder of the letter contained a number of other errands for his wife to perform: 'And further yf Richard Swifte be cum home or fortune to cum shortly, I will that he resorte to me at Begham or Tonbridge with all dylygence. Such news as ye have in those partyes I pray you sende me parte by this berer.' Then, as an afterthought, he added: 'And farther I pray you sende me word in wryting who hathe resorted unto you syns my departuer from you to speke with me.' He signed it: 'Per your husbend Thomas Crumwell.' If the letter is lacking in affection, it does at least prove that Cromwell trusted Elizabeth to act on his behalf and to report the comings and goings at their home during his absence. The way in which Cromwell addresses his wife suggests more fondness than the contents of the letter itself. It is inscribed: 'To my well beloved wyf Elyzabeth Crumwell agenst the Freyers Augustines in London be this given.'[51]

Elizabeth clearly benefited from her husband's rising status because she received gifts from men eager to win his favour. One such individual was William Bareth, who in November 1525 sent Mrs Cromwell six plovers 'for to drynke a quart of wyn withal'.[52] But there is little other record of her daily life at Austin Friars, or that of their three children. Anne, Grace and Gregory would probably have remained at home during their early childhood, and it was common for wives to superintend this phase of their children's education. In most affluent households, boys would be appointed a tutor by the age of seven. Gregory was Cromwell's only son and heir, so it is likely that his father would have been keen to invest in his education. As well as studying Latin, Greek, arithmetic, classical and religious texts, he would have been groomed from an early age for his future career. The evidence suggests that his father intended him to enter the same professions of law and trade in which he himself was building up such a profitable business.

Gregory may have been taught for a time by John Palgrave (or Palsgrave), former tutor to the king's daughter, Mary. In 1525 Palgrave had been appointed tutor to the king's illegitimate son, Henry Fitzroy, at Bridewell Palace, close to Cromwell's house in the city, so Gregory may have joined him there. Palgrave's programme of studies was ambitious. Influenced by some of the greatest scholars of the age, including Thomas More, Thomas Elyot and Stephen Gardiner, it included languages, the classics, law and music. But he fell foul of Wolsey and was removed from his post the following year.

By contrast, the education of daughters remained the responsibility of mothers throughout their childhood, and only the most privileged or enlightened households would invest in a tutor for them. Girls tended to live at home until they reached adulthood, and their studies were generally limited to sewing, embroidery, dancing, music and riding. The primary aim of their upbringing was to shape them into godly and moral young women, adept at household management and social skills. Given that their ambitions were restricted to marriage, the more effectively a young girl was schooled in these 'wifely' accomplishments, the more likely her father was to find her a good husband. Later in the century, the Calvinist preacher John Knox declared: 'Woman in her greatest perfection was made to serve and obey man'. He described the female sex as 'weake, fraile, impacient, feble and foolish . . . experience hath declared them to be unconstant, variable, cruell and lacking the spirit of counsel and regiment'.[53] Learning for its own sake was not encouraged: what pleasure could a woman possibly take in intellectual stimulation? Katherine Pole, Countess of Huntingdon, considered that her four daughters had left her care 'literate, although not overstuffed with learning'. This was a natural and satisfactory state as far as men were concerned. A woman with a good education was compared to a madman with a sword: she would be a danger to herself and to others.

There were some exceptions to this general rule. Sir Thomas More saw to it that all his daughters received an education equal to that of young men. He also tutored his wife in music and literature in order to improve upon the education she had received at home. Henry VIII's younger daughter, Elizabeth, would become a gifted and precocious scholar, learning several languages by the age of eight, including Greek and Latin. By contrast, two of his wives, Jane Seymour and Katherine Howard, were barely literate.

As an ambitious man of business, Cromwell would have planned to make good marriages for his daughters, and would therefore have ensured that they acquired the usual wifely accomplishments. But it is hard to imagine that he did not also share with them the benefits of his own cosmopolitan and cultured background. His later career would prove that he took a keen interest in the religious education of children of both genders. Moreover, in the will Cromwell drew up in 1529 he made special provision for Anne and Grace's education, bequeathing eleven pounds for 'the vertewous educacyon and bringing up' of both girls until they reached maturity,[54] which suggests that he took more of an interest in his daughters' upbringing than was usual for the time. Cromwell himself had been raised in a predominantly female household and had had a difficult relationship with his father. Evidence from his later career indicates that he had a positive view of women. Some of his most regular correspondents were women, and he worked assiduously to advance the cause of many wives, widows and daughters who sought his help.[55]

We have glimpses of how Cromwell liked to spend the precious few leisure hours that his service to Wolsey afforded him. When he dined at home, it would have been with his wife and children: family meals were always eaten together. There were just two main meals a day: dinner, which was served at eleven, and supper between five and six in the evening. Banquets were held on special occasions, which would extend the mealtimes (as well as the menu) significantly. The Cromwells would have been able to afford what was considered a good diet in Tudor times, with plenty of roast and boiled meat, poultry, fish, bread, ale and wine. Fruit and vegetables were eaten sparingly, and a household manual of 1500 warned readers to 'Beware of green sallettes & rawe fruytes for they wyll make your soverayne seke [sick].' Fruit was believed to worsen the effects of the plague, so the sale of it was banned during one particularly virulent outbreak.[56]

In most ordinary households, meals were served on wooden tableware. The main 'plate' was a thin square wooden board with a large central hollow that contained the meat and gravy. An inventory of Cromwell's house shows that this tableware was replaced with pewter as he grew in wealth during the later 1520s. Perhaps he sought to emulate the magnificent banquets regularly given by his master. George Cavendish describes the exquisite tableware upon which the food was served to Wolsey's household and guests. On display in one large cupboard were 'six desks [shelves] high, full of gold plate, very sumptuous, and of the newest fashions, and upon the nethermost desk garnished all with gold, most curiously wrought'.[57]

As well as enjoying art, literature and music, Cromwell was also a keen gardener and, perhaps thanks to the court circles in which he now moved, developed a love of falconry. He was also an affable and generous host. Ambassador Chapuys, who rented a house close to Cromwell's after he took up his post in England in 1529, described him as 'hospitable, liberal with his property and with gracious words, magnificent in his household and in building'. On one occasion, he recalled his reception by Cromwell, 'which was, as usual, most kind', and on another he noted that Cromwell had 'according to his usual laudable custom, received us with great kindness and cordiality'.[58] Despite being an adversary, Chapuys also acknowledged that Cromwell was 'a person of good cheer, gracious in words and generous in actions'. His sentiments were echoed by Thomas Alvard, a servant of Wolsey, who was effusive in his praise: 'Of your housekeeping, it is showed me there is never an Englishman, the King's grace except, that doth keep and feast Englishmen and strangers as ye do.'[59]

An inventory of Austin Friars taken in June 1527 offers a tantalising hint of the style in which Cromwell and his family lived.[60] This extraordinarily detailed and extensive list of 'Master Crumwell's goods in his house' includes everything from furniture, furnishings, clothes and jewels, to the number of sheets in his cupboards and pewter dishes on his tables. There is even a description of 'an old chair of easement' that stood in one of the bedrooms. The whole is a testament to Cromwell's good taste.

It is clear that by then the Cromwells were living in some comfort. Austin Friars had three wings, with the principal rooms at the front, overlooking the churchyard, and a hall and gallery forming a link to the service wing at the rear. This latter included a kitchen, buttery, larder and wood house: clearly this was a residence for entertaining, not just living in. The private chambers were on the first floor, the bedrooms (of which there were eight) on the second and servants' garrets were in the roof. There was also a well-appointed cellar in the basement.

Every room was decorated according to the latest tastes and

fashions. The ground-floor parlour, to which Cromwell's guests would have been shown upon arrival, was particularly imposing, being carpeted and fitted with a long table and a screen. The hall, which was entered through a 'portal' or grand doorway, was where Cromwell would have entertained favoured or important guests. It was here that the luxury of his furnishings was shown off to most dazzling effect. Even the most distinguished ambassador could not fail to have been impressed by the 'great gilt chair' upon which the master of the house sat – a throne for his own personal palace. There were three smaller gilt chairs 'for women', twelve gilt stools and footstools, a gilt table, cupboard and mirror. The floor was covered with rich carpets, and the room was scattered with lavish cushions embroidered with the red rose of Lancaster. Cromwell's loyalty to his other master was demonstrated by 'My lord Cardinal's arms, gilt in canvas'. He also displayed the arms of his first noble client, the Marquess of Dorset. Meanwhile, a portrait of the Emperor Charles V was a more surprisingly decisive inclusion, given that the English king was constantly flitting between a pro-Imperial and pro-French foreign policy. But Cromwell clearly felt able to express his personal preference in his own home – even though it was hardly a private residence. The records attest that he hosted meetings of the Privy Council here when his career was at its height.

Both the hall and the parlour were decorated with a series of religious images, including representations of Lucretia Romana. According to legend, the virtuous Lucretia was the object of desire for the sexually rapacious Prince Tarquin, whose behaviour sparked the downfall of the Roman monarchy. Although such a tale was well known at the time the inventory was taken, and would probably have inspired works of art in other important households, it is interesting to speculate whether Cromwell removed the paintings when he was a servant of Henry VIII during the 1530s, by which time life (in the form of Anne Boleyn) had come to imitate art a little too closely.[61]

The grandest bedroom at Austin Friars was the New Chamber, in which Cromwell and his wife would have slept. Its centrepiece was an ornate bed with feather mattress flanked with red and green curtains and gilt bells, and standing on a rich woollen carpet. Numerous gowns belonging to the couple are described, all fashioned from satin, velvet and other rich fabrics, and trimmed with a host of different furs. Cromwell himself had no fewer than sixteen doublets, including two in crimson satin, one in tawny taffeta and one in black velvet. He also had numerous pairs of hose, gloves, caps and other accessories, all made from the finest materials. As well as his ordinary day wear, he had a 'brown-blue' riding-coat and a nightgown trimmed with fox fur. His wife Elizabeth was richly decked out too in dresses of russet, tawny and black satin and velvet, with necklaces, purses and hats to match, including 'a coif of Venice gold' – one of many treasures that displayed Cromwell's love of all things Italian.

Their clothes were bedecked with expensive jewels. Cromwell was particularly fond of gold rings, and twenty different ones are described in the inventory. Among them was 'a gold ring, with a table diamond' and 'a gold ring, with a turquoise like a heart', both of which were 'upon my master's finger' when the inventory was taken. There was also a 'great table ruby', a large pearl with a gold pin and 'a diamond triangle, set in gold'. His other valuables included an impressive array of gold and silver tableware. There were silver goblets, spoons and salt cellars, a gilt cup and ale pot, and a delicate glass cup garnished with silver.

The less public rooms contained items that may have been closer to Cromwell's personal tastes. Inside one of the parlours was 'a cloth stained with the images of a man and a woman, lovers'. There was also a table flanked with Wolsey's arms, and the fact that these were on display in both the public and private rooms of Cromwell's house suggests the strength of his loyalty to his master. There were two maps of the world as well – one in another parlour and one in the servants' quarters – as might be expected from such a well-travelled owner. He had chosen an appropriate theme for one of his tapestries, which was described as: 'a border of arras work, with a picture of Occupation and Idleness'.

The servants' rooms were more comfortable than might be expected, with tapestries and pictures on the walls, a carved gilt bed with a feather mattress, and a new wainscot cupboard. In a room adjoining one of the bedchambers was a great ship chest, bound with flat bars of iron from Flemish foundries, all covered with yellow leather. This was one of several such chests in the house, which indicates that many – or most – of Cromwell's valuables could have been hidden away from view.

The contents of the kitchen hint at a rich and varied diet for the Cromwell household and their guests. A 'great round spit' stood in front of the fire, and there were numerous pots, pans, platters, knives, kettles, ale and wine pots. The 'great copper for capons', 'flesh hook' and 'garlick mortar' provide a glimpse into some of the ingredients that were used in the many dishes that came out of the kitchen on a daily basis. It was apparently with good reason that Cromwell was noted for his lavish hospitality.

There was a small garden (one-twentieth of an acre, or 220 metres squared) to the north of the house. The inventory provides no further details of this, although if it remained unchanged by the time a survey of the property was taken in the seventeenth century, it comprised two square knot gardens, which were popular in the Tudor period, surrounded by gravel paths. There was also an arched bower structure in the north-east corner of the garden.[62]

Cromwell's house was sufficiently well appointed for him to receive important guests, and the fact that he was noted for his generous hospitality proves that he was willing to invest considerable sums in feasting and entertainment. He retained a small orchestra of around twelve musicians, and his account books refer to 'Mr Bryan's minstrels'.[63] He also sponsored a theatre company. 'My Lord Cromwell's players' gave performances at his own house and also toured the country, visiting places as far afield as Barnstaple in Devon and Thetford Priory in Norfolk.[64]

Despite the undeniable comfort in which Cromwell and his family lived, there is an underlying sense of modesty, if not quite austerity. His upbringing and youth, which had seen him begging on the streets of Florence, had given him a natural thriftiness that he never entirely relinquished. While his noble companions at court lavished enormous sums on outdoing each other in ostentation, he spent money strategically, where it would have greatest impact. He did this so effectively that it fooled even his regular acquaintances into thinking that he lived as luxuriously as any duke. 'He lives splendidly,' remarked Chapuys, 'and [is] remarkably fond of pomp and ostentation in his household and in building.'[65] In fact, when he was not entertaining important guests, Cromwell's account books attest that he was content to live quite simply. It was an indication as much of his pragmatism as of his self-control. The vast majority of his time was spent at court and in his places of business, so why should he waste money on creating a household that was fit for continual show and entertainment? He was no Wolsey, whose homes and palaces were little short of a rival court. The centre of Cromwell's power was the court itself.

His reputation, gained over the centuries, as a greedy, grasping bureaucrat is also undermined by evidence that he gave generously to the poor of London. A business contact, Lawrence Giles, sent greetings to Cromwell and his wife, and thanked him for his kindness, assuring him that God provides for those who help the poor, 'as I understand . . . your mastership is provided'.[66] This is corroborated by the Spanish Chronicle. Written before 1552 by a Spanish merchant living in London (possibly Antonio de Guaras, who came to England with Eustace Chapuys in 1529), it is riddled with inaccuracies and written with a strong Imperial bias. Nevertheless, the author was almost certainly an eyewitness to some of the events he described so it does have some merit. He later reflected that Cromwell was greatly loved by the people of the capital, which suggests that his generosity was both consistent and well known. Londoners also recognised and admired the fact that, unlike most members of the richer classes, he had earned his money by hard work, not inheritance.

CHAPTER 3

'Nōt withoute sorow'

AROUND THE TIME that the Cromwells moved to Austin Friars, a new face appeared at court. In 1522 the ambitious politician and diplomat Thomas Boleyn had secured a place for the younger of his two daughters, Anne, then aged about twenty-one, in Catherine of Aragon's household. Having taken up her appointment, Anne swiftly established herself as one of the leading ladies of the court. What set her apart was her style and sophistication, both of which had been honed to perfection at one of the most glamorous courts in the world. From the outset, she and her sister Mary had been groomed to make marriages that would boost their family's aristocratic credentials and enable their father Thomas to move further up the political ladder. He had used his political contacts to secure places for both girls in the household of Mary Tudor, sister of Henry VIII, who had married the aged King Louis XII in October 1514.

The Boleyn girls had made an impression at the French court, but in very different ways. Mary soon gained a reputation – deserved or not – for sexual licence. Anne, meanwhile, thrived in the lively and intellectually stimulating French court and developed a love of learning that continued throughout her life. Among her closest companions was Margaret of Navarre, sister of Francis I, who encouraged Anne's interest in literature and poetry. It was in France that Anne also developed a love of lively conversation, a skill that would make her stand out from the quieter, more placid ladies at the English court when she made her entrance there.

So entirely did Anne embrace French manners, language and customs that the court poet, Lancelot de Carles, observed: 'She became so graceful that you would never have taken her for an Englishwoman, but for a French woman born.'[1] Anne was widely admired for her exquisite taste and the elegance of her dress, earning the praise of Pierre de Brantôme, a seasoned courtier, who noted that all the fashionable ladies at court tried to emulate her style. Possessing a 'gracefulness that rivalled Venus', she was, he concluded, 'the fairest and most bewitching of all the lovely dames of the French court'.[2]

King Louis died just three months after the wedding (some said the exertion of satisfying his young bride had led to his demise), and his widow hastily returned to England. Both Boleyn girls remained in France for several years. Mary became the mistress of the new king, Francis I. He was said to have called her his 'English mare' and 'hackney', whom he had the pleasure of riding on many occasions, although her reputation may have been unjustly besmirched. In late 1519 Mary was recalled to England and joined her father at court. Soon afterwards, she was married to William Carey, but this did not stop the English king from taking her as his mistress.

Her sister Anne had acquired a taste for life in France, however, and so remained there for a further two years after Mary's departure. Her father called her back at the beginning of 1522 because there were plans to marry her to her cousin, James Butler. Thomas Boleyn could not have guessed how much higher Anne would aim in her choice of husband. Shortly after her arrival, Anne took part in a court pageant organised by Cardinal Wolsey for the king on Shrove Tuesday 1522, in which she played the part of Perseverance – particularly fitting given the events that later unfolded.

Anne Boleyn's entry to the royal court held no apparent significance for Cromwell, who was increasingly preoccupied by the demands of his flourishing career. In 1524 he was appointed to the distinguished but unpopular role of subsidy commissioner in Middlesex, which involved calculating the value of people's lands and goods for taxation. At the same time, his success in the business of common law led to his election as a member of Gray's Inn. As his reputation grew, he received an increasing number of requests from high-profile clients. They included Thomas Wriothesley, who hailed from an ambitious family that had previously enjoyed the patronage of the Duke of Buckingham and fifth Earl of Northumberland. Educated at Cambridge under the auspices of the respected scholar and future courtier Stephen Gardiner, Wriothesley was noted for his mental capacity, integrity and striking good looks. It was later said of him that 'he was an earnest follower of whatsoever he took in hand, and very seldom did miss where either wit or travail were able to bring his purpose to pass.'[3] The Spanish Chronicle, meanwhile, describes him as 'one of the wisest men in the kingdom'.[4] Wriothesley chose a career at court over a degree, and in 1524, at the age of just nineteen, he enlisted Cromwell's legal services. But the client–servant relationship was soon reversed as he carried out a range of administrative tasks at court for Cromwell, whom he referred to as 'master'. He was also appointed the king's messenger and made it his business to become acquainted with all the affairs at court. He was, in short, a useful man to know – although not one to trust entirely. Nevertheless, Cromwell came to appreciate his intelligence and diligence, and during the years ahead he employed him on a number of increasingly important missions, both at home and abroad.

Another of Cromwell's clients proved even more significant for his future career. In February 1524 a Yorkshire knight called Sir Robert Ughtred sold the manor of Kexby, close to the city of York, to John Aleyn, a London alderman and senior member of the Mercers' Company. No sooner had he acquired it, than Aleyn appointed Cromwell to handle its sale to Cardinal Wolsey. Thomas Heneage, one of Wolsey's principal agents in the sale, was so impressed by his conveyancing skills that he asked Cromwell to represent him in a number of his own transactions. The two men soon struck up a close friendship.

In January 1525 Wolsey gave Cromwell a commission that would have far-reaching consequences. He appointed him to help survey six monasteries that were to be converted for the use of Cardinal's College at Oxford. Cromwell subsequently worked on the dissolution of a further thirty small religious houses in order to fund the beautification of the college and the foundation of Wolsey's grammar school at Ipswich.[5] Both building projects were extravagant and the costs exorbitant. Diverting the revenue from religious houses to similar building projects was not unprecedented, but it had never been attempted on this scale before. It was an extraordinarily complex task, requiring an intimate knowledge of the law. As well as surveying and estimating the value of the monasteries' property, Cromwell would have to make careful inventories of them, before finally stripping them of their furnishings and riches, and selling or leasing their lands. The fact that he had already proved himself skilled at conveyancing marked him out as the man for the job.

During the next two years, he and a team of assistants worked assiduously in selling the lands and goods of the thirty monasteries. With typical attention to detail and not wishing to leave anything to chance, Cromwell personally superintended the surrender and dissolutions. This was an enormous task, and one that would prove invaluable experience for him in future. By August 1526 the documents relating to the houses that had been suppressed to fund Cardinal College in Oxford filled thirty-four bags. Commenting upon his thoroughness in the task, an anonymous contemporary chronicler observed: 'This Cromwell was so diligent that he managed to inquire into everything, and the poor abbots, in doubt what was the object, and in the hope of ingratiating themselves with the Cardinal, sent him large sums of money by Cromwell.'[6]

Two years later, Cromwell was able to report: 'I according to your most gracyous commaundement have repayred unto the late monasterye of Wallingforde Where I founde aswell all the ornamenttes of the churche as all other ymplementtes of houseolde clerely conueyed awaye and nothing remaining. Sauyng only the euydences [evidence] Which I sorted and conueyed unto your colledge at Oxforde.'[7] The scale of the task, and the burden it had placed on Cromwell, is clear from a letter he wrote to Stephen Gardiner in January 1529. He asked that Gardiner might explain his absence to Wolsey, pleading: 'I have certen bokes to be don and accomplisshed concerning his colledge in Gipswich.' These 'bokes' included a bewildering array of letters patents, deeds and titles relating to the transfer of the monastic lands. Cromwell realised that there had never been a better opportunity to prove his worth, so he had no intention of delegating any of this work to others. He admitted that although not all the documentation was 'yet in readiness nor perfected to my mind', he hoped to finish it 'tomorrow at night or Wednesday by noon', at which time he would take it straight to 'my lord his grace'.[8]

Cromwell's involvement in the dissolution of the thirty monasteries occurred at a significant moment in the religious life of England. In September 1525 William Tyndale translated and published an English version of the Bible. Until that time, the vast majority of the population had had no access to the word of God, most Bibles being available only in Latin. Although there had been earlier translations, Tyndale's was the first to take advantage of the new printing press, which made it available on an unprecedented scale. It also drew upon the teachings of Martin Luther, whose radical theology had been gaining ground in parts of Europe.

That Cromwell had been inspired by radical reformist beliefs in carrying out his duties for Wolsey at this stage is doubtful. His assiduity seems to have been motivated more by a desire to prove his worth and earn a profit both for his master and himself than by any religious convictions. Nevertheless, he had shown a keen interest in the Bible ever since reading the translation by Erasmus during his travels in Italy in 1517–18. This visit had coincided with the rise of Protestant theology in Germany under the leadership of Martin Luther, whose *Ninety-Five Theses* had appeared in 1517. As well as questioning papal authority, Luther denounced the corruption of the Roman Catholic Church, particularly the worship of saints and relics, and the sale of indulgences, whereby a man could 'buy' God's forgiveness. Instead, he taught that salvation was attainable by faith alone. This was the central doctrine of the movement that became known as Protestantism.

Such ideas gradually filtered into England with the help of 'radical' preachers such as William Tyndale, Miles Coverdale, Thomas Bilney and Robert Barnes. When the latter delivered a sermon at Cambridge on Christmas Eve 1525, the city rapidly became a seedbed for reformist beliefs, and a centre – along with London – for the distribution of Protestant books. Among the abuses of the Roman Catholic faith that the reformists denounced was the corruption often found in the monastic houses. They promoted the study of the scriptures and an altogether more personal relationship with God, free from the trappings of the Roman Catholic Church – notably the Pope himself. Cromwell did not immediately espouse such beliefs, although he was at least open to them. But he would become increasingly warm to the reformist faith as his career progressed – and as it served both his private and political interests to do so.

Another member of Wolsey's staff was a man who would in the future become one of Cromwell's deadliest enemies: the Cambridge scholar and theologian, Stephen Gardiner. He entered Wolsey's service around 1524, aged about thirty, and soon began building up an impressive portfolio of ecclesiastical posts as a result. An expert in canon law, he proved indispensable not only to Wolsey but also to Henry VIII. He was a skilled diplomat too and accompanied Wolsey on his embassy to France in 1527. The cardinal was so impressed with him that he refused to relinquish him to his royal master, although Gardiner did become increasingly involved with the king's business. Gardiner was known for his cunning and double-handedness. Foxe, who was no admirer, claimed that he 'was moost cruell, so was he also of a mooste subtile and craftye witte, gapynge rounde aboute to get occasion to let and hynder the Gospell'. He concluded that he 'semed suche a man, to be borne for no other purpose, but onely for the destruction of the good'.[9] Gardiner once referred to himself as 'wily Winchester', following his appointment to that bishopric in 1531.[10] One hostile source claimed that his evil nature was reflected in his appearance: 'This doctor had a swart colour, an hanging look, frowning brows, eyes an inch within the head, a nose hooked like a buzzard, wide nostrils like a horse, ever snuffing into the wind, a sparrow mouth, great paws like the devil, talauntes on his feet like a grype, two inches larger than the natural toes.'[11] Although Gardiner himself insisted: 'I have never thought of returning evil upon anyone,' his relationship with Cromwell would prove the falseness of this statement.[12]

Meanwhile, Cromwell was also keeping a close eye on the building of his master's new colleges at Oxford and Ipswich, drawing up all the necessary deeds and scrutinising the craftsmen's accounts to the last penny. In addition, he personally superintended the workmen, paying regular visits to both colleges in order to inspect the works. The dean of the Ipswich college reported to Wolsey that Cromwell 'took great pains' to ensure that all the treasures and furnishings from the suppressed houses were carried into his master's new building with the utmost care. By April 1528 he was able to report to his master: 'The buyldinges of your noble colledge [at Oxford] most prosperouslye and magnyfycentlye dothe arryse in suche wise that to every mannes judgement the lyke thereof was never sene ne ymagened having consideracyon to the largeness beautee sumptuous Curyous and most substauncyall buylding of the same.' He added that the daily services in the chapel were 'so devuoute solempe and full of Armonye that in myne opynyon it hathe fewe peres'.[13]

The latter remark hints at a degree of piety on Cromwell's part, although this did not stop him and his men from going about their business with a ruthlessness that shocked their contemporaries. John Foxe later recorded that Cromwell 'procured to himself much grudge with divers of the superstitious sort, and with some also of noble calling about the king'.[14] Before long, Henry himself heard of the matter, and demanded that Wolsey supervise the work of his servants more closely. 'I have herd the Kyng, and noble men, speke thinges incredible of thactes of Mr Alayn [John Alen, later Archbishop of Dublin] and Cromwell,' observed the king's secretary, Dr William Knight, in a letter to the cardinal.

According to his critics, Cromwell was not only ruthless: he was corrupt. In an attempt by Wolsey's enemies to discredit the dissolution, Cromwell was accused of diverting some of the funds he received into his own pocket. Although he might reasonably have expected to receive gifts as a form of payment for his services, it does seem that he overstepped the mark. If a monastery was rich enough to pay him a bribe, then it might escape suppression. Meanwhile, the spoils from the less fortunate ones often lined Cromwell's own pockets rather than helping to pay for the new colleges. Farmers and other laymen whose lands had been lost as part of the dissolution could petition Cromwell for their return, which would be granted only if the bribe they offered was large enough. Little wonder that by August 1527 he had stirred up so much ill feeling that it was said that a 'sanctuary man' named Pen 'lay in wait to murder Cromwell'.[15]

Cardinal Pole, meanwhile, reported the rumour that Wolsey's despised agent had been sent to prison and would shortly be punished for his crimes.[16] This was repeated in the anonymous Spanish Chronicle. It claims that an outraged Henry summoned Cromwell to account for his crimes:

> As soon as the King knew that this Cromwell had brought with him so much money robbed from the abbeys, the King sent for him, and said to him, 'Come hither; what are these robberies you have committed in the abbeys?' and Cromwell answered him very boldly, 'May it please your Majesty, I have not committed any robbery, and I have done nothing but what I was ordered to do by my master the Cardinal. The money I bring was sent of their own free will by the abbots of the monasteries as a gift to the Cardinal, and your Majesty well knows that the Cardinal did as he liked, and I did as he told me, and therefore I bring these thirty thousand pounds sterling for the Cardinal.' The King thereupon took a great fancy to this Cromwell, and spoke to him in this fashion, 'Go to, Cromwell, thou art much cleverer than anyone thinks', and instead of sending him to be hanged as everybody expected, he gave him a slap on the shoulder and said to him, 'Henceforward thou shalt be my secretary.' This was the beginning of the rise of this Cromwell, who afterwards became more powerful than the Cardinal himself.[17]

Although entertaining and based upon elements of truth, this account conflated the events of Cromwell's rise to power, and the record of his alleged conversation with the king is not found in any other contemporary source.

In fact, it was more likely to have been Wolsey than the king who knew of Cromwell's shadier dealings, and he was more than happy to turn a blind eye to such things. After all, his new assistant had excelled himself in what was an enormously ambitious and complex task. Cavendish reported: 'Mayster Cromwell executed his office the whiche he had over the londs of the colleges, so justly and exactly that he was had in great estimacion for his witty behaviour therin, and also for the trew, faythfull, and dylygent servyce extendyd towardes my lord his mayster.'[18] Although Cromwell never held a senior formal position in Wolsey's household and was rarely involved in matters of state (officially, at least), the fact that he increasingly supervised the cardinal's legal affairs and was able to exercise extensive ecclesiastical patronage gave him considerable power. Soon, he was besieged by many supplicants for the cardinal's favour. Addressing him in terms of the utmost deference, such as 'the right worshipful Mr. Cromwell' and 'Councillor to my Lord Legate', petitioners did not just use him as a conduit, but realised that in order to secure Wolsey's good graces they had first to secure his.[19] Although many of Cromwell's supplicants were poor men who stood to lose their homes or livelihoods as a result of the dissolution of the monastic houses, an increasing number of them were men of power and influence, such as the Abbot of York and John Bourchier, second Baron Berners.

At the same time as rising to the status of the cardinal's principal adviser, Cromwell was able to develop his private legal practice, becoming one of the most prosperous lawyers in the capital. Indeed, the two careers were complementary: Wolsey's name carried so much weight that clients scrambled for association with his chief agent.

Wolsey would soon be in dire need of his new protégé's assistance because events at court were taking an unexpected and disturbing turn. By 1526, Anne Boleyn had been in service to the queen for four years. She remained unmarried, her planned betrothal to James Butler having come to nothing. But there had been no shortage of other suitors. Now in her mid-twenties, Anne had grown in allure.[20] Her slim, petite stature gave her an appealing fragility, and she had luscious dark brown hair, which she grew very long. Her most striking feature, though, were her eyes, which were exceptionally dark and seductive, 'inviting conversation'. 'Her eyes, which are black and beautiful,' reported the Venetian ambassador, 'take great effect on those who served [her].' But for all that, Anne was not a conventional beauty. 'Madam Anne is not one of the handsomest women in the world,' sneered the same ambassador, 'she is of middling stature, swarthy complexion, long neck, wide mouth, bosom not much raised.'[21] Her skin was olive-coloured and marked by small moles at a time when flawless, pale complexions were admired. She also had small breasts, a large Adam's apple 'like a man's', and, most famously, the appearance of a sixth finger on one of her hands.[22]

But it was undoubtedly Anne's personal charisma and grace, rather than her physical appearance, that gave her an indefinable, irresistible sex appeal. Writing during Elizabeth I's reign, George Wyatt observed that her looks 'appeared much more excellent by her favour passing sweet and cheerful; and . . . also increased by her noble presence of shape and fashion, representing both mildness and majesty more than can be expressed'. While the women at court all tried to copy her style, the men were beguiled by her flirtatious, provocative manner, and her brazen self-confidence. Wyatt said of her: 'For behaviour, manners, attire and tongue she excelled them all.'[23] Unlike her elder sister, however, Anne kept a strict rein on her desires. She pushed the boundaries of flirtation as far as she could without damaging her reputation, and retained an aloofness that only served to increase her appeal.

But there was one suitor whom Anne did not keep at bay. Henry Percy was the son and heir of the Earl of Northumberland, one of the most powerful nobles in the country. He had been sent at a young age to serve as a page in Cardinal Wolsey's household, and would therefore have become acquainted with Cromwell. The cardinal had a low opinion of the young lord, and scorned his lack of financial sense. Having no respect for his noble birth, he was a bullying and controlling master.

His service to Wolsey introduced Percy into court circles, as his father had no doubt intended, and he soon formed a passionate attachment to Mistress Boleyn. For as much as she liked to play the *belle dame sans merci*, Anne was not devoid of emotion, and she fell deeply in love with Percy. Theirs was a forbidden courtship, however, for the Earl of Northumberland had long since planned to marry his son to Lady Mary Talbot, daughter of the Earl of Shrewsbury. For all her popularity at court, Anne was still a mere knight's daughter and by no means a sufficiently good match for his son. But Percy and Anne were determined to be together, and were therefore betrothed in secret.

Nothing remained hidden at the Tudor court for long, and when news of the betrothal broke, it put Wolsey in an extremely awkward position. Not only was the Earl of Northumberland incensed that the cardinal had not kept a close enough eye on Percy to prevent the betrayal, but the king himself objected to the match. Henry had every right to be offended: given the importance of the earldom of Northumberland, his permission had to be sought for the marriage of its heir. Wolsey furiously upbraided the young lord in front of his household and summoned his father to take him away from court before he could cause any more trouble. Percy was married to Mary Talbot shortly afterwards.

Wolsey's biographer, George Cavendish, claimed that the cardinal had put a stop to Lord Percy's relationship with Anne at the behest of the king, who had already fallen passionately in love with her himself. However, the timing makes this unlikely. Their betrothal was broken off by the end of 1523, and it was not for another three years that Anne was talked of as the king's new inamorata.

The early relationship between Henry VIII and Anne Boleyn showed little sign of the intensity that it would later develop. The very fact that Anne had been at court for some four years before there was any sign of an attachment suggests that it was hardly a case of love at first sight. Besides, for at least some of that time, Henry had been occupying himself with Anne's elder sister, Mary. But Anne was made of very different stuff to her sister – and the various other mistresses who had gone before her. Far from being seduced by the heady prospect of becoming the King of England's lover, she resolved from the moment that his attentions began to hold out for a much greater prize. She would not be a mere mistress: she would be queen. It was an extraordinarily audacious plan, even for one born of such an ambitious family. Anne had not even enjoyed sufficient status to marry the Earl of Northumberland's son, and yet she had now set her sights on marrying the king. There was also the small fact that Henry already had a queen – and a popular one at that. But Anne rightly judged that he was tiring of a wife who, at forty, was some five years older than himself and now unlikely to bear him the son he so desperately needed. By contrast, she herself was still young and with every prospect of fertility.

Keeping the king at arm's length proved a masterstroke. Henry loved the thrill of the chase as much in his private life as he did in the hunt. If he had bedded Anne straight away, she would have been soon discarded and forgotten. Her refusal to yield increased her allure tenfold and drove the king wild with frustrated lust and 'violent passion'.[24] Before long, this mighty and all-powerful monarch had been reduced to the status of a lovesick puppy. Writing in 1527, Henry complained that he had 'been more than a year wounded by the dart of love, and not yet sure whether I shall fail or find a place in your affection', begging Anne to 'give yourself, body and heart, to me'.[25] He even promised to make her his 'sole mistress', a privilege that he had afforded to no other woman before. This was hardly enough to tempt Anne, who retorted: 'I would rather lose my life than my honesty . . . Your mistress I will not be.' She played the king with all the skill of a puppeteer, giving him just enough encouragement to keep him interested, but rebuffing him if he tried to overstep the mark. Thus, one moment Henry was writing with gleeful anticipation of the prospect of kissing Anne's 'pretty duggs [breasts]', and the next he was lamenting how far he was from the 'sun', adding mischievously, 'yet the heat is all the greater'.[26]

It did not take Anne long to bring her royal suitor around to the idea of ending his marriage to Catherine. By the end of 1527, he had promised to make her his wife. And he knew exactly who he would commission to bring it all about. Wolsey was summoned to attend the king in his privy chamber. When his master instructed him to begin proceedings for a divorce from the queen, the cardinal was said to have sunk to his knees and begged Henry to reconsider, remaining in that position for more than an hour as he used every persuasion he could muster.[27] But it was no use: the king remained implacable. Although the cardinal was well aware of his master's infatuation with Mistress Boleyn, he had apparently no idea that she lay at the heart of his master's decision, for in agreeing to do his bidding, he remarked that he hoped a suitable princess could be found to replace Catherine.

But any hopes that Henry may have cherished of a swift annulment would soon prove ill-founded. Frustrated by Wolsey's inability to resolve matters, Henry began to suspect that his chief minister was deliberately employing delaying tactics. There may have been a grain of truth in this. The cardinal knew his royal master better than anyone, and probably judged that his passion for Anne would fade as quickly as it had for many other ladies at court. But he also knew how dangerous it was to disobey the king's commands and therefore begged Henry that, whatever reports to the contrary he received concerning his management of the business, he should 'conceive none opinion of me but that in this matter and in all other things that may touch your honor and surety I shall be as constant as any living creature'.[28]

It is not clear to what extent, if at all, Cromwell assisted his master in trying to secure the divorce. But since he had already proved his immense skill in legal matters, it is likely that the cardinal set him to work in preparing the ground. The key premise for the annulment was the questionable validity of Henry's marriage to Catherine, given that she was the widow of his brother Arthur. According to the Bible: 'If a man shall take his brother's wife, it is an unclean thing ... they shall be childless.'[29] The fact that Henry and Catherine had a living daughter, Mary, was beside the point: it was sons that counted. Catherine, though, steadfastly maintained that her marriage to Arthur had never been consummated, so she had been free to marry his brother. On 17 May 1727 Wolsey convened a secret tribunal which the king attended to answer charges of cohabiting with his brother's wife. It achieved nothing, and the hearing was disbanded at the end of the month.

Wolsey was skirting around the issue, and Henry knew it. The divorce could only be granted with Pope Clement VII's sanction, so his efforts ought to be focused in that direction. But to complicate matters, the Pope was a prisoner of the Holy Roman Emperor, Charles V, whose mutinous troops had sacked Rome in the same month as Wolsey's tribunal. Not only did this limit the Pope's capacity for action, but his captor, Charles, was the nephew of Catherine of Aragon so he was unlikely to do anything that might cause the Emperor offence. Henry duly declared war on Charles at the beginning of 1528, but this produced no effect.

Further catastrophe struck in late May, when the sweating sickness broke out in London. This most virulent of diseases, which had claimed many thousands of lives ever since the first recorded outbreak in 1485, rapidly assumed epidemic proportions, sweeping across the entire country in a matter of weeks. Dr Caius, a contemporary physician, described its characteristically rapid progress: 'In the year of our Lord God 1485, shortly after the 7th day of August . . . there chanced a disease among the people, lasting the rest of that month and all September, which for the sudden sharpness and unwont cruelness passed the pestilence.' While some victims survived for up to fourteen days, the sickness

> immediately killed some in opening their windows, some in playing with children in their street doors; some in one hour, many in two, it destroyed; and at the longest to them that merrily dined, it gave a sorrowful supper. As it found them, so it took them; some in sleep, some in wake, some in mirth, some in care, some fasting and some full, some busy and some idle; and in one house sometime three, sometime five, sometime more, sometime all; of the which if the half in every town escaped, it was thought great favor. This disease, because it most did stand in sweating from the beginning until the ending, was called here *The Sweating Sickness*; and because it first began in England, it was named in other countries 'The English sweat.'[30]

The cause of the disease remains unknown, but it tended to afflict the richer members of society more than the poor. Erasmus attributed it to inadequate ventilation, clay floors and the unchanged, rotting rushes with which rooms were commonly strewn. He also claimed that excessive consumption at mealtimes was a contributory factor, as well as the use of too much salt.

The onset of the disease would be marked by a feeling of apprehension, followed by violent cold shivers, dizziness and severe pains in the head and neck. Having been unable to keep warm, the sufferer would then experience hot sweats, palpitations, intense thirst and delirium. In the final stages, they would be overwhelmed with exhaustion and an urge to sleep. 'This disease . . . is the easiest in the world to die of,' concluded the French ambassador, Cardinal du Bellay, in June 1528.[31]

The mortality looked set to be very great in the capital during this latest epidemic, and there was widespread panic. 'About two thousand only have been attacked by it in London,' reported du Bellay, although he added that those who had so far escaped 'might be seen as thick as flies hurrying out of the streets and the shops into the houses, to take the sweat the instant they were seized by the distemper . . . I assure you that the priests there have a better time of it than the physicians, except that there is not enough of them to bury the dead . . . Twelve years ago, when the same thing happened, ten thousand persons died in ten or twelve days, it is said: but it was not so sharp as it is now beginning to be . . . Everybody is terribly alarmed.'[32]

Henry VIII, ever fearful of infection, ordered that the court be broken up. He hastily left London and fled to a succession of residences in the country. To his horror, he learned that his beloved Anne had contracted the disease. She was swiftly conveyed to her father's estate at Hever Castle in Kent, where her life hung in the balance for several days. For all his declarations of undying love, Henry stayed away and instead contented himself with writing to her. He was obliged to live a virtually solitary existence, for an alarming number of his closest attendants had started to fall ill too, including Henry Norris, William FitzWilliam and William Paget.

Meanwhile, Wolsey had bravely decided to stay in London, only moving as far as Hampton Court, where he continued to conduct his tortuous negotiations for the king's 'Great Matter'. Several members of his household fell prey to the sweat, and a letter that the cardinal wrote to his royal master at this time suggests that he too may have been a victim. He assured Henry: 'If it shall fortune the same to be the last word that ever I shall speak or write unto your Highness, I dare boldly say and affirm your Grace hath had of me a most loving, true and faithful servant.'[33]

Although Cromwell managed to avoid infection, his wife was not so fortunate. Elizabeth died that summer, almost certainly of the same disease that was decimating the capital's population. The last reference to her is in a letter from Richard Cave, a close associate of the Cromwells, on 18 June 1528. He recommended himself to Thomas and his wife, and thanked the former for his 'good cheer' when he was last with him. The letter was written from 'Stanford', which was probably Stamford in Lincolnshire, so it is possible that Elizabeth was already dead by the time he wrote it and that news had not yet reached him.[34]

Given that Cromwell was capable of intense loyalty and affection to those closest to him, he must have been grief-stricken by the loss of his wife – and no doubt shocked by its suddenness. Although the surviving records provide only a few tantalising details of the Cromwells' marriage, which is perhaps inevitable given that Elizabeth died before her husband had risen to real prominence at court, they seem to have enjoyed a harmonious marriage. The reference by Cromwell to his 'well beloved wyf' was more than just the usual niceties of address. She had borne him three children, had established a well-run household at Austin Friars and had acted on his behalf when business took him away from home. The fact that he had been content for her mother to come and live with them is a further indication of affection. The will that Cromwell drafted a year later suggests that he still cherished the memory of his 'late Wyff'. Among his most generous bequests were those to her mother, Mercy Pryor, her sister Joan and her children, and other members of Elizabeth's family.[35]

But there is also evidence – albeit obscure – that Cromwell may have had an illegitimate daughter. Jane Cromwell appears in the archives of the county of Chester. Little is known about her, except that she married William Hough of Leighton in Wirral, Cheshire, some time between 1535 and 1540. Girls were often married as young as twelve years old, but even if the latter date for Jane's marriage is accepted, she must have been conceived while Cromwell's wife was still alive. Jane's husband, a staunch Catholic, was the son of Richard Hough, who was Cromwell's agent in Cheshire from 1534 to 1540. It is therefore likely that Cromwell arranged their marriage, which was a good one for a girl of Jane's obscure origins. But he would arguably have performed this favour for any loyal servant, and there is little other than the girl's surname to suggest that she might have been his daughter. She could equally have been the daughter of one of his sisters, who then adopted his name in the same way as his nephew Richard did – in order to enhance her prospects.

The sources provide no other hint of infidelity on Cromwell's part. Nor do they suggest that he took any mistresses after Elizabeth's death. When he was invited to stay with the Duke of Norfolk in York in 1537, his prospective host quipped: 'And if ye lust not to dally with my wife', he would be happy to supply for his comfort 'a young woman with pretty proper tetins [breasts]'.[36] This says more about Norfolk's sexual licence than Cromwell's. The duke, whose wife had cause to complain about the 'harlot' Bess Holland, clearly kept other willing mistresses in his household. By contrast, Cromwell appeared to have strict moral standards. In his will, he requested a priest 'of continent and good living' to pray for his soul, and he would later abhor the tales that were brought to him of vice and infidelity among the occupants of the religious houses. John Foxe concurred that he was 'of suche vertue, as not without sorow we may wyshe for euen in the mooste noble families nowe a dayes'.[37]

Cromwell's son Gregory seems to have left home shortly after Elizabeth's death, ostensibly to begin his education but possibly also to avoid infection. There is no record that his sisters followed suit: their maternal grandmother probably superintended their upbringing at home after the death of their mother. Gregory was placed in the care of Margaret Vernon, Prioress of Little Marlow, a modest house of Benedictine nuns in Buckinghamshire. It was by no means unusual for gentlemen to place their young children in the care of nuns. Cromwell's choice may have had more to do with the prioress than the place. Margaret Vernon was a close friend of his. They had probably met through Wolsey, with whom Margaret was well acquainted, and their intimate and chatty correspondence suggests mutual respect, even affection. The prioress had evidently benefited from Cromwell's protection in the past, for in one of her many letters to him she recalled: 'Your mastership knoweth right well that there was by my enemies so many high and slanderous words and your mastership had made so great instant labour for me.'[38]

Although it was not considered appropriate for boys to stay in nunneries beyond the age of nine or ten, Margaret later claimed that Cromwell had promised that she should superintend Gregory's care until he was twelve years old.[39] While the nuns could teach girls, they were only permitted to supervise boys, who were usually accompanied by a male tutor. This was certainly the case with Gregory, who was taught by a succession of distinguished tutors appointed by his father.

The first scholar to direct Gregory's studies at Little Marlow was John Chekyng of Pembroke College, Cambridge, who sent regular reports to Cromwell of his son's progress. Although Cromwell had high hopes for the boy, he was something of a disappointment – at least academically. In his first dispatch of 27 July 1528 Chekyng noted that his charge 'works and plays alternately. He is rather slow, but diligent.' Perhaps in a fit of professional jealousy, Chekyng claimed that he was appalled by how badly tutored Gregory had been, so that he could hardly conjugate three verbs when first committed to his care, 'though he repeated the rules by rote'. He added that as a result of Palgrave's style of teaching, he did not believe that Gregory would ever make a scholar and that he would have to 'unteach him nearly all he has learned'. But he assured Cromwell that his son was 'now studying the things most conducive to the reading of authors, and spends the rest of the day in forming letters'.[40]

A letter from Gregory himself was included with that of his tutor. The rather erratic spelling and grammar suggests that Chekyng's assessment had been accurate, but the affectionate little letter also makes clear just how close the bond was between father and son. 'Most dere father,' Gregory begins, 'I humbly recomend me unto yow, and hertily beseche yow of yowr daly blessyng, naturally bowndon thayreunto, for the wiche and other yowr manifowld benefittys to me colatyt, I am and schalbe yowr daly bedman, interely desyryng the continwans of the same, trusting soo to accomplysse and fulfyll yowr parentall commandments in the passage of myne erudicion, that yow my good father schall tharewith be ryght wel contentyd, by God's helpe, the wiche with hys grace Hee send hus. Amen.' He signed the letter: 'By yowr vigelant sone, Gregori Cromewell.'[41]

Gregory apparently made rapid progress under Chekyng's watchful eye. In the tutor's next letter, written in November 1528, he notes that 'Little Gregory is becoming great in letters.' Gregory had been joined by a boy named Christopher, who may have been his cousin, Christopher Wellyfed. The boy was evidently supported by Cromwell because among the contemporary records is an account by Christopher to Cromwell dated 15 June 1530, detailing his expenditure 'from the Feast of the Annunciation to that of John the Baptist'.[42] Gregory benefited from the influence of this boy, who Chekyng noted 'does not require much stirring up'. A boisterous and apparently accident-prone child, Christopher had started a fire in his lodgings soon after arriving. He had fallen asleep while reading by candlelight, and the candle had fallen on to the straw mattress below. The resulting fire had consumed a new feather bed and bolster, sheets, and several items of clothing (including two doublets and hose) belonging to Christopher and Nicholas Sadler – probably a younger brother or other relative of Cromwell's secretary and close friend, Ralph Sadler. If the walls of their chamber had not been plastered, Chekyng confided to Cromwell, 'we had had mor harme'. By November 1530 Christopher had left Little Marlow, having run up expenses that a rueful Chekyng admitted were 'something large'.[43]

Cromwell continued to support his nephew after he had completed his studies. A brief reference in a letter of June 1533 from Cromwell's cousin, Nicholas Glossop, implies that Cromwell had arranged for Christopher to spend some time at Cambrai, although the purpose of his visit is not specified.[44] Although his nephew was evidently no great scholar, Cromwell later helped him secure a career in the Church – something that Christopher had, rather unpredictably, expressed a desire to pursue. Cromwell also arranged an advantageous marriage for his niece, Alice Wellyfed. Their parents, Cromwell's sister Elizabeth and her husband William, both died in 1533, so Cromwell perhaps felt a heightened sense of responsibility for their welfare thereafter. Family ties remained of prime importance to him and would do so throughout his increasingly flourishing career.

Meanwhile, Chekyng sent assurances to Cromwell that Gregory had continued to improve and would be 'loaded with Latin' by the next time he saw him.[45] Cromwell was clearly very assiduous about his son's care, fearful no doubt that he too would succumb to some terrible sickness or disease. On the rare occasions when he could be spared from court, he visited Gregory at Little Marlow, and received regular reports of his welfare at other times. In one letter, Chekyng assured him that Gregory was being kept warm during the onset of winter with thick cloaks and blazing fires. He also thanked Cromwell for sending a bundle of cloth the day before, which was no doubt intended to provide winter clothes for his son. The tutor added that various reports had been spread about Cromwell in Cambridge, which he was glad had 'proved false'.[46] It is not clear what this referred to, but it is an indication of Cromwell's growing prominence that his dealings were being talked about outside London.

Chekyng's loyalty was poorly repaid. Diligent though he was as to his son's welfare, Cromwell was sometimes slow to pay the tutor what was due to him for board, lodging and tuition. On 28 June 1528 Chekyng wrote a respectful but insistent letter, begging to know whether Cromwell had received his account because he was in debt and being pressed for money from other quarters. There is no record of whether Cromwell settled the account on this occasion, but relations between the two men had deteriorated significantly by the following summer. Cromwell had evidently complained about the standard of Chekyng's teaching, claiming that his 'folks' had 'profited nothing' from his care. The tutor wrote an indignant reply, reminding Cromwell of the many other pupils who had benefited from his instruction and assuring him that he would gladly relinquish Cromwell's protégés, 'for if I never have 1*d*. advantage by any scholer, I trust to have a poor living'. He claimed to have laid out forty shillings every six weeks for the boys, and the fact that Cromwell repaid him so infrequently meant that he was constantly in debt.[47]

Cromwell's treatment of Chekyng might suggest a miserly side to his character. That he was eager to bolster his riches, and careful to preserve them once gained, is evidenced by his voluminous business correspondence. It made sound financial sense to settle accounts as late as possible, but the fact that he applied this principle to Gregory's education belies the care that he otherwise showed towards his son. He wanted the boy to receive the best possible education, but he was apparently not willing to pay for it – or at least, not in a timely manner.

It is possible, though, that Cromwell blamed Chekyng for his son's slow progress and withheld the money until he saw better results. He may also have been so preoccupied with court affairs that he sometimes neglected his own. Chekyng's would not be the only debt that he overlooked. One account tells of an old woman who had been owed money by Cromwell for some time. When she reminded him of it, he immediately repaid the debt in full and gave her a yearly pension of four pounds and a livery in recompense. Moreover, there are numerous reports of his generosity towards the poor and other charitable causes. It therefore seems unlikely that his slowness in settling Gregory's tuition fees was due simply to a natural miserliness.

The many demands of Cromwell's political and legal career had allowed him little time to grieve for either the death of his wife or the departure of his son. Certainly there would have been no more than the briefest of respites from his official duties. Once the sweating sickness had retreated and it was safe for the king to return to London, the plans for his divorce had resumed in earnest. In October

Cardinal Campeggio arrived from Rome. He had been appointed legate by the Pope and entrusted to decide upon the case for the divorce on his behalf. As well as listening to many lengthy arguments from Henry and Wolsey, he also held an audience with the queen. Catherine showed him the papal dispensation that had been granted by an earlier Pope, sanctioning her marriage to Henry despite the fact that she had been married to his brother. Campeggio seized upon this as an excuse to invalidate his commission, which in turn occasioned further delays.

By then, Wolsey was clinging on to power by his fingertips. Angered by his failure to bring proceedings to a swift – and positive – conclusion, Anne Boleyn turned against the cardinal, accusing him of deliberately causing delays and obstacles. 'I cannot comprehend, and the king still less, how your reverent lordship, after having allured us by so many fine promises about divorce, can have repented of your purpose,' she upbraided him. Henry, too, was losing patience, and ordered a covert investigation into his adviser's activities. Wolsey complained to his royal master that he was 'greatly suspected of all men herein'.[48] But he doggedly pursued the increasingly tortuous negotiations with the papal legate, and in June 1529 convened a trial at Blackfriars to prove the illegality of Henry's marriage. The trial was adjourned by Campeggio on 30 July in order to allow a petition from Queen Catherine to reach the Pope in Rome.

It is perhaps an indication of how vulnerable Cromwell felt that he had drawn up his will during the trial.[49] He appointed Ralph Sadler as executor – a sign of the enormous trust that he now placed in his secretary. Written on 12 July 1529, its principal beneficiaries were his children: Anne, Grace and Gregory. The latter figured most prominently, as might be expected for Cromwell's only son and heir. He bequeathed the boy the substantial sum of 666 pounds (equivalent to more than £200,000 today), which he stipulated should be used to purchase land. He judged that the income from this should be sufficient to pay for 'the educacyon and fynding honestly of my saide Soon [*sic*] Gregory in vertue good lerning and Maners untill such tyme as he shall cum to the full age of xxii yeres.' He added that his executors should 'be good unto my saide Son Gregory and to see he do lose no tyme but to se him verteously ordered & brought up according to my trust'. Cromwell ordered that a further 200 pounds be given to Gregory when he reached the age of twenty-four, and supplemented this generous bequest with some of his most valuable household items.

Cromwell also made provision for his daughters. That Anne and Grace were remembered in his will when he might have been expected to focus solely upon his male heir suggests that he was close to them. The affectionate reference in Cromwell's own hand to his 'litill Doughters Anne and Grace' implies that they were very young when the will was drawn up. To both girls, Cromwell bequeathed 100 marks (equivalent to around £20,000 today) when they came of age or were married.

The document is the only record we have of the two girls' existence. It is also the only record of their death. The provisions their father had made for them in his will were crossed out at a later date. How much later is not certain. The cause and date of their deaths are not recorded, but they seem to have died within a short time of each other. It is possible that they, like their mother, fell prey to the sweating sickness, outbreaks of which had continued to appear in the capital periodically after 1528, or to some other virulent disease. Cromwell must have been greatly grieved that both his daughters were taken from him so young (the eldest could have been no more than fourteen years old) and in such quick succession, and would have missed their presence keenly. It may have been to ease the loss that he invited his sister and brother-in-law, Elizabeth and William Wellyfed, to come and live with him at Austin Friars. William proved a useful addition to the household, keeping an eye on the servants during Cromwell's frequent absences on court business.[50]

Cromwell remembered all his closest friends and family in his will. To Ralph Sadler he bequeathed 200 marks (about £40,000), along with 'my Seconde gowne Jaquet and Doblet and all my bokes'. His old friend Stephen Vaughan received a similar bequest. Elizabeth and William Wellyfed were bequeathed an annual allowance of twenty pounds (more than £6,000). As well as these personal bequests were the usual charitable ones, which Cromwell did not stint upon.

Around the same time as he drew up his will, Cromwell also made arrangements for the care of his niece – presumably a daughter of his sister, Katherine Williams. Katherine was already dead by this time because the will refers to his 'onlye Suster' Elizabeth.[51] The recipient of the letter he drafted soon afterwards is not named, but judging from the almost bullying tone in which his master addressed him he was evidently an agent or servant. Cromwell began with a sharp reprimand, saying that he 'mervayle gretlye that ye haue made no better spede for your chaplain In whos Fauours I haue wryten vnto Mr Chaunceler of Wynchester'. With a swift change of tone, he continued: 'Syr I praye you be so good vnto me as to lett me send my systers daughter vnto the Jentylwoman your wyff and that ye wyll on my behalf desyre her to take her and to bryng her vpp for the which her goodnes yf she wylbe content so to doo I shold rekyn my self moste bounden both to you and here and besydes the payment For her borde I wyll so content your wyffe as I trust she shalbe woll pleasyd.'[52] His generosity towards his family suggests an abiding loyalty and affection. Despite the many other more pressing demands upon his time, he never forgot the ties of his youth, and now that he was in a position to help members of his family he never missed an opportunity to do so.

The collapse of the Blackfriars trial dangerously weakened Wolsey's position. It had been his last chance to secure the divorce, and he had no other weapons in his armoury. Although he had done his utmost and achieved more than many other men would have been capable of, he was increasingly used as a scapegoat in the failure to resolve the king's 'Great Matter'. 'He would promise muche and performe lytle,' claimed one scathing commentator. Meanwhile, a gleeful Chapuys reported to his master: 'It is generally and almost publicly stated that the affairs of the cardinal are getting worse and worse every day.'[53]

Hall's chronicle records that shortly afterwards a book containing no fewer than thirty-four articles against Wolsey was presented to Henry, who 'perceiued the high pride and coueteousnes of the

Cardinal, and saw openly with what dissimulacion and clokyng, he had handeled the kynges causes: how he with faire liying words, had blynded and defrauded.'[54] For a time, the king refused to act against his minister, perhaps mindful of the loyal service he had shown him ever since his accession twenty years before. But Anne continued to pile on the pressure, and on 9 October 1529 Wolsey was indicted for *praemunire* – a law that prohibited the assertion of papal jurisdiction against the supremacy of the monarch – in the Court of the King's Bench. He resigned the great seal nine days later.

On 22 October Wolsey surrendered all his property to the crown. With admirable composure, he declared: 'I would all the world knew that I have nothing but it is his [Henry's] of right, for by him, and of him I have received all that I have: therefore it is of convenience and reason, that I render unto His majestie the same againe with all my hart.' Even then, Henry protected him against complete ruin. Wolsey was offered the choice of answering to the king or parliament. Perhaps recognising the vestiges of affection that his royal master still felt towards him, he chose the former. But Henry's affection was notoriously fickle, and courtiers were quick to conclude that Wolsey's prospects were not favourable. On the same day that Wolsey surrendered his property, the French ambassador, Jean du Bellay, reported: 'Wolsey has just been put out of his house, and all his goods taken into the King's hands. Besides the robberies of which they charge him, and the troubles occasioned by him between Christian princes, they accuse him of so many other things that he is quite undone.'[55]

When the cardinal left York Place and entered his barge, he saw to his dismay that crowds had gathered on the banks, expecting to see him taken to the Tower. They were disappointed, for he had been ordered to his house at Esher. Nevertheless, it was a humiliating moment for the man who had been so high in the king's favour for so long, and it was with a heavy heart that he and his remaining attendants (including Cromwell) made their way westwards along the Thames. But Cavendish claims that they were overtaken at Putney, close to Cromwell's first home, by Henry Norris, groom of the stool, who brought him Henry's ring and a message telling him 'to be of good chere for he was as myche in his highenes favor as ever he was'.[56] Overwhelmed with relief and gratitude, Wolsey knelt in the mud to thank him for the joyful news. He gave Norris his cross and sent the king his fool, Sexton (known as 'Patch'), as a gift.

By the end of October, du Bellay was already confidently predicting that 'it is not improbable that he [Wolsey] may regain his authority'.[57] But he and his household had spent a miserable few weeks at Esher, devoid of furnishings and in great fear of what the future might hold. Cromwell had stood by his master throughout, desperate to help him try to regain the king's favour. Despite Henry's gesture of goodwill, though, Wolsey knew that even he could not stay the tide for long. It was only a matter of time before he would have to fight not just for his reputation, but for his life.

CHAPTER 4

'Make or marre'

ON THE MORNING of All Hallows' Day 1529 Wolsey's gentleman-usher and biographer, George Cavendish, encountered a distraught Cromwell in a window embrasure of the great chamber at Wolsey's residence in Esher. With tears pouring down his cheeks, he clutched his primer and recited 'our lady mattens'. It was a rare display of emotion and piety – 'a strange sight in him afore', as Cavendish himself admitted – and betrays the strength of Cromwell's affection for and loyalty to his master the cardinal. The scene was later recreated (with some embellishment) by Shakespeare in his history play, *Henry VIII*, when a tearful Cromwell bids his master farewell:

> Must I, then, leave you? must I needs forego
> So good, so noble and so true a master?
> Bear witness, all that have not hearts of iron,
> With what a sorrow Cromwell leaves his lord.
> The king shall have my service: but my prayers
> For ever and for ever shall be yours.[1]

But Cromwell's tears were for himself, too. When Cavendish asked him if he was distraught because of Wolsey, he replied: 'Nay, it is for my unhappy adventure. For I am like to lose all that I have laboured for, all the daies of my life, for doing of my master true and diligent service . . . this I knowe well, that I am disdained withal for my master's sake . . . An evill name once gotten will not lightly be put away.'[2] By the time of Wolsey's fall, Cromwell was recognised as the most senior and trusted of the cardinal's advisers. And yet, without a formal office or income from his employment in Wolsey's household, his influence rested entirely on his master's survival. All the efforts he had made on the cardinal's behalf during the past decade had apparently been in vain. His fate – and his reputation – were so closely tied to his master's that his cherished hopes of a dazzling career at court were all but dashed. He had, in short, backed the wrong horse. Worse still, without the cardinal's protection, he now faced alone the wrath of all the enemies he had made as a result of the monastic dissolutions. Rumours were already circulating that he had been thrown into the Tower. How long would it be before they became a reality?

Self-pity did not sit easily with Cromwell, though, and he soon regained his composure, declaring to Cavendish (as much, perhaps, as to himself): 'I do entend (god wyllyng) this after none [afternoon], whan my lord hathe dyned to ride to london and so to the Court, where I wyll other [either] make or marre or I come agayn, I wyll put my self in the prese [press] to se what any man is Able to lay to my charge of ontrouthe or mysdemeanor.'[3] He was as good as his word. After advising Wolsey on the winding-up of his excessive household, he set off for London, accompanied by his faithful servant Ralph Sadler. Shortly afterwards, on the night of 1–2 November, Sir John Russell, first Earl of Bedford and a trusted member of Henry's government, arrived at Esher, soaking wet, on a secret errand authenticated, again, by Henry's ring. A short while later, Wolsey was overjoyed to receive another sign of his royal master's favour in the form of 'plenty of howsshold stuff, vessell and plate And of all thynges necessary.'[4]

It is unlikely that Cromwell had been able to secure these comforts for his master so speedily. Nevertheless, he had wasted no time in promoting Wolsey's cause. Just a few days after arriving in London, Cromwell had been returned as a burgess (a representative of a borough) in the new parliament that had opened on 4 November. It is ironic that the principal means by which he had achieved this was through the influence of Thomas Howard, third Duke of Norfolk, a leading councillor and Wolsey's deadliest enemy.

The fifty-six-year-old Norfolk was one of the most distinguished and longest-serving members of Henry's court. His first marriage to Anne, who as the fourth surviving daughter of Edward IV was Henry VIII's aunt, had won him access to the most exclusive royal circles. He had served Henry VII faithfully throughout his reign, proving an able soldier and leader of men, and continued to enjoy favour in the next reign. A year after his accession Henry VIII made Howard a Knight of the Garter, the highest order of chivalry in the land and an honour that he would justify when he played a prominent role in defeating the Scots at Flodden in 1513. The following year he was made Earl of Surrey, and on the death of his father in 1524 he succeeded to the dukedom of Norfolk. When his niece, Anne Boleyn, ensnared the king's affections, it served to enhance Norfolk's standing at court even more.

'He ys a ernest man, a bold man and a witty, in all his matters,' observed one contemporary.[5] 'Witty' meant sharp rather than humorous: unlike Cromwell, Norfolk was not known for his sparkling wit or conversation. Proud and arrogant, he also possessed a violent temper and lashed out at anyone who caused offence. Jealously guarding his favour with the king, he harboured a bitter hatred towards those who rivalled his own influence. Holbein's portrait of him, painted around 1539 when he was sixty-six years old, shows him with a stern, menacing face and cold, dark staring eyes. Physically, he was the opposite of Cromwell. The Venetian ambassador described him as 'small and spare in person, his hair black'.[6] He was always the most outspoken advocate for an aggressive, warlike foreign policy, which had set him at odds with Wolsey, who tended to be more cautious. Norfolk had in any case taken a dim view of this low-born upstart, whom he believed had no place in either the council or the court. He would take a similar view of Wolsey's protégé. That Cromwell should now seek his assistance is an indication of his own audacity.

Cromwell rightly judged that Norfolk's star would have risen in direct inverse proportion to Wolsey's fall, and he apparently had no scruple in petitioning his master's adversary. Indeed, with Norfolk in the ascendancy, securing his favour was an essential prerequisite for promoting Cromwell's interests at court. But if pragmatism had once more won out over principle, this was not a sign that Cromwell had abandoned his old master: befriending his enemy was simply a means to an end.

Norfolk secured the king's consent for Cromwell's entry into parliament, but this was granted on condition that Cromwell could get himself elected to a local seat, as was required for members of the Commons, and that he would comply with royal instructions. The former was a challenge at this late stage, particularly as he lacked a patron. But Cromwell made the most of the few tenuous court connections he did have. His first recourse was to instruct Sadler to persuade Thomas Russhe, a friend of Wolsey's (and, according to Cavendish, of Cromwell too) who had connections to the Willoughby family, to help him obtain the Suffolk seat of Orford. When this failed, Cromwell called upon Sir William Paulet, Wolsey's steward for the bishopric of Winchester, who had the authority to nominate members to seats in that diocese. Shortly afterwards, he was returned as the new member for Taunton.

Cromwell participated in the business of the house from 4 November until the first session closed on 17 December. During this time, he sat on a committee that had been established to investigate the misuse of the king's protection by merchants. More significantly, he may also have played a leading role in the Commons' campaign against the corruption of the clergy. It is ironic that it was the parliament that had been convened to deal with the collapse of Wolsey's policy that marked the beginning of his protégé's public career. It was also highly innovatory: Cromwell had become the first statesman in English history to build his rise to power on membership of the House of Commons. He shrewdly judged that this would provide him with immunity from hostile attacks, as well as an excellent base from which to launch political action. But he also knew that parliamentary membership was not enough: to gain real power, he needed to win favour with the king and secure a formal position in his service.

Eager though he was to carve out his own political career, Cromwell had far from forgotten his former master. Cavendish claims that it was in this same parliament of 1529 that Cromwell successfully defended Wolsey against a bill of attainder (by which those who offended against the king could be deprived of their lands or even their lives), although the proceedings against the cardinal had been heard in the Court of the King's Bench in October. Since that court had failed to achieve an attainder, it is possible that a confession by Wolsey had been submitted to this parliament instead. Certainly an aggressive stance was taken by the new Lord Chancellor, Sir Thomas More, who had filled Wolsey's shoes. He denounced 'the great wether which is of late fallen'.[7] Wolsey's adversaries proceeded to record his faults in a series of forty-four articles, which were presented to the king on 1 December. They included violating the liberties of the Church, subverting the 'due course and order' of the law, and – most serious of all – claiming equality with the king. The cardinal, no doubt under intense pressure, had put his signature to the document, thereby acknowledging his guilt and preventing any restoration of his titles and offices. It was probably at this point that Cromwell spoke in his defence. He may even have done so at the request of the king, who still felt enough affection towards Wolsey not to see him attainted. This, together with Wolsey's submission, was enough to avoid an attainder. By the time parliament was adjourned on 17 December, Wolsey's position was secure – for now. Although he had forfeited his other offices, he remained Archbishop of York and papal legate. The latter offered him some protection from charges of treason, but it was far from infallible. He wrote to Cromwell in buoyant mood, arguing that by his submission the king had received more than he would otherwise have had, and hoping that now his affairs might be settled.

Cromwell's loyalty towards Wolsey is commendable. Even if Henry was reluctant to mete out the ultimate punishment for the cardinal's failure to secure a divorce, acting in support of the disgraced minister was still a highly risky business. Scores of Wolsey's other servants had immediately distanced themselves from him, anxious to protect their own position. One of the first to jump ship had been the cardinal's secretary, Stephen Gardiner, who conveniently chose to forget the many offices and preferments he had gained from this service, and became the king's secretary in July 1529. By September, he was writing to his former master to tell him that the king was reluctant to grant him an audience – clearly he himself had done little to persuade him. As soon as Wolsey was out of the way, Gardiner manoeuvred himself into a position to secure the newly vacant see of Winchester, the wealthiest in England. Cromwell's secretary, Ralph Sadler, confided to him a short while later that he had visited Gardiner to ask him to help the cardinal, but he 'said he knew nothing at all about my lord's Grace'. Sadler shrewdly predicted: 'I think he will do little or nothing to my Lord's [Wolsey's] avail, or to that of any of his friends, more than he may not choose for very shame, considering the advancements and promotion that he hath had at my Lord's hand. I have small trust in him.'[8]

Sir Thomas Heneage proved similarly fickle. A promising young protégé of Wolsey, the cardinal had later secured a position for him in the privy chamber so that he might help counteract the rise of the Boleyn faction. He had acted as a go-between for Wolsey and Anne, but his master came to distrust him – with good reason. When Wolsey fell from favour, Heneage was quick to disassociate himself from him. In response to the cardinal's plea for help, he callously told him to 'content yourself with that you have', adding the insincere assurance that 'the king will be good and gracious to your Grace.'[9]

In contrast, Cromwell refused to abandon his old master, even though it threatened to bring his newly won position in parliament to an abrupt end. With unflinching loyalty, he proceeded to act as an intermediary for the cardinal with the king, travelling between Wolsey's residence and the court, relaying messages and petitions. His prospects of success were grim indeed. He had precious few allies, and even they lacked any real influence. They included Sir Richard Page, who had begun his career in Wolsey's service before being appointed a gentleman of the privy chamber in 1516. He had continued to serve Wolsey's interests, however, and had therefore become well acquainted with Cromwell, who was sufficiently convinced of his loyalty to continue the association. Sir John Russell, who had enjoyed Wolsey's favour for some time, also proved willing to help further Cromwell's interests.

Nevertheless, Wolsey's enemies, triumphant at his fall, now dominated the court. Principal among them was the Duke of Norfolk. Given his kinship to Anne Boleyn, he had a close vested interest in the king's 'Great Matter'. As the highest-ranking nobleman in the country, he also had a natural disdain for the man whom he regarded as a base-born upstart. Together with his nephew George Boleyn, Viscount Rochford and the Duke of Suffolk, he was determined to engineer Wolsey's complete destruction. 'Dayly they wold send hyme some thyng or do some thyng ayenst hyme,' observed Cavendish, 'wherin they thought that they myght geve hyme a cause of heveness or lamentacion.'[10]

Cromwell alone was Wolsey's defender. In speaking on behalf of a man whom it was every day expected would be formally accused of treason, he was tainted by association. At the end of October 1529 Stephen Vaughan had written to him in a state of great anxiety: 'I commend me unto you and am greatly in doubt how you are entreated in this sudden overthrow of my lord your master [Wolsey]. I never longed to hear from you as now . . . You are more hated for your master's sake than for anything which I think you have wrongfully done against any man.' Vaughan had evidently predicted the catastrophe that befell Wolsey, for he added that he had 'wished very much' to tell Cromwell before he left London 'how much he feared what has come to pass, but durst not write it'. He was no fair-weather friend, though, and assured Cromwell: 'Like as a true heart is never overthrown with no tempest, like so cannot the same in your trouble but be now much more thristye [thirsty] to know your state . . . If there be any service in the world which I may do for you, let me have knowledge and be assured of me as of yourself.' He ended with a more positive assurance: 'Though I hear many things of you which please me no, yet do I doubt but your truth and wisdom shall deliver you from danger.'[11] Feeling embattled and vulnerable, Cromwell must have appreciated his friend's show of loyalty. But in truth, no matter how well-intentioned Vaughan was, there was little protection or influence he could bring to bear from the Netherlands. Cromwell was therefore forced to contemplate the bleak prospect of being surrounded by many powerful enemies at court, and precious few allies.

That Cromwell's name was still inextricably bound up with that of the disgraced cardinal is also suggested by the rash of letters from Wolsey's old clients, begging his protégé to take over their affairs. Wolsey's indictment under the statute of *praemunire* affected all those who had received grants of land from him because this not only nullified his own holdings, but those of his beneficiaries. Many of them now wrote in panic to Cromwell, desperate to protect their assets. They included William Page of Horsmonden in Kent, who had been granted some former monastic land by Wolsey and was now being challenged for it by its former owner. Page had therefore been advised by Sir Thomas Neville, a prominent lawyer and trusted royal councillor, to seek Cromwell's assistance.[12] Yet, far from eschewing anything connected with his former master, Cromwell seemed actively to promote their association. He even incorporated some of Wolsey's coat of arms into his own as a bold – and brave – statement of his enduring loyalty.

As soon as parliament was adjourned on 17 December, Wolsey wrote to Cromwell begging him to join him at Esher: 'As you love me, repair here this day, at the breaking up of the Parliament. I have to communicate to you touching my comfort, and need your advice on certain things requiring expedition, to be solicited there.' Cromwell evidently demurred, for a short while later Wolsey wrote again, urging him: 'I have certain things to communicate to you respecting yourself which you will be glad to hear.' Panic-stricken, he claimed that one of Cromwell's letters had been intercepted and never reached Esher, although this may have been a tactic to persuade his protégé to visit. He assured Cromwell that he was 'Myn onely ayder in thys myn intollerable anxiete and hevynes', and that he would trust no one else to solicit his causes, leaving them entirely in Cromwell's hands.[13]

The stress of the situation soon took its toll on Wolsey's health. A few days later, he fell ill. Now approaching his sixties, he had been in poor health for some time, having been treated for a variety of ailments which included the stone (probably gallstones), fevers, jaundice, throat infections, colic and dropsy. His fall from power sparked a rapid deterioration in his condition, causing him to lose his appetite and sleep badly. The onset of what may have been diabetes (which manifested itself by diarrhoea and vomiting) was aggravated by his refusal to eat regular meals. The cardinal blamed his condition on Cromwell's failure to visit, telling him: 'The forbearing and putting over of your coming hither hath so increased my sorrow, and put me in such anxiety of mynd, that this night my breath and wind, by sighing, was so short that I was by the space of three hours as one that should have died.' He mournfully added: 'If I be not removed to a drier air, and that shortly, there is little hope.' Although undoubtedly suffering, Wolsey made the most of his illness to persuade Cromwell to visit. 'If you love my life, break away this evening and come hither, to the intent I may open my mind unto you, and instruct you of the same, which I cannot commit to writing.' He ended with a plaintive entreaty that his servant should 'take some pain now for me, and forsake me not in this my extreme need . . . Now is the time to show whether you love me or not.'[14]

Wolsey's illness seems to have affected his mental state, for as well as entreating Cromwell to beg the king's favour, he also urged him to seek Anne Boleyn's mediation. 'Yf the desspleasure of my lady Anne be [some]what asswagyd, as I pray God the same may be, then yt shuld [be devised t]hat by sume convenyent meane she be further laboryd, [for th]ys ys the only helpe and remedy. All possyble means [must be used for] atteynyng of hyr favor.'[15] There could have been few persons at court less likely to intercede for the beleaguered cardinal than the woman who had been instrumental in his downfall. But Cromwell made the most of Wolsey's poor health to win her sympathy, and that of her royal suitor, for the beleaguered cardinal. Henry immediately dispatched his own physician, Dr William Butts, to attend Wolsey and also sent another ring as a sign of his affection. Anne sensed the need for diplomacy and sent him a token of her own. Buoyed up by these signs of favour, Wolsey made an apparently miraculous recovery.[16] He attempted a rapprochement with Anne at once, perhaps fooled into thinking that her concern for him had been genuine. He therefore granted her beloved brother, George, an annuity of 200 pounds from the lands of the bishopric of Winchester, and the same amount from

St Albans. This was almost certainly Cromwell's idea. He appreciated – as his master did not – that even some of the most influential nobles at court were financially dependent upon the crown and had little disposable income of their own. Their positions in the dazzling court of Henry VIII demanded a show of outward splendour that most could ill afford. As well as the grant to George Boleyn, Cromwell also arranged for Henry Norris's salary to be increased from 100 pounds to 200 pounds, and for Sir John Russell's annuity to be more than doubled.[17]

Although he arranged these gifts on Wolsey's behalf, Cromwell also benefited from them. With the cardinal confined away from the court at Esher, his agent received all the thanks, and a good portion of the resulting favour. That this had been a conscious strategy on his part is suggested by the fact that the majority of the gifts were to the Boleyns, whose antipathy towards Wolsey was so strong that it could hardly have been dissipated by a few hundred pounds bestowed here and there. But they might well have looked favourably upon the bestower. Little wonder, then, that when Wolsey followed up the grant to George Boleyn with a letter to Lady Anne, this went unanswered. Cromwell ruefully admitted: 'She gave kind words, but will not promise to speak to the King for you.' It is unlikely that he ventured further with Anne. Cromwell cautioned Wolsey: 'None dares speak to the King on his [Wolsey's] part for fear of Madame Anne's displeasure.' He was right. The Imperial ambassador, Eustace Chapuys, who had arrived at court in September 1529, informed his master, Charles V, that Anne was furious with Sir John Russell for commending Wolsey to the king. 'The lady had been very angry and refused to speak with him. Norfolk told him of her displeasure, and that she was irritated against himself because he had not done as much against him [Wolsey] as much as he might.'[18]

Charles V had appointed Chapuys to serve as his ambassador so that he might act as chief adviser to his aunt, Catherine of Aragon. Chapuys more than fulfilled his brief. A highly devout and conscientious man, he immediately struck up a close relationship with the beleaguered queen, and his visits brought her great comfort. She entrusted him with many messages to her nephew, and both she and her daughter Mary came to view him more as a much loved friend than an official adviser. For his part, Chapuys would grow genuinely fond of the two women, seeing himself as their only champion, and he threw himself fully behind their cause. In so doing, he developed a deep and implacable hatred of 'the Concubine', Anne Boleyn, and of all who aided her quest for the throne – Cromwell included.

Although officially they were sworn enemies, the two men had a great deal in common. Both were trained lawyers with a keen intellect and love of learning. They were also exceptionally shrewd and quickly appraised the most significant points of any situation. As they became better acquainted, Cromwell and Chapuys would remain sparring partners rather than friends, although their correspondence does suggest that they developed a grudging respect for each other as time went on. The ambassador once referred to 'the love I bore him [Cromwell]' in a letter to his master.[19] Cromwell would prove a good neighbour when, in October 1533, a fire broke out at the Imperial embassy, destroying Chapuys's clothes, furniture and valuables. The ambassador wrote at once to his master, bewailing this 'terrible and almost irreparable blow to me, who must be completely ruined in consequence!'. He added, however, that his neighbour Cromwell 'has sent to offer his help as regards my own private affairs'. Chapuys 'politely declined', but seemed touched by the offer.[20]

As Cromwell became more established at court, the apparently contradictory objectives of carving out a career while defending the most hated man there gradually became more aligned. Cavendish recalls: 'Master Cromwell, perceiving an occasion and a time given him to work for himself, and to bring the thing to pass which he long wished for, intended to work so in these matters to serve their desires, that he might the sooner bring his own enterprise to purpose . . . and so by their witty heads the two men worked together to bring by their policies Mr Cromwell in place and estate where he might do hymself good and my lord much profit.'[21] Becoming a regular visitor to court, even on such a difficult errand, enabled

Cromwell to build up his contacts there. Moreover, in taking charge of the disposal of Wolsey's lands, he was able to demonstrate his skill in legal affairs. Above all, though, the role of Wolsey's chief apologist brought Cromwell into ever more frequent contact with the king himself. At first, lacking both title and connections, he had been obliged to cultivate men who were already close to Henry. His choice was natural: the king's lawyers. It was the Attorney-General, Sir Christopher Hales, with whom Cromwell struck up a particularly close relationship, and who may have recommended him to the king.

Ironically, Henry was perhaps the only man at court who felt any affection towards the disgraced cardinal. At the end of December 1529 Ralph Sadler reported to his master that 'My Lord's [Wolsey's] hinderers and enemies have had time with the King before his friends', but added that he 'trusts their purpose will be prevented'.[22] Sadler's faith was justified. Henry was willing to lend a sympathetic ear to Cromwell's petitions on behalf of his master. These early exchanges gave Cromwell the chance to employ his considerable charm to win over the king, as well as to prove his usefulness in business matters. He did so to great effect. Less than a month after Wolsey's fall, a friend of Cromwell's had heard 'comfortable tydynges that you be in favour hilie [highly] with the Kynges grace, lordes and comunalytie aswell spirituall as temporall'.[23]

Although Wolsey's enemies had been quick to seize the initiative in court and council after his departure, there remained an unofficial vacancy that Henry himself was keen to see filled. The cardinal had been his mainstay ever since his accession in 1509. He had liberated the new king from the tedious business of government by proving himself indispensable in all matters – from diplomacy and foreign policy to justice, taxation and the Church. He was the first true polymath of Henry's government, and now the king needed another. Cromwell, perhaps with coaching from his old master, needed to demonstrate quickly that he could fill his shoes. The fact that he had so much in common with Wolsey was a significant advantage. It cannot have escaped the king's notice that Cromwell was also of humble stock and had clawed his way out of obscurity by a combination of immense skill and hard work, proving himself adept in a host of different businesses. In modern parlance, he might be termed a micro-manager: he certainly did not like to delegate. This may have derived from an arrogant belief that he alone could execute matters effectively, as well as from a natural (and often justified) suspicion of the motives of others.

Neither can the similarity of their characters have escaped the king's notice. Cromwell possessed the same exceptional shrewdness and clear-sightedness – perhaps even more so than his mentor – as well as the irresistible combination of charm, humour and irreverence that had kept Henry in thrall to the cardinal for so many years. He may not have enjoyed the benefits of a formal education, but he had learned to write and speak in as articulate and persuasive a manner as his better born counterparts – so much so that he would gain renown as a great orator throughout the court. Although he once declared that 'he would not, for anything in this world, be held as a liar or dissembler', he was already a master of diplomacy and deception, of saying one thing and meaning another.[24] In short, Cromwell was the ideal courtier. To boost his credentials still further, he had quickly learned the courtly pursuits of hunting and hawking, knowing that both were essential if he was to secure close and regular access to the king. He could also shoot well with a longbow. Such pastimes had the useful subsidiary benefit of enabling him to conduct informal business with other members of the court. Chapuys's letters are full of references to Cromwell inviting him to go hunting, and offering to give him a good horse for the task – a gift that the ambassador consistently declined. He also reported that Cromwell kept hawks at his house and liked to watch them fly in the evenings after dinner.

But Cromwell knew that, even had he wished to do so, he could not erase his lowly birth by trying to act the courtier. Instead, he made a virtue of his humble origins. Although he could flatter and fawn as convincingly as a seasoned courtier, he preferred to talk frankly, without embellishments. 'I know how desirous you are that people should speak to you openly and in a straightforward manner,' the Imperial ambassador told him.[25] Furthermore, Cromwell drew attention to his background as a means of convincing Henry that he considered himself utterly unworthy in the presence of such a mighty sovereign. It was a theme that Henry, ever vulnerable to flattery, soon warmed to. 'Most humblye prostrate at the Fete of your Magnifycence [I] beseche your highnes to pardon my boldnes [in] this wrytyng to your grace,' Cromwell concluded one dispatch, 'which onlye procedythe for the trowthe dewtye allegaunce and loue I doo bere to your mageste and the Common welth of this your Realme as our lorde knowyth vnto whom I shall as I am most bounden Incessantlye praye for the contenewans & prosperous conseruacyon of your most excellent most Royall and Imperyall estate long to Indure.'[26] But the king did not wish to be surrounded by men who would simply flatter and fawn: he wanted an adviser brave enough to challenge him and tell him the truth, as well as do his bidding. Thomas Cromwell was the perfect man to fill the void created by Wolsey's departure.

That both men were of such humble origins was more than a coincidence. Wolsey's rise to greatness was unprecedented, and could have rested as an extraordinary anomaly had it not been for the fact that no sooner had his career ended than the king chose another low-born man to take his place. This begs the question of whether Henry chose them precisely *because* of their backgrounds, not in spite of them. Did their upbringing give them significant skills that their noble colleagues lacked? Certainly, they were both highly skilled, self-taught men with a range of practical experience that would prove highly useful in their royal service. They were also extremely industrious with an enormous capacity for hard work – something that could not be said of most noble courtiers, whose positions had come to them by right, not by a hard-fought struggle. To aspire to a career in the king's service required considerable vision and ambition: it was a dream that would have seemed completely out of reach for the vast majority of ordinary subjects. This same ambition was the driving force for both men once they had gained a foothold in Henry's service; it gave them the energy and motivation to continue striving for even greater advancement, and as such gave them an edge over their more complacent rivals.

But Cromwell had to demonstrate that he was more than a mere clone of the cardinal: after all, no matter how high the latter had risen in Henry's favour, he had ultimately failed in a number of important tasks – not least securing the king's divorce from Catherine of Aragon. If Cromwell was to succeed where his master had failed, then helping to achieve this latter ambition was crucial. His prolific ability in legal matters was already acknowledged at court, and it cannot have taken Henry long to realise that it might usefully be applied to his 'Great Matter'. Legend has it that during one of their earliest meetings, Cromwell whispered into his sovereign's ear a scheme for all the revolutions that would take place in Church and government during the 1530s, whereupon Henry immediately ordered him to put it into action. The reality was probably rather different. Although the king undoubtedly spotted Cromwell's potential, what he was looking for in a new chief adviser had changed significantly since Wolsey first came to power. Then, Henry had been a pleasure-seeking young man, happy to entrust the business of government to Wolsey so that he might focus on more diverting pastimes. This arrangement had worked well for almost twenty years, but Wolsey's failure to secure the divorce had forced his master to take a more active interest in government – and he was not minded to relinquish that. What he wanted now was someone who could carry out his instructions, rather than direct proceedings themselves.

It was perhaps inevitable that contemporaries would draw comparisons between Cromwell and Wolsey, and speculate whether the former would succeed where his old master had failed. While many (noble) courtiers whispered disparaging remarks about yet another low-born servant having risen to prominence so soon after the last, Ambassador Chapuys used the comparison to flatter Cromwell. He told Charles V: 'I resolved, after some familiar sentences which passed between us, the better to gain him to our side, to pay him the compliment of saying that I had often regretted he did not come under his master's knowledge and favour at the same time as the Cardinal, for being, as he was, a more able and talented man than the latter, and there being now so many opportunities to gain credit and power, he might undoubtedly have become a greater man than the Cardinal, whilst the King's affairs would have gone on much better.' Chapuys concluded 'that I considered the King, his master, very lucky in possessing such a man as himself under present circumstances and in these troubled times'.[27] Cromwell himself must have been as eager to learn from, and surpass, his predecessor as he was to escape the constant comparisons between these two commoners in the king's service.

Impressive though Cromwell's reputation as a lawyer already was, Henry was unlikely to entrust such a weighty commission as the divorce to a man who, to him at least, was unproven. He therefore set Cromwell to work on an extremely complex legal matter that would test his much vaunted abilities. Although Wolsey had forfeited all his properties and goods to the crown upon resigning his office, the legal position of his colleges was complicated. They continued to function for almost a year after the cardinal's fall, albeit under increasingly straitened circumstances, thanks to the forfeiture of their revenues and possessions. But while the king could seize their valuables with no difficulty, the same could not be said of their lands. This was because the building of the colleges had been financed by the dissolution of the thirty or so monasteries that Cromwell had helped to administer. This dissolution, in turn, had only been possible with the Pope's sanction, which stipulated that the proceeds should be used to fund educational establishments. Henry himself had ratified this, vowing to protect the colleges from legal challenge. He was therefore reluctant to go back publicly on his promise and convert the lands to secular use. But his lawyers had found a loophole that enabled him to do so, and he eventually agreed that they could act on it. From around June 1530, commissioners were appointed and inquests held to administer the transfer of the monastic estates to the crown. And as Cromwell had been responsible for the original conveyancing, he was a natural choice to oversee the process.

The exact date at which Cromwell formally entered the king's service is not certain. The first reference to it is found in a letter that Wolsey wrote to him in August 1530, in which he mentions

Cromwell's 'opportunities of access to the King's presence'.[28] But other correspondence makes it clear that he was, if not actually in service, then at least in favour with the king several months before that. On 3 February 1530 his old friend Stephen Vaughan, who had been so fearful for Cromwell's reputation after Wolsey's fall, wrote to congratulate him on having secured Henry's good graces, assuring him: 'You now sail in a sure haven.' He could not help adding the warning, though, that: 'A merry semblance of weather often trusteth men into dangerous seas, not thinking to be suddenly oppressed with tempest, when unawares they be prevented and brought in great jeopardy.'[29]

Vaughan also provided a rare glimpse into his friend's personal life, for he added a wish to be commended to Cromwell's mother. If he was referring to Katherine Cromwell, this is the only time she had been mentioned in contemporary records since Thomas's childhood, so the assumption has often been that he broke contact with both his parents after leaving Putney for the Continent as a youth. His father Walter probably died while Cromwell was still travelling, and although his mother had outlived him and had married again, she would have been a very old woman by now – at least by the standards of the day. In fact, it is likely that by 1530 Katherine was already dead and that Vaughan was referring to Cromwell's mother-in-law, Mercy Pryor. Vaughan had a great liking for the woman, whom he referred to as 'after you, my most singular friend'.[30]

Vaughan was not the only contemporary who noted Cromwell's rapid rise in royal favour. As early as May 1530, the Princess Mary was seeking his intercession with her own father, assuring him: 'I am advertised that all such men shall first resort unto you to know the king my father's pleasure.'[31] The following month, Sir John Russell informed Cromwell that he was high in Henry's favour after helping the Lord Chamberlain, William Lord Sandys, to become keeper of Farnham Castle, one of the cardinal's forfeited properties. 'After your departure from the Kyng his grace hadd very good Comunycacion of you,' he wrote, 'whiche I shall advertise you at our next metyng.'[32]

CHAPTER 5

'The frailty of human affairs'

THE COURT, WHICH, by now, was home to Thomas Cromwell, was one of the most dazzling in the world. According to one envious foreign visitor, Henry's court was the most 'magnificent, excellent and triumphant' that had ever been seen in England. Its primary function was to house the monarch, but by the early sixteenth century it had become the nation's political and cultural nucleus, the home of government, a melting pot of scholars, artists and the greatest minds of the age. The epitome of style and sophistication, it dictated fashion in dress, art and architecture for the entire country.

Henry VIII owned more palaces than any other English monarch. Principal among these were the lavish houses situated on the banks of the River Thames: from the rambling Whitehall Palace to the imposing Tower of London and the splendour of Hampton Court, his palaces were the envy of the world. Bedecked with the finest tapestries, richly coloured silks and velvets, gold and silver plate, exquisite sculptures and paintings, they would have presented an awe-inspiring sight for even the most seasoned of courtiers. Furniture was heavily gilded, tapestries were shot through with lavish amounts of gold thread, and everything else was so brightly painted that it might be considered gaudy to modern tastes. Even the floors were painted or tiled in vivid colours. Although most of the interiors have been lost, it is still possible to experience some of the awe and wonder when, for example, standing in the middle of Henry's vast great hall at Hampton Court and gazing up at the extraordinary craftsmanship of the original hammerbeam roof, complete with 'eavesdroppers' – small figureheads looking down on the courtiers below, intended as a reminder that everything was overheard within the confines of the court.

Henry spent most of the year in London, and his palaces there housed by far the greatest number of occupants. Hundreds if not thousands of courtiers would be crowded into the public rooms. The business of feeding and accommodating them all was of necessity run like a military operation. During the summer months, or when there was the threat of plague in the capital, the king and a select number of favoured courtiers would go on 'progress' to his houses outside London, or those belonging to distinguished nobles and councillors. They would stay for just long enough to eat the host out of house and home before moving on to the next residence in a vast, unwieldy train of carts, wagons, horses and attendants. It was an itinerant court, with the king and his entourage moving an average of thirty times a year – although this decreased slightly as he became less physically robust in his later years.

The royal palaces were built to a more or less consistent plan, which reflected the shift from the overwhelmingly public life of medieval monarchs to a greater desire for privacy among the Tudors. Thus, there was an increasing division between the public or 'state' rooms, such as the great hall, and the king's private suite of rooms. He and his wife had separate apartments which were organised in a ceremonial or processional route that became ever more private or exclusive as it went on. The outer rooms included a great watching chamber and presence chamber. These were usually followed by the privy chamber – the king's inner sanctum, where he would take his meals, converse with guests, work on state business or relax. Beyond that lay the privy or 'secret' lodgings, which included the king's formal and second bedchamber, his closet (which could take the form of a private oratory or study) and close stool.

Because only the most favoured courtiers gained access to the privy chamber, it assumed considerable political importance, rivalled only by the Privy Council. The latter typically comprised nineteen or so members and met almost every day to debate and decide upon all matters of government. The staff of the privy chamber increased during Henry's reign and were, inevitably, in continual service. The friction between the personal or informal authority of the privy chamber staff, who might petition the king and influence his policy during his 'off duty' hours, and the formal or 'official' powers of the Privy Councillors became increasingly marked as the reign wore on. A clever courtier would try to ensure that he had a foot in both camps.

The jockeying for position between members of the household and council was only part of the story, however. As Henry's reign progressed, the court became increasingly riven by factions. These groups of influential courtiers and councillors would form at different times and over different issues: from foreign policy to the question of the king's marriage. Their power struggles came to dominate life in both the formal and informal arenas of Henry's court. It was with ample justification that Sir Francis Bryan observed there was an 'overplus' of 'malice and displeasures'. Alliances were forged and broken with bewildering speed, and if a particular faction looked set to lose royal favour, its members defected with little recourse to loyalty or principle. A man's word was by no means his bond, and nobody could be completely trusted – however earnest they might seem. Many criticised this way of life. John Husee, an agent of Lady Lisle, echoed Bryan when he warned: 'Every man [should] beware the flattering of the court.' Meanwhile, Henry's future queen, Jane Seymour, described it as a place that was 'full of pride, envy, indignation, mocking, scorning and derision'.[1]

Henry VIII liked to surround himself with like-minded courtiers. Men such as Charles Brandon, Duke of Suffolk, Sir Anthony Browne and William Compton were his constant companions. They not only shared his interests, they physically resembled him: tall, large-framed, imposing. It has been said that the king consciously sought out men who were the mirror image of himself. Judging from the Holbein portrait, Cromwell was not dissimilar – in build at least – to his royal master. By the time Cromwell entered his service, Henry had lost his youthful athleticism and had grown considerably in girth. Cromwell, too, had a frame that could best be described as portly. Unlike his royal master, there is no evidence that he had ever displayed sporting prowess, although he had been fit enough for military service in his youth. Either way, both men had now settled down to the comforts of middle age, with waistlines to match.

That so many people should clamour to spend their lives in such a dangerously volatile place as the royal court would be perplexing had the rewards not been at least as great as the risks – and in some cases considerably greater. Even though Henry's grip on the reins of court and government was by no means as tight as his father's had been, he was still the principal source of power and preferment. Close and regular access to the king was therefore an essential prerequisite for any aspiring courtier – a fact that Cromwell knew only too well. He once confided to Chapuys: 'It was only now that he had known the frailty of human affairs, especially of those of the Court, of which he had before his eyes several examples that might be called domestic, and he always laid his account that if fate fell upon him as upon his predecessors he would arm himself with patience, and leave the rest to God; and that it was quite true, as I said, that he must rely upon God's help not to fall into mischief.'[2] To adopt such a philosophical attitude was entirely sensible, but the years ahead would test Cromwell's sanguinity to its limits.

By early 1530, Cromwell was clearly a rising star at court. But the preceding few months had not just been about feathering his own nest: he had worked consistently to rehabilitate Wolsey with the king so that he might avoid being attainted for treason. The disgraced cardinal had been effusive in his thanks, and variously referred to his former protégé as 'myn only comfort', 'my only help', 'mine own good Thomas' and 'my onely refugy and aide'.[3] For all his gratitude, though, the cardinal had unrealistic expectations of what his protégé could achieve. Refusing to accept that his glory days were over, he constantly sought a return to royal favour and claimed that Cromwell was the only means by which he could achieve this. 'At the reverens of God leve me not nowe, for yf ye do I shal nat longe lyve in thys wrechyd world,' he pleaded in one dispatch. 'Ye woll nat beleve how I am alteryd, for that I have herd nothing from yow of your procedyngs and expeditions in my maters.'[4]

For all these fine words, Wolsey had been the most demanding of all the supplicants for Cromwell's favour. Although he claimed to care nothing for 'the good and muck of thys [wo]rld', and desired 'only to make a convenient portion for the entertainment of his house, and to do good to his poor servants and kinsfolk', he was clearly unable to adjust to his straitened circumstances. He insisted that the minimum he could live on was £4,000 a year – a staggering sum for the time and equivalent to £1.3 million today. He even asked Cromwell to send him some quails for his supper. A rather exasperated Cromwell refused on the basis that there was nobody who was prepared to deliver them to the cardinal. An inventory of Wolsey's goods taken around this time reveals the extraordinary luxury in which he had lived for the previous decade. It included rich tapestries and velvet hangings, twenty-seven feather beds, 157 woollen mattresses, eighty-eight pillows stuffed with down feathers, embroidered silk sheets, 'cloth of gold' cushion covers, Venetian carpets, crystal and gold glasses, gilt cups and plates, and innumerable other riches and adornments.

It is easy to imagine Cromwell's exasperation as he read the increasingly insistent and unrealistic messages from his former master. Wolsey had placed him in a position that would have been intolerable for a less able or persuasive man. But Cromwell had learned the art of diplomacy from his years on the Continent, as well as his service to Wolsey, and he was already an excellent judge of the king's character and moods. This was proved on 12 February 1530, when he secured Henry's pardon for Wolsey.[5] Shortly afterwards, his former master was restored to the archbishopric of York, with all its possessions except York Place. This was an extraordinary achievement. In a little over four months, Cromwell had transformed Wolsey's position from disgraced minister on the verge of a conviction for treason, to one of the foremost prelates in the land once more. He had done so from a standing start, with no position and precious few contacts in a court filled with the cardinal's enemies. Now, not only Wolsey but also Cromwell himself enjoyed the king's good graces.

Still Wolsey was not satisfied. A less ambitious man might have been content to secure nothing more than a pardon so that he could spend the rest of his life in peace, if not prosperity. But the cardinal was too used to riches and luxury, and he sent a series of peevish letters to Cromwell, urging him to protect his assets. He was particularly keen to retain the bishopric of Winchester and the abbey of St Albans – or, if the king saw fit to take them from him, he wanted Cromwell to secure him a pension. 'For God be my judge, I never thought, and so I was assured at the making of my submission, to depart from any of my promotions; for the rigour of the law, for any offence that can be arrected unto me, deserveth no such punishment; and so, trusting in the King's goodness, I am come to this point. I hope his Grace will consider the same accordingly. I have had fair words, but little comfortable deeds.'[6] Although he paid lip service to penitence, the cardinal was full of self-righteous indignation and urged Cromwell to make Henry see sense. 'As touching the Articles laid unto me, whereof a great part be untrue, and those which be true are of such sort that by the doing of them no malice nor untruth can be justly arrected unto me, neither to the Prince's person, nor to the realm.' The tactics that Wolsey advised Cromwell to employ with the king provide a glimpse into his own relationship with Henry, for he urged him to set aside deference and 'Take [bo]ldnes unto yow.'[7]

Such tactics might have worked for Wolsey at the height of his powers, but Cromwell was not yet close enough to the king and therefore opted for a more diplomatic approach. He assured Wolsey: 'As touching the process against your Grace out of the Exchequer and all other matters and suits brought against you, I have pleaded your pardon, which is allowed in all the King's courts, and by the same your Grace discharged of all manner causes at the King's suit.' Still Wolsey was not content. Although he had been pardoned, his York lands were not immediately returned to him and he urged Cromwell to find out what was happening. His former protégé entreated him to be patient because it would take time for the necessary legalities to be concluded. 'This will be very displeasant to you, but it is best to suffer it, for, if they should not be found, you could not hold your bishopric quiet, notwithstanding your pardon; for your restitution made by your pardon is clearly void, for that the King did restitute your Grace before he was entitled by matter of record. When these offices shall be found, your pardon shall be good and stand in perfect effect.'[8]

The Duke of Norfolk was incensed that the cardinal had escaped further reprisals. When Sir John Russell opined that Wolsey would now look to return to court, the duke 'began to swear very loudly that rather than suffer this he would eat him up alive'. In the event, he contented himself with getting the cardinal well away from court. At the beginning of March, he ordered him – through Cromwell – to depart for York. Reluctant to be so far from court, Wolsey delayed his departure. But by April 1530 he had run out of excuses and was obliged to set out on the long journey north. He made a slow – and, some said, stately – progress up north, stopping at several houses along the way. Although pleading poverty, he travelled in 'such sumptuous fashion that some men thought he was of as good courage as in times past'. But on reaching York, he told Henry that he was 'unfurnished, to my extreme heaviness, of everything that I and my poor folks should be entertained with . . . I have neither corn nor cattle, ne any other thing to keep household with, nor know not where to borrow anything in these parts towards the provision of the same.' As a result, he concluded, he was 'wrapped in misery and need on every side; not knowing where to be succoured or relieved, but only at your Highness' most merciful and charitable hands'.[9]

Cromwell was running out of patience. Wolsey had constantly complained of his failure to visit him at Esher and now he assumed the role of one who had been entirely neglected. Although the cardinal's responses tended towards the melodramatic, his accusation that Cromwell no longer cared for him had a grain of truth to it. Cromwell was undoubtedly still working on Wolsey's behalf, but increasingly he advised the cardinal to petition other members of the council for assistance.[10] He also began simply to relay what the king and others had said, rather than sweetening his dispatches with assurances of better times to come. In one letter, he even passed on a message from the Duke of Norfolk, who 'willeth you for the present to be content, and not much to molest the King . . .

for, as he supposeth, the time is not meet for it.' Cromwell also warned the cardinal that Henry had 'showed me how it is come to his knowledge that your Grace should have certain words of him and other noblemen unto my lord of Norfolk since the time of your adversities, which words should sound to make sedition betwixt him and my lord of Norfolk.' He added that although Wolsey was still respected in some areas, his enemies 'deprave all', and cautioned: 'Sir, some there be that do allege that your Grace doth keep too great a house and family, and that ye are continually abuilding. For the love of God, therefore, have a respect, and refrain.'[11] This would have been enough to frighten most men into keeping a low profile, but Wolsey persisted in his attempts to regain what he saw as his rightful property and riches.

Although Cromwell continued to work on the cardinal's behalf, their relationship became increasingly fraught with tension. Cromwell's loyalty to his former master had cost him dearly, not just in reputation but in cash. And he was not a man to overlook a debt. In July 1530 he told the cardinal that furthering his cause 'hath been very chargeable' to him, and that he could not sustain it any longer. He claimed: 'I am 1,000l. worse than I was when your troubles began.' This prompted Wolsey to send his former protégé some recompense. Cromwell did not acknowledge this in person, but asked his secretary, Ralph Sadler, to do so. It was hardly a gracious acceptance. Sadler informed Wolsey that his master 'hath accepted his token, which yet was not so great a reward as he expected'.[12]

By the time Wolsey took up residence at Cawood Castle, a few miles south of York, it was Michaelmas, 29 September. Shortly afterwards, he learned that the king had started to take possession of his college lands, as well as those of St Albans and Winchester. But because the cardinal had been attainted by *praemunire*, any grants that Henry made from the revenues of the colleges would only be valid while Wolsey was still living. This is when Cromwell spied his advantage – or, as Cavendish put it: 'perceyved an occasion given him by time to helpe himselfe'. Only a lawyer of his exceptional skill could chart a way through the tortuous processes involved in securing the grants on a longer term basis. The recipients of the grants were therefore obliged to seek Cromwell's assistance – and pay handsomely for it. 'There was none other shifte but to obtaine my lord's confirmation of their patents,' observed Cavendish. 'Then began every man both noble and gentleman who had any patents out of Winchester and St Albans to make suite to Mr Cromwell to solicit their cause to my lorde to get therin his confirmation, and for his paines therin bothe worthily to reward him and every man to shewe him such pleasures as should be at all times in their small powers, whereof they assured him.'

Cromwell exploited the situation to the full, winning both financial and political gain. 'Nowe began matters, to worke to brynge Mayster Cromwell into estimacion, in suche sort as was afterward myche to his encrease of dygnyte,' related Cavendish. All those men who had before sought Wolsey's intervention 'made now earnest travell to Mayster Cromwell for these purposes, who refused none to make promyse that he wold do hys best in that case, and havyng a great occasion of accesse to the kyng for the disposicion of divers londes wherof he had the order and governaunce; by means wherof and by his witty demeanor, he grewe contynually in to the kinges favour.' According to Cavendish, Cromwell could not have taken more advantage of the situation than he did: by solving a thorny legal conundrum to everyone's benefit (except, perhaps, his former master's) he had catapulted himself to a place of great esteem and influence at court. 'Thus rase hys name and frendly acceptaunce with all men. The fame of his honestie and wisdome sounded so in the kynges eares that . . . he perceived to be in hyme no lesse wysdome than fame had made of hyme report . . . and the conference that he had with the kyng therin, enforced the kyng to repute hyme a very wyse man, and a meate instrument to serve his grace, as it after came to passe.'[13]

Wolsey was greatly aggrieved upon hearing of the seizure of his beloved lands. Cromwell himself reported that 'the Cardinal takes the suppressing and dismembering of his colleges very heavily.' At first, Wolsey was meek in his sorrow, recommending his 'poore estat and Collegys to your and other goode friendes helpe and releff'. But as he witnessed his life's work being dismantled, the cardinal's accustomed sangfroid gave way to distress, and he entreated the king 'humbly and on my knees with weeping eyes' to spare Oxford College at least. He sent a similar message to Cromwell, lamenting that he 'cannot write for weeping and sorrow'. He added thanks for 'all the pains' his protégé had taken, promising to 'requite him' when he could.[14] When no answer came, however, Wolsey's distress turned to resentment – much of which was levelled at Cromwell. Rumours had apparently reached Wolsey that his former protégé had betrayed him by profiting from the dispersal of his lands. The cardinal had complained of this to others, which provoked Cromwell to write a furious letter, demanding to know if he still enjoyed the cardinal's confidence.

> I am informed your Grace hath me in some diffidence, as if I did dissemble with you, or procure anything contrary to your profit and honour. I much muse that your Grace should so think, or report it secretly, considering the pains I have taken ... Wherefore I beseech you to speak without feigning, if you have such conceit, that I may clear myself. I reckoned that your Grace would have written plainly unto me of such thing, rather than secretly to have misreported me . . . But I shall bear your Grace no less good will . . . Let God judge between us. Truly your Grace in some things overshooteth yourself; there is reg[ard] to be given what things ye utter, and to whom.[15]

Cromwell had shrewdly judged that attack was the best form of defence. Chastened, Wolsey meekly assured him that he had realised how ill-founded the rumours were after friends had informed him of Cromwell's loyalty in all his dealings. 'The Cardinal strives to clear himself to Cromwell,' it was reported, 'protesting that he suspects him not, and that may appear by his deeds, for that he useth no man's help nor counsel but his ... he hath asked of their common friends how Cromwell hath behaved himself towards him, and, to his great comfort, hath found him faithful.' Wolsey ended with an impassioned plea, beseeching Cromwell 'with weeping tears to continue stedfast, and give no credit to the false suggestions of such as would sow variance between us, and so leave me destitute of all help'. More letters were to follow, all grovelling in tone. 'Myne owne lovyng Mr. Crumwell', he began one in August 1530, and went on to praise his protégé's 'gentle heart'.[16]

Cromwell replied with a letter of consolation that was so lacking in conviction that it bordered on insulting. He must have known that the assurances he made were entirely without foundation, but he was no doubt eager to cover up the profit he had made from the whole sorry affair. 'It may please your grace to quiet yourself and to take the fynding of these offices pacientlie and uppon the retourne of the same there shalbe such orders taken that your grace shall not be interrupted in the receyving of your revenues ne otherwise be molested in any maner case for any new sute.' In another missive, he concluded: 'I entreat your Grace to be content, and let your Prince execute his pleasure.'[17] By implying that this was all the king's work, rather than his own, Cromwell cleverly deflected any lingering resentment that Wolsey may have had towards him.

As well as revealing the cracks in the relationship between Wolsey and Cromwell, the episode had demonstrated just how susceptible the two men were to court intrigue. Even though Wolsey was well away from the court and with apparently little chance of regaining any influence there, his alliance with Cromwell was still viewed as a threat by their enemies, who were intent upon destroying it altogether. Even as far from court as Ipswich, one of Cromwell's correspondents reported: 'You would be astonished at the lies told of you and me in these parts.'[18] The same was apparently true of Cawood, where there was no shortage of informants willing to blacken Cromwell's character to his former master.

Wolsey's relationship with Cromwell never fully recovered. The latter's correspondence reveals his increasing frustration at the cardinal's inability to accept reality. But his loyalty had not been entirely obliterated by the quest for personal and political gain. Although he could not stop the king from taking possession of the colleges, he knew how close they were to Wolsey's heart and therefore did what he could to help the residents therein. A grateful John Clerke, Canon of Cardinal's College, Oxford, sent Cromwell a pair of gloves on 21 December in acknowledgement of his kindness towards Clerke and his brother. Cromwell was also on civil enough terms with Wolsey by 21 October to ask him to employ his kinsman, a Dr Karbott – who 'though somewhat simple in appearance . . . will do well if put in trust'. He added a recommendation on behalf of one of Wolsey's young servants, Nicholas Gifford, and provided a typically shrewd appraisal of the man's character: 'Though young and somewhat wild, he is disposed to truth, [hone]ste, and hardyness, and will love your Grace with all his heart.'[19]

In concerning himself with the minutiae of Wolsey's household, Cromwell might have been fooled into thinking that the cardinal's own interests were limited to that sphere. But as well as attending to the business of his diocese, it was rumoured that Wolsey had once more started to meddle in politics. According to his adversaries, he entered negotiations with both the emperor and the French king with the intention of securing a papal interdict that Henry should relinquish Anne Boleyn. Whether the cardinal really had acted so recklessly is a matter for debate. Given that he was so desperate to regain the king's favour, it seems unlikely. Moreover, his name was prominent in a list of ecclesiastical and lay magnates who petitioned the Pope to grant the king's divorce in July. But when, on 23 October, reports reached Henry of a papal brief prohibiting his remarriage and ordering him to dismiss Anne Boleyn from court, the finger of suspicion was pointed firmly at Wolsey.

The king was quick to act. On 1 November he dispatched William Walsh, a gentleman of the privy chamber, to arrest the cardinal on charges of high treason and convey him with all speed to the Tower of London. The French envoy hinted that the rumours had been started by a member of Wolsey's own household: 'The King says he has intrigued against them, both in and out of the kingdom, and has told me where and how, and that one and perhaps more of his servants have discovered it, and accused him.' Wolsey duly set out for London, but his progress was hampered by a fresh bout of sickness, which drove him to a state of near collapse. Barely able to stay on his mule, on the evening of 26 November he arrived at Leicester Abbey, where he greeted the abbot with the words: 'Father abbott I ame come hether to leave my bones among you.' Early the following morning, he made his final confession, uttering the famous lament: 'I se the matter ayenst me howe it is framed, But if I had served god as dyligently as I have don the kyng he wold not have geven me over in my grey heares.'[20] He died shortly afterwards.

Wolsey's enemies, anxious to ensure that there would be no rehabilitation of the cardinal's reputation in death, were quick to denounce him. As well as laying the blame for the stalemate over the king's divorce firmly at his door, they argued that nothing better could be expected of one of such humble origins. The French envoy sneered that: 'he thought ever that so pompeos and ambysyous a harte, spronge out of so vyle a stocke wold once shewe forthe the basenes of his nature, and most comonlye against Him that hath raysed him from lowe degree to highe dignytye.' In short, breeding – or lack of it – will out. Chapuys, meanwhile, reported to his Imperial master: 'The cardinal of York died on St Andrew's Day about 40 miles from here, at a place where the last king Richard was defeated and killed. Both lie buried in the same church, which the people begin already to call "the Tyrants' grave".'[21]

Cromwell must have received the news of his old patron's death with mixed emotions. As well as sadness at the passing of the man who had been his master for many years and the means of his rise at court, he might have felt some relief that the invidious position in which he had been placed since Wolsey's fall was now at an end. Yet there was also the danger that his own standing with the king might be damaged by the cardinal's final, irredeemable, fall from grace. Such fears were soon ended when, in the closing weeks of 1530, Cromwell was appointed a member of the Privy Council.

Quite what had prompted this move was a matter for speculation among contemporary commentators. Foxe claims that Cromwell's sudden promotion was thanks to some well-timed comments he made being overheard by influential members of Henry's treasury: 'It happened where as Cromewell was, that there was talke of the kynges substaunce and treasure. Then sayde Cromwell, if the kynge woulde admytte my counsayle, I woulde bryng to passe that he alone shoulde sone become the rychest Prynce of all christian Prynces. These wordes the more they semed to tende to the kynges profyte, the soner as it happened it was brought vnto the kynges eares. From that tyme forwarde Cromewel beganne to be better knowen and dearer vnto the kyng.'[22]

The Imperial ambassador, Eustace Chapuys, tells a different story. He claims that Sir John Wallop, a diplomat and politician, had levelled various insults and threats at Cromwell upon the death of Wolsey. Cromwell had felt sufficiently embattled to seek the king's protection. In the private audience that followed, he promised to make Henry the richest king in England's history. The king was so impressed by this offer that he immediately appointed Cromwell to the council, although he told nobody about it for four months. The Spanish Chronicle concurs that 'Cromwell was always inventing means whereby the King might be enriched and the crown aggrandized.'[23]

Although they differ in detail, Foxe and Chapuys agree that Cromwell rose to favour as a result of convincing his royal master that he would make him a rich man. Such a tactic was entirely commensurate with Cromwell's natural self-confidence with rulers, which bordered on the audacious. He had already demonstrated this during the meeting he had orchestrated with the Pope in 1517. By the end of 1530, he had been around Henry long enough to judge that he would respond well to a similar approach. From now on, he would enjoy increasingly privileged – often exclusive – access to Henry. John Foxe described him as 'the mooste secret and deare councellour vnto the kyng'.[24]

Cromwell's appointment to the council was a significant step forward in his career at court, propelling him into the king's circle of trusted advisers. Even though he was a lesser member of that body and chiefly employed in legal business, he was not slow in expressing his views on all matters. The Spanish Chronicle claimed that 'always . . . he was the first to speak' in council meetings. This was entirely characteristic of Cromwell's style. Chapuys once noted an unusual occasion when Cromwell 'remained, contrary to his usual habit, silent and thoughtful for some time'. On another, he had interrupted an august gathering of men by saying: 'Enough of that, and let us go to business.'[25] The advent of such an opinionated, outspoken and – worst of all – low-born upstart was no doubt irksome to the more noble and well-established members, such as Archbishop Warham and Wolsey's old adversaries, the dukes of Norfolk and Suffolk. The ascerbic George Cavendish penned the following verse on Cromwell's sudden emergence in the council:

> With royal egles a kight may not flie;
> Allthoughe a jaye may chatter in a golden cage,
> Yet will the eagles disdayne his parentage.[26]

By contrast, Holinshed claimed that Cromwell's lowly birth made his rapid rise to favour even more impressive: 'By him it well appeared, that the excellencie of heroicall vertues, which aduance men to fame and honor, resteth not onelie in birth and bloud, as a priuilege appropriate and alonelie annexed vnto noble houses, but remaineth at the disposition of almightie God the giuer & disposer of all gifts, who raiseth the poore manie times from the basest degree, and setteth him vp with princes.'[27]

Norfolk had wasted no time in seizing power in the wake of Wolsey's fall. By November 1530, the Venetian ambassador was able to report that the king 'makes use of him in all negotiations more than any other person . . . and every employment devolves to him'.[28] Although he had helped Cromwell to a position in parliament the year before, he was no ally: indeed, he rapidly transferred his enmity from Wolsey to Cromwell. Meanwhile, another of the cardinal's former protégés, Stephen Gardiner, also became a bitter enemy of Cromwell around this time. He had confidently expected the king to transfer his favour from the late cardinal to himself, and when this fell to Cromwell instead, he developed an implacable and enduring hatred towards the new minister. Although they maintained a veneer of cordiality in their correspondence, as the niceties of court etiquette dictated, the hostility occasionally broke through. In one dispatch, Cromwell upbraided Gardiner for 'your said lettres not soo freendely conceyved, as I thinke my merities towardes youe haue deserued'. In another, he accused his rival of behaving 'colerikly' and 'melancoulily' towards him.[29]

But – for now at least – the presence of two such dangerous and determined adversaries did not prevent Cromwell's rise in royal favour. Henry was quick to spot Cromwell's potential, and further promotion soon followed his appointment to the council. Early the following year, he began to act as receiver-general and supervisor of the college lands that had been acquired from the late cardinal. He was officially confirmed in this position a year later, on 9 January 1532.

Having learned from Wolsey's example, Cromwell set about making himself as indispensable as possible to the king. He managed the sale and receipt of royal land, supervised building works at the Tower of London and Westminster, heard appeals and decided the fate of prisoners and felons who were brought before him, and involved himself in various other matters of law enforcement. It is a sign of his perceived influence with the king that he was soon besieged by a bewildering number of requests for assistance. Some of the highest ranking men at court now swallowed their pride and sought the help of this blacksmith's son. Among them was Henry's closest friend and brother-in-law, the Duke of Suffolk, and Henry Bourchier, second Earl of Essex.

Despite the increasing demands of his service at court, Cromwell maintained his private legal practice throughout this time – perhaps mindful that this would sustain him if everything else crumbled to dust. But for the moment there seemed little prospect of that. Both his private and public businesses were booming. Requests for his legal assistance poured in from every quarter: corporate bodies, religious houses and individuals paid him considerable sums for his services. In August 1526 an alderman named George Monoux had assured Cromwell that if his 'grete matier' was brought to a successful conclusion, he would pay him twenty marks (equivalent to around £4,500 in modern currency).[30]

Cromwell also continued his private money-lending business, which was proving extremely lucrative. One of his debtors was a man named Thomas Allen, who borrowed the considerable sum of one hundred pounds. When he failed to repay this, Cromwell wrote to inform him that: 'For lacke and defaulte whereof ye haue forfaited to the kinges highnes the Somme of one thousande markes which me thinketh ye ought substaunciallye to loke vppon for the king is no person to be deluded nor mocked with all.'[31] This letter proves that no matter how many demands there now were on Cromwell's time thanks to his new appointments in government, he continued to keep a close eye on his private business matters. He also evidently used his two careers to complement each other: if one of his debtors failed to pay, then he would threaten them with the king's wrath.

In January 1531 parliament was reconvened.[32] Although there had been few sessions since Cromwell's first entry to the Commons in 1523, his influence was now predominant. By the end of the session in March 1531 he took home with him no fewer than twenty-nine bills that had reached the statute book – most of which, it seems, had been instigated by him. By the summer, news had reached as far as Derbyshire that 'one Mr Cromwell penned certain matters in the Parliament house, which no man gainsaid.'[33] The king himself was now fully aware of Cromwell's abilities, and it was probably around this time that he began actively to seek his assistance in the most pressing issue of the day.

The first indication that Cromwell had become involved in the king's 'Great Matter' was when he drafted some legislation concerning it. However, for a time there was nothing to suggest that he was in any way influencing proceedings: he appeared to be simply acting as Henry's agent and draftsman, working quietly and assiduously to carry out a policy that had been formulated elsewhere. All that was about to change.

Cardinal Pole provides an account of the conversation that passed between Henry and Cromwell when they first discussed the 'grete matier'. Having begun by excusing himself for daring to offer an opinion on so weighty an issue, and one of which he professed to be entirely ignorant, he claimed that the strength of his loyalty to the king would not allow him to be silent when there was a chance

– however small – that he might be of help. Cromwell then laid the entire blame for the failure to secure a divorce on the shoulders of Henry's advisers. They had given too much credence to the opinions of the 'common herd' rather than the 'wise and learned', all of whom were in favour of the divorce. Considering that the only real obstacle was the Pope, the answer to the conundrum was simple: to renounce the authority of Rome, as the Lutherans had done in Germany.

For centuries, the Pope and his councils had decided doctrine, held final jurisdiction over Church law, received Church taxes and had the final say in the appointment of bishops. That England was part of the papal fold had, until now, been largely accepted – albeit with increasing dissatisfaction by those who favoured the annulment of the king's marriage. Now, according to Pole, Cromwell made the king see that a break with Rome was not only desirable, it was eminently achievable. England was like a monster with two heads, he said. If the king made himself head of the Church, then the papal head would be struck off and his subjects (the clergy included) would answer to Henry alone. Pole claimed that the king was so delighted with Cromwell's scheme that he told him to carry it out immediately.[34]

However compelling Pole's account, it is not corroborated by any other source. Most of the leading contemporary commentators at court – notably the Imperial ambassador, Chapuys – saw the events that unfolded between 1530 and 1533 as the king's own work. Yet it is possible – likely, even – that throughout this time Cromwell had been working quietly behind the scenes. Henry himself would hardly have wished to admit that he had been advised on such a drastic course of action by a political ingénu – and a low-born one at that. It would have seriously undermined his own credibility. Far better that the measures be seen as emanating from himself. Respect for his authority was so great by this time that a policy introduced in his name was assured of much greater success than if it had been fronted by a new member of his council. That Cromwell's influence had been concealed for the first three years of his career in Henry's service is also suggested by the fact that he 'burst into prominence' so suddenly and with such assured authority that the groundwork must have been prepared for some time. Chapuys was not the only ambassador at court to appreciate this fact.[35]

Tempting though it is to believe that in one brief meeting with the king Cromwell planted the idea of rejecting papal authority in Henry's mind, and thus set in train a series of cataclysmic events that would change the political and religious landscape of England for ever, the notion probably took hold gradually, and thanks to other influences than Cromwell alone. Frustrated by the Pope's refusal to grant his divorce, Henry began to lend an ever more willing ear to a host of different experts drawn from legal and academic circles who argued for his right to complete jurisdiction over the English Church. Nevertheless, Cromwell now argued for it more convincingly and set out a clearer strategy for achieving it than anyone had done before. He gave fresh impetus to what was rapidly becoming a quagmire of endless debate and negotiation.

From 1530, a team of scholars led by Dr Edward Fox worked assiduously to find the justification for the emerging idea of royal supremacy over the Church among a host of ancient texts – including the Bible itself. The sources that they gathered, known as the *Collectanea satis copiosa*, were used as proof that since Anglo-Saxon times the kings of England had enjoyed absolute spiritual authority, as well as secular. Their interpretation of the texts did not bear close scrutiny, but it was enough to fuel the flames of the king's reforming zeal. He had started a crusade against papal authority and would stop at nothing until it had achieved his ultimate goal: divorce from Catherine and marriage to Anne.

Aware of the hostility that the English clergy had already shown towards the notion of a divorce, Henry decided to bully them into submission. In late January 1531 he issued a writ of *praemunire* against the entire English clergy and demanded a subsidy of 100,000 pounds (equivalent to more than £32 million today) from the Convocation of Canterbury in return for a general pardon. Some of the leading clerics of the day put up a fierce resistance, but they were no match for the king, who added five new articles, including the demand that they recognise him as supreme head of the Church in England.

As the debate raged between Church and king, the chief protagonists soon emerged. Leading the resistance from the former was the most senior churchman in the land: William Warham, Archbishop of Canterbury, along with the staunch conservative, Bishop John Fisher. The king's cause was championed by two men: Thomas Audley, speaker of the Commons, and Thomas Cromwell.

That Cromwell was leading the charge for the king is a sign of how far he had risen – and how fast. In little over a year, he had been transformed from the newest member of parliament with relatively minor administrative responsibilities, to one of the key players in the most important, controversial and pressing issue of the day: an issue that had already assumed not just national, but international significance. Realising that Henry's bullying tactics were achieving little beyond the creation of a stalemate, Cromwell launched a charm offensive on Warham and his supporters, assuring them that the king was not taking on any new powers. Rightly suspicious, they held firm. Cromwell then changed tack and persuaded convocation, a representative assembly of clergy, to accept a watered-down version of the title, whereby the king was recognised as supreme head only as far as the law of Christ allowed. They duly agreed to Henry's articles and the payment of the subsidy on 8 March 1531. It was a legal nicety, but one of enormous significance. The royal supremacy was now recognised in law, and if the king's powers over the Church were still somewhat vague, this meant that they had the potential for extension. At a stroke, Cromwell had secured the short-term agreement needed to progress the divorce, while laying the foundations for religious and political change of truly revolutionary proportions. That he was responsible for such a significant moment in England's history was not lost on contemporaries. A century later, Strype observed: 'Secretary Crumwell had the great stroke in all this. And all these counsels and methods were struck out of his head. For which, as he received the curses, and drew upon himself the hatred of many, so, many more, well affected to a reformation of superstitions in the Church, extolled him as highly.'[36]

Although Cromwell was increasingly preoccupied by his burgeoning career at court, he remained closely involved in his son

Gregory's education and was in regular correspondence with the boy's guardian, Margaret Vernon. Chekyng had been replaced by a tutor named Copland, who was making good progress with the boy. Nicholas Sadler, whose education Cromwell was funding too, had also had a beneficial effect upon Gregory's studies. Margaret Vernon reported to Cromwell in 1531: 'Your son and his master are in good health, and now prosper in learning more in one day than before in a week, by reason of Nich. Saddelar, who is of very good conditions. Mr. Copland every morning gives each of them a laten [Latin lesson], the which Nicholas doth bear away, as well Gregory's lesson as his own, and maketh the same Gregory perfect against his time of rendering. The master takes such comfort that he is with them three times a day.' In another, she assured Cromwell: 'Your son is in good health, and is a very good scholar, and can construe his paternoster and creed. When you next come to me I doubt not that you shall like him very well.'[37]

Margaret was particularly concerned for Gregory's religious education. Cromwell had evidently promised to send a priest for the purpose, but when he did not arrive Margaret found someone who she believed would be better suited to the task. She urged Cromwell: 'Let me know your pleasure speedily, for I would that your child should lose no more time. The gentleman you promised would be much to your charge, and not do so well for the child . . . You promised that I should have the governance of the child till he was 12 years old. By that time he shall speak for himself if any wrong be offered him, for as yet he cannot, except by my maintenance; and if he had a master who disdained my meddling it would be great unquietness to me.'[38] By the time Margaret wrote this letter in 1531, Gregory, then aged about eleven, seems to have conducted most of his studies at Cambridge. As well as Mr Copland, his tutors included Henry Lockwood, Master of Christ's College, and John Hunt, a lawyer and graduate of Wolsey's college at Oxford. The latter's expertise was no doubt intended to help Gregory follow in his legal footsteps.

Shortly before the beginning of the Michaelmas term on 29 September 1531, the king issued instructions 'unto his trustie

Counsailer Thomas Cromwell, to be declared, on his behalf, to his Lerned Counsaill, and indelayedlie to be put in execucyon, the Terme of Saynt Michael in the 23ti yere of his moct vicotoryous reigne'.[39] This was a confirmation of Cromwell's meteoric rise to power: he had joined the inner ring of the council. Just two months later, the Venetian ambassador included Cromwell as seventh in a list of leading councillors. The only men above him were the likes of Norfolk, Suffolk and others of the highest pedigree. Cromwell was the sole commoner, yet he had been given wider powers than many of his colleagues. They included supervising criminal prosecution, customs duties and payments due to the king, as well as drafting parliamentary legislation on matters as wide-ranging as treason and sewers. At the same time, working closely with Audley, he took control of the king's legal and parliamentary affairs. By the following spring, he had also begun to gain influence over elections to the Commons.

Cromwell now turned his full attention to the matter that offered even greater rewards and was closest to the king's heart. If he could secure the divorce from Catherine of Aragon, then his position at court would be unrivalled and – surely – unassailable.

CHAPTER 6

The King's 'Great Matter'

In the same year that Cromwell was appointed to the inner ring of the king's council, Catherine of Aragon was banished from court. Her position there had long since become intolerable, but she would never have left of her own accord. Resolutely clinging to the belief that her marriage was indissoluble, she repaid her husband's coldness with unswerving loyalty and devotion, and resisted his increasing pressure for an annulment with maddening stubbornness. When it became clear that she was not going to give him what he wanted, Henry's coldness towards her turned to cruelty, and he tried to bully her into submission.

His mistress was no less tormenting. The longer that Anne Boleyn's liaison with the king continued, the greater her influence at court became. A foreign visitor to the court noted with some astonishment: 'There is now living with him [the king] a young woman of noble birth, though many say of bad character, whose will is law to him.'[1] Anne was constantly in the king's presence: she ate with him, prayed with him, hunted with him and danced with him. The only thing she still refused to do was to sleep with him. As her status grew, so did her pride and haughtiness. She even began hurling insults at the queen, in whose household she continued to serve. Anne was once heard to proclaim loudly that she wished all Spaniards at the bottom of the sea. On another occasion, she told one of her fellow ladies-in-waiting that 'she did not care anything for the Queen, and would rather see her hanged than acknowledge her as mistress.'[2]

Anne was so jealous of any sign of affection between the king and queen that anyone would have thought she was the spurned wife and Catherine the cherished mistress. As the tedious negotiations for an annulment dragged on, her behaviour became increasingly erratic and she lashed out at the slightest provocation. When she discovered that Catherine was still mending her husband's shirts, she flew into a jealous rage. Henry's sexual frustration mingled with Anne's increasing bouts of temper to often explosive effect. Keenly aware that time was passing her by and that she ought to have been wedded and bedded long before now, Anne threatened to relinquish the king altogether. Still besotted, Henry soothed away her threats with assurances that he would soon arrange matters so that they might marry. But his mistress was making some dangerous enemies at court. She was also alienating swathes of the population, who had great sympathy for Catherine and derided Anne as the 'Great Whore'.

Catherine's daughter, Mary, who was fifteen years old when her mother was banished from court, was also the subject of pity. Until Henry became obsessed with Anne Boleyn, she had been his cherished only child, 'much beloved by her father', according to the Venetian ambassador.[3] He had proudly shown her off to foreign ambassadors, who all praised her beauty and intelligence. Her long red hair was 'as beautiful as ever seen on human head', and another observer complimented her delicate, 'well proportioned' figure, as well as her 'pretty face . . . with a very beautiful complexion'. Gasparo Spinelli, a Venetian dignitary, told of how the young princess had danced with the French ambassador, 'who considered her very handsome, and admirable by reason of her great and uncommon mental endowments'.[4]

When Mary first learned of her father's infatuation with Anne Boleyn, it did not cause her any immediate concern; there had been mistresses before and no doubt there would be more to follow. But her ally Chapuys warned that Anne 'is the person who governs everything, and whom the King is unable to control'.[5] Nonetheless, Mary clung doggedly to the belief that her mother's position was unassailable. The events that followed therefore came as a terrible shock.

In a studied insult to the beleaguered queen, when she was forced to leave court in 1531 her old rooms were given to the woman who had taken her place. Anne was now queen in all but name. Mary was steadfast in her loyalty to her mother and longed to be with her, but the king cruelly kept them apart. She made no secret of her hatred for the 'concubine', although she was careful to profess her continuing devotion to her father. Anne, though, was determined to oust Mary from Henry's affections, just as she had Catherine. She tried to poison the king's mind against his daughter, and treated Mary with barely concealed disdain. 'The said Anne has boasted that she will have the said Princess for her lady's maid . . . or to marry her to some varlet,' reported Chapuys, 'but that is only to make her eat humble pie.'[6]

The psychological toll of watching her parents' marriage unravel and the ever more cruel indignities inflicted upon her mother, who was forced to live in a succession of remote and uncomfortable houses, had a devastating effect upon the young girl's health. Mary suffered bouts of nausea and on one occasion was unable to keep any food down for three weeks, which caused great alarm among her attendants. In the spring of 1531, when she was recovering from one of her frequent stomach upsets, she wrote to her father, saying that nothing would speed her recovery more than to visit him at Greenwich. Her request was peremptorily refused, which Chapuys believed was 'to gratify the lady [Anne], who hates her as much as the Queen, or more so, chiefly because she sees the King has some affection for her'.[7]

At the same time as trying to rid the court of Catherine and Mary's influence, Anne also championed the royal supremacy, realising that this held the key to the divorce. Until now, apart from the dealings he had had with her to promote Wolsey's cause, Cromwell had retained some distance from Anne, perhaps waiting to see which way the tide would turn. Anne Boleyn's hatred for the cardinal, and the prominent part she had played in his downfall, made her a natural enemy of Cromwell. And yet, she was almost as great a pragmatist as he was, and was not about to sacrifice personal gain for principles. Besides, their views on the solution to the king's 'Great Matter' were now closely aligned. Cromwell was therefore gradually drawn into Anne's orbit. Recognising Cromwell's considerable abilities in the law, as well as his skill as a 'fixer' at court, she began to seek him out. By 1533, she was referring to him as 'her man'.

That Cromwell appeared to share Anne's interest in religious reform was a convenient, if unlooked for, benefit. On the other hand, the fact that Anne was the niece of one of Cromwell's chief adversaries did not deter either of them. Indeed, according to Chapuys, it was a positive advantage. 'I hear from a reliable source that day and night is the Lady working to bring about the duke of Norfolk's disgrace with the King,' he reported, 'whether it be owing to his having spoken too freely about her, or because Cromwell wishes to bring down the aristocracy of this kingdom, and is about to begin by him, I can not say.'[8] The notion that Cromwell sought the destruction of the entire nobility of England owes more to the ambassador's prejudice against this low-born adventurer than to reality. At most, Cromwell may have realised that there was no love lost between Norfolk and his niece, and that he might therefore profit from allying with the latter. But for Cromwell, alliance with Anne was only ever a means to an end. He had by this time almost certainly determined upon resolving the conundrum of the king's 'Great Matter'. The fact that this aligned with Anne's own desires was incidental: Cromwell was motivated by service to his royal master first, and himself second.

The contemporary records do not reveal the extent of their collaboration at this time. It is possible that Anne recognised Cromwell's potential, and that together they mapped out the means for achieving their mutual aim. But Cromwell continued to act for, and take his instructions from the king alone.

On 15 January 1532 the third session of the so-called 'Reformation Parliament' began. It had originally been scheduled for the previous October, but had been delayed because of indecision among Henry's ministers as to how to drive forward the reforms. This same uncertainty marked the legislation that resulted from the session. Cromwell and his team drafted one bill that proposed to grant convocation the power to annul the royal marriage, while another sought to remove its independent jurisdiction. At the same time, Anne's uncle, the Duke of Norfolk, tried to pressure influential peers into supporting the notion that the annulment could be granted by parliament, without the need for papal approval. Both efforts failed. In the end, all that was achieved was indirect action in the form of the 'Act for the Conditional Restraint of Annates'. This was an attempt to put pressure on the Pope by ending the payments (or annates) made to Rome by senior clerics of the first year's revenue from their benefices. Cromwell probably drafted the bill, but he was sceptical about its likely success, confiding to Gardiner that 'for what ende or effecte it will succede suerlie I know not'.[9] His pessimism was misplaced. Together with all the other measures he had introduced in order to bring the clergy under the direct control of the king, this Act proved a decisive step forward in the break with Rome.

The Act also swelled the coffers of the royal treasury – something that Cromwell had consciously aimed to do since entering the king's service. Thanks to his skilful manipulation of events, he ensured that most of the measures that contributed towards the break with Rome also had the supposedly unlooked-for benefit of increasing the wealth of the crown. In one of his numerous memoranda, Cromwell noted that the funds resulting from the seizure of the annates would now be redirected to the royal coffers, and gave a rather vague explanation of how they would be spent: 'Th'enhabitauntes and peple of this realme shall pay yerely unto the kyng for ever, in lieu or stede of smoke pence, whiche they were wont to pay to the busshop of rome, for every hed or house a certayne small thyng for and towardes the defense of thys Realme, whiche may be ymployed in makyng of forteresses throughout the Realme.'[10]

Quite how rich this, and other measures by Cromwell, had made his royal master was suggested by Chapuys, who in December 1534 reported to Charles V: 'The King, besides the 30,000 pounds which he newly obtained from the clergy, and an ordinary fifteenth from the laity, which was granted him last year, and which may amount to 28,000 pounds, has just imposed a tax by authority of Parliament, of the twentieth penny of all goods of his subjects, and that foreigners shall pay double, which will amount to a great sum.' The ambassador was in no doubt who was responsible: 'These are devices of Cromwell, who boasts that he will make his master more wealthy than all the other princes of Christendom.' Carlo Capello, the Venetian ambassador, concurred that Cromwell had made his king a rich man, and provided an even higher estimate of the latter's income. 'The King's predecessor had a revenue of some 400,000 ducats, and whilst I was in England, the present King . . . may have increased this sum to 700,000 ducats, of which Secretary Cromwell was and is in great part the author; and now lately by these annats, and by the church benefices which he has absorbed, that sum will have been doubled; so at this present his annual revenue amounts well nigh to a million and a half.'[11]

A further indication of the king's newfound wealth is the fact that, throughout the period of Cromwell's ascendancy, the coinage was never debased. This method of replenishing the royal coffers had first been employed by his former master, Wolsey, and involved reducing the amount of silver or gold in a coin so that more coins could be made but their real value was diminished. It is to Cromwell's credit that he was determined to stamp out this practice and restore the coinage to its true value. His primary motivation in doing so was to protect England's trading interests, for he knew that these would be undermined if the value of English money was called into question. He therefore arranged for a proclamation to be issued 'for the false and clipped Coyne going in this Realme with a greate punishment to every person that is founde with any false or counterfeit moneye'.[12]

Cromwell's efforts with regard to the coinage did little to win over the English people, however. They became increasingly convinced that he was acting not in their interests, but solely in his own. Commenting on Cromwell's fiscal policies, Chapuys observed: 'He does not consider that by this means he alienates the hearts of the subjects, who are enraged and in despair, but they are so oppressed and cast down, that without foreign assistance it is no use their complaining, and it will not be Cromwell's fault, if they are not oppressed further.' According to his account, not only was Cromwell making some dangerous enemies by his aggressive policies, but by encouraging Henry to behave like an absolute monarch, he was alienating large swathes of his subjects against their king.[13]

Undeterred, Cromwell now began a campaign systematically to undermine the power of the Church in England, perceiving this as the only means to establish royal supremacy. Complaints about clerical abuses had already been voiced in the 1529 parliament, and Cromwell resurrected these in the 'supplication against the ordinaries'. Among the accusations levied against the 'ordinaries' (or clerics) were the excessive fees raised by the Church courts, the punishment of minor offences with excommunication, and the large number of holy days that were observed with insufficient devotion. Most significantly, though, it described Henry as 'the only head, sovereign, lord, protector, and defender', and forced convocation to define what it understood by 'headship as far as the law of Christ allows' – the mealy-mouthed compromise that had made them agree to the statute of *praemunire* a year before.[14]

The supplication was presented to the king on 18 March 1532. No further action was taken, but when the Convocation of Canterbury reconvened on 12 April, the first item on the agenda was how to respond to the supplication. Bishop Gardiner, who had until that time proved loyal to the king, now apparently turned his coat by drafting a robust reply on behalf of convocation, declaring: 'We, your most humble servants, may not submit the execution of our charges and duty, certainly prescribed by God, to your highness' assent.'[15] In a barely concealed attack on Cromwell, it went on to denounce the 'sinister information and importunate labours and persuasions of evil disposed persons, pretending themselves to be thereunto moved by the zeal of justice and reformation, [who] may induce right wise, sad, and constant men to suppose such things to be true, as be not so indeed.'[16] Gardiner and his colleagues had played right into Cromwell's hands. The king was so outraged by their defiance that he proceeded to bully them into submission. On 11 May he made a speech in parliament accusing them of little short of treason: 'We thought that the clergy of our realm had been our subjects wholly, but now we have well perceived that they be but half our subjects, yea, and scarce our subjects; for all the prelates at their consecration make an oath to the Pope, clean contrary to the oath that they make to us, so that they seem to be his subjects, and not ours. The copy of both oaths I deliver here to you, requiring you to invent some order, that we be not thus deluded of our spiritual subjects.'[17]

Four days later, under threat of another *praemunire* charge, convocation capitulated, reluctantly signing what has become known as the Submission of the Clergy. In so doing, the clergy had accepted that the law of the Church would in future depend on the consent of the king, in the same way as secular laws required his consent in parliament. This constituted a major victory for Cromwell's reforms – and paved the way for the break from Rome.

As a devout and orthodox Catholic, Sir Thomas More had increasingly sided with the clergy against the king's religious reforms. He was also deeply opposed to the divorce, and had fought assiduously on the queen's behalf. Although Henry remained fond of him for a time, when More made it clear that he would continue to fight for what he saw as the true faith and Church in England, he made a dangerous adversary of the king. For the previous seven years More had waged a fierce war against the rise of heresy, denouncing the teachings of Luther and his fraternity, publishing strongly worded tracts in defence of the orthodox faith, and organising raids on the houses of known heretics. In May 1532, he resigned as Lord Chancellor. Now that he was no longer part of government, he stepped up his campaign with renewed vigour. During the next year and a half he published five major works against Protestant doctrine and the erosion of the Church's power. As well as antagonising the king, this set More on a collision course with Cromwell.

More's son-in-law, William Roper, recounts that Cromwell visited the former Chancellor at his home in Chelsea. He carried a message from the king, no doubt urging More to conform, but the latter used Cromwell's visit as an opportunity to advise him on how best to deal with Henry. 'You shall, in your councell-givinge unto his grace, ever tell him what he oughte to doe, but never what he is able to doe . . . For yf the lyone knewe his owne strengthe, harde were it for any man to rule him.'[18] This is a fascinating insight into the way More and his fellow councillors had tried to manage Henry. It implies that they, not he, had directed policy and had manipulated him into agreeing to their will. According to More, it was a form of damage limitation: if the king alone had dictated matters, it would have wreaked chaos and disorder, even tyranny.

Cromwell's response to More is not recorded. By now, he had the measure of Henry and his court and was probably ill-disposed to accept the advice of this bastion of the old order, whose stubborn idealism had lost him his office. Nevertheless, the years that followed would prove that Cromwell's way of handling the king was not entirely dissimilar to that which More had espoused. He once wryly observed to Chapuys: 'The king, my master, is a great king, but very fond of having things his own way.'[19] The trick, perhaps, was in making Henry believe that he had.

Although Cromwell had undoubtedly been motivated by political necessity in engineering the break with Rome, there is evidence of an emerging religious conviction that increasingly dictated the course of his actions against the orthodox Catholic Church. This constituted a marked shift in his beliefs. His will of 1529 suggests that at least up until that time, any personal piety he had was along traditional lines. He had requested intercession by the saints and had left money for masses to be said for his soul by the five orders of friars within the city of London.[20] His unusually public display of piety after Wolsey's fall later that year, when Cavendish reported hearing him recite 'our lady mattens', also adhered to the orthodox faith. In a letter he wrote to Wolsey in May 1530, he was openly critical of the new reformist faith, declaring: 'The fame is that Luther is departed this life. I would he had never been born.'[21] The inventory of Austin Friars taken in 1527 contains clues that point towards Cromwell's conservative religious tastes. In one of the chambers was 'a relic closed in crystal, garnished with silver and gilt, like a fish', and in Cromwell's own bedroom there was 'a carved and gilt altar table of the Nativity of our Lord'. Images of the Virgin Mary were also scattered about the house.[22]

Yet the seeds of reformist beliefs may already have been planted in Cromwell's mind. According to Cavendish, on the same evening as his tearful outburst at Esher, Cromwell also unleashed a tirade of anti-clerical resentment. Likewise, when the disgraced cardinal admitted that he had no money to pay his lay servants, Cromwell demanded that his chaplains make a contribution. Complaining bitterly about the 'profettes and avuntages' enjoyed by the priests, he argued that Wolsey's lay servants had 'taken myche more payn for you in oon day than all your Idell chapleyns hathe don in a yere'.[23] These sentiments may have been inspired by such influential reformers as Stephen Vaughan and Miles Coverdale, both of whom were his close friends. The latter was a neighbour of Cromwell's at Austin Friars and had been mentored by the Cambridge scholar Robert Barnes, who taught that the true religion could only emerge through the study of scripture. This coined the word 'evangelical' because it was founded upon the Good News or the *Evangelion* of the scriptures. 'Evangelical' thus applied to most religious reformists emerging in England at this time. 'Protestant' was a term not widely used until the reign of Mary I, and 'Lutheran' related more precisely to the more radical teachings of Martin Luther.

Coverdale had written to Cromwell around 1527, possibly earlier, asking for books to help advance his studies, and praising Cromwell 'for the fervent zeall, that yow have to vertu and godly study'.[24] In a similar vein, another of Cromwell's friends, John Oliver, had written to thank him for evenings he had spent at his house in 1531 or 1532, 'where in verie dede I did here such communicacion which were the verie cause of the begynnynge of my conversion'. The pair would apparently spend hours poring over evangelical texts and translations of the New Testament, and Oliver affirmed that he 'found allwaies the conclusions you mayntenyd at yor borde to be consonent with the hollie worde of god'.[25] Foxe concurred that Cromwell 'was moste studious of hym selfe in a flagrant zeale to set forwarde the truthe of the Gospel, sekyng all meanes and wayes to beate down false Religion and to aduaunce the true'.[26]

As his influence with the king increased during the 1530s, Cromwell began to encourage Henry to consider evangelical reforms. This was a bold move: he was well aware that the king abhorred Luther and had resisted doctrinal change in the past. He therefore proceeded with a measure of caution – at least initially. In early 1531 he persuaded his royal master to allow William Tyndale safe passage back to England. This is testament to Cromwell's powers of persuasion, as well as his standing with the king, because Henry had denounced Tyndale as a heretic only a few months before. Cromwell's friend Stephen Vaughan was dispatched to Antwerp in order to find Tyndale and begin negotiations for his return. Tyndale proved reluctant at first, claiming that news he received of events in England made him afraid to go back. Even the avuncular Vaughan failed to persuade him, and he admitted to Cromwell: 'He will not listen to me, as he greatly suspects me.'[27]

Eventually, Vaughan's charm began to work, and the reformer warmed to the idea. Everything was proceeding well until Vaughan included a copy of Tyndale's *Answer* to Thomas More with a letter he wrote to the king. Tyndale had been openly critical of the Lord Chancellor's work, and he himself had rightly predicted that this would anger the king. Henry furiously demanded that Cromwell order Vaughan to have nothing more to do with Tyndale. Cromwell wrote to his friend accordingly. Playing down Henry's anger, he assured Vaughan that the king 'was right well pleased and right acceptablie considered your diligence and payn[es] taken in the wryting and sending of the saide boke', but admitted: 'his highnes nothyng lyked the sayd boke being fyllyd with Scedycyous Slaunderous lyes and Fantastycall oppynyon[s].' The king, he said, feared that 'the evill doctryne of so perverse and malycyous a person' would 'Seduce deceyve and disquiet the people and comenwelth of this realme', and was therefore 'veray glad that he is out of his Realme'. Cromwell ended with a more urgent entreaty: 'I hertelie pray you . . . for the loue of god . . . exhorte you vtterlie to forsake leve and withdraw your affectyon from the saide Tyndale and all his secte.'[28] However, Vaughan's reply suggests that he may have added a secret postscript, urging him to keep the channels of communication open. Vaughan had two further meetings with Tyndale in May and June that year, before Cromwell gave up hope of bringing the matter to a successful conclusion. Indeed, he acquiesced with the king's request to dispatch Sir Thomas Elyot to arrest the reformer and bring him back to England.

CHAPTER 7

'The suddaine rising of some men'

'ALL MY HOPE is in you,' Wolsey's illegitimate son, Thomas Winter, wrote to Cromwell in October 1532. 'You are now placed in that position which I and all your friends have long wished for and you have attained that dignity that you can serve them as you please.'[1] The year 1532 would be a golden one for Cromwell. By the end of it, he would have amassed so many appointments and privileges at his royal master's hands that he would control the entire domestic administration of England. The day after Sir Thomas More's resignation, the king showed his favour towards his chief adversary by granting Cromwell and his son Gregory the lordship of Romney in Newport, south Wales. Cromwell's wealth increased in direct proportion to his influence with the king. His meticulously kept accounts include innumerable references to well-filled purses, gloves, cheeses and other gifts left in his apartments by men eager for preferment.[2]

An indication of Cromwell's growing wealth is the fact that in 1532 he and his household took over two large properties on Throgmorton Street within the precinct of Austin Friars, close to where they were living.[3] He obtained a ninety-nine-year lease of his current house and garden in June, together with the adjacent house and warehouse. He also leased a property further south called the Swanne that fronted onto Throgmorton Street, which was owned by the friary but lay outside its precinct. He would buy this property from the friary two years later, together with an adjacent plot of land bordering the street, which meant that he now owned a substantial area of land and buildings close to his current house. In addition, Cromwell bought land and property behind his house so that he was able to create a huge garden.[4]

Without pausing to seek permission, Cromwell proceeded to move the fences of his neighbours' gardens back by twenty-two feet, and offered neither warning nor compensation. 'This house [i.e. Cromwell's] being finished, and having some reasonable plot of ground left for a Garden, he caused the pales of the Gardens adioyning to the north parte thereof on a sodain to be taken downe, 22 feet to be measured forth right into the north of every man's ground, a line there to bee drawen, a trench to bee cast, a foundation laid, and a highe bricke wall to bee builded.' Even more audaciously, he put the house of Thomas Stow (father of the antiquarian, John) on rollers and moved it, and then started to build a new house for himself on the land that had been thus vacated. An outraged John Stow recorded how all this had happened 'ere my Father heard thereof: no warning was given him, nor any other answere when hee spake to the surveyors of that worke but that their Mayster Sir Thomas commaunded them so to doe.' It is an indication of Cromwell's widely recognised influence at court that nobody dared utter so much as a whisper in protest. 'No many durst go to argue the matter,' observed Stow, 'but each man lost his land, and my Father payde his whole rent . . . for that halfe which was left.' He could not resist adding: 'The suddaine rising of some men, causeth them to forget themselves.'[5]

Building work was still continuing to the house in September 1535, when Cromwell's agent, Thomas Thacker, reported: 'The wall of the kitchen towards the street, the windows of freestone, with the scullery and other offices is clearly finished. The carpenter is raising the roofs and all is complete except the windows of the side of the hall towards the court. Your own lodging, with the chamber and gallery above, are finished and plastered and want only glazing.'[6]

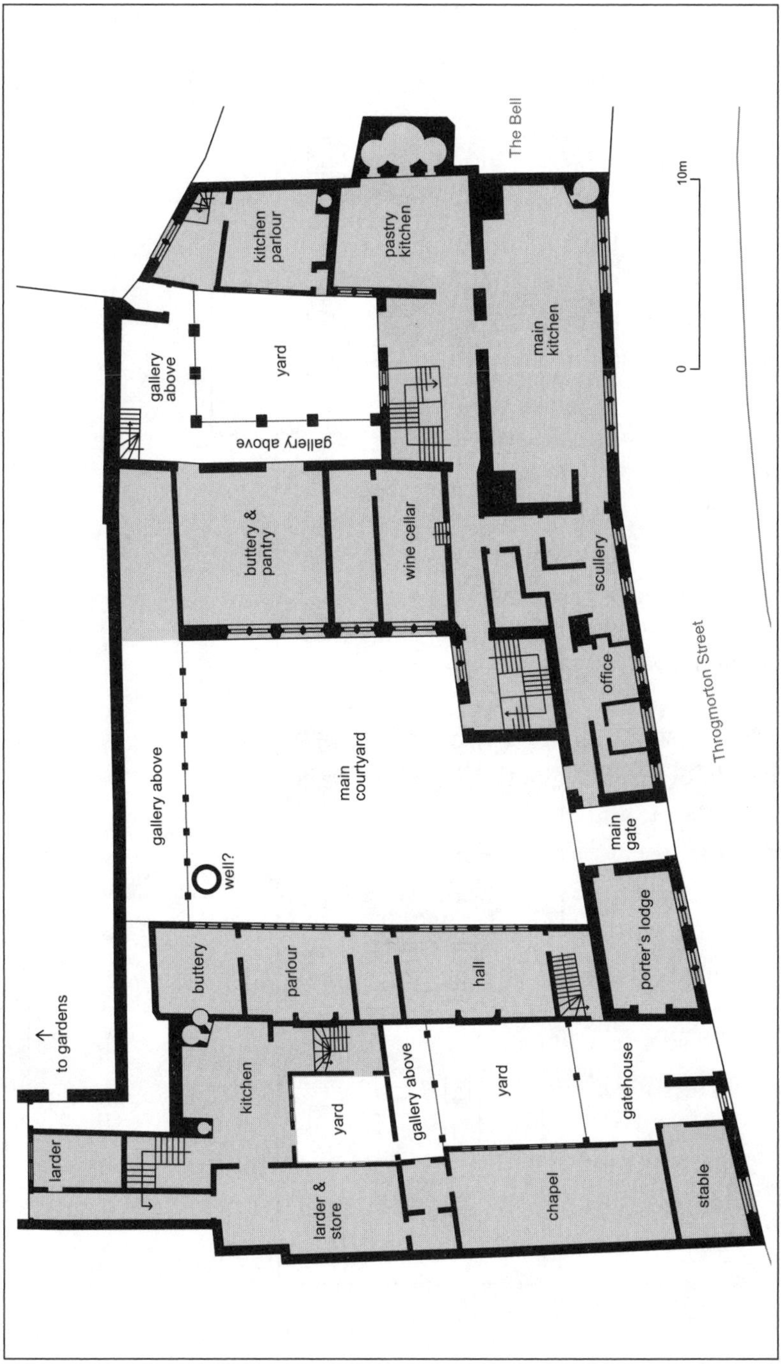

Detailed ground floor plan of Thomas Cromwell's new mansion at Austin Friars (scale 1:500)

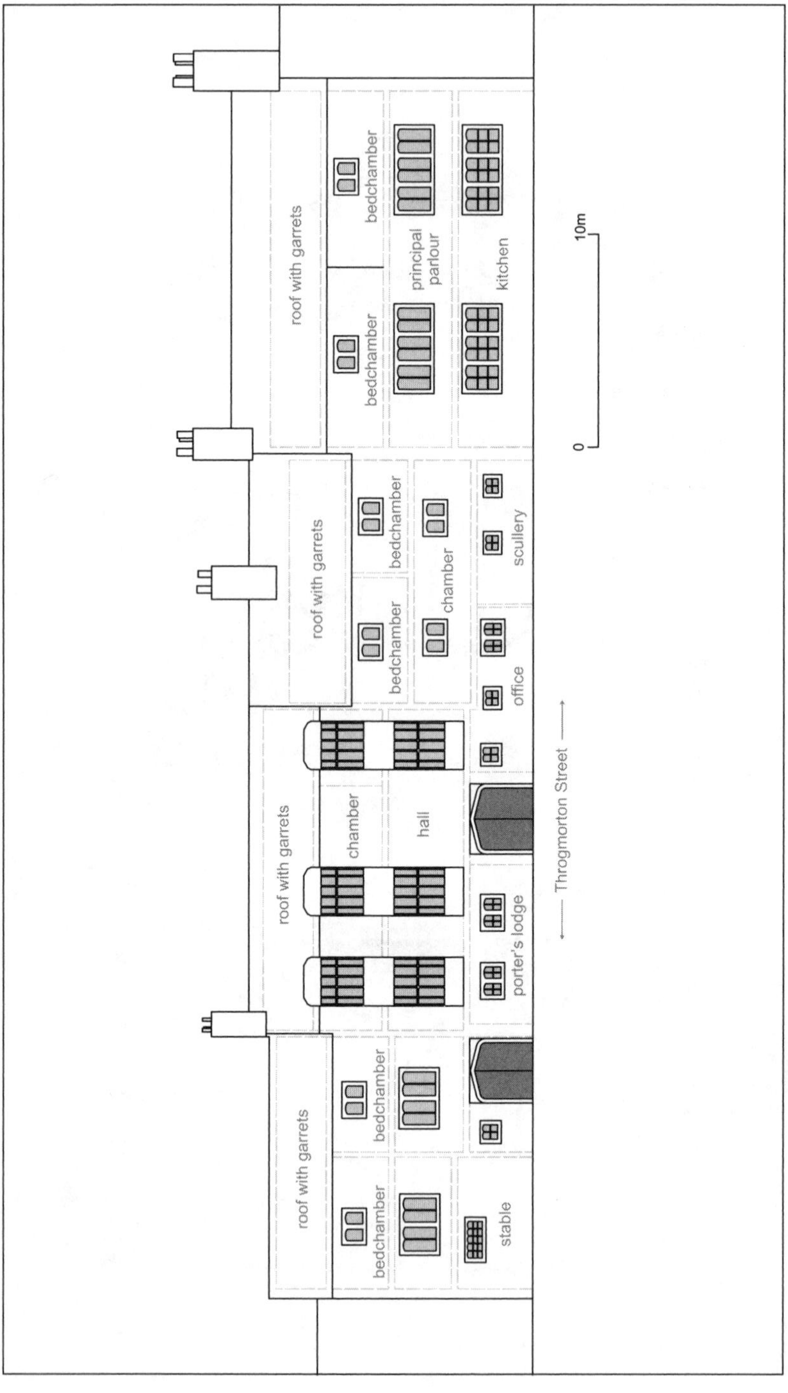

Reconstructed elevation of Thomas Cromwell's new mansion at Austin Friars (scale 1:350)

Cromwell's latest residence was on such an ambitious scale that it took several years to complete, even though at the height of the building there were ninety-eight workers on site.[7] In February 1536 Chapuys told his master that he intended to return from his morning worship at the Augustinian friary 'through the house which he [Cromwell] is building, as it would be my most direct road home'.[8] When it was eventually finished in July 1539, at a cost of at least 1,000 pounds (more than £300,000 today), it was one of the largest private residences in the entire capital. Stow admitted that the result was impressive: 'On the south side, and at the west end of this church, many fair houses are built; namely, in Throgmorton Street, one very large and spacious, built in the place of old and small tenements by Thomas Cromwell.'[9]

The mansion was three storeys high and built of brick, with walls that were two feet thick in places. It was timber-framed, with a tiled roof and three large oriel windows spanning the first and second floors. Arranged around three courtyards, it had fifty rooms – more than three times as many as Cromwell's original Austin Friars house. It contained a chapel, extensive kitchens and private chambers and bedchambers. The centrepiece was a spectacular series of halls to which important guests would have been conveyed via the grand staircase. The hall that overlooked the street was heated and had four bay windows. They were hung with fine tapestries by Flemish weavers. There is little detail of the other decoration in the public rooms, but the bedrooms were all lavishly furnished, with four-poster beds covered with cloth of gold, damask or velvet. The huge garden contained formal square knots or beds, intersected by paths and walkways, and the maze shown on a seventeenth-century survey was probably part of Cromwell's new garden. His leisure pursuits were also given free rein here, for there was a 'diceing' house, a bowling alley and several summer houses.

Cromwell's extensive new residence was required for more than just status: his ever expanding household had been rapidly running out of accommodation and working space. Members of Cromwell's family also needed to be housed. His only surviving child, Gregory, had been studying at Cambridge for the past four years and returned home – fleetingly – in 1533, when he was about thirteen years old. He had benefited from an excellent education and had come to share his father's interests and beliefs, thanks at least in part to the influence of his tutors and his fellow pupil, Nicholas Sadler, who was a known adherent of the reformist faith.

There had been no question that Gregory would remain at Cambridge to study for a degree: such a course was usually reserved for those young men who intended to enter the Church. Besides, Cromwell was keen that Gregory should benefit from the same practical experience that he himself had gained during his youth. He therefore assigned his son to the care of various influential friends whom he believed could enhance his spiritual, intellectual and – above all – practical abilities. They included Rowland Lee, Bishop of Coventry and Lichfield and a close associate of Cromwell. Although he had a fearsome reputation for administering brutal justice, Lee was said to have treated the boy as if he 'were his owne naturall sonne'.[10] Gregory subsequently went to stay with Sir Richard Southwell, a Privy Councillor, at his estate at Woodrising Manor in Norfolk.

Gregory was accompanied to each new residence by his tutor, Henry Dowes, a man of considerable intellectual ability. In collaboration with Cromwell, Dowes compiled an extensive curriculum of study for the boy, which included French, Latin, English, accounting, music and Roman and Greek history. Perhaps not surprisingly, given his father's predilection for humanist teachings, the works of Erasmus figured prominently in his studies. But Gregory followed the observances of the traditional faith too: Dowes refers to his pupil hearing mass.[11] Gregory also practised the longbow, played the lute and virginals and came to share his father's love of hunting, hawking and riding. Together with his cousin, Christopher Wellyfed, who had apparently rejoined him for a time, Gregory escaped on a hunt during breaks in his studies and when any other opportunity presented itself. In a letter to Cromwell, Dowes admiringly noted: 'for his recreation he [Gregory] useth to hawke and hunte, and shote in his long bowe, which frameth and succedeth so well with hime that he semeth to be therunto given by nature.'[12]

Gregory's heart clearly lay more with outdoor sports than with academic study. In September 1534 Henry Dowes ruefully admitted to Cromwell that he had used every effort to focus Gregory on his studies, 'but forcause summer was spent in the service of the wild gods, it is so much to be regarded after what fashion youth is brought up.'[13] Even though Dowes assured his master that Gregory was spending several hours a day in reading and writing, and that when they went out riding Dowes made sure to tell him a Greek or Roman story on the way, Cromwell was not satisfied. He urged Dowes to be much stricter with the boy and deny him the pleasures of the chase so that he might concentrate on improving his mind. By April of the following year, Dowes was able to report: 'Mr. Gregory and his company are in good health and busy in learning. His improvement is greater than at any time here before, partly because he is brought into some awe and dread, and is ready to give himself to learning when required; partly because those things which formerly alienated his mind from study are now withdrawn.' Although he admitted that 'the ripeness of his wit, which is not of that hasty sort that by and by do bring forth their fruit, grows to a greater docility,' he assured Cromwell: 'The hours of his study for the French tongue, writing, playing at weapons, casting accounts, pastimes of instruments, have been devised by Mr. Southwell, who spares no pains, daily hearing him read in the English tongue, advertising him of their true pronunciation, explaining the etymology of those words we have borrowed from the French or the Latin, not even so commonly used in our quotidian speech . . . If he continues in this way, this summer shall be consecrated to Apollo and the Muses, as was the last to the wild goddess Diana.'[14]

Gregory had also become close to his cousin, Richard Williams, son of Cromwell's sister Katherine and her husband Morgan, whom he saw on his visits to Austin Friars. Born in Wales either in or before 1502, Richard was at least eighteen years older than his cousin, and there seems to have been an element of hero worship in Gregory's relationship with him. He certainly had much to admire: Richard was an impressive young man. Trained as a soldier, he excelled in jousting and other tournament sports favoured at court. He also shared his uncle's sharp intellect and cunning, and the two men enjoyed a natural affinity. Cromwell seems to have taken over his nephew's care soon after the death of his sister Katherine, and Richard adopted his surname.

Cromwell soon realised his nephew's potential. It was almost certainly thanks to his influence that Richard was appointed to the service of Thomas Grey, Marquess of Dorset, whom Cromwell himself had served early in his career. He evidently introduced his nephew at court soon after he himself had begun to rise to prominence there. Richard rapidly won favour with the king, perhaps because of his prowess in the tournament arena, and he was appointed to the Privy Council in 1531. He also seems to have acted as a messenger on his uncle's behalf. He was probably the 'kynnesman this berer' to whom Cromwell referred in a letter to Gardiner written in January 1532. So pleased was Cromwell with his nephew that he not only promoted his interests but those of Richard's friends. Several years after he first took over Richard's care, he wrote to his associate, Rowland Lee, Bishop of Coventry and Lichfield, asking that he might assign an office in the church of Lichfield to Richard, so that he in turn might give it to 'a nere frende of his'.[15]

Cromwell, his son and nephew comprised a small, close-knit family. The letters that Gregory and Richard wrote to the elder Cromwell suggest a genuine affection. Richard would later write to his uncle bemoaning their separation: 'I never more desired anything than, since your departure, to see you, nor thought time longer in your absence.' Gregory was no less effusive in a letter asking for his father's blessing, which he described as 'more treasure unto me then all the abundance of worldly goods'. There is no sense of any rivalry between the two young men for Cromwell's affection. Richard left his cousin 'a great horse' in his will.[16]

Cromwell's family was far outnumbered by the growing number of staff at Austin Friars. Although the vast majority of the correspondence from Cromwell's household concerns the business transactions in which they were involved, there is evidence of the personal lives of its members. The attention of the ever assiduous Ralph Sadler had been distracted by the arrival of a new servant in 1530. Ellen (or Helen) Barre had suffered a miserable marriage to Matthew, a London tradesman who frittered away his money on drink and abandoned his wife and two children. Having tried for some time to trace him, Ellen eventually presumed him dead and took the position of laundress in Cromwell's household. She and Sadler soon formed a strong attachment and within a few months of meeting they were married. But in 1545, after fifteen years of marriage and with seven children by Sadler (three sons, the eldest of whom was named Thomas in honour of the master, and four daughters), Ellen discovered to her horror that her estranged first husband was still alive. She was therefore guilty of bigamy. A drunken Barre had been overheard by one of Thomas Wriothesley's servants boasting that he was Lady Sadler's husband. Barre was immediately seized and interrogated. When the truth of his claims was established, Sadler's only option was to petition parliament. Thanks to his experience and influence as a Privy Councillor, he had little difficulty in securing a private bill, passed on 24 December, legitimising his children. But Lady Sadler remained legally Barre's wife and it may have been years before this was resolved. Sadler was deeply attached to his wife and 'took his matter very heavily'.[17]

Another of Cromwell's close servants and protégés, Thomas Avery, returned to Austin Friars in 1532. Avery had benefited from his education with Stephen Vaughan, who wrote to Cromwell in February to advise him that the boy was on his way back and had reached Zeeland. He urged his friend: 'Receive him again as the first-fruit of my rude education. If he were neglected, the sap would be spilt, and the flowers lost that might spring hereafter.'[18] Avery did not remain in Cromwell's household for long after his return, for in November 1533 he was writing from the household of Gertrude, Marchioness of Exeter, in whose service Cromwell had placed him. But all this was intended as a training-ground for the young man, whose potential – like Richard's – he had been quick to spot. He therefore intended him for his own household.

A shrewd judge of men, Cromwell certainly had a gift for spotting potential among his family and servants. By the early 1530s, when his career at court was beginning to flourish, he could rely on a growing band of talented, loyal and trustworthy young men, all eager and quick to learn the tricks of Cromwell's trade. As the seventeenth-century historian John Strype observed: 'He retained many persons of great quickness and abilities, and preferred them to the King, who employed them in his frequent messages and dispatches abroad into other kingdoms.' This same shrewd judgement enabled Cromwell to single out other members of his acquaintance as being worthy of advancement. 'He preferred more men of worth and integrity, whether Lay or Clergy, in his time, than any other in great place and favour at Court had done,' remarked Strype. In his regular lengthy dispatches to Charles V, Ambassador Chapuys made many references to Cromwell's various servants and messengers. 'He never ceases sending me messages through a confidential friend of his,' he reported in one, 'who has called on me several times for the last fortnight.'[19]

Serving as Cromwell's apprentice had become one of the surest means of securing a profitable career at court. His household, in common with those of other important members of the court, had become a semi-official department of government, filled with secretaries, clerks, accountants and other officials whose job it was to administer the wealth of correspondence, writs, draft Acts and other documentation connected with Cromwell's court business, as well as the legal cases, trading matters and financial dealings of his private enterprises. At its height, it comprised a staggering 400 members of staff, many of whom had formerly served Wolsey. Cromwell had no doubt picked out the men who had proved their worth in the cardinal's service.[20] All the servants were decked out in Cromwell's livery. This was typically understated, being grey in colour, with the gentlemen servants wearing velvet and the yeomen clad in long tunics with 'their skirts large enough for their friends to sit upon them'. On special occasions, their master invested in more ostentatious attire, such as the London muster in 1540, when his servants marched from Mile End in 'coates of white cloth, the armes of this Citie, to witte, a red crosse, and a sword on the breaste and backe'.[21]

The trappings of service to Cromwell signified more than mere status. In contrast to the other great Tudor households, which acted as finishing schools for members of the upper classes, working for Cromwell was no sinecure. Anyone who hoped to gain employment with this rising star of Henry's government must prove himself capable of undertaking a myriad of tasks with a high degree of competence. He must also be willing to work the same long hours as his master. Nevertheless, Cromwell treated the members of his household well, ensuring that they were all properly housed, clothed, fed and governed. The fact that he later reflected that he had retained all these men 'at my great Charge' suggests they were well paid.[22] John Stow claimed: 'A man thought himself fortunate if he could call himself a servant of Cromwell.' His views were echoed by John Foxe, who was impressed by what 'a kind and loving master he was to his servants.' This is corroborated by the story of an audacious boy from Cumberland who was so desperate to become a member of Cromwell's household that he bought himself a coat of livery in Cromwell's colours and turned up one day in 1535 when Thomas Legh was conducting some monastic visitations, begging the agent to let him tag along.[23]

As well as his immediate circle at Austin Friars, Cromwell also maintained ties with more distant members of his family and friends. They included his cousin, Nicholas Glossop (his mother's nephew), who in June 1533 wrote to beg for Cromwell's assistance. A member of the Guild of Taylors, Glossop faced financial ruin when, on the death of his master, the guild proposed withdrawing his annuity of twenty-six shillings and eight pence per year. 'I am almost four-score years old, impotent, lame of the gout and cramp, and one of my eyes is gone,' he pleaded. He also sent his cousin '12 Banbury cheeses, half hard and half soft, and wish they were worth 20,000*l*.' Reminding Cromwell of their family connection, he stated, 'My mistress your mother was my aunt', and also referred to Cromwell's nephew, Christopher Wellyfed, for whom he had provided 'a feather-bed with a bolster'. Cromwell was swift to act upon the letter. He wrote at once to the Merchant Taylors about his cousin's annuity: 'I request that you will continue it for my sake, and increase it by thirteen shillings four pence a year.' That he acted out of genuine concern rather than grudging agreement is suggested by the sense of urgency he conveyed, telling the guild: 'I wish to have your answer on the morrow of the next court day.'[24]

Despite making time for private and family concerns, Cromwell never failed in his duties to the king – and was rewarded richly for it. On 14 April 1532 he was made Master of the Jewels. As well as being his first office, this deceptively minor appointment gave him access to the royal coffers and allowed him to administer government finance from the funds brought under his control. John Strype observed that this appointment signalled that Cromwell had 'grown in great favour with the King'.[25]

It was around this time that Hans Holbein painted Cromwell's portrait. That Cromwell should commission the most celebrated court painter of the age to take his likeness is an indication of how far he had risen. The low-born son of a Putney blacksmith had now taken his place among kings, dukes and earls in securing immortality as a sitter for Hans Holbein. The painting may have been commissioned to celebrate Cromwell's recent appointment, since the paper on top of the pile is inscribed 'To Master Cromwell, trusty and well-beloved master of our jewel house'.

Another lucrative position followed on 16 July, when he became clerk of the hanaper, an office in the department of the chancery, for which he received fees and other moneys for the sealing of charters, patents, writs and the like. Cromwell would receive no fewer than seventeen further appointments during the remainder of his ascendancy at court, and even though most of these were comparatively modest, the income that arose from them was far from it. As the decade progressed, Cromwell amassed such riches that he became one of the wealthiest men in England. It has been estimated that by 1537 his annual income was around 12,000 pounds – equivalent to more than £3.5 million in today's money.

Cromwell was quick to capitalise on his new roles as a means not only of generating income for himself, but of securing even more regular contact with his sovereign. In September 1532 he wrote to inform Henry of progress in making a new jewel-encrusted collar that the king had designed. He assured his master: 'I haue wyllyd your goldsmyth not to procede to the making of any thing In perffeccyon vntill your gracious pleasure shalbe Ferther knowen for the which purpose both he and I shall repayre vnto your highnes on Saterday night or Sondaye in the morning.'[26] Eager though he was to ensure his royal master received the most lavish jewels and adornments, Cromwell himself eschewed the outward trappings of power. Titles and offices were all very well for the authority and riches they gave him, but – unlike the vast majority of his contemporaries – he did not hanker after pomp and ostentation in his own dress and ceremonies. That he did not attempt to erase his lowly birth in this way reveals both his naturally frugal nature, as well as a sense of security that his power derived from inner skill, not outer show. He had also learned from his former master, Wolsey, that too much pomp and ostentation could lead to trouble.

His titles, however, did seem to give Cromwell a new confidence in dealing with his more noble colleagues in government. Thus he wrote to the Duke of Suffolk, one of the most distinguished and longest-serving members of Henry's circle, requiring him to surrender his patent of Earl Marshal, which had been granted to the Duke of Norfolk. Although Suffolk was granted the justiceship of some forests close to the Trent in return, he was clearly aggrieved at this change. Cromwell condescendingly assured him: 'His majesty supposes and perfectly perceives that your grace hath much more estimation and zeal to nourish kindness and love between my said lord of Norfolk and you . . . which undoubtedly is highly to his gracious contentment to see and perceive so great and honourable personages [among] his subjects so lovingly and friendly, the one to love the other.' Cromwell no doubt secretly delighted in the antagonism that he knew this move would create between the dukes, and in the fact that he – the lowest-born member of Henry's council – should be given the role of peacemaker. He ended by asking Suffolk 'to repayre to the Courte with Resonable spede' adding a half-hearted apology for his 'bolde & Rude wryting'.[27]

Cromwell's newfound powers were anathema to his blue-blooded rivals. As the seventeenth-century Church historian Thomas Fuller shrewdly observed: 'This was the cause why he was envied of the nobility, being by birth so much beneath them and by preferment so high above most of them. Besides, many of his advancements were interpreted not so much as honours to him as injuries to others, as being either in use improper or in equity unfit or in right unjust or in conscience unlawful for him to accept.'[28] Cromwell was content to let them think the worst. Although he might privately relish his adversaries' fury, his focus was always on business, not one-upmanship.

By the summer of 1532, it was clear that Cromwell had become intricately involved in foreign, as well as domestic affairs. In May and June he sent two letters to the king, relaying certain information that he had managed to glean from his contacts abroad. This included a meeting of the English ambassadors with those of the emperor, as well as reports he had received from Rome and Venice about the likelihood of a Turkish invasion of Italy. The network of contacts and agents that Cromwell had so carefully built up over the preceding years now stood him in excellent stead. Henry realised that here was a man who might keep him better informed of continental affairs than most others.

The death of Archbishop Warham in August 1532 removed another conservative opponent at court, and paved the way for an appointment that would prove enormously beneficial for Cromwell's reforms. Some four years Cromwell's junior, Thomas Cranmer was of slightly more distinguished origins, being the son of a Nottinghamshire esquire – albeit an impoverished one. Educated at Cambridge, he had been among the bright young scholars whom Wolsey had tried to procure for his new college at Oxford. Cranmer had resisted, but he later accepted an invitation from the cardinal to join the English diplomatic mission to the Emperor Charles V in Spain. Cranmer proved so able in this task that he was granted the honour of a meeting with the king on his return, who showered him with gifts, including rings of gold and silver. From that moment, Cranmer became a stout advocate for Henry's divorce from Catherine of Aragon. Although he returned to Cambridge, he seems to have been enlisted by Wolsey for various business matters. For example, in October 1528 he travelled from London to Ipswich bearing a letter from Cromwell to William Capon, dean of Wolsey's new college at Ipswich. By then the two men would almost certainly have been acquainted, but it was only after Wolsey's fall that their collaboration really got under way.

Cranmer was admired for his calm and sanguine nature – not

qualities that were found in abundance at Henry's court. 'He was a man of such temperature of nature, or rather so mortified, that no manner of prosperity or adversity could alter or change his accustomed conditions . . . Notwithstanding privately with his secret friends he would shed forth many bitter tears, lamenting the misery and calamities of the world.'[29] Cromwell would soon become one of the 'secret friends' to whom this commentator was referring.

After the collapse of Cardinal Campeggi's hearing in the summer of 1529, Cranmer had suggested switching focus from the legal case at Rome towards a general canvassing of university theologians throughout Europe. As well as removing the Pope from the equation, this strategy had the added benefit of being more cost-effective than the protracted and futile negotiations that Wolsey had spearheaded. The king had acquiesced, and Cranmer had undertaken the task with alacrity. Realising his potential, the Boleyn family had quickly taken Cranmer under their wing, offering him lodgings in Thomas Boleyn's newly acquired Durham Place, a lavish Thames-side mansion on the Strand, so that he might have quietude to apply 'his minde concerninge the Kinges question'.[30] Such was Henry's own faith in Cranmer that in 1530 he dispatched him to Rome as part of a team of envoys whose task was to gather university opinions. It was a fruitless mission, but Cranmer did not suffer by association and on his return to England he was put to work on the *Collectanea* and other academic treatises in support of the divorce.

Although Cranmer had embarked on his theological career as a conservative, his efforts on the king's behalf had encouraged him to question papal authority. A diplomatic mission to Germany in 1532 fanned the flames of his nascent evangelical beliefs. While there, he met several leading Lutherans, including Andreas Osiander. This meeting would prove significant in more ways than one. On a visit to Osiander, Cranmer met the niece of the pastor's wife, a young woman called Margaret. Apparently instantly smitten, he married her within a very short time of their first meeting. This is an indication not just of his love for Margaret, but of his new faith, for the evangelicals rejected the old tradition of clerical celibacy. Nevertheless, it was with some alarm that he learned in the autumn,

parliament was recalled to pass the necessary legislation. It is a testament to the careful groundwork that Cromwell had spent the past three years preparing that he was able to act so speedily. But he was taking no chances. He therefore ensured that the new parliament would be filled with men known to be favourable to the divorce. He also had his confederate, Sir Thomas Audley, appointed Lord Chancellor, which meant he would now officiate over the House of Lords.

The session began on 4 February, and Cromwell wasted no time in bringing forward a new bill that restricted the right to make appeals to Rome. What this meant in practice was that the king's word, and that of his Archbishop of Canterbury, would be final and unchallengeable. Acutely aware that his entire career – perhaps even his life – rested upon the success of this measure, Cromwell disregarded all opposition. Even the king's comments on the draft bill were ignored. Cromwell also drew up lists of all those who dared to speak out. His memory was as long for opponents as it was for friends, and the men who tried to obstruct his path to glory would live to regret it. Among them was Sir George Throckmorton, who had already made an enemy of the king by expressing his fear that if the marriage to Anne went ahead (he did not know it already had) it would trouble Henry's conscience because, quite apart from the matter of the king's first wife, he had 'meddled both with the mother and sister' of Anne Boleyn. The king exclaimed, 'Never with the mother!' and Cromwell was quick to add: 'Nor with the sister either – and therefore put that out of your head.' This exchange ensured a swift exit from court for Throckmorton – at Cromwell's instigation. A letter that Throckmorton wrote to Cromwell on 29 October that year makes it clear that he had been instructed 'to live at home, serve God, and meddle little'.[31]

While Cromwell was dictating the deliberations in parliament, Cranmer was consecrated Archbishop of Canterbury on 30 March. Immediately afterwards, another significant barrier to the divorce was removed when convocation agreed that the king's marriage to Catherine had been unlawful. Then, during the first week of April, Cromwell succeeded in making law the Act in Restraint of Appeals.

Described as 'Cromwell's masterpiece in statute-making', the famous preamble to the Act pronounced that the realm of England was an empire, ruled by the king as supreme head, with complete mastery over the bodies and souls of his subjects.[32] The surviving drafts of the bill reveal some disagreement between Cromwell and his royal master about the nature of the latter's authority, with Henry insisting that his jurisdiction over the Church emanated from his 'imperial' crown. The fact that Cromwell removed such references probably indicates less a difference of opinion on the constitution than a typically pragmatic attempt to reduce clerical opposition. He realised that by emphasising the threat that appeals to Rome constituted to the king's temporal position, the Act stood a much greater chance of acceptance by the clergy. From now on, no subject of the king – Catherine of Aragon included – could appeal to Rome as a higher authority.

The final pieces of the jigsaw were now moved swiftly into place. On 11 April Cranmer sent the king a pro forma challenge to the validity of his marriage to Catherine. The next day, Cromwell was appointed Chancellor of the Exchequer – an indication of his great favour with the king, as well as his aptitude for the position. On 10 May a formal trial was invoked to consider the legitimacy of the king's first marriage. Within a fortnight, it had concluded that the marriage between Catherine and Arthur had been consummated, so her subsequent union with his brother had been unlawful. On 28 May Cranmer pronounced Henry's marriage to Anne to be lawful, and four days later she was crowned queen in a staggeringly ostentatious ceremony, aimed at quelling any doubts as to her legitimacy. But the hostility towards the new queen was so great among her subjects that it would take more than an impressive display of pomp and pageantry to change their minds. Chapuys described the coronation as 'a cold, meagre and uncomfortable thing, to the great dissatisfaction, not only of the common people, but also of the rest'.[33] Dissatisfaction soon turned to open mockery. All along the processional route Henry and Anne's initials were displayed intertwined. But this cipher was turned to parody with cries of 'HA HA' among the disdainful crowds as Anne's procession passed by.

As a public relations exercise, the coronation had failed miserably. But Cromwell was determined that the resentful English people must not be allowed to undermine the legislation that he had fought so hard to achieve. He therefore attempted to bully them into accepting their new queen. This marks a discernible shift in his attitude towards his opponents, which was almost certainly born of the fact that he was now higher in the king's favour than he had ever been. In May 1533 Chapuys told his master that Cromwell 'manages all his [Henry's] affairs', and in another dispatch that month described him as 'the oldest among the councillors and he who now enjoys most credit with the King'.[34] The Scottish theologian Alexander Ales referred to him as: 'Lord Crumwell, the King's ear and mind, to whom he had entrusted the entire government of the country'.[35] Chapuys confirmed Cromwell's pre-eminence later that year when he reported that the mighty Norfolk was now obliged to bend his opinions to those of his rival. The duke had previously been one of the most outspoken advocates of the 'old religion' at court. It was thus with some surprise that his fellow councillors listened to an outburst in which he denounced the Pope with '1,000 blasphemies, calling him an unhappy whoreson, a liar and a wicked man, and that it should cost him wife and children, his own person, and all that he possessed, or that he would be revenged on him'. Chapuys wryly added: 'He has a good deal changed his tune, for it was he alone [in] the Court who showed himself the best of Catholics, and who favoured most the authority of the Pope; but he must act in this way not to lose his remaining influence, which apparently does not extend much further than Cromwell wishes; for which reason, I understand, he is wonderfully sick of the Court.'[36]

CHAPTER 8

'Hevy wordes and terrible thretes'

IN PUSHING THROUGH the legislation to release England from papal authority and give the king his divorce, Cromwell had fulfilled his end of the bargain. Queen Anne, however, had failed to fulfil hers. In late August 1533 she had entered her confinement at Greenwich Palace, observing all the prescribed rituals to ensure the successful delivery of a prince. Her chambers had been hung with heavy tapestries, every chink of natural light had been blotted out (even down to stuffing the keyholes with material), and she had been served only by women. The conventions had been laid down the previous century by Henry's grandmother, Lady Margaret Beaufort, and had been strictly observed ever since. Confidently predicting the birth of a son who would silence her enemies once and for all, Anne had ordered letters to be drafted that thanked God for sending her 'good speed, in the deliverance and bringing forth of a prince'.[1]

But the child that was born in the early hours of 7 September was not the expected son and heir. It was a girl. Henry was devastated. He had overturned the entire religious and political life of England in order to marry Anne, on the promise that she would give him the prince upon whom the stability of his realm depended. But instead, she had produced nothing more than another useless girl. Surely God had shown his hand: his new marriage was cursed. All the celebrations that had been planned to mark the arrival of a new Tudor prince were cancelled. Chapuys reported with barely concealed glee that 'the King's mistress was delivered of a daughter, to the great regret both of him and the lady, and to the great reproach of physicians, astrologers, sorcerers, and sorceresses, who affirmed that it would be a male child. But the people are doubly glad that it is a daughter rather than a son, and delight to mock those who put faith in such divinations, and to see them so full of shame.' He later added that the new queen had shown 'great disappointment and anger' at the birth of her daughter. Suppressing his fury and disappointment, when visiting his new daughter for the first time, Henry told Anne: 'You and I are both young, and by God's grace, boys will follow.'[2] It was not a reassurance so much as a threat, and Anne knew it.

The infant princess was christened Elizabeth at a ceremony marked by all the usual observances, but which, according to Chapuys, was 'cold and disagreeable'. Like her mother, the child soon became the subject of hatred. Two friars were arrested for saying that the princess had been christened in hot water, 'but it was not hot enough'. Meanwhile the Spanish referred to the 'concubine's daughter' as the 'little whore' or 'little bastard', and gloated that she represented God's punishment for the English king's expulsion of papal authority.[3] The king had little choice but to acknowledge the child as his heir, and the Act of Succession that Cromwell forced through parliament early the following year formally recognised her as such. In so doing, it supplanted the king's elder daughter (now known simply as the Lady Mary), who was rendered illegitimate by the annulment of his marriage to her mother. It also set Mary and Cromwell on a collision course.

Mary Tudor and Thomas Cromwell were diametrically opposed in every way that mattered. She was a staunch Roman Catholic: he a reformist who had masterminded England's break from Rome; she was the daughter of Henry VIII's first queen: he had engineered the king's marriage to his second. Thanks to Cromwell, Mary had suffered the misery and humiliation of being demoted from heir to the throne to illegitimate outcast. And yet, on the surface at least, relations between the two were cordial. Their letters were filled with respectful, even affectionate sentiments. Cromwell was always ready with flattery and assurances of assistance, such as when he avowed that 'not only did the King cherish the Princess, his daughter, immensely, but he loved her 100 times more than his last born [Elizabeth].'[4]

Their correspondence should not be taken at face value, however. Even the fiercest of enemies would disguise their antipathy with the elaborate, courtly language of the Tudor age. Cromwell's friend and protégé, Thomas Wyatt, wrote a poem about such 'Dissembling Words', wryly observing:

> Throughout the world if it were sought,
> Fair words enough a man shall find;
> They be good cheap, they cost right nought,
> Their substance is but only wind;
> But well to say and so to mean,
> That sweet accord is seldom seen.[5]

Chapuys, a seasoned diplomat and courtier, was all too well aware of the fact. 'Although Cromwell has always given me to understand that he had great affection for the Princess,' he told Charles V, 'no deed of his has yet come to warrant his words and professions.'[6] Beneath the apparent cordiality between Cromwell and Mary in the aftermath of the divorce lay a bitter conflict over Mary's stubborn refusal to acknowledge the invalidity of her parents' marriage and accept her father's new status as supreme head of the Church. In the aggressive campaign that Cromwell had waged ever since the parliament of 1533 to subdue all resistance to his reforms, it was vital that the king's elder daughter be seen to submit. As a figurehead for the opposition – both in England and abroad – she constituted a dangerous threat to Cromwell's regime. He therefore did everything he could to persuade her to relent.

It was at least partly at Cromwell's instigation that Mary's privileges were gradually eroded and she was deprived not only of the company of her mother, but of her friends and allies. Chapuys's many requests to visit Mary were often rebuffed by the minister, who became adept at creating delays and excuses. The frustrated ambassador complained in November 1533 that Cromwell had proved both elusive and non-committal on the subject: 'I sent to Cromwell by one of his own servants, being unable for several reasons to talk with him in person, what remonstrances I could. He replied that neither he nor anyone else could tell me in detail what he had learned of the intentions of the king in council, but he assured me in general that the king is an honourable and virtuous prince and wishes to preserve the friendship of the emperor and to treat the queen and the princess well. He said that after he had talked with the king he could perhaps give a more specific reply.'[7]

On another occasion, Cromwell cancelled the ambassador's visit to Austin Friars at short notice, claiming that he was needed at court. But Chapuys was reliably informed that he had subsequently ridden off to one of his other houses. At other times, Cromwell would entice the ambassador with 'fair words' and warm assurances, but he was always careful to avoid committing any promises to paper. It was a tactic that Chapuys himself would later employ when dealing with the king, noting: 'I had likewise taken pattern by Cromwell himself, who had never given me anything in writing.'[8] Mary, though, had inherited her mother's tenacity and withstood all Cromwell's attempts to undermine her position. She and her supporters remained a thorn in his side for the next three years.

In the complex world of Henrician politics and diplomacy, however, relationships were rarely either consistently hostile or harmonious. Even though Cromwell had been the chief architect of the annulment of Henry and Catherine's marriage, he felt some sympathy for the rejected queen and her daughter, and his correspondence attests that he sometimes provided for their comfort. Catherine and he were the same age, and both were driven by a fierce loyalty to the king. Cromwell certainly gave Chapuys enough genuine hope of his good intentions to inspire the diplomat to try to win the secretary over to Catherine's cause. He confided to his Imperial master in July 1533: 'Should I perceive the least sign of his [Cromwell's] choosing to follow the right path, I shall not fail to . . . make him feel how much he would gain in personal safety, and increase his power and reputation, if he would help in the Queen's restoration.'[9] It was both a promise and a threat, but there is no evidence to suggest that Cromwell intended to heed it – for now, at least. At the time it was written, his favour with the king was at an all-time high, the woman whom he had helped to the throne was pregnant with what she claimed was a male heir, and everything was set fair for the new regime.

But Cromwell was ever one to hedge his bets and keep as many potential allies in play as possible. During the weeks and months that followed, he therefore appeared to listen favourably to the ambassador's attempts to persuade him. 'He might be sure that the Queen once reinstated, he would find her both kind and grateful, and much better disposed to favour him than I could say,' related Chapuys to his master in August 1533.

> This speech of mine Cromwell took in very good part. He thanked me immensely for the good advice tendered, as well as for the affection shewn by me to the King and to himself . . . and he promised me over and over again that as regarded himself he would do his best, and that he hoped everything would turn out well in the end. He did not on that occasion hold the usual language respecting your Majesty and the Queen, nor did he advise, as at other times, that you should both yield and consent to the King's marriage. And certainly if any faith is to be attached to Cromwell's words, and the King's present absence from the Lady be taken into consideration, one might say that there is some shew of repentance in that quarter.[10]

For all his hopeful demeanour, Chapuys knew that he was negotiating from a position of inferiority. Cromwell, not he, held sway at Henry's court and could attach himself to whichever cause seemed most likely to serve his own ends. The ambassador soon became disillusioned. 'Cromwell's words are very fair indeed,' he told the emperor, 'but his deeds are bad, and his will and intentions beyond comparison worse.'[11]

The birth of a new princess did not deter Cromwell from implementing the reforms that her parents' marriage had prompted. He employed his considerable network of informants in gathering evidence against those who objected to the new laws and sympathised with the former queen. In July 1533 he had learned of the arrival in England of two friars who intended to whip up popular resentment against the king's new marriage. His spies informed him that the friars also carried letters to certain people believed to be sympathetic to the old regime, as well as to Catherine herself. He wasted no time in reporting all this to his royal master. Rather than immediately apprehending the friars, Cromwell advised 'that theye Fyrste sholde be sufferyd to speke with her [Catherine] and suche other of hers as woolde peraduenture delyuer to them anything wherby theyr Ferther practysys myght be persayuyd [perceived] and so thayr Cankeryd Intenttes myght be therbye dyscyfferyd'. His advice was evidently followed, for in the next dispatch he reported: 'Touching the Freres obseruantes [Friars Observants] that were with the princes[s] dowagier, being subtillie conueyed from thens were first espied at Ware by such espialles as I leyed for that purpose, and hauyng good awayte leyed vppon them were from thens dogged to London, and there (notwithstonding many wyles and cauteles by them invented to escape) were taken and deteyned till my cummyng home.' He went on to describe how he had personally interrogated the friars, and although he 'coulde gather nothing of anye momente or grete importaunce', he was confident that they would confess under torture.[12]

Although Cromwell had successfully quelled this opposition, there was plenty of home-grown resistance to his reforms. One of the most outspoken dissenters, a nun called Elizabeth Barton, had claimed to have had visions of the disasters that would ensue if the king married Anne. She had enjoyed the protection of the elderly Archbishop Warham, but his death in 1532 had left her vulnerable and she had therefore been easy prey for Cromwell. Together with Cranmer, he brought pressure to bear upon her with some intense questioning. When Elizabeth held firm, Cromwell ordered both her and her supporters to be rounded up and thrown into the Tower in 1533. In so doing, he was sending a clear signal to all would-be opponents to the new regime.

Among those with whom Elizabeth Barton was found to have colluded was Bishop John Fisher. He had conducted several interviews with the nun, but had failed to report any of her disloyal prophecies to the king, which was now taken as a sign of neglect of duty to the sovereign. Cromwell himself wrote to upbraid the bishop in February 1534, having already spoken 'hevy wordes and terrible thretes' to him.[13] In a lengthy and strongly worded dispatch, he accused Fisher of having 'conceyvid a greate opinion of the holines of the woman' and of having asked her only 'Idle questions', rather than examining her closely as a potential traitor. This, said Cromwell, was at best 'negligent' and at worst suggested complicity on the part of the bishop. 'Ye have been in greate defaut hering belevyng and conceling suche thinges as tended to the destruction of the prince,' he warned. It is an indication of how confident he was in the king's favour that he dared to predict how his royal master would have reacted if Fisher had been upfront about the nun's seditious revelations: 'I beleue that I know the kinges goodnes and natural gentilnes so well, that his grace wold not so vnkyndly handle you, as you vnkyndly write of him, onles ye gave him other causes thanbe expressed in your letters.'[14]

Cromwell did not stop there. He resolved to use the opportunity presented by Elizabeth Barton's arrest to draw other high-profile adversaries into his net. Driven by his determination to secure the king's supremacy, he proved his aptitude for clear strategic thinking, which set him apart from the religious and political idealists who surrounded him. The records do not reveal the extent to which Henry was applying pressure on Cromwell to eradicate any opponents to the reforms. But even if he was, Cromwell did not flinch from delivering the *coup de grâce*. This was the first real test of his mettle and he did not disappoint his royal master.

Principal among the opponents upon whom Cromwell now set his sights was Sir Thomas More. The former Lord Chancellor was accused of having conspired with Elizabeth Barton. More's dealing with her was less significant than Fisher's, but Cromwell was a master at spinning a tangled legal web out of the most insubstantial of threads. When More confessed to having met and written to the nun, therefore, much was made of it in the subsequent investigation. Cromwell personally interrogated More, but even his skill could not find enough of a case to answer, as Chapuys reported: 'As the King did not find, as it seems he hoped, an occasion for doing him more harm, he has taken away his salary.' The ambassador shrewdly added: 'The persecution of these men [More and Fisher] is only because of their having taken the Queen's [Catherine's] part.'[15]

While his bullying tactics succeeded in quelling opposition within England for the time being, they triggered a complete breakdown in diplomatic relations with Rome. When he heard of the controversy, Clement VII refused to issue any more papal bills for the appointment of English bishops. Far from persuading Cromwell to adopt a more conciliatory stance, however, this prompted him to unleash all the resources at his disposal to discredit the papacy. With Henry's sanction, he began one of the fiercest and ugliest smear campaigns in English history, attacking the Pope from the pulpit and the printing press. A painting of the four evangelists stoning the Pope may have been commissioned at his prompting. At the same time, he drafted the necessary legislation to break all remaining ties between England and Rome. Parliament was summoned early in 1534, and under Cromwell's close scrutiny it passed the Act of Succession, which declared Mary illegitimate and recognised Elizabeth (and any other children that Anne Boleyn might have) as heirs to the throne. The same session passed the Dispensations Act, outlawing the payments that households owning a certain amount of land had traditionally been obliged to pay to Rome. This was complemented by the second Act in Restraint of Annates, which diverted payments formerly made by the Church away from the Pope and into the royal coffers. The submission of the clergy, which had been passed by convocation two years before, was also confirmed by statute. By the end of the session on 30 March, the break with Rome had been finally, incontrovertibly, achieved.

As a reward, the following month Henry confirmed Cromwell as his principal secretary and chief minister. He had held both these positions in all but name for some time, but this hardly detracted from the significance of the appointment.

Cromwell, buoyed up by this sign of favour, was unrelenting in his efforts to subdue opposition. Although the members of both parliamentary houses had been obliged to swear an oath accepting the Act of Succession before the session closed, Cromwell rightly judged that this was not enough. For the Act to take full effect, all Henry's subjects must formally acknowledge the legitimacy of the king's marriage to Anne Boleyn. This was an unprecedented move: never before had the entire country been forced to do the king's bidding in this way. Cromwell intended it as a means of winkling out all the dissenters who had so far escaped reprisals. By compelling them to swear an oath in favour of the marriage, rather than simply declining to express their opinion either way, he drove the resistance from a dangerous, underground movement out into the open where he and his enforcers could deal with it.

He started with the capital. On 13 April the London clergy were presented with, and accepted, the oath. But it was not long before a number of high-profile figures came forward in opposition. Principal among them were Sir Thomas More and John Fisher, both of whom refused to accept the oath. More was immediately arrested and was thrown into the Tower on 17 April. Fisher joined him there four days later. The former Chancellor wrote a long letter to his daughter Margaret, in which he explained his reasons for refusing to submit, and described the shock waves that this refusal had produced throughout the council. Nobody appeared more outraged than Cromwell. 'Master Secretary sware a great oath that he had lever [rather] that his only son had lost his head than that More should have thus refused the oath, for the King would now conceive a great suspicion against him, and think that the matter of the nun of Canterbury was contrived by his drift.'[16]

For all his bluff and bluster, however, Cromwell must have secretly rejoiced at having manoeuvred his adversary into such an invidious position. Shortly after the arrest of More and Fisher, he wrote to Cranmer, who had attempted to resolve the situation peaceably by suggesting that the two men need only swear to the oath, and not to its preamble. Cromwell pointed out that 'if their othe should be so taken it were an occasion to all men to refuse the hole or at the lest the lyke. For in case they be sworn to the succession and not to the preamble it is to be thought that it might be taken not onelie as a confirmacion of the Bisshop of Rome his auctoryte but also

Thomas Cromwell (c. 1485-1540) by Hans Holbein. This portrait may have been commissioned to celebrate Cromwell's appointment as Master of the Jewels in 1532. The letter on top of the pile is inscribed 'To Master Cromwell, trusty and well-beloved master of our jewel house'.

St Botolph's Church, Boston, known locally as 'Boston Stump'. Cromwell travelled to Rome in 1517 in order to obtain permission from the Pope to sell Indulgences at the church, which was a lucrative business.

The Pope selling Indulgences, 1521. Taken from *Passional Christi und Antichristi* by Philipp Melancthon, a leading reformer and critic of the practice.

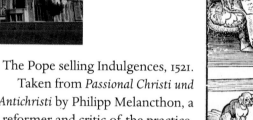

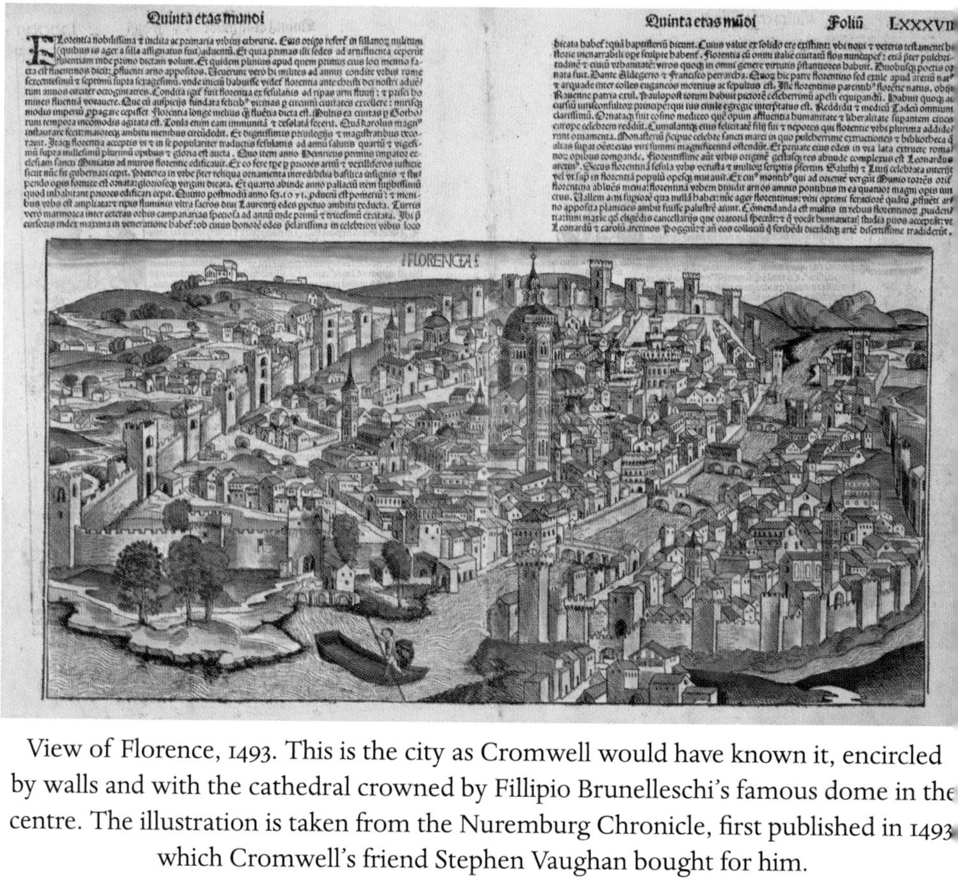

View of Florence, 1493. This is the city as Cromwell would have known it, encircled by walls and with the cathedral crowned by Fillipio Brunelleschi's famous dome in the centre. The illustration is taken from the Nuremburg Chronicle, first published in 1493 which Cromwell's friend Stephen Vaughan bought for him.

Cardinal Thomas Wolsey (c.1470/1-1530). This portrait commemorates the founding of Cardinal's College (later renamed Christ Church College) at Oxford University in 1525.

Henry VIII (1491-1547) in Parliament, 1523. This parliament, which sat from April to August 1523, was Cromwell's first. As he was then an unknown, it is unlikely that he is represented in this illustration, which is taken from *The Wriothesley Garter Book*. His patron, Thomas Wolsey, can be seen to the right of the King, with a Cardinal's hat above him.

Henry VIII by Joos van Cleve, c.1530-1535. This portrait was painted when Cromwell was rising rapidly in the King's service. Now in his early to mid-forties, Henry has started to gain weight but still retains some of his youthful attractiveness.

Catherine of Aragon (1485-1536) by Lucas Horenbout, c.1525. This portrait is symbolic of Catherine's piety. She offers her monkey a coin, but instead he chooses her cross.

Anne Boleyn (c.1500-1536). There are few contemporary portraits of Anne, and this one derives from an earlier version. She wears the French hood which she made fashionable at court, as well as her famous 'B' pendant.

Henry VIII dining in his Presence Chamber. The King is seated beneath a canopy and surrounded by his court. The figures on the left holding staves are his senior court officers.

Hampton Court Palace. Originally built by Cardinal Wolsey, when he fell from favour it was acquired by Henry VIII. The King immediately set about extending the already vast palace, adding the now famous Great Hall.

Allegory of the Reformation from John Foxe's *Actes and Monuments*. The illustration symbolises Henry's victory over Pope Clement, who lies prostrate beneath his feet. Cromwell and Cranmer are shown on Henry's right, receiving the Bible.

The Four Evangelists Stoning the Pope, by Girolamo da Treviso the Younger, c.1538-154
This is one of several anti-papal pictures owned by Henry VIII which aimed to reinforc
his supremacy over the English church.

Sir Thomas More (1478-1535) by Hans Holbein, 1527. The chain More is wearing symbolises his service to the King, rather than a specific office. He was appointed Lord Chancellor two years after this was painted.

John Fisher, Bishop of Rochester (c.1469-1535) by Hans Holbein. A stalwart religious conservative, Fisher was one of Cromwell's most bitter opponents.

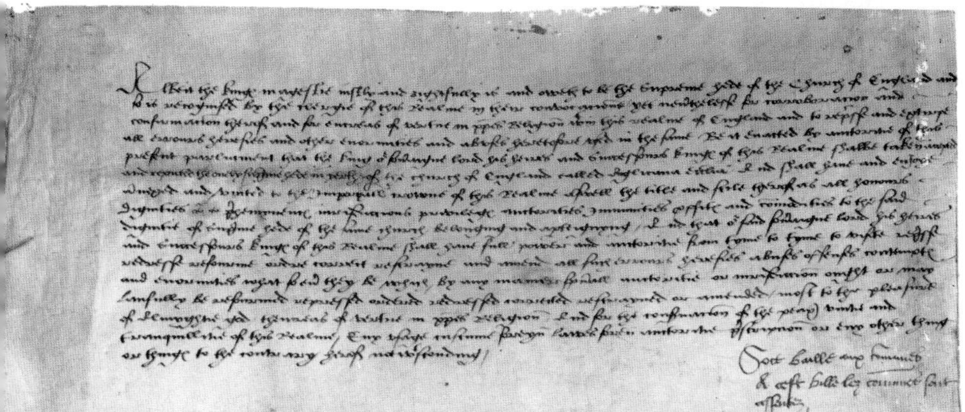

The Act of Supremacy, 1534. In recognising Henry VIII, not the Pope, as head of the church in England, this paved the way for his divorce from Catherine of Aragon.

Valor Ecclesiasticus, 1535. Literally meaning 'The Value of the Churc this survey was commissioned by Cromwell in his new role as Viceregent in Spirituals.

Thomas Cromwell (undated). Although based on Holbein's original, this portrait shows Cromwell in a less flattering light. It was probably commissioned after his death.

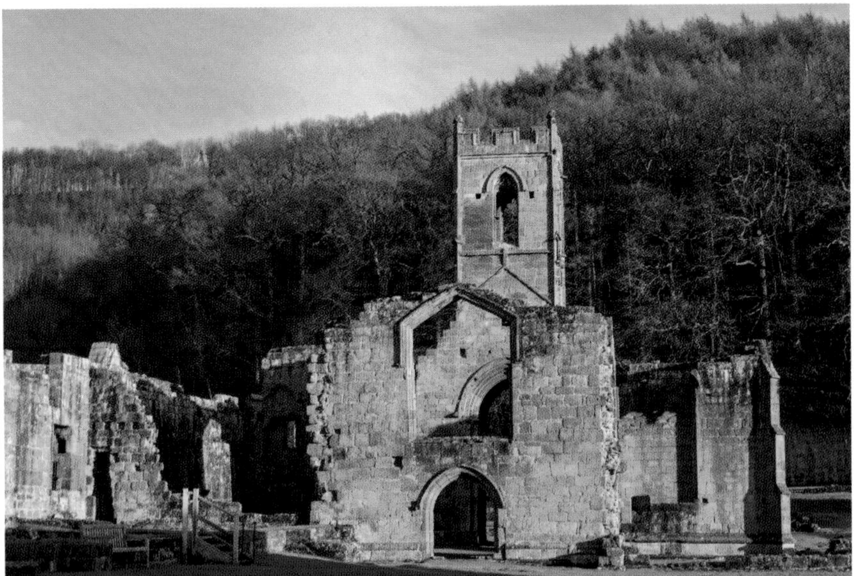

Mount Grace Priory, North Yorkshire. Founded in the late fourteenth century, Mount Grace was one of only ten Carthusian houses in England. It was dissolved in 1539.

as a reprobacion of the kinges second mariage.' Cromwell urged that 'no such thinges should be brought into the heddes of the people by the ensample of the saide Bisshop of Rochester and Mr More.' That he should thus refer to Sir Thomas More is an indication of the disdain he felt towards the former Chancellor. But his letter also reveals a degree of exasperation with Cranmer, whose eagerness to avoid conflict made him an unreliable ally at times. He warned the archbishop: 'His grace specyallye trustyth that ye wyll in no wyse Suppose attempt or move hym to the Contrarye.'[17]

Meanwhile, on 18 April an order was issued requiring all the citizens of London to swear, which they duly did. But Cromwell was determined to eradicate any possibility of further resistance, and therefore decided upon a very public – and very brutal – display of strength. Elizabeth Barton and her supporters had remained holed up in the Tower since their arrest the previous year. Chapuys had smugly reported that the judiciary had been extremely reluctant to convict her – a sure sign of their faithfulness to the old religion. They had therefore become potent symbols of resistance to Cromwell's reforms, and he was determined to make an example of them.

Bypassing any further resistance from the judiciary, Cromwell resorted to his favoured route of parliamentary action, securing treason verdicts through an Act of Attainder. He subsequently ordered that Elizabeth Barton and five of her supporters (all of whom were members of the clergy) be dragged from the Tower to Tyburn in full public view, where they were to meet a traitor's death. Elizabeth had won considerable notoriety in the capital and would have been an instantly recognisable figure to the crowds who gathered to witness the gruesome spectacle. The official punishment for a female traitor was burning, but Cromwell made the concession that she be hanged and then her head hacked off. Her supporters were less fortunate: they endured the horrors of a traitor's death, although their corpses were decapitated rather than quartered.

The executions marked a turning point not just in the progress of Cromwell's reforms, but in the administration of justice. They proved the extent both of his powers and of his ruthlessness. He was prepared to crush anyone who opposed him, as well as those who had become unwittingly tangled up in events. Even those closest to Cromwell were shocked by this new brutality. The Attorney-General, Sir Christopher Hales, had become embroiled in the controversy when Cromwell had ordered him to arrest four men who were suspected of colluding with Elizabeth Barton. He had begged his friend: 'If no cause appear to the contrary, I pray you send home the religious men as soon as you can.' His plea had fallen on deaf ears, but he had tried again three days before the executions, urging Cromwell: 'for God's sake be ye mean to the King's highness to be merciful to them all.'[18] But the case of Barton and her supporters was just the beginning. Soon, the summary arrest and execution of opponents to the new regime would seem more commonplace than shocking.

The reason for Cromwell's apparently sudden shift to an altogether more brutal strategy has been the cause of some debate. Hostile contemporaries were quick to attribute it to his natural ruthlessness, which he had been careful to conceal until now. But the evidence suggests that he was acting out of his accustomed pragmatism, rather than a tyrannical impulse. The force of opposition he had encountered from the likes of More and Fisher had hardened his resolve to push forward his reforms. It had also made him keenly aware of how dangerous and prevalent his adversaries were. It was clear that there could be no compromise: the two sides were too diametrically opposed. Fighting for his reforms so ferociously was an act of self-preservation as much as of statecraft. Although he might be high in favour with the king now, he knew all too well how swiftly Henry's attitude could change. He was therefore a good deal more vulnerable than his titles and authority suggested. In such circumstances, attack was the best – indeed, the only – form of defence.

The model that had been tested in London was now transferred to the rest of the country. Cromwell organised commissions to go into every shire to secure oaths of acceptance. He was no longer satisfied with acceptance of the Act of Succession: realising that the greatest resistance came from the clergy, he demanded that all new bishops also formally acknowledge the royal supremacy. Ecclesiastical bodies and colleges, including those of the universities, were obliged to swear corporate oaths along the same lines, and individual members of the clergy signed declarations that 'the bishop of Rome has no greater power conferred on him by God in this realm than any other foreign bishop.'[19] Meanwhile, most ordinary laymen grudgingly accepted the form of words presented to them by the commissioners, even if they continued to express their dissent afterwards. Recognising this, Cromwell introduced a shockingly harsh new treason Act when parliament met in November 1534. It was now treasonous to speak of rebellion against the royal family, to deny their titles, or to call the king a heretic, tyrant, infidel or usurper.

In the same parliament, Cromwell forced through the Act of Supremacy, which clarified and confirmed the king's position as 'Supreme Head on earth of the Church of England', and stipulated that he and his heirs 'shall have full power and authority from time to time to visit, repress, redress, reform, order, correct, restrain, and amend all such errors, heresies, abuses, offences, contempts, and enormities, whatsoever they be . . . any usage, custom, foreign laws, foreign authority, prescription, or any other thing or things to the contrary hereof notwithstanding'.[20] Meanwhile, the Act for Payment of First Fruits and Tenths put a heavy new burden of taxation upon the clergy. Cromwell calculated that it would yield an average yearly income of 40,000 pounds – equivalent to around £12.5 million today.

Cromwell's new laws took swift and brutal effect. Those clergy who dared to speak out against the king from their pulpits ended up in the Tower or were forced into exile abroad. Neither did the ordinary members of society escape reprisal. Cromwell personally investigated accusations against even the humblest of subjects. No charwoman or blacksmith could criticise the king or praise the Pope and expect to get away with it. But Cromwell knew that this grass-roots opposition was a reliable barometer of the public mood towards the new regime. That is why he took such a careful, detailed interest in every allegation, every rumour. In October 1534 he wrote to the Privy Council about a 'veray evill disposed persone' who had been arrested. He urged them not to put him to death until he had been 'examyned' so that 'we may knowe the hoole and profound bothom of his cancred hert.'[21] As well as widespread dissent against Cromwell's religious reforms, he found that there was also enduring hatred of the new queen. Even two years after Henry had married Anne Boleyn, a Suffolk woman named Margaret Chanseler spoke out against the divorce and called the queen a 'noughtty' and 'goggyll yed [eyed] hoore', and prayed that she would have no more children.[22] Margaret escaped punishment, but not before there had been a full enquiry during which the witnesses were interrogated by no fewer than ten Justices of the Peace, including the Abbot of Bury St Edmunds.

The north of England had traditionally proved the most persistent opponent to royal authority. The greater the distance from court, the less allegiance the subjects seemed to feel towards their king. The region was also a stronghold for Roman Catholicism and clung even more tightly to the trappings of the old religion than the rest of the country. The great Yorkshire abbeys such as Fountains and Mount Grace stood as symbols of northern traditions – and resistance. Cromwell knew that if his reforms were to succeed, he had to bring the northern counties under more direct royal control. His strategy was to undermine the powerful nobles who dominated the area, and he began by picking off the weakest of them. Henry Percy, sixth Earl of Northumberland and the former lover of Queen Anne, held the key post of Lieutenant of the North. But he was debt-ridden and ineffective, his authority was restricted to the middle and eastern marches, and even this was declining. Cromwell therefore focused upon the area under his jurisdiction before moving on to the north-west. Here, too, he was able to exploit a weak and divided region. Feuding between the two dominant families, the Dacres and the Cliffords, made their government much less effective than it might have been. Cromwell deliberately stirred up more trouble between them. He had William, third Baron Dacre, charged with treason on the dubious grounds that he had developed close relations with the Scottish lords across the border, even though this had proved to be in England's interests rather than his own. Dacre was acquitted by his peers at the trial in July 1534, but by then

Cromwell had succeeded in breaking his control of the western marches. He proceeded to have Henry Clifford, first Earl of Cumberland, appointed warden there two months later.

In bringing the north to heel, Cromwell did not neglect the other outlying parts of the kingdom. Although Henry had nominal control over Ireland, his predecessors had only ever enjoyed limited success in enforcing their authority there. As in the north of England, powerful local lords predominated. Cromwell therefore resorted to his favoured policy of placing trusted advocates of royal authority in key positions. The most important of these was that of deputy, which since 1532 had been held by the ninth Earl of Kildare, an associate of the Duke of Norfolk. But when the earl was incapacitated by a gunshot wound later that year, Cromwell seized his chance. He began cultivating Kildare's rivals, the Butlers and Archbishop Alen of Dublin, and in September 1533 he had the earl recalled to England. Cromwell was quick to replace him with men favourable to his regime and he filled the Dublin council with his supporters. He also had Sir William Skeffington appointed as deputy. As a result, by the end of May 1534 there was widespread acceptance of the royal supremacy.

But this was by no means the end of the matter. On 11 June Kildare's son, Thomas, Lord Offaly (known as 'Silken Thomas'), denounced the king's policies before the council and started a rebellion. Again, Cromwell was quick to act. On 29 June he had Kildare thrown into the Tower, where he died two months later. This spurred Offaly on to mount a full-scale revolt. He and his supporters butchered Archbishop Alen, together with all his chaplains and servants, as they attempted to escape to England on 27 July. They then stormed Dublin Castle. Offaly and his fellow rebels held on to power for a year before surrendering on 24 August 1535. He was escorted to London and sent straight to the Tower.

It has been claimed that from this time until his fall, Cromwell was the 'virtual ruler' of Ireland.[23] Certainly, the king seemed content to entrust him with the direction of Irish affairs. The appointment of officers and the regulation of financial matters, together with everything else connected with the country, were now within

Cromwell's domain. He exerted royal authority with as scrupulous an attention to detail as he did in England, sending numerous dispatches to his commissioners there.[24]

With power came corruption. Cromwell seems to have employed more bribes in Ireland than anywhere else. One courtier claimed he was 'the grettest bribour' in the country.[25] The wealthy and influential Butler family, kinsmen of the Duke of Norfolk, were said to have paid Cromwell substantial sums in order to avoid their castles being searched by the royal agents. Such rapacity provoked widespread resentment against the king's chief minister in Ireland. It was even rumoured that he would be assassinated. 'My Lorde Pryvee Seale hathe wrought to his awne confusion and dethe, and of late tyme was veray nere the same, and escapid veray narrowly,' claimed George Paulet. 'By his meanes and solicitation, all the Kinges profictes and revenues [have been] gevyn away by sinister meanes.' He estimated that Henry had six times as much revenue as any of his predecessors, but that 'all is consumyd, and goon to noght, by meanes of my Lorde Prive Seale.'[26] The king, however, was apparently content for his minister to profit from his management of Irish affairs. Provided he kept the country under royal control, then he might be rewarded for his pains in this way.

Cromwell faced a similar challenge to royal authority in Wales, although its closer proximity to England made it somewhat easier to deal with. Nevertheless, opposition to the Cromwellian regime was strong among a population that clung tightly to its traditions and privileges. In 1534 he appointed Rowland Lee, the newly elected Bishop of Coventry and Lichfield, as president of the council in the Welsh marches. Lee, who had studied law at Cambridge before entering the Church, had been active in the service of Cardinal Wolsey. After the latter's fall, he transferred his service to Cromwell and the two soon became friends. As one of the king's chaplains, Lee became active in royal business and was a valuable ecclesiastical ally to Cromwell in pushing forward Henry's divorce from Catherine of Aragon. He was also rumoured to have conducted the secret wedding ceremony with Anne Boleyn, although this is not substantiated by the sources. In 1533 he had been dispatched to the northern counties to persuade convocation there to support the divorce, and had also helped bring Elizabeth Barton and her supporters to trial.

Lee had therefore more than proven his loyalty to Cromwell's regime, and there could have been no better man to oversee the implementation of the new reforms in Wales. As president, he succeeded the Catholic Bishop of Exeter, John Veysey, who was also deprived of his see. Cromwell enhanced Lee's powers still further by giving him the authority to apprehend felons who had hitherto escaped justice by exploiting the independent jurisdictions of the marcher lordships. Lee wasted no time in exercising his new powers, and he soon won a reputation for swift and brutal justice. He became known as the hanging judge, and the Welsh chronicler Elis Gruffudd claimed that he had 5,000 felons executed within the space of six years. Although this was undoubtedly an exaggeration, Lee commanded such fear and respect that he soon brought the recalcitrant Welsh to heel.

In a dispatch to Charles V of December 1534, Chapuys, who had some sympathy with the Welsh thanks to their loyalty towards Catherine of Aragon and her daughter Mary, described the widespread resentment that Lee's regime had caused in that country: 'The distress of the people is incredible, and the anxiety they have to declare themselves, especially the Welsh, from whom by act of parliament the King has just taken away their native laws, customs and privileges, which is the very thing they can endure least patiently. I wonder how the King dared to do it during these troubles in Ireland, except that God wishes so to blind him.'[27]

Although Cromwell appointed trusted servants such as Lee to important strategic posts, he relinquished little personal control over the execution of his new laws. As a result, he accrued an enormous burden of administration, paperwork and investigation. His friend Stephen Vaughan wrote to him in late 1534, pleading that he might reform the judicial system so that he did not have to exhaust himself 'with the continual travail of common causes'.[28] The fact that he found time to do this while also driving through the reforms at government level is a testament to his considerable assiduity, perfectionism and – perhaps – paranoia. Although he surrounded himself with able servants and advisers, he never fully trusted anyone. He had seen too many men (his former master included) fall prey to the dangerous, pervasive intrigues of the Tudor court, where a man might justifiably leap at his own shadow.

Proof of this came just a few months after Vaughan's letter. Despite the closeness of their friendship, it was still vulnerable to the intrigues of Cromwell's enemies at court, who were eager to deprive him of allies. They whipped up a controversy between the two men, convincing Vaughan that his old friend was playing him false. When he discovered this, Cromwell wrote at once to Vaughan, upbraiding him for having so little faith in his loyalty. 'Perceyuing by your letteres how gret a suspicion ye haue conceyuid of my frendeship and old amytie towardes you (whereof I cannot but mervaile) I must nedes playnelie say unto you, that ye are farre ouershotte in that behalf . . . I haue euer ben your grete Frende without euer making any semblaunce or gyuyng you cause to thinke the contrary.' He insisted: 'Ye shall assuredlye Fynde me aswell redy to do you good now as I ever was Advising you therefore [not] to conceyue any like suspicion in your Frende till you haue cause which I am sure ye have not had nor shall have at my hande.' Cromwell also warned Vaughan to be careful what he wrote in future because: 'Being absent from the Courte your letteres addressed unto me chaunced amongst others to com to the handes of the kinges highnes who in myn absence both opened and redde them.'[29]

The friendship between Cromwell and Vaughan seems to have been restored after this exchange, but their correspondence was conducted on a more cautious footing in future. Disregarding his friend's pleas to shift some of the burden of work on to others, Cromwell continued with his campaign against those who opposed the reforms. Largely as a result of his diligence in bringing dissenters to justice, it has been calculated that 883 people were accused of treason between 1532 and 1540, of whom 308 were executed. Henry's elder daughter earned the nickname 'Bloody Mary' for burning 283 Protestants during her five-year reign. Cromwell's tally may have been higher, but it gives a misleading impression of the brutality of his regime. The vast majority of those who were put to death had been involved in open rebellion against the crown, or were men who, like the Duke of Buckingham, had become embroiled in dynastic or court politics. In fact, the acquittal of Margaret Chanseler, who had spoken out against the king's marriage to Anne Boleyn, was by no means unusual. Out of the hundreds of people who were investigated for speaking out against the supremacy, only sixty-three were punished. It was a period of instability, not – yet – tyranny.

CHAPTER 9

'Good master secretary'

CROMWELL'S INEXORABLE RISE at court continued throughout 1534. 'The credit and authority which he enjoys with this King just now is really incredible,' Chapuys reported to Charles V that year, 'as great indeed as the Cardinal ever enjoyed, besides which he is daily receiving fresh bounties from him.'[1] Cromwell had already proved his ability as principal secretary, and it was a position for which he was ideally suited, given his attention to detail and enormous capacity for hard work. No matter how many offices the king conferred upon him, he treated none of them as a sinecure. If the work associated with each position became too onerous, then he would pass both the office and the associated fees on to someone else.

Such diligence set Cromwell apart from most other men in Henry's court, who vied with each other for new titles but were not so eager to take on the associated duties. By contrast, Cromwell and his ever expanding household of clerks, secretaries and messengers ensured that the tasks required by each office were carried out with the utmost efficiency. His voluminous papers and correspondence reveal the attention to detail for which he became renowned. That Cromwell took each of his posts (major and minor) so seriously provides an interesting contrast to the much vaunted image of the corrupt, grasping official who was driven solely by the desire for personal gain. Even his old sparring partner, Chapuys, was forced to admire the conscientiousness of this perpetually busy official, and referred to Cromwell's 'multifarious engagements' in a dispatch to his master. On another occasion, the minister had complained to him 'that for no money in the world would he consent to have so much work in hand as he has had ever since our last meeting'.[2]

Cromwell used his position as principal secretary to introduce radical innovation in the royal finances. In 1534 he drafted the Subsidy Act, which for the first time enabled taxation to be raised not just for war, but for the achievement of peace. He also expended a great deal of time and effort in masterminding reforms to improve the 'common weal'. In contrast to many of his other changes, these social reforms were motivated by evangelical and humanistic ideals, rather than financial gain for the crown. The antiquarian John Stow (who was no fan of Cromwell) described how 'in that declining time of charity', he often saw him providing 'bread, meate and drinke sufficient' for 200 poor people twice a day outside his gate. Eustace Chapuys agreed that he was 'very liberal' with his money, and a widow named Joanna Creke praised him for his 'abundant charity'.[3]

Cromwell painstakingly recorded all the ideas he wished to discuss with the king in a series of 'remembrances' (or memoranda). These still survive and give a fascinating glimpse into the brilliant, agile mind of a true polymath. Among the numerous schemes he presented (or planned to present) to his royal master were proposals for reforms in education, poor relief, trade, industry, agriculture and the common law. Not all these initiatives succeeded, but those that did secured Cromwell's position as one of the greatest economic and social reformers that England has ever seen.

An indication of Cromwell's startling productivity is the sheer volume of statutes passed during his ascendancy. His papers are filled with drafts of the Acts that he planned to introduce into parliament, and his memoranda contain still more. Between 1509 and 1531, 203 Acts were passed during nine sessions of parliament. By contrast, between 1532 and 1540 when Cromwell was at the height of his powers, there were 333 Acts during eight sessions. The space taken up by this legislation is also significant. The twenty-two years of Henry's reign before Cromwell's dominance saw the drafting of 416 pages of statutes – a total that Cromwell almost equalled (409) in just eight years.[4] All Cromwell's statutes were extraordinary in their level of detail and ran to many hundreds of pages, which reveals as much about his assiduity in legal affairs as the legislative importance of the content of each statute.

In September 1534 Cromwell was briefly distracted from his prolific state business by the arrival of an altogether unexpected visitor at the English court. She was Mary Boleyn, sister of the queen. Mary had been absent for some time; indeed, little had been heard of her since she had accompanied Anne to France late in 1532. Her arrival now caused a great stir, for she had left the court a widow and returned visibly pregnant. This was no bastard child, though, for Mary admitted that she had been married in secret to the lowly William Stafford. Anne was furious and immediately had her banished from court. She was in no mood to be humiliated by her sister, for she had suffered either a miscarriage or stillbirth that summer, and was taunted by the knowledge that her husband the king had taken up with a new mistress, the so-called 'Imperial Lady', who openly supported Catherine of Aragon and her daughter Mary.

Anne's reaction was no passing fit of spite. She refused to see or speak to her sister, and persuaded the king not to lift the banishment. In desperation, Mary wrote to Cromwell, begging him to intercede with her sister and the king. Referring to herself as 'a poor banished creature', she lamented: 'I am sure it is not unknown to you the high displeasure that both he and I have, both of the king's highness and the queen's grace, by reason of our marriage without their knowledge.' She went on to plead that they had acted only out of love, not malice. 'Good master secretary, consider, that he was young, and love overcame reason; and for my part I saw so much honesty in him, that I loved him as well as he did me . . . For well I might have had a greater man of birth and a higher, but I assure you I could never have had one that should have loved me so well, nor a more honest man.' Drawing attention to the fact that her husband's personal qualities made up for his humble birth may have been an attempt to win Cromwell's sympathy: the implied compliment to himself was obvious.

Mary's letter makes it clear just how great Cromwell's influence at court had become. With the king and queen turning a deaf ear to her pleadings, he was the surest means to secure her reinstatement. She referred to the many other people whom he had helped when she begged him to 'show part of your goodness to us as well as you do to all the world besides'. Mary continued:

> Good master secretary, this shall be my suit to you, that, for the love that well I know you do bear to all my blood . . . sue for us to the king's highness, and beseech his highness, which ever was wont to take pity, to have pity on us; and, that it will please his grace of his goodness to speak to the queen's grace for us; for, so far as I can perceive, her grace is so highly displeased with us both that, without the king be so good lord to us as to withdraw his rigour and sue for us, we are never like to recover her grace's favour: which is too heavy to bear. And seeing there is no remedy, for God's sake help us.

For all her anguish that Anne would not forgive her, there was clearly an element of rivalry between the two sisters, for Mary could not resist adding: 'I had rather beg my bread with him [Stafford] than be the greatest queen in Christendom.'

Although Mary rightly judged that if anyone would be able to help her out of her predicament, it was Cromwell, she was obviously out of touch with court politics for she also asked him to persuade the Duke of Norfolk and her brother, Lord Rochford, to be good to her because 'they are so cruel against us.'[5] Cromwell was the person least likely to persuade Norfolk to do anything by this stage, and there is no evidence that he ever enjoyed Rochford's friendship or trust. Indeed, Mary had misjudged the extent to which Cromwell would be prepared to make any effort on her behalf. It was hardly in his interest to do so. His alliance with the queen was tenuous at best, and meddling in a matter that had already caused her extreme outrage and embarrassment might well make an enemy of her for good. Neither did the king want his old mistress back at court – he was far too preoccupied with his new one, as well as with a marriage that had started to cause him more grief than pleasure. In such circumstances, Cromwell would only have undertaken such a thankless and potentially risky task if it had been on a friend's behalf. He might have been acquainted with Mary before she left court, but she could hardly be counted as one of his intimates. If Cromwell replied to her, his letter has not survived. Certainly, there is no evidence that he was moved to take any action, and Mary was obliged to stay away from court.[6]

Around the same time as the Mary Boleyn controversy, Cromwell had a chance encounter with another figure from his past. This one was altogether more welcome. According to the contemporary Italian novelist Matteo Bandello, the Florentine merchant Francesco Frescobaldi arrived in London at some point between 1533 and 1535 to collect some debts that were owed to him. It is an indication of how much he had fallen on hard times that he was obliged to make such a journey. Cromwell was said to have recognised his old master in the streets while riding to court 'and on a sudden quitting his Horse (to the wonder of all his Attendants) he went and most affectionately embrac'd him; and scarcely refraining from Tears, he ask'd him whether he was not Francis Frescobald, the Florentine; yes Sir (said he) and Your Humble Servant, "My Servant, (quoth Cromwell) no, as you have not formerly been my Servant, so I will not account you any other than my special friend."'[7] He promptly took him to Austin Friars, gave him dinner, and wasted no time in ordering an investigation to track down Frescobaldi's debtors. Calling one of his servants, he told him: 'Look who these be that are set down in this schedule and see thou find them all out, be they where they may in this island, and give them to understand that, except they pay their whole debt within fifteen days' time, I will put my hand to the matter, and that to their hurt and displeasance; wherefore let them consider that I am their creditor.'[8] Such was Cromwell's influence (and menace) that within days all the debts had been paid and Francesco was able to return to Italy with money in his pocket – both from his debtors and his old protégé, who had insisted on giving him 1,600 ducats plus another thirty-six in payment for the money, clothes and horse that Frescobaldi had given him all those years before in Florence. It is a touching tale that, though unauthenticated, illustrates the intense loyalty that Cromwell showed towards his former masters. He was renowned for never forgetting old friends or those who had done him a kindness, no matter how lowly or lacking in influence they might be.

Cromwell's kindness towards Frescobaldi may have also been due to his enduring affection for Italy. Some years later, when the Venetians were seeking the renewal of permission to import wool from England, the Doge and Senate told their ambassador to approach 'the Magnifico Cromwell' because they did 'not doubt that the secretary will easily procure what they wish'.[9] Bandello later wistfully observed: 'Had he loved the nobility of his country as he seemed to love foreigners, belike he had yet been alive.'[10]

Cromwell's loyalty was not exclusively reserved for his Italian acquaintances, however. In 1529 his old friend Stephen Vaughan had fallen foul of the Merchant Adventurers because of a religious controversy. The governor of the company had had him hauled before the Bishop of London on charges of heresy. At the time, Cromwell had been unable to help his friend because he had been battling for survival in the wake of Wolsey's fall, but as soon as he had clawed his way to power at court, he ensured that the charges would be dropped and Vaughan was able to rebuild his career. Cromwell subsequently purchased the priory of St Mary Spital in Shoreditch, London, for Vaughan and his new wife Margery, and also secured the latter an appointment as silk-woman to Anne Boleyn. He continued to take a close interest in Vaughan's welfare, and when he learned that he was owed a year's wages by the king, he wrote a strong letter to Audley demanding that these be paid.[11]

In October 1534 Cromwell was appointed Master of the Rolls – one of the highest judicial positions in the land. It also brought with it a grand and ancient residence: the Rolls House on Chancery Lane. In 1233 Henry III had erected a Carthusian house on the site for converted Jews. Edward III annexed the house to the newly created office of Custos Rotulorum (Master of the Rolls) in 1377. The master was responsible for keeping the 'rolls' or records of the Court of Chancery, which had jurisdiction over all matters of equity, and a far greater remit than the common law courts. From the late fourteenth century, it accepted cases from private individuals, and as a result the number of hearings quadrupled during the following century. The Masters of the Rolls were generally priests, and often the king's chaplains. Cromwell was one of the first secular holders of the office.

Cromwell's correspondence indicates that he made frequent use of the Rolls House. Soon, there was such a crowd of visitors amassed outside that it was difficult to gain entry. In July 1536 his old friend Margaret Vernon, formerly Prioress of Little Marlow and custodian of his son Gregory, wrote to complain: 'I have been frequently at the Rolls to speak with you, but by reason of the great multitude of suitors and lack of friendship in your mastership's house, I am kept back and cannot come to your presence.'[12] Cromwell had, in effect, established a court of his own, filled with supplicants for his favour, political contacts, ambassadors and envoys. It was upon his household, almost as much as the king's, that power and patronage were centred. In his poem about Cromwell, George Cavendish had him complaining that after his promotions: 'Than [then] folowed me sewters like a swarme of bees.'[13]

Acquiring the Rolls House eased the growing problem of accommodating Cromwell's sizeable household, and he wasted no time in transferring some of his servants there.[14] But more space was needed. He had already bought an impressive new house known as the Great Place, which was next to St Dunstan's Church at Stepney Green, east of London. Some time before 1535, Cromwell had either leased Great Place to his nephew, Richard Cromwell, or bought him a new house nearby. He now also acquired a house in Hackney and set about a series of improvements. 'I have viewed your house at Hackney,' wrote his agent Thomas Croke in 1535. 'The kitchen is finished except the paving. The wet and dry larders and the filling of the pool in the garden are well forward.' Shortly afterwards, in September that year, another of his agents, John Williamson, reported: 'Your place at Hackney is in a good stay, except the garden which is in digging.' A report from Thomas Thacker on the same day gives a glimpse into the scale of Cromwell's property development, and the care with which each of his houses was appointed.

> Your households at the Rolls, Friars Austin, Hackney and Stepneth are in good health. The stairs (in this last house) from your lodging down to the gallery is finished with a window where the jakes was, very well done. Your building at Hackney goes forward, the brickwork of the kitchen with the chimney is finished to the roof; the roof set up and tiles upon it; the enlarging of the buttery and scullery brought above the ground. The roofs thereof are framing with all speed; your lodgings trimmed with windows, glass and hangings – a goodly place, in my opinion.[15]

As well as his London homes, Cromwell had what for him was a house in the country – although lying at Ewhurst in Surrey it was still within easy reach of the capital. The ever vigilant Thacker had not overlooked this in his recent survey of Cromwell's homes: 'On Sunday last I went to Ewhurst and viewed there the goodly frames. The double floors of your hall and solar under it are finished. Certain goods must be transported to Ewhurst from the Thames waterside. Carriage is scarce because of hay time and harvest, but the parson of Ewhurst says that we shall have the carts next week.'[16] Again, Cromwell undertook major improvements to the house because no fewer than 600 loads of bricks were transported there. He also owned land in the manor of Wimbledon, close to the place of his birth. From 1534 he leased the manor of Allfarthing in Wandsworth from the king, and five years later he bought the nearby manor of Dunsford from the Duke of Suffolk. In addition to these, Cromwell had a home at Mortlake. It was here, and at Austin Friars, where his in-laws and most of his domestic staff lived. The other properties tended to be filled with his clerks, secretaries and other household staff.

Cromwell owned a considerable amount of land in addition to his properties. During the 1530s he steadily accumulated large monastic lands and royal grants. Most of these were centred on Essex, Kent and Sussex, and by the end of the decade Cromwell was one of the greatest landowners in those counties. But he also owned land as far west as Cornwall and as far north as Lincolnshire. In 1535 his accounts gave his total annual income from landed properties as 417 pounds (almost £130,000 today), although the rapid increase in land and property prices during modern times means that in real terms it would have been worth a great deal more today. Moreover, Cromwell's land acquisition rose sharply in the second half of the decade, when he seemed to focus upon this as more than just a useful subsidiary to his other business interests. His associated income would therefore have increased in parallel.[17]

Thanks to his growing portfolio of property, not to mention the palaces in which he was allocated accommodation, Cromwell lived a peripatetic existence. Judging from the places where he wrote his letters, he did not spend much time at Ewhurst or Hackney, for the majority are signed from Austin Friars, the Rolls House and Stepney. By the middle of the 1530s, therefore, Cromwell had an impressive portfolio of property, as befitted a courtier of his standing and influence. His agents kept a close eye on the spending at each house, which suggests that they were far from being extravagant show homes, such as his old master Wolsey might have possessed, stuffed full of priceless treasures that Cromwell would rarely enjoy – and which ran the risk of being stolen. They were carefully chosen, practical and well-built investments that were no doubt intended to help support Cromwell when he finally retired from court – not that he showed any signs of intending to do so. They were also necessary to accommodate his ever expanding household, although Cromwell was frugal enough to distinguish between those servants he needed with him at all times, and those who could live in their own houses. While his secretary Ralph Sadler lived in Cromwell's houses for much of the time, he also had a handsome home of his own built in Hackney – Sutton House – where he lodged his large family. This still survives today.

Meanwhile, another of Cromwell's young protégés had returned to his household around this time and did find room there. Thomas Avery had completed his apprenticeship in the household of the Marchioness of Exeter, and by September 1535 he was employed as Cromwell's private cofferer or purse-keeper. This involved managing Cromwell's household expenses and dispensing money to the servants. Although it did not carry the same political weight as Sadler's appointment, it was nonetheless a position of great responsibility, for large sums of money would have passed through his hands on a regular basis.[18]

As well as his household staff, Cromwell also liked to be surrounded by the leading intellectuals and reformists at his various residences. The presence of men such as William Marshall, Richard Morison and Thomas Starkey made his household a veritable melting-pot of innovative, enlightened initiatives. 'He always retayned vnto hym, and had about hym suche as could be founde to be helpers & furtherers of the same [religion],' observed Foxe, 'in the nomber of whom were sundry and dyuerse freshe and quicke wyttes, pertainyng to his famyly, by whose industrie and ingenious labours, diverse excellent both ballades and bookes were contrived and set abroade, concernyng the suppression of the Pope and all Popyshe idolatrie.'[19] Starkey, meanwhile, recalled the conversations 'of God, of nature and of other politic and wordly things' which he and his fellow guests enjoyed at Cromwell's supper parties. The lawyer John Oliver agreed that the 'dinners and suppers, where I indeed did hear such communications which were the very cause of the beginning of my conversion' to the Gospel.[20]

Those who were lucky enough to receive an invitation to dine at Austin Friars, Stepney or one of Cromwell's other London houses would be guaranteed a sumptuous feast. As well as the bewildering array of different meats and fish favoured by the Tudor court, such as venison, pheasant, capon, swan, rabbit, oxen, cod, oysters and cockles, Cromwell's cook also used such exotic delicacies as ginger, nutmeg, figs, oranges and marzipan. Artichokes were evidently a particular favourite, and were supplied by the royal gardens at Hampton Court, along with beans, cherries, quinces, gooseberries and apples. Guests with a sweet tooth were treated to tarts from the royal kitchens or puddings from 'Mrs Bigges'. All this was washed down with lavish quantities of wine from the royal cellars. In June 1537 Cromwell paid Mr Hill, 'serjeant' of the king's cellar, 400 pounds (more than £120,000) for his supplies.[21]

The fact that Cromwell's socialising had a serious purpose suggests that even in his so-called leisure hours his mind was focused on business. Although he continued to enjoy hawking in the evenings, he often invited Chapuys on such occasions so that they might discuss affairs of state as they watched the hawks chase their prey. His stables housed nearly a hundred horses, although he preferred to ride to court on a mule – as had his old patron, Wolsey. He was evidently fond of birds because he later invested in 'a cage of canary birds' for his house, and he also kept greyhounds. Other, more unusual, animals are listed in his accounts too. He received an elk from Lubecker, four live beavers from Danzig, and in July 1539 paid nineteen shillings for a velvet collar for an unidentified 'strange beast' which he gave to the king as a present.[22]

Cromwell's accounts also reveal that he liked to gamble, particularly at dice, and regularly lost substantial sums. Between 1537 and 1539, for example, his losses amounted to almost £50,000 in modern money. He gambled on card games as well, and his companions on such occasions included Sir William Paulet, Sir Richard Rich and the Lord Mayor of London. In addition, Cromwell regularly played with his royal master, who was addicted to such pastimes, and suffered a series of expensive (and possibly tactical) defeats.[23]

Keen to provide every entertainment expected of a courtier host, Cromwell employed a jester at his household. He may have been inspired by a visit from the king's favourite fool, Will Somers, who received a payment for his services. Cromwell went to some considerable trouble to find a jester of the same calibre as Somers. In November 1538 he dispatched one of his servants to Calais to collect 'Anthony the fool'. The following month he spent thirty-four shillings and six pence on 'bells for Anthony's coat', and a few months after that, a hosier was commissioned to make some stockings, presumably in suitably garish colours.[24]

Cromwell evidently had a flair for entertaining because he was sometimes tasked with arranging the lavish court masques that his royal master so loved. This was always at his own expense, but he did not stint on any of the details. For one particularly sumptuous performance, the Italian engineer Giovanni Portinari was commissioned to build the set at a cost of more than twenty-five pounds (equivalent to £8,000), a milliner was paid just shy of eleven pounds

(£3,600) 'for the stuff of the masque of King Arthur's knights', and the wife of Cromwell's friend Stephen Vaughan made some of the costumes out of the finest silk. Cromwell himself took part in at least one of these masques: in January 1537 a tailor was paid the equivalent of 4,000 pounds to make the costume for 'my Lord's part of the masque'.[25] Regrettably, the accounts provide no further details about the costume, or the part that Cromwell played. But the fact that he entered into such frivolities with apparent enthusiasm contradicts the commonly held view of him as a humourless bureaucrat.

By the close of the year 1534, the extent of Cromwell's powers was evident to all. Not only had he wrested control of domestic and religious affairs, he was also instrumental in dictating the king's foreign policy. Here, he was as pragmatic as in all his other dealings, although the general tenor of his approach was an aversion to committing his sovereign to expensive military campaigns overseas. While he was careful to keep all the foreign powers in play without absolutely allying with, or antagonising, any of them, the fact that he had masterminded the king's divorce from Catherine of Aragon and the break with Rome set him firmly at odds with Catherine's nephew, Charles V. This in turn led to speculation that he would forge an alliance with France – the natural enemy of the emperor. In December 1534 Chapuys reported: 'I am told that Cromwell, since the Admiral's [Norfolk's] departure, boasted in good company that he had begun to weave a web from which your majesty could not extricate yourself in a whole year. The French ambassador, I am told, has spoken of it lately more openly and like a Frenchman, saying that your majesty after doing so many injuries to the King his master had offered him for sole recompense some marriage, and that his wrongs would have to be redressed, and what had been violently taken from him restored.'[26]

Meanwhile, relations between Henry and the papacy appeared to be improving, thanks in no small part to the death of Clement VII and the accession of the apparently more amenable Paul III in October 1534. Cromwell was quick to capitalise upon this welcome development. In April 1535 he wrote to an envoy in Rome, reiterating the justice of Henry's divorce from Catherine of Aragon which, he

CHAPTER 10

Dissolution

SUCCESS HAD COME rather late to Cromwell. By 1535 he was approaching fifty – a time when most men would have been leading a sedentary life or would have already gone to the grave, the average life expectancy at this time being just thirty-five.[1] He was therefore older than many of his peers in court and council. But it had been worth the wait, and by carefully engineering his rise to greatness during the preceding years, always with an eye to maintaining his private business interests as a safeguard, Cromwell had apparently established a firm foundation for even greater achievements.

Although he was physically robust, judging from his earlier career as a soldier and the frequent references to his hunting expeditions, from the middle of the 1530s his health began to falter. According to Bandello, Cromwell had 'endured all bodily fatigue with patience', but he was not as resilient as he once had been.[2] A combination of age and the innumerable hours he had spent poring over legal documents was no doubt to blame for Cromwell's failing eyesight, and his accounts attest that he was wearing spectacles by the time he reached his fifties. More serious complaints followed. In March 1535 Chapuys noted that he had been due to call on the secretary, but 'heard that he is worse than yesterday, and therefore can not see any one'. Cromwell complained of 'a rheum, which had caused a swelling of his cheek and eye'. The ever sceptical Chapuys opined that this 'slight indisposition' was 'some capricious move', but a month later Cromwell was too sick to attend court and the king himself paid him a visit at home. Although he professed that this 'has had the effect of carrying away the relics of his illness', he was only well enough to return to his duties in late April, and on 5 May Chapuys reported that this had been Cromwell's only visit to court since his illness.[3]

Meanwhile, Cromwell's official duties had been unrelenting. On 21 January 1535 Henry had appointed him Viceregent in Spirituals, or vicar-general. This gave him considerable new powers over the Church. Aware of how successful his principal secretary had been in both monitoring and, where necessary, obliterating public resistance to his supremacy, the king was eager to extend this enforcement to the clergy. Even so, he could not have envisaged the scale of the reforms his minister would implement. The appointment set in train a revolution that would shake England to its core.

Cromwell was now fully on the offensive and stridently self-confident in all his dealings, including those with the most senior clergymen in the land, as Chapuys reported early in 1535: 'Cromwell does not cease to harass the bishops, even the good ones like Winchester and some others, whom he called lately before the Council to ask them if the King could not make and unmake bishops at pleasure; who were obliged to say Yes, else they should have been deprived of their dignities.' The ambassador added that Cromwell had boasted to an informant that 'the Council had been summoned only to entrap the bishops.'[4]

Cromwell's attitude towards his high-born rivals had undergone a gradual but marked shift as his career progressed during the early 1530s. Principal among them were Norfolk and Gardiner. When he had first risen to prominence in Henry's service, he had treated his rivals with a cautious reserve, even aloofness, which to the untrained eye could have suggested a degree of grudging respect for his social superiors. But as his favour with the king had become more secure, and his confidence in the extent of his own powers had grown ever greater, his attitude had changed to one of open hostility and, at times, disdain. He may not have been their social equal, but he was their political superior and he was determined that they should acknowledge the fact.

The way in which, during the course of 1535, Cromwell neutralised the threat posed by his major rivals is a testament as much to his self-assurance as to his deftness in negotiating his way through the tortuous factional politics of the court. One of the principal means by which he had outmanoeuvred his rivals was to engineer their frequent absence from court on various domestic and diplomatic missions. Access to the king had long been the essential prerequisite for power and influence. Without it, no matter how many titles or privileges a man enjoyed, he would always be more vulnerable to the intrigues of his enemies, who might undermine his favour with a well-timed word in the king's ear. That is why Cromwell ensured that he himself would be almost constantly at his sovereign's side. He even managed to secure a suite of rooms at court 'to which he [Henry] can, when he likes, have access through certain galleries without being seen'.[5] In addition, Cromwell had built up a strong network of agents and spies across the country and abroad, upon whom he could rely to represent him and keep him supplied with information. It was an invaluable system of delegation that enabled him to maintain his presence at court. If business ever did call him away, then he would make sure he was back in the royal presence within a matter of days.

At the same time, Cromwell succeeded in removing his chief opponents from court – one of them permanently. He started with Norfolk. Chapuys had already observed two years earlier that Cromwell's influence had started to irritate the Duke of Norfolk so much that he had declared himself sick of the court. In spring 1535 Norfolk finally retired to his estate at Kenninghall and stayed there for some considerable time. He was apparently not prepared to tolerate playing second fiddle to a low-born upstart, and probably also needed time to plan a counter-attack.

Norfolk's absence significantly weakened the position of his main ally. Stephen Gardiner's antipathy towards Cromwell had deepened when he had been obliged to resign the secretaryship to him in April 1534. This proved a bitter pill to swallow and the prelate was intent upon revenge from that day forward. His correspondence with Cromwell gives little hint of this, however: jealousy and resentment were masked by professions of deference and admiration. In July 1534 he wrote to the new 'Master Secretary . . . my especial frende' with his 'most harty commendations', assuring him: 'The good successe of my poore affayres hath been, by your frendly handeling, soo prosperous and pleasaunte unto me, and the continuaunce of your amitie soo ferme and stable, that in such matiers as bringe me in doubte and perplexitie of mynde, I always thinke ye may best and, as I veryly trust, wyl redyest procure, as ye have doon in other like cases, my convenient resolution in the same.'[6]

The two men soon abandoned this pretence of cordiality. By now, their hostility was known to everyone at court. 'There was continuall emulation betwene them twoo, and mortall dissention, such as . . . happened betwene the wolves and the lambes,' observed John Foxe, 'for bothe of theim beyng greatly in the kynges fauour, the one beyng muche more feared [Gardiner], the other was muche better beloued [Cromwell]. Eyther of them excellyng in dexteritie of wytte, howebeit, the vertues in the one farre exceaded the other.'[7]

Cromwell seemed to enjoy taunting – even bullying – Gardiner in front of the other council members. The prelate later recalled one occasion when he had been summoned to Hampton Court to take part in a debate about whether the king's 'will and pleasure' should be regarded as law, as Cromwell insisted it should. '"Come on my Lord of Winchester," quod he [Cromwell] . . . "Aunswer the King here . . . but speake plainly and direccly, and shrink not, man!"' Furious at being so humiliated, Gardiner refused to answer Cromwell but addressed the king himself, giving a typically ambivalent reply. 'The King turned his back and left the matter after, til the Lord Cromwel turned the cat in the panne afore company, when he was angry with me, and charged me as though I had played his parte.'[8] On another occasion, Cromwell pretended hurt and dismay when Gardiner accused him of acting against his interests. 'Your said letters [were] not so friendly conceived, as I think my merits towards you have deserved,' he chided him, adding that it was 'only your fantasy that I should rather of my self than otherwise promote the matter.'[9]

Although he seemed to have the upper hand, Cromwell knew that Gardiner was a dangerous adversary, particularly when allied to the likes of Norfolk. He therefore engineered the bishop's departure from court on an embassy to France. Gardiner took up this post in October 1535 and would remain there for three years, enabling Cromwell to augment his position even further at his rival's expense, as Foxe gleefully observed: 'Afterwarde he brought . . . the byshop of Wynchester hym selfe, although he was the kynges chiefe councellour, to an order, frustratyng and preventyng all his enterpryses and complayntes, by a marveilous provydence, but specially in those thynges whyche dyd tende to the ruyne and decaye of good men, and such as favoured the Gospel, vnto whom Cromwel was alwayes as a shyld [shield] against the pestiferous enterpryses of Wynchester.'[10] As it transpired, neither Norfolk nor Gardiner was completely vanquished, but for now their rival was firmly in the ascendancy.

As vicar-general, Cromwell had been commissioned to organise two thoroughgoing visitations: one of all the churches, monasteries and clergy in the land, and the other of the monasteries alone. He delegated this task to a number of trusted and carefully selected men, whom he dispatched to religious houses across the country with instructions to assess the quality of the religious life within. In particular, they were encouraged to report on any abuses, corruption, immorality or 'superstitious' practices they encountered. They found much to report.

The vast majority of the six hundred or so monastic communities across England had been founded in the eleventh and twelfth centuries, when a wave of monastic enthusiasm had swept across western Europe. By the time Cromwell focused his attention on them, they had played a prominent part in the lives of rural and urban communities across the country for up to half a millennium. The role of the monasteries extended well beyond ministering to people's spiritual needs. They were renowned centres of learning and culture, provided medical care to the sick, succour to the poor and destitute, and offered employment to many hundreds of laymen. Above all, they were the largest landowners in the country, with property and estates far exceeding those of the king himself. It was this fact that drew them to the attention of Cromwell.

The monasteries had arguably been in decline – with some notable exceptions – for many years. 'Riddled by worldliness and deadened by routine', they had all but ceased to fulfil their original religious, social and economic functions.[11] Their former intellectual vigour had deteriorated, their charitable purpose was negligible, and few men now included bequests for prayers to be said by the religious orders. A significant number of monks adhered only loosely to their vows, and vice and corruption were commonplace in many institutions. It was with some justification that Foxe condemned them as 'dennes of slouth and idlenes'.[12] This picture of monastic decline was contradicted by pockets of genuine piety and spiritual rigour, particularly among the orders of friars, but there was certainly enough evidence of abuse to inspire Cromwell's reforms.

In April 1535 he made a cautious start which belied the intensity that his campaign would soon develop. Conscious that Archbishop Cranmer was also undertaking a visitation, Cromwell focused instead on writing in the king's name to the bishops, nobility and Justices of the Peace in every shire, instructing them to imprison any clergyman who had been 'seduced with filthy and corrupt abominations of the bishop of Rome or his disciples or adherents'. He added a letter of his own, referring to himself as 'an eye to the prince', whose task it was 'to foresee and in time provide remedy for such abuses . . . as might else, with a little sufferance engender more evil in his public weal than could after be redubbed with much labour'.[13]

These letters carried Cromwell's stamp, as well as the king's, which is a sign of how great his influence had become – and of how much his authority was feared. Cavendish described him as one whom 'all others dyd excell in extort[ing] power and insacyat [insatiate] tyrannye'. On 3 June the Venetian ambassador in England disapprovingly remarked that although 'this Cromwell was a person of low origin and condition; he is now Secretary of State, the King's prime minister, and has supreme authority.'[14] On the same day, Cromwell issued a circular letter to every bishop in the land ordering them to preach in support of the supremacy, and ensure that the clergy in their dioceses did the same.

But Cromwell knew that such letters, even if closely observed, lacked the impact required to terrify the clergy into obedience. He had to flex the muscles of the Henrician regime more visibly – and more terrifyingly. Just a few weeks after the letters had been dispatched, a series of executions was organised to make an example of those clerics still loyal to the Pope. On 4 May 1535 three Carthusian priors, a learned monk and the vicar of Isleworth were all executed at Tyburn. Shortly afterwards, three other members of the order – Houghton, Hale and Reynolds – were hauled before the courts. The jury had looked set to acquit them, but Cromwell probably brought pressure to bear so that they returned a guilty verdict. The men remained outspoken in their defiance. Hale had called the king a 'tyrant', and told his accusers: 'If thou will deeply look upon his life, thou shalt find it more foul and more stinking than a sow, wallowing and defiling herself in any filthy place.' Reynolds, meanwhile, dared to tell Cromwell that all 'good men' in the kingdom believed, as they did, that the king had no right to call himself head of the English Church. Determined to punish such open defiance, Cromwell ensured that all three men would meet the most horrific death of all. They were taken to Tyburn and hanged 'with great ropes' in their habits, then disembowelled while still conscious. Finally they were beheaded and quartered. As an extra refinement of torture, it was ordered that 'one saw the other's execution fully carried out before he died.' Yet, as one eyewitness noted: 'No change was noticed in their colour or tone of speech, and while the execution was going on they preached and exhorted the bystanders with the greatest boldness to do well and obey the King in everything that was not against the honour of God and the Church.'[15]

Their steadfastness betrayed the strength of feeling against Cromwell's reforms, and as such constituted a warning. But it was one that the principal secretary chose to ignore. Instead, he stepped up his campaign against all those who dared to speak ill of the new regime. His spies were everywhere. The court records for 1535 contain numerous cases of ordinary men and women having uttered derogatory words against their monarch, which were then twisted into treason. An eighty-year-old husbandman from Worcestershire was reported to have blamed a run of bad weather on the king, saying that it had all started with his 'busines' – although what this referred to was not clear in the report. The punishments for these misdemeanours were terrifyingly harsh. If the authorities deemed that the words had been seditious, the perpetrators could be put to death. Henry's subjects could no longer express their opinions – even if they did not act upon them – without fear of reprisal.

Taking such a close interest in the lives of even the lowliest of men and punishing any whisper of insurrection was a means that Cromwell himself admitted was 'for the putting the Kynges Subiectes and other in more terroure ande Feare'. His policy now was to win obedience through intimidation, not persuasion. Foxe tells how Cromwell once encountered a friar who was still wearing his cowl, even after his religious house had been suppressed. 'Will not that cowl of yours be left off yet?' he demanded. 'If I hear, by one o'clock, that this apparel be not changed, then shalt thou be hanged immediately.' The terrified friar acquiesced at once. This tale may have been exaggerated or even invented, but it reflects the fact that Cromwell had developed a fearsome reputation. And this extended beyond the religious sphere. When a gang of ruffians heard that he and his entourage were approaching, they were said to have scattered in panic.[16]

But for all the effectiveness of his threats (real or imagined) and minor convictions in terrifying the population, Cromwell needed a more high-profile example. John Fisher had been languishing in the Tower for more than a year, during which time he had been subjected to intense pressure either to affirm or deny the king's position as supreme head of the English Church. He eventually uttered a denial – which, thanks to Cromwell's new Act, constituted high treason. Fisher was duly tried, convicted and sentenced to death. That this stalwart of Henrician England had been brought to such a pass was deeply shocking. Now aged sixty-six, Fisher had served the Tudors ever since he had come to the notice of Henry VIII's pious grandmother, Lady Margaret Beaufort. He was one of the most influential churchmen of the age, and a powerful figurehead for the traditional faith. But all that counted for nothing: he was to meet his end as a traitor. On 22 June he was conveyed to Tower Hill and executed in front of a stunned and silent crowd.

Shocking though it was, Fisher's death was soon eclipsed by that of another prominent advocate of the old religion. Like Fisher, Sir Thomas More had been incarcerated in the Tower since his arrest in April 1534. For as long as he remained there, in open defiance of the king's demands, he was an embarrassing and dangerous figurehead for other opponents to the royal supremacy and divorce. His opposition could of course be silenced by force. But executing More would also make a martyr out of him, and drum up even more sympathy and support for the 'true' religion. Various councillors had been dispatched to try to make him change his mind, but to no avail. Even his wife had failed to make him see reason, chastising him: 'I marveyle that you, that have beene alwayes hitherto taken for soe wise a man, will nowe soe playe the foole to lye here in this close filthye prisonne, and be contente thus to be shutt upp amongst myse and rattes, when you might be abroade at your libertie.'[17]

It was therefore left to Cromwell to take on the task. His eagerness to secure More's acquiescence was due to more than mere loyalty to the king, however. Although they were diametrically opposed on matters of faith and doctrine, the similarity of their interests and careers had fostered a certain respect between these two great adversaries, and, for all his apparent ruthlessness, Cromwell had no desire to see More sent to the block. Besides, it would send a much more powerful message to the conservatives if he persuaded their most influential figurehead to conform.

During numerous visits to More's cell in the Bell Tower, often accompanied by Ralph Sadler, Cromwell employed all his lawyer's skills of reasoning and persuasion to break down his resistance. One of his visits was deliberately timed to follow the incarceration of the Carthusian monks, news of which would certainly have reached More. But the prospect of their fate had by no means weakened his own resolve: if anything, it had strengthened it. In vain, Cromwell urged that 'as the Kyngis Hyghnesse wolde be gracyous to them that he founde comformable, so his Grace wolde folow the course of hys laws toward such as he shall fynde obstinate.' In a clear reference to the monks who were awaiting execution, Cromwell warned that More's 'demeanour in that matter was of a thyng that of likelyhode made now other men so styffe therin as they be'.[18]

But, weary from his fourteen months in a cold, damp prison, death held little fear for More: indeed, he seemed to welcome it. He confided to his daughter Margaret: 'I am . . . the Kyngis trew faythfull subject and daily bedesman and pray for hys Hyghnesse and all hys and all the realme. I do nobody harme, I say none harme, I thynk none harme, but wysh everye bodye good. And yf thys be not ynough to kepe a man alyve in good fayth I long not to lyve.'[19] Having realised that his attempts were futile, Cromwell arranged for More to be tried on 1 July 1535. Although More had originally been imprisoned for refusing to recognise the Act of Succession, the basis of his indictment was that he had denied the royal supremacy, which had been put in place several months after his incarceration in the Tower. The foundation of the trial was therefore shaky, to say the least. But the outcome was never in doubt. Richard Rich, a brilliant if unscrupulous lawyer and administrator who had risen to the position of Solicitor-General, testified that More had rejected the king's title on 12 June 1535. Even if he had not, then in the eyes of those who sat in judgement, his very silence had been enough to condemn him. The Attorney-General, Sir Christopher Hales, claimed that More's reticence was 'a sure token and demonstration of a corrupt and perverse nature, maligning and repyning against the statute'.[20]

Once the jury had passed sentence, More was at last free to speak his mind. After accusing Rich of perjury, he went on to repudiate the concept of royal supremacy, describing it as 'directly repugnant to the lawes of God and his holye Churche'. England's separation from Rome had, he said, fractured the body of Christ. Furthermore, the new Church of England was too narrow and confined when compared to the universal Church of Rome: 'For of the aforesaide holy Bisshopps I have, for every Bisshopp of yours, above one hundred; And for one Councell or Parliament of yours (God knoweth what maner of one), I have all the councels made these thousande yeres. And for this one kingdome, I have all other christian Realmes.'[21] It may have alleviated his conscience, but More's impassioned speech did nothing to halt the natural course of justice. He was condemned to die a traitor's death, but this was commuted to beheading in deference to More's former status as Lord Chancellor. This sentence was carried out at the Tower on 6 July 1535, with Cromwell in attendance. Standing on the scaffold, moments from death, More urged the watching crowds to remember that he was to suffer 'in and for the faith of the holy chatholick churche'.[22]

As Cromwell had feared, More was immediately declared a martyr – not just among the English dissenters, but across Europe. Emperor Charles V remonstrated with the English ambassador to the imperial court, Sir Thomas Elyot, saying that he 'wold rather have lost the best city of our dominions then have lost such a worthy counsellour'.[23] To counter this, Cromwell hastily instructed Sir John Wallop the English ambassador in France, to justify the executions to King Francis, who had shown equal 'ingrate and vnkynde Demeanure' towards his English counterpart. 'Ye shall sey to the saide Frensh Kyng that the same were not so mervelous extreme as he alledgeth,' he told him. 'Mr. More and the Bisshop of Rochestser . . . secretely practised aswell within the realme as without to move and styrre discension and to sowe sedycyon within the realme, intending thereby not onelye the distruction of the kyng but also the hole subversion of his highnes realme.' Cromwell concluded that 'it shall and may well appere to all the worlde that they having such malice roted in their hertes ayenst their prynce and Souereigne and the total Destruction of the commen weale of this realme, were well worthie if they had a thousand lyves to haue suffered x [ten] tymes a more terrible Deth and execucion then any of them Did suffer.' Cleverly portraying Francis and Henry as brothers-in-arms against the overweening power of the Pope, he urged the French king to consider 'the usurped auctoryte of the bisshop of Rome who Daylie goth about to suppresse and subdue kynges and prynces and their auctorytee gyuen to them by goddes worde'.[24]

But Francis was not to be so easily swayed by such a rousing speech. He and Charles persisted in their censure of the executions. This was only the beginning. More's name would be revered for decades to come. Writing in Mainz in 1550, Maurice Chauncy included accounts of More and Fisher in his influential and popular history of martyrs, as did the Italian Niccolo Circignani in 1584. Meanwhile, in England, even More's detractors admitted that his example would continue to inspire future generations. In his famous *Book of Martyrs*, published in 1563, John Foxe rightly predicted that More would be made a saint.[25]

Sir Thomas More's execution drew the battle lines between those of the new and old faiths more clearly than ever before. And if it sent a warning shot to a man whose rise to power had been similar, then Cromwell did not show it. Instead, the demise of his fellow lawyer seems to have inspired him to push forward his religious reforms with renewed vigour. He was joined in this by the king himself. Henry took his new role as supreme head of the English Church very seriously: it had been more than just a convenient (if convoluted) way of ridding himself of his first wife. He had always taken a keen interest in theology and, like More, had been a devotee of Erasmus. Even if he did not entirely share Cromwell's increasingly evangelical opinions against the corruptions of the Church, he was prepared to lend them a willing ear – for now at least.

Before he could undertake the visitations with which he had been commissioned on being made vicar-general, Cromwell first had to implement a census of Church lands and revenues. In early April 1535 he included a note in one of his 'remembrances' to 'remember all the jewels of the monasteries in England and specially the cross of emeralds at St Paul's'.[26] The survey that followed, known as the *Valor Ecclesiasticus* (literally, the 'value of the Church'), was the most detailed since Domesday Book in 1086. Completed within a year, it told Cromwell and his royal master, in staggeringly accurate detail, the value of all ecclesiastical lands and holdings in England. It may originally have been intended primarily as a means of taxing Church property more effectively, and to a lesser extent as a tool of reference in rooting out corruption, but it soon became a tempting prospect of what the royal coffers stood to gain if the religious houses were dissolved. One contemporary source estimated that the monasteries held 'two-thirds of the nation' in land and estates.[27]

From the summer of 1535, Cromwell turned his full attention to the monasteries. On 23 July he joined the king and queen on their progress to the West Country. This was one of the rare times he left London. With the notable exception of his youth and the brief sojourn in Calais in late 1532, Cromwell had never strayed from the capital for more than a few days – and even then it was to places a few miles away, such as Windsor. Unlike his noble colleagues, he did not spend substantial periods of each year at his country estate. His professional and personal lives were focused on London, and he showed no predilection to be anywhere else.

This progress must therefore have been something of an ordeal for Cromwell, but he made the best of it. He travelled with the royal couple for two full months and allowed himself no respite during this time. His voluminous correspondence attests to the meandering route the court took around the west of England, for he carefully inscribed each letter with the name of the place where they were staying. Beginning at Winchcombe in Gloucestershire, they travelled to Tewkesbury Abbey, Berkeley and Thornbury castles, Bromham and Winchester. Their route was very deliberate. Persuaded by Anne (and perhaps Cromwell), Henry decided to set aside the usual pleasures of the progress and use the trip as a means of drumming up support for his religious reforms. He therefore visited towns that were known to be favourable to reform, and while there he made very public rewards to the local gentry.

Meanwhile, Cromwell made the most of being in the West Country by launching his own visitation of religious houses there. With typical attention to detail, he even investigated a few himself. Chapuys reported: 'Wherever the King goes, Cromwell, who accompanies him, goes about visiting the abbeys in the neighbourhood, taking inventories of their lands and revenues, amply instructing the people in this new sect, and dismissing from the said abbeys, convents, or nunneries all those men or women who had professed before reaching the age of 25, the rest being at liberty to quit or remain, as they please.'[28]

Cromwell's experience that summer would be enough to inspire him to increase the pace of reform dramatically as soon as he returned to court. In this, it seemed he had the perfect ally. Queen Anne had for some time been championing the religious reforms that were gathering ground at her husband's court. She introduced Henry to William Tyndale's writings and kept a copy of his English translation of the New Testament in her suite for anyone who wished to read it. She also made a show of befriending a number of leading reformers at court, and it was through her influence that they were later appointed to powerful bishoprics. It was said that men such as Hugh Latimer, Nicholas Shaxton, Thomas Goodrich and even Thomas Cranmer owed their positions to her. A posthumous account of Anne, written by the reformist cleric William Latymer, described her as 'well read in the scriptures' and 'a patron of Protestants'.[29]

In speaking out so openly for the reformist religion, Anne was making some dangerous enemies at court. The Catholics were in no doubt that the king's alarmingly radical religious reforms were at her instigation. Eustace Chapuys reported to his master, Charles V, that 'the concubine' had told the king 'he is more bound to her than man can be to woman, for she extricated him from a state of sin . . . and that without her he would not have reformed the Church to his own great profit and that of all the people.'[30] But her beliefs were also bringing her increasingly into line with the king's chief minister. United in a common cause, she and Cromwell made a formidable double act. Their views differed in one crucial respect, however: while the minister had an eye to the profit that the crown stood to gain from the monasteries, the queen believed their riches should be diverted to charitable causes. For now, this difference mattered little. But it had sown a seed of discord that would soon have fatal consequences.

The collaboration between Cromwell and Anne on religious reform was presumably forged through regular meetings and conversations, some of them perhaps in secret. They were careful not to correspond about their reformist views, but in a rare surviving letter from Anne to Cromwell it is clear that they were working towards the same aim. The letter bears the month but not the year, although it was certainly written after Anne became queen. She addresses Cromwell with the standard royal greeting to a favourite: 'Trustie and right welbiloued we grete you well.' She goes on to say that the bearer of the letter, Richard Herman, was a merchant and citizen of Antwerp but had been expelled 'for nothing ells . . . but oonly for that that he dyd . . . helpe to the settyng forthe of the Newe Testamente in Englisshe'. This, Anne concluded, was hardly a just cause for expulsion, and she therefore required Cromwell 'with all spede and favoure convenient ye woll cause this good and honeste marchaunte, being my Lordis true faithfull and loving subjecte, restored to his pristine fredome, libertie and felowshipe'.[31]

Anne had need of allies at this time. Although on the surface all was well with the royal couple as they made their progress through the west of England, the king had rapidly tired of his new wife. Her failure to produce a male heir after two years of marriage had dangerously weakened her position. As if to demonstrate her vulnerability, Henry had arranged that one of the final calling points for their summer journey should be Wolfhall. The Wiltshire home of Sir John Seymour and his family, Wolfhall (or 'Wulfhall') was situated in Savernake Forest. A medieval manor house, it was one of the more modest residences in which the court stayed that summer, but its significance was far greater than the rest. The Seymours were of an ancient lineage that stretched back to the time of William the Conqueror. Sir John's wife Margery was of equally distinguished birth, being descended from Edward III. Their sons, Edward and Thomas, were already carving out careers for themselves at court. But it was their eldest daughter, Jane, upon whom the king had started to lavish his attention.

Jane Seymour had first appeared at court around 1529, when she had been appointed a lady-in-waiting to Queen Catherine, whom she greatly admired. After Catherine's exile from court, Jane had been transferred to the service of Anne Boleyn. At first, she had apparently attracted little notice – either from the king or anyone else at court. This is perhaps not surprising. True, Jane had her pedigree to recommend her, but she had little else. She was plain and sallow-faced, 'so fair that one would call her rather pale than otherwise'.[32] A portrait painted of her around 1536 shows her to have had a large, plump face with a double chin. Her eyes are small and beady, and her lips thin and closely compressed. One onlooker at court dismissed her as being 'of middle stature and no great beauty'.[33] Neither did she have the sparkling wit and intelligence of her rival: in fact, she was barely literate and her recorded utterances are few. Even Chapuys, who was predisposed to favour this rival to the hated 'Concubine', was at a loss to explain what Henry saw in her. He could only conclude that she must have a fine 'enigme', meaning 'riddle' or 'secret', which in Tudor times referred to the female genitalia.[34]

It was not until late 1534 that Jane had begun to be talked of as the king's latest inamorata. The ever vigilant Chapuys noted in October that the king had become 'attached' to 'a young lady' of the court.[35] She was then about twenty-seven years old, some seven or eight years younger than her royal mistress. If Jane was no great beauty, then neither – by then – was Anne. The considerable strain under which she had laboured as she tried in vain to claw back her power at court after Elizabeth's birth had started to show on her face. A portrait of around 1535 forms a startling contrast to that painted just two years before, when Anne was at the height of her powers. Her famously seductive eyes have become sunken and tired; her high cheekbones have disappeared beneath skin that is beginning to sag; and her pretty, smiling lips that the king once longed to kiss have grown thin and pinched with disappointment. That same year, in a dispatch to the Doge and Senate, the Venetian ambassador described the thirty-five-year-old queen as 'that thin old woman'. In a similar vein, Ambassador Chapuys remarked that the prospect of replacing Anne with Jane was 'by many a one compared to the joy and pleasure a man feels in getting rid of a thin, old, and vicious hack in the hope of getting soon a fine horse to ride'.[36]

Jane was the perfect antidote to a queen who, from Henry's perspective, was rapidly becoming tiresome. While Anne was tempestuous and outspoken, Jane appeared meek, docile and placid: 'as gentle a lady as ever I knew', according to one courtier. The king himself described her as 'gentle and inclined to peace'.[37] Other courtiers were quick to draw comparisons with the queen. John Russell, Earl of Bedford, remarked that the 'kyng hath come out of hell into heaven for the gentellness of this [Jane] and the cursidness and unhappyness in the other [Anne]'.[38]

Although those who were hostile to Queen Anne wasted no time in flattering the king's new love, there was as yet nothing to suggest that Jane Seymour would become anything other than his mistress. It would have taken a far-sighted courtier to predict that she would be Anne's downfall. Certainly, Cromwell showed no sign of switching his allegiance from the queen at this stage. Aware that his royal master's passion for Anne had cooled, he more than anyone knew how much had been sacrificed to bring their marriage to pass, so it must have seemed inconceivable that it would be so quickly overturned. For now, therefore, the minister stood firmly in the Boleyn camp.

Inspired by his visit to the West Country, on his return to court in September Cromwell suspended the authority of every bishop in the country so that the six canon lawyers he had appointed as his agents could complete their surveys. He also invoked his powers as Viceregent to establish a new court that gradually restored power to individual bishops, but made it clear that they would henceforth be officers of the state. This meant that when the king died, so too would their powers. As a further incentive to obedience, Cromwell restricted their privileges by withholding certain rights, such as those of visitation and probate, which carried with them lucrative fees.

At the same time, the visitations to churches and monasteries by his agents were also gathering pace. Two of the most hated were Thomas Legh and John ap Rice, whose arrogance and severity aroused widespread resentment. Soon Cromwell was besieged with letters of complaint at the unscrupulous methods they used to exact damning evidence from the houses they visited. 'The Commissioners found means to make divers monasteries obnoxious,' claimed one observer. Brutal though they were, their methods were also effective. Under pressure from Legh, one monk attested in a letter to Cromwell that the inmates of his house cared little for religion, but turned up at matins 'as dronck as myss and [played] sume at cardes, sume at dyyss'. Meanwhile, Richard Layton, an agent of Cromwell, condemned the inhabitants of one of the Sussex monasteries he visited as 'the blake [black] sort of dyvelisshe monkes' whom he said were 'paste amendment'.[39]

Layton and Legh proved so adept at hunting out corruption that Cromwell subsequently dispatched them to Yorkshire, one of the strongholds of the old religion. Their investigation was as thorough as it was unrelenting. 'Ther ys nother monasterie, selle, priorie, nor any other religiouse howse in the north but other [either] doctor Lee or I have familier acqwayntance within x or xii mylles of hit,' Layton reported to their master. 'We knowe and have experiens bothe of the fassion off the contre and the rudenes of the pepull . . . ther is matter sufficient to detecte and opyn all coloryde sanctitie, all supersticiouse rewlles of pretensyde religion, and other abusys detestable of all sorttes.'[40]

Cromwell was no doubt well pleased with the reports that his commissioners sent him at court. The evidence they provided was exactly what he needed to justify, and accelerate, a full-scale reformation of the religious life in England. Quite how accurate the reports were may not have greatly mattered to the minister, but it is interesting to consider. Undoubtedly, Cromwell's commissioners found genuine evidence of laxity and corruption in many of the houses they visited. The heads of these houses were elected by the monks themselves, who often chose those who would allow the inmates to lead an easy life. In some of the richer houses, an inappropriate level of luxury was enjoyed by the brethren. There are also tales of sexual profligacy which suggest that the vow of celibacy was far from universally upheld. Yet there is also a suspicious uniformity to the reports that reached Cromwell's desk, which could suggest that they were embellished or even fabricated in some cases.

John Foxe, however, was in no doubt that in attempting to reform and, increasingly, remove England's monastic communities, Cromwell had performed a great and noble service. 'Throughe a Devine methode or policie of wyt and reason received, suffred, deluded, brake of, and repressed all the pollicies traynes, malice and hatred of fryers, monkes, religious menne and priestes, of which sorte there was a great rabbell in Englande. Theyr houses he subverted throughout all the Realme.' Writing in the reign of Elizabeth I, by which time Cromwell's reforms had become more established, he reflected with horror on what might have happened if they had not: 'I thynke all we are bounde unto that one man, in that otherwyse we shoulde haue bene myserable, and yet ther is some hope left of the recovery of religion, the great flockes of monkes beyng banyshed, which els at this daye woulde have possessed Englande in so great nomber, that ten Cromewels woulde hereafter scarsly suffice to banysh them againe.'[41]

Although, with the advantage of hindsight, it is clear that Cromwell had for some time been carefully but deliberately moving the pieces into place for a thoroughgoing revolution, it was not until early in 1536 that he admitted as much. In one of his numerous memos to himself, he wrote concerning the 'abomination of religious persons throughout this realm, and a reformation to be devised therein'.[42] The scale of this reformation was realised in the parliament that was called shortly afterwards. Between 4 February and 6 March the final session of the so-called Reformation Parliament introduced a bill to dissolve all religious houses with a gross income of less than 200 pounds (equivalent to £65,000 today) per annum. This was supported by his commissioners' reports, which told a sordid tale of vice and corruption in these smaller religious houses. These reports gave Cromwell the justification he needed to push ahead with the dissolution and helped to offset any suspicion that it was motivated by greed on his or the king's part. By 18 March the bill had passed through both houses as the Act for the Suppression of the Lesser Monasteries: 'Whereupon the said Lords and Commons by great deliberation finally be resolved that it is and shall be much more to the pleasure of Almighty God and for the honour of this his realm that the possessions of such spiritual religious houses, now being spent, spoiled and wasted for the increase and maintenance of sin, should be used and converted to better uses.'[43]

Shortly afterwards, another Act was passed establishing a Court of Augmentations of the king's revenue. This court had the power to collect the lands, property and goods of the suppressed abbeys, and dispose of them in whatever way would be most profitable to the crown. Principal among its thirty or so staff were friends and servants of Cromwell. The new vicar-general was determined to control the funds that were about to come flooding into the royal treasury.

The legislation that Cromwell had forced through parliament was underpinned by a reformation in government administration that amounted to what the historian Geoffrey Elton claimed was of revolutionary proportions. During Cromwell's tenure, the medieval system of government, which was based very much on the household and individual advisers, was gradually replaced by the creation of a bureaucratic government with departments related to specific tasks and staffed by capable people who worked to a series of rules and procedures. Not only did this create a more efficient administration, it also considerably reduced the potential for one or more individuals to dominate the government. This is somewhat ironic, given that in creating this system, Cromwell was able to make himself indispensable to the king.

With the new legislation in place, commissions were sent to the highest-ranking men in each county, authorising them to investigate the state of each religious house in their area. They were to take detailed inventories and estimates of the wealth of those houses, as well as the number of monks who would need employment elsewhere were their establishment to be dissolved. It is interesting to note that the reports these men sent back to Cromwell were far more favourable about the state of the religious houses than those compiled by the likes of Layton and Legh.

Cromwell was undoubtedly motivated at least partly by the financial gain to be had from these lesser houses. 'Seeing himself so quickly raised to the place of secretary to the King, and being one of the greatest heretics in the kingdom, he said to the King, who he saw was bent upon aggrandizing the Crown, "May it please your Majesty, I have a note of all the revenues and treasures held by the abbeys, and it seems to me that your Majesty could take away a great many of them, and apply the revenues to the crown,"' the Spanish Chronicle relates. '"But how can this be done, Cromwell?" said the King. "I will tell your Majesty. I will present a letter to Parliament in your name asking them to grant you all the abbeys which have less than three thousand ducats, and your Majesty can then appropriate a great revenue to the Crown, and send the abbots to the richer abbeys."'

The dissolution gathered ground with bewildering speed. 'Cromwell was no sluggard,' observed the Spanish Chronicle, 'for he immediately sent collectors to unmake the abbeys.'[44] Once a report had been received by the Court of Augmentations, an order would be issued for the dissolution of the house in question and the diversion of its riches to the crown. A receiver was then appointed to strip the church of its treasures – from the vestments and gold plate to the bells and pews. Even the lead from the roof would be stripped off. Scores of men (many of them brought from the capital, local workmen being reluctant to undertake the task) were employed to strip each house bare before destroying it. The description of their work by one of Cromwell's officials conjures up an image of a swarm of vultures descending on a newly fallen corpse. 'We are pluckyng down an hygher vaute borne up by fower [four] thicke and grose pillars xiiii fote fro[m] syde to syde, abowt in circumference xlv fote . . . we browght from London xvij persons, 3 carpentars, 2 smythes, 2 plummars, and on[e] that kepith the fornace. Every of these attendith to hys own office: x of them hewed the walles abowte, amonge the whych ther were 3 carpentars: thiese made proctes to undersette wher the other cutte away, thother brake and cutte the waules.'[45]

The piecemeal destruction of these beautiful religious houses, many of which had stood for hundreds of years, must have been devastating for those who lived nearby. The monasteries would have been the largest and most magnificent buildings for miles around, dominating the landscape in which they were situated. They would have inspired awe and reverence among the local population. In stripping them of their treasures and taking them down brick by brick, Cromwell's men were committing what must have been seen as an act of the most shocking vandalism. It also symbolised, in the most brutal way possible, the progress of his despised reforms.

The memory was still raw more than half a century later, when a man whose father and uncle had witnessed the destruction of their local monastery described the impact it had had on them and their neighbours: 'It would have made an heart of flint to have melted and wept to have seen the breaking up of the House, and their sorrowful departing; and the sudden spoil that fell the same day of their departure from the House. And every person had everything good cheap; except the poor Monks, Friars and Nuns, that had no money to bestow of anything.' As well as Cromwell's men, there were scores of looters who seized the chance to share in the spoils: '[They] took what they found, and filched it away . . . It would have pitied any heart to see what tearing up of the lead there was, and plucking up of boards, and throwing down of the spares; . . . and the tombs in the Church [were] all broken . . . and all things of price either spoiled, carped away, or defaced to the uttermost.'[46] The Spanish Chronicle also bewailed the wholesale destruction: 'A great quantity of plate and revenues was got from them, without counting the large quantity stolen by the Commissioners, and great was the damage done to the realm by the destruction of these abbeys.'[47]

Although the impact of the dissolution was most visible in rural areas, it left its mark on England's cities too. Principal among them was London, from where the Venetian ambassador reported in 1554: 'On the banks of the river there are many large palaces, making a very fine show, but the city is much disfigured by the ruins of a multitude of churches and monasteries belonging heretofore to friars and nuns.'[48]

In all, 376 houses were suppressed in this first phase of the dissolution. The total amount raised from the sale of the jewels, plate, lead and other valuables that were seized was estimated at 100,000 pounds, equivalent to more than £32 million today. The annual incomes of the houses, meanwhile, brought the crown a further 32,000 pounds (£10.3 million). This was a sizeable portion of the 250,000 pounds that the king routinely received into his treasury each year.

Even now, though, the full potential of the dissolution was not realised. The greatest prizes were undoubtedly the larger, wealthier religious houses, but Cromwell's commissioners had been at pains to praise the consistently high moral standards that existed there.

Moreover, several of the smaller houses were eventually spared (after the payment of substantial fines), and many of the inhabitants who wished to continue in their religious calling were allowed to do so. Henry even went so far as to re-found two houses in his own name: Bisham Abbey in Berkshire and Stixwould Priory in Lincolnshire. This has been interpreted as a sign that there had been no masterplan for the wholesale destruction of the monasteries. While this could be true, the clarity and far-sightedness of Cromwell's policies render it unlikely that he acted in a reactionary, rather than premeditated, way. More feasible is that, having witnessed first-hand the resistance that his initial reforms were meeting from large swathes of the population, he adopted a softly-softly approach in these early stages of the Reformation. His caution may have had another justification. One of the fiercest opponents to this small-scale dissolution of the monasteries was the queen herself.

CHAPTER 11

'A more gracious mistress'

CROMWELL HAD ENJOYED a seemingly inexorable rise since he first entered Henry VIII's service in 1530. By early 1536, the world seemed to lie at his feet. He had persuaded parliament to pass legislation that consolidated all his reforms and had truly revolutionary implications for the future. His standing at court had never been higher, and neither had his favour with the king.

By contrast, Queen Anne had enjoyed only brief periods in the sun, each overshadowed by setbacks of varying degrees of seriousness. Worst of all, the birth of her unwanted daughter, Elizabeth, had not been followed by the promised male heir. Indeed, Anne had failed to give birth to a healthy child of either gender, and had suffered at least two miscarriages. The dawn of the year 1536 seemed to augur much happier prospects, however. Anne was pregnant once more, and the child growing inside her had survived those perilous early weeks. Hopes soared that she would at last give Henry the son he craved. More glad tidings soon followed. The new queen had never thrown off the shackles of the old, and there was enduring and widespread sympathy for the beleaguered Catherine, who steadfastly maintained the validity of her marriage to Henry. For as long as she lived, the 'Great Whore' would never be accepted by the English people. But Catherine's health had deteriorated rapidly in recent months, not helped by the miserable conditions in which she had been forced to live. At the end of December 1535, Cromwell had reported to Gardiner that 'the douagier is in greate daunger.'[1] He was right. It was with great rejoicing that Anne learned of her old rival's death on 7 January 1536.

Cromwell must also have received the news with satisfaction. His letter to Gardiner the following day had more than an air of triumph about it. He could not resist making a veiled reference to what he had long tried to prove was Catherine's 'sin' of marrying her late husband's brother when he reported 'the departure yesterdaye of the princesse douagier whose soule god pardon'. Catherine stood for everything he had spent his career at court unpicking, and had remained a figurehead for resistance to his regime. So convenient was her death, indeed, that Chapuys even speculated that the minister may have had a hand in it. He recalled a sinister threat that Cromwell had apparently made in August 1534, when he had remarked: 'The death of the Queen and Princess would put an end to all disputes [between Henry VIII and Charles V].' The ambassador concluded: 'You will thus see that their aim is to get rid of these ladies.'[2]

Chapuys's suspicions against Cromwell had been heightened by the fact that the minister had made sure to spy on the former queen and her household. When the ambassador had visited her shortly before her death, he had been accompanied by a 'friend of Cromwell's whom the King had sent to accompany me, or rather to spy and note all that was said and done'. It was Cromwell who informed the ambassador of Catherine's death a few days later. Chapuys immediately wrote to his master, confiding his certainty that there had been foul play.

> The Queen's illness began about five weeks ago, as I then wrote to your Majesty, and the attack was renewed on the morrow of Christmas day. It was a pain in the stomach, so violent that she could retain no food. I asked her physician several times if there was any suspicion of poison. He said he was afraid it was so, for after she had drunk some Welsh beer she had been worse, and that it must have been a slow and subtle poison for he could not discover evidences of simple and pure poison; but on opening her, indications will be seen.

More than six weeks later, Chapuys was still voicing his suspicions against the king's chief minister: 'I forgot to write that among the news brought by Cromwell, he said it was reported in France that the good Queen had been poisoned, and that the French alleged the said report came from the Spaniards; which news he could not report to me without some change of colour and bearing.'[3]

Chapuys was sufficiently convinced by Cromwell's blushes to conduct his own discreet investigation into the matter. He became even more convinced of foul play when he heard the account of the man who had been appointed to 'open' the queen – namely, to remove her vital organs prior to embalming. This man had 'in great secrecy as a thing which would cost his life' told the Bishop of Llandaff, Catherine's confessor, what had happened, and the ambassador had persuaded the bishop to pass on the information to him. According to the man's account:

> The Queen died two hours after midday, and eight hours afterwards she was opened by command of those who had charge of it on the part of the King, and no one was allowed to be present, not even her confessor or physician, but only the candle-maker of the house and one servant and a compagnon, who opened her, and although it was not their business, and they were no surgeons, yet they have often done such a duty . . . He had found the body and all the internal organs as sound as possible except the heart, which was quite black and hideous, and even after he had washed it three times it did not change colour. He divided it through the middle and found the interior of the same colour, which also would not change on being washed, and also some black round thing which clung closely to the outside of the heart. On my man asking the physician if she had died of poison he replied that the thing was too evident by what had been said to the Bishop her confessor, and if that had not been disclosed the thing was sufficiently clear from the report and circumstances of the illness.[4]

Rumours of poison often accompanied the death of royals and other high-profile figures, and there is no reason to give this one any more credence than others. Nevertheless, the notion that Cromwell had Catherine murdered has convinced recent commentators, as well as contemporary ones. The editor of his correspondence is among them. 'If the Queen was murdered, there is every reason to think that Cromwell was chiefly responsible for the crime,' he asserted. 'To a man of his character and training such a step would have been far less repugnant than to Henry, had he once assured himself that it was indispensable to his purposes. He had had sufficient experience of the Italy of Alexander VI and Caesar Borgia to render him quite callous to the ordinary sentiments of humanity in such matters.' Merriman argues that England's position in Europe had reached such a dangerous impasse, with the prospect of allied Franco-Imperial forces launching an invasion against the heretical English king, that Cromwell could well have taken 'desperate measures' to avoid it. He concedes, though, that he could not have acted without his master's complicity: 'It is mere folly to suppose that Cromwell would have attempted to murder the Queen without the King's full consent. It is more than probable however that – if poison it was – it was he who put the idea into Henry's mind, and took the responsibility for its execution upon himself.'[5]

Cromwell certainly wasted no time in capitalising on the advantage that Catherine's death had presented. On Henry's orders, he arranged for the news to be communicated to the French king, making it clear that he was no longer in a position to dictate to his English neighbour. Cromwell duly issued instructions to Gardiner and Wallop on 8 January, telling them frankly that Catherine's death had removed 'the onelie matier of the unkyndenes' between his master and the emperor. He also ordered them in their 'conferences and procedynges with the frensh kyng and his counsaile' to behave 'the more aloof and be the more Froyt and colde in relentyng to any their overtures or requestes'. At the same time, Cromwell was quick to point out to Chapuys that in removing the only cause of resentment between their two masters, the former queen's death was the best thing that could have happened. He even went so far as to assure one of the ambassador's messengers cheerfully that it would be 'no such great evil as people supposed' if the Lady Mary followed her mother to the grave, 'and that the King his master had already well discussed all the ill effects that could possibly arise from it, and that he was well able to answer for everything.'[6]

Convenient though Catherine's death undoubtedly was for Cromwell, the idea that he hastened it is unlikely. Certainly it is not supported by any reliable evidence. The only suggestion that he was involved is provided by Chapuys, who was bound to be suspicious of the man who orchestrated her downfall. But a little over a week later, the ambassador was speculating that there was someone at court with an arguably stronger motive than Cromwell for getting rid of the former queen. Her successor Anne had never won the love of the English people, who had continued to see Catherine as their rightful queen. Neither had she succeeded in retaining the affections of the king, who had become increasingly frustrated by her inability to bear him a son. Just one week after conjecturing that Cromwell was behind the old queen's death, Chapuys was wildly speculating that the culprit was Anne, who had long wanted both Catherine and her daughter Mary out of the way.

> I don't suppose [suspect] the King but the Concubine (who has often sworn the death of both, and who will never be at rest till she has gained her end, suspecting that owing to the King's fickleness there is no stability in her position as long as either of the said ladies lives), will have even better means than before of executing her accursed purpose by administering poison, because they would be less on their guard; and, moreover, she might do it without suspicion, for it would be supposed when the said ladies had agreed to everything that the King wished and were reconciled and favourably treated after they had renounced their rights, there could be no fear of their doing any mischief, and thus no suspicion would arise of their having received foul play.[7]

In fact, the former queen had been in poor health for some time, and modern medical analysis has suggested that her symptoms were consistent with cancer, the disease that would also cause the death of her daughter Mary. Moreover, aged fifty-one, Catherine had had a long life by Tudor standards – certainly longer than the majority of other women. If she had known, as she lay dying at Kimbolton, that Cromwell would be tasked by Henry to arrange her funeral, it would hardly have given her any comfort. Cromwell performed the delicate task with customary efficiency, adhering to his master's instructions that the expense should not be too great, but still ensuring that due respect would be paid to the former queen. Only Chapuys saw cause to grumble that Catherine had not been buried in the most sacred part of Peterborough Cathedral.

Meanwhile, for Anne Boleyn, her rival's demise crowned her triumph and seemed to assure a dazzling future as Queen of England. The king was apparently no less joyful than his second wife upon hearing of Catherine's death. Cromwell reported that 'his Maiestie is mery and in perfite health.' Henry was relieved that the burden of doubt and guilt caused by throwing off his first wife had at last been lifted. Furthermore, for one who set great store by these things, it was surely a sign that God had not forsaken him after all. Lavish entertainments were held at court, and Henry appeared 'clad all over in yellow from top to toe' with his wife and their daughter at his side, and was 'like one transported with joy'.[8]

But Anne's triumph would be short-lived. In a cruelly ironic twist of fate, on the very same day (29 January) that Catherine was laid to rest at Peterborough Cathedral, Anne miscarried. This time, God had surely shown his hand: the fifteen-week-old foetus had all the appearance of a boy. Chapuys was quick to convey the news to his Imperial master. With barely suppressed triumph, he told Charles: 'the Concubine had an abortion which seemed to be a male child which she had not borne three and a half months, and on which the King has shown great distress.' His conclusion was brutal but accurate: 'She has miscarried of her saviour.'[9]

Things now began to unravel rapidly for Anne. Henry made little secret of his resentment and distaste towards her. 'For more than three months this King has not spoken ten times to the Concubine . . . when formerly he could not leave her for an hour,' reported a gleeful Chapuys in February 1536. 'When she miscarried he scarcely said anything to her, except that he saw clearly that God did not wish to give him male children.' Others noted that although he tried to maintain appearances at court, in private he 'shrank from her'. Worse still, for Anne, was the fact that her royal husband had already found a new favourite to replace her. Anne herself knew it: indeed, she claimed that the discovery of his love for Jane Seymour had caused her to miscarry. 'The love she bore him was far greater than that of the late Queen,' she avowed, 'so that her heart broke when she saw that he loved others.'[10]

In the immediate aftermath of Anne's crisis, Cromwell appeared to remain loyal to her cause. On 24 February an outraged Chapuys reported that the secretary had commanded Princess Mary to relinquish a cross that her mother had given her. Although Cromwell had been at pains to point out that this was 'by the King's command and in his name', Chapuys clearly had his doubts.[11] But he was soon to change his mind.

On 1 April Chapuys told Charles V that he had heard 'that this King's mistress and Secretary Cromwell were on bad terms just now', and that there had even been talk of a new marriage for the king – which Cromwell, presumably, was busy arranging.[12] He had hastened to see the minister at once so that he might discover the truth of the statement. He wanted to know whether, as was rumoured, Henry really intended to abandon his second wife and marry the daughter of the King of France. In order to cajole Cromwell into confiding in him, Chapuys assured him that 'although a more lawful marriage should follow, and male issue from it would be to the prejudice of the Princess, yet the affection I bore to the honor and tranquillity of the King and kingdom, and towards him particularly, made me desire another mistress, not for hatred that I bore to this one, who had never done me any harm.' Cromwell 'appeared to take all this in good part'. Far from supporting the marriage that he had worked so hard to bring about, he denied any involvement in it: 'He then began to defend himself, saying he had never been the cause of this marriage, although, seeing the King determined upon it, he had smoothed the way.' At the same time, however, Cromwell attempted to play down the rumours: 'Notwithstanding that the King was still inclined to pay attention to ladies, yet he believed he would henceforth live honorably and chastely, continuing in his marriage.' Chapuys was surprised by the sudden change in Cromwell's demeanour:

> This he said so coldly as to make me suspect the contrary, especially as he said so, not knowing what countenance to put on. He leaned against the window in which we were, putting his hand before his mouth to avoid smiling or to conceal it, saying afterwards that the French might be assured of one thing, that if the King his master were to take another wife, he would not seek for her among them. He then said that when an answer came from your Majesty upon the subject of our communication we should discuss everything and do some good work.

Although Cromwell had almost certainly decided to break with the queen at this point, his ambiguity was deliberate: the situation at court was more volatile than ever, and much as the king might seem to despise his second wife at present, Cromwell knew full well that he could be passionately in love with her again the next day. Nevertheless, the secretary was keen to part on good terms with Chapuys. 'At last, when I was going to leave, he said to me that although I had formerly refused a present of a horse he wished to give me, that now I could not do so without suspicion of ill-will,' reported the ambassador, 'and he offered me one that the earl of Sussex had presented to him the day before; and for all I could say to excuse myself, I was obliged to accept it.'[13]

That Cromwell should so quickly abandon his alliance with Anne is perhaps surprising. After all, they had enjoyed a successful association for at least five years. It had been largely thanks to Cromwell that Anne had realised her ambition of becoming queen, and her passion for religious reform had given them further common ground. But theirs had always been a somewhat uneasy alliance. While quick to recognise his usefulness, Anne – in contrast to her husband – had never shown any great liking for Cromwell, or appreciation of his personal qualities. According to Chapuys, Cromwell had confided 'that were the Lady to know the familiar terms on which he and I are, she would surely try to cause us both some annoyance, and that only three days ago she and he had had words together, the Lady telling him, among other things, that she would like to see his head off his shoulders.'[14] The ambassador had been shocked by this remark, but he was clearly aware that relations between the queen and the secretary were fractious. He told Cromwell: 'I could not but wish him a more gracious mistress, and one more grateful for the inestimable services he had done the King, and that he must beware of enraging her, else he must never expect perfect reconciliation.' The ambassador feared that Anne would be Cromwell's downfall, just as she had been Wolsey's. 'I told Cromwell that I had for some time forborne to visit him that he might not incur suspicion of his mistress for the talk he had previously held with me . . . in which case I hoped he would see to it better than did the Cardinal, as I had great belief in his dexterity and prudence.'[15]

For his part, Cromwell had only furthered Anne's cause for as long as it was aligned with that of the king. He felt no personal loyalty or affection towards her and, like Henry, was no doubt tiring of her increasingly hysterical outbursts. Where Cromwell was concerned, politics would always win out over passion and principles. It is an indication of how secure he felt in the king's favour, as well as his appreciation of the latter's increasing coolness towards his second wife, that he showed little fear at her threats. He told Chapuys: 'I trust so much on my master, that I fancy she cannot do me any harm.'[16]

It was Cromwell's dissolution of the lesser monasteries that had first set them on an open collision course. For as much as she favoured reform, Anne increasingly found it distasteful that the proceeds from the suppressed religious houses should be diverted to the crown's coffers rather than to charitable causes. Alexander Ales, a Scottish reformer who was closely acquainted with Cromwell, claimed that he and his supporters 'hated the Queen, because she had sharply rebuked them and threatened to inform the King that under the guise of the Gospel and religion they were advancing their own interests, that they had put everything up for sale and had received bribes to confer ecclesiastical benefices upon unworthy persons, the enemies of the true doctrine, permitting the godly to be oppressed and deprived of their just rewards.'[17]

Despite the increasing hostility between Anne and Cromwell, they had until now kept up appearances of accord enough to fool most courtiers. Even Chapuys suspected that Cromwell's claim that she intended his death was 'an invention', and concluded: 'All I can say is, that everyone here considers him Anne's right hand, as I myself told him some time ago.'[18] But their simmering hostility was about to break out into open aggression. Less than a fortnight after the Act for the Suppression of the Lesser Monasteries had been passed, Anne took decisive and aggressive action. On Passion Sunday (2 April) 1536 she instructed her almoner, John Skip, to preach a sermon that was a thinly veiled attack on Cromwell. In a service attended by the king and his court, Skip 'explained and defended the ancient ceremonies of the Church . . . defending the clergy from their defamers and from the immoderate zeal of men in holding up to public reprobation the faults of any single clergyman as if it were the fault of all.' Warming to the theme, his criticism of the principal secretary became ever more obvious as he 'insisted on the need of a king being wise in himself and resisting evil counsellors who tempted him to ignoble actions'. He also condemned the same 'evil counsellors' who 'suggested alteration in established customs', and went on to tell the story of Haman, the evil and avaricious enemy of Queen Esther in the Old Testament, who persecutes the Jews and tries to divert their riches to the royal treasury. This story ends with Haman facing death on the very scaffold that he had built for his rival, the queen's protector. The almoner concluded that a king's councillor 'ought to take good heed what advice he gave in altering ancient things' and 'lamented the decay of the universities and insisted on the necessity of learning'.[19]

Determined to use the sermon to discourage her husband from betraying her with Jane Seymour, Anne also instructed Skip to tell the story of how Solomon 'lost his true nobility towards the end of his life by sensual and carnal appetite in the taking of many wives and concubines'. Various (favourable) comparisons had been made in the past between Henry and Solomon, so the inference would hardly have been lost on him. Both the king and his chief minister left the chapel in a rage. Skip was immediately interrogated and upbraided for 'preaching seditious doctrines and slandering the King's Highness, his counsellors, his lords and nobles and his whole

Parliament'. He escaped without further reprisals. For all their fury, Henry and Cromwell knew that he had merely served as a puppet to the queen.

But Anne was not finished yet. This opening blow was strengthened by her having apparently enlisted the help of Cranmer, who wrote to Cromwell on 22 April supporting the queen's views on the dissolution of the monasteries. That one of his foremost allies should thus be won over to his enemy's cause must have shaken Cromwell to the core. Barely had he had a chance to catch his breath than Anne proceeded to undermine his policy of favouring the Holy Roman Empire over France. She insisted that Charles V be made to accept the royal supremacy – something that she knew full well the emperor, as a faithful Roman Catholic (and nephew of the late Queen Catherine), would never do. Forcing the matter would therefore sour England's relations with Charles and leave no other option than alliance with his great rival, Francis I. If Anne had been lashing out alone, she could have been contained. But to Cromwell's dismay, and that of the Imperial ambassador, she appeared to be fully supported by her husband.

All this spelled grave danger for Cromwell, and he knew it. She had brought down his former patron, Cardinal Wolsey, who had seemed invincible. Now all her ire was focused on him. The words that she had once uttered about the king's first daughter, Mary, could have equally applied to him: 'She is my death, or I am hers.'[20] Cromwell had to act quickly in order to regain the initiative. His first step was to align himself more closely with the faction of conservative courtiers, led by Sir Nicholas Carew and with the Seymour brothers among their ranks. Carew and his followers had for some time been plotting to oust the 'usurper queen' and replace her with Jane Seymour, whom they could more easily bend to their will. Carew was head of an ancient noble family and had been a courtier since childhood. He counted the Duke of Suffolk among his friends, and was also one of Henry VIII's closest favourites. So intimate was he with the king that Wolsey had had him charged with over-familiarity. Although he played an active part in the Reformation Parliament, his family was deeply conservative and had strong ties of loyalty to Catherine of Aragon and her daughter. Realising that it was hopeless to try to reinstate the former, Carew had chosen the less direct route of promoting Jane Seymour. He had offered her lodgings at his house at Beddington, south of London, where the king paid her regular night-time visits. He had also sent letters of encouragement to the Lady Mary, telling her 'to be of good cheer, for shortly the opposite party would put water in their wine'.[21]

Even as early as July 1535, Cromwell had begun to make friendly overtures towards members of Carew's faction. In that month he had sent Richard Rich to warn the Duke of Suffolk of the king's displeasure at the 'decay' of certain houses that the duke claimed to have restored, as well as a number of other gripes. He instructed Rich: 'to say somwhat to the saide Duke in this matier alledging vnto him that as I am, alwayes haue been, and euer wilbe his graces poure frende so I requere him not to stycke with [i.e. object to] the kinges highnes in this matier . . . I pray you shew him on my behalf that my poure and frendelie aduise is that his grace shall liberally wryte to the kinges highnes in this matier so as his highnes may thereby perceyue the saide Dukes gentill herte and naturall zele towardes his maieste aswell in this as in all other thinges.'[22]

It is an indication of how much Cromwell wanted to be rid of Anne, as well as of the extent of his pragmatism, that he was prepared to put his weight behind a body of men who were so diametrically opposed to his own principles, and who until now had proved his most steadfast enemies at court. They were committed traditionalists in both religion and politics, promoting conservative Catholicism and a government dominated by the aristocracy. Cromwell, by contrast, was a radical religious and political reformer who had won his position at court by skill and hard work, not by birth. Yet he evidently judged that there was little choice but to make what he could of this unlikely and, frankly, distasteful alliance. Neither could Carew and his supporters have looked upon it more favourably. They despised Cromwell as a low-born, unscrupulous interloper who had won more favour with the king than he ever had a right to. But they also recognised that he was the source of real power at court so they, too, were prepared to set aside their principles in the pursuit of gain.

That Cromwell was obliged to play the dangerous game of factional politics also says much about his relationship with the king. Although Henry had raised him to a position of unparalleled influence at court, Cromwell was by no means as close to him as Wolsey had been. There had been a natural affinity between the king and the cardinal that the latter's protégé and successor could not emulate. This was not a failing on Cromwell's part: he had more than enough political guile and charisma to secure the king's favour. Rather, Henry was determined to retain control over every aspect of government in which he took a close interest. Admittedly, this still gave Cromwell a considerable amount of influence: his royal master was content to let him lead on issues about which he had little concern. The king was also ready to listen to his chief minister's advice, and to give assent to policies that aligned with his own objectives. But he would never again give a minister as free a rein as Wolsey had enjoyed. Henry had learned a great deal from that experience, and Cromwell was paying the price. Cromwell was always careful to sign his letters to the king in the most deferential manner, variously describing himself as 'Your majesties most bownden' or 'humble subiect & servant'.[23] Reginald Pole's claim, made in August 1536, that Cromwell 'ruled' Henry was wide of the mark.[24] The king would later boast to his then secretary, William Petre: 'It is I that made both Cromwell, Wriothesley and Paget good Secretaries, and so I must do to thee.'[25]

An illustration of this came with the realignment of England's foreign policy in the aftermath of Catherine of Aragon's death. This had prompted an immediate improvement in relations with her nephew, Charles V, just as Cromwell had so confidently predicted to Chapuys. But, eager to prevent an Anglo-Imperial alliance, Francis I had also started to make friendly overtures towards Henry VIII. The latter had been delighted at being restored to such a favourable position, and was keen to keep both powers in play. Cromwell recorded that the English ambassadors at the Spanish and French courts had been instructed to give 'an answer soo general that it doth neither refuse their alliance, ne moche encorage them, to conceyve that they maye without difficultie obteyn their desire'.[26] But – for the first time in his career – Cromwell had disregarded his royal master's command. Favouring an alliance with the emperor, the principal secretary began to stir up trouble between the English and French kings. He gleefully reported to Gardiner that Henry had humiliated the French ambassador in front of the court. 'I wold your lordship had this day hard [heard] the kings grace handle the ambassador of fraunce he made suche repetycion of hys graces most frendly overtures and procedynges towardes them and of their unfr[e]ndely facyons towards him.'[27]

But it was when Cromwell made a point of voicing his disdain for France during a conference with Chapuys that he really overstepped the mark. That he knew the risk he was taking in acting on his own initiative and against the king's will is implied by the great pains he took to meet the ambassador in secret. He sent a message asking that Chapuys would meet him at the Augustinian friary close to both their houses. The ambassador declined, saying that he wished to go and celebrate masses 'for the soul of the good Queen', and suggested Cromwell write to him instead. The principal secretary explained that he could not do so because he was anxious 'to avoid the suspicion of the French and because he wished only to speak to me of himself and not by command of the King, and therefore he begged I would choose some place less *suspect* where we could talk together, and he would tell me things of great importance for the services of your Majesty and the King.'[28]

Chapuys eventually agreed to call in on Cromwell, as if on a whim, as he walked home from church. He relayed what passed between them in great detail to his master. Cromwell, he said, had shown him great courtesy, assuring him that 'he had continually done his best to prevent anything being treated with the French to your prejudice.' He went on to say that 'the King his master desired nothing more earnestly than your friendship, to which he was not only naturally inclined himself but strongly urged by his Council.' The ambassador, clearly not convinced by these fine words, gave a polite but non-committal reply. This prompted Cromwell to make even stronger assurances of his commitment to the Imperial cause: 'He showed such great anger that he could hardly explain himself, saying that the French had played such tricks upon the King that he would rather be hanged on the highest steeple of London than have done or thought the half of them.' Referring to negotiations that Henry's envoys were undertaking in Germany and Denmark, he told Chapuys that 'he was ready to forfeit his head if it were found that anything had been treated in those countries to the prejudice of your Majesty' and that 'he thought the King his master would do all your Majesty wished.' Cromwell went on to boast that Chapuys 'should consider the wonders he had done here since he had had the government of the King's affairs'.[29]

But the principal secretary knew that no matter how pre-eminent he was at court, he could not treat with Charles V on his own authority: 'Cromwell said that I might feel quite assured there was no dissimulation in what he had said, and it would be very foolish in him to attempt it, for nothing could be gained thereby for his master; and as what he had said came of himself without commission from his master, I might see that he had no power to make any overture, which must come of your Majesty.'[30] This was a clever move on Cromwell's part. He had been careful not to exceed his authority by forging an alliance, but had encouraged Chapuys to urge his master to do so.

The ambassador remained sceptical. He had too long an experience of dealing with Cromwell to take the wily minister at his word. For a time, it seemed that Chapuys was right to suspect Cromwell's sincerity: he had ventured nothing beyond fine words and promises. However, on 21 April the ambassador reported that he had had another conference with Cromwell, and had found him 'firm, and as determined as ever to complete things begun'. Chapuys presented him with letters from the emperor, 'which he kissed and received with great reverence', apparently overwhelmed that such a mighty potentate should pay such attention to 'un petit compagnon'. This show of modesty was somewhat undermined by what Chapuys felt to be a hardening in Cromwell's manner towards an Anglo-Imperial

an audience for Chapuys with the king. Henry welcomed the ambassador with apparently genuine warmth. But when, accompanied by Cromwell and Audley, he took Chapuys to his private chamber, things suddenly turned sour. Chapuys told the king of the conversations he had had with Cromwell about the benefits of an Imperial alliance, and Henry's demeanour became abruptly and dangerously hostile. He brought their conversation to an end shortly afterwards.

While Chapuys went to converse with one of Jane Seymour's brothers, 'always keeping an eye upon the gestures of the King and those with him', there erupted a heated argument between Henry and his chief minister. 'There seemed to be some dispute and considerable anger, as I thought, between the King and Cromwell; and after a considerable time Cromwell grumbling left the conference in the window where the King was, excusing himself that he was so very thirsty that he was quite exhausted, as he really was with pure vexation, and sat down upon a coffer out of sight of the King, where he sent for something to drink.' Not long afterwards, Henry emerged into the throng of the court, as Chapuys reported: 'I know not whether to come near me, or to see where Cromwell was.' Barely containing his anger, he brusquely told the ambassador that the terms of the proposed alliance with the emperor were so weighty that he could not consider them unless they were set down in writing. Chapuys protested that he had never asked such a thing before because he had always proved true to his word. Besides, he said: 'I had taken example of Cromwell, who had never given me anything in writing.' The king brushed aside his protests and 'insisted wonderfully on having the said writing, and said several times very obstinately that he would give no reply'. Nevertheless, he went on to give a full and very angry reply, refuting each of the terms that Cromwell had carefully drawn up with Chapuys. Recalling all the wrongs that the emperor had done him during the previous years, he angrily denounced his 'great ingratitude', claiming that without Henry's support he would not have acquired such an extensive empire. 'The Chancellor and Cromwell appeared to regret these answers, and in spite of the King's gestures to them that they should applaud him, neither of them would say three words,' Chapuys reported. To stand in defiance of the king was a bold move and betrayed how much Cromwell wanted the alliance. He might also have found it too humiliating to back down in front of the court, given that everyone knew him to be the most powerful member of it. Eventually, the audience was brought to a conclusion with Henry promising to look back over the treaties he had forged with Charles in the past, after which he would give the Imperial ambassador his further opinion.[34]

The ambassador immediately left court, with Cromwell following hot on his heels. The pair met up at the same place where they had begun their day together, midway between Westminster and Greenwich. 'There we expressed our mutual regret, which was great on both sides, especially on that of Cromwell, who was hardly able to speak for sorrow, and had never been more mortified in his life than with the said reply.' Cromwell told Chapuys that he had already spoken to his royal master about the matter and had assured him 'that if he had known what has taken place in this affair, he would not have meddled with it for all the gold in England, and that henceforth he would not treat with ambassadors without having a colleague.' The ambassador reflected: 'He has certainly shown himself in this an honest man; for although he knew it displeased his master, and that he incurred some danger, he would not retract anything he had said to me.'[35]

What Cromwell then confided to Chapuys is one of the clearest illustrations of his relationship with the king: 'Although he had always pretended that what he said to me was of his own suggestion, yet he had neither said nor done anything without express command from the King.' If these words are taken at face value, they support the theory that no matter how much power Cromwell might have attained at court, his authority was always strictly limited by that of the king. This is supported by the language employed in many of Cromwell's surviving letters, which are littered with such phrases as 'the kinges highnes desireth you . . .', 'the kinges highnes pleasure and commandment is . . .', and 'his magestye hathe willid me to sygnyfie unto youe that his graciouse pleasur and commaundyment is . . .'.[36] In trying to forge an alliance with the emperor without the king's express command, Cromwell had overreached himself.

It was a lesson that the principal secretary had learned the hard way. Cautious and shrewd though he was, he had allowed his ambition to blind him to the reality of the situation. Perhaps his former master, Wolsey, would have got away with such an audacious move, but Henry would never allow another minister to enjoy the same level of autonomy as the fallen cardinal. The episode left Cromwell chastened and disillusioned. 'On my asking him what could have made this variation in the King's will, he said he could not imagine what spirit it was, and that at least I had given him no occasion, for the King himself was satisfied with the moderate language I had used; and he concluded that princes have spirits or properties which are hidden and unknown to all others. By which conversations Cromwell showed covertly his dissatisfaction at the strange contradictions of his master.' It was small consolation that, as Cromwell told Chapuys, the king had had an audience with the French ambassador, who 'came back from Court as mortified as I was the day before'. As Chapuys prepared to take his leave, a dejected Cromwell reflected: 'that he who trusts in the word of princes, who say and unsay things, and promises himself anything from them, is not over wise, as he had found on Tuesday last.'[37]

The whole sorry episode had not only taught Cromwell a salutary lesson about the reality of his position, it had also effected a discernible shift in his relationship with the king. True, Cromwell still enjoyed unparalleled power and influence at court, but his former buoyancy and confidence in dealing with his royal master had been replaced by a growing deference and uncertainty. He was increasingly apologetic when proffering advice to his sovereign, assuring him on one occasion: 'Thies I do not write as thinking your grace nedeth any warnyng thereof being of so highe and excellent witt prudence and long experience. But that I wold declare unto your maiestie howe I doo for my part take the thinges and as I thinke other men shuld tak them.'[38]

At the same time, there was an increasing disdain in Henry's attitude towards Cromwell. In May 1535 Chapuys had reported to the emperor that due to the sheer volume of work, Cromwell had made an uncharacteristic mistake. The king had instructed him to show the ambassador a letter that he had written to his envoy in France, but Cromwell had forgotten to do so. When he learned of this, Henry upbraided his minister as 'a fool and a man without discretion'.[39] According to one source, the king would even resort to physical intimidation in order to keep Cromwell firmly in his place. 'As for my Lord Prevye Sealle, I wold not be in his case for all that ever he hathe,' declared George Paulet during his imprisonment for slandering Cromwell in 1538, 'for the King beknaveth him twice a weke, and sometyme knocke him well aboute the pate; and yet when he hathe bene well pomeld about the hedde, and shaken up, as it were a dogge, he will come out into the great chambre, shaking of the bushe with as mery a countenaunce as thoughe he mought rule all the roste.' He added that 'the Kinges Majestie hath called my Lorde Prevye Seale villain, knave, bobbyd him aboutes the hedde, and thruste him out of the prevye chambre', but that Cromwell would 'laugh' at such treatment.[40]

There are no other reports to corroborate the notion that Henry used violence against Cromwell, and Paulet's claims may have been the ill-founded slander that they were purported to be. Nevertheless, he was well acquainted with the court, being the brother of the Lord Chamberlain, Sir William Paulet, and an associate of William FitzWilliam. He had been a regular eyewitness to some of Cromwell's dealings at court, and wryly observed: 'I, standing at the lower ende of the chambre, perceive theise matiers well ynogh, and laughe at his facion and ruffes.'[41] Moreover, Cromwell himself once confessed to Chapuys that he had been too afraid to relay an unpalatable piece of news to the king in person, so had sent him a message instead. The ambassador added: 'Cromwell sent me this word as if it were a great secret.'[42] It is not hard to imagine the increasingly irascible and paranoid Henry lashing out at his low-born minister in this way – determined, perhaps, to emphasise the gulf in their social status as a means of reinforcing his own authority.

Although he had developed a fearsome reputation himself, and had been a self-confessed 'ruffian' in his younger days, there is no hint that Cromwell ever lost his temper with the king. Of course, if he had retaliated physically, this would have been tantamount to treason, which was incentive enough to keep his cool. But the evidence suggests that Cromwell was on the whole a peaceable man. His bouts of temper were rare and, as one acquaintance noted, lasted only a 'little while'.[43] Older than many of his colleagues, and with a great deal more experience of the harshness and brutality of life, the hot-headedness of his youth had given way to a calmer, more measured outlook. He was, if not unshockable, then at least philosophical about the constant twists of fortune that accompanied life in general, and court life in particular. As Cavendish wryly observed, Cromwell had been 'set uppe on the toppe of the whele', the implication being that he might suddenly find himself at the bottom.[44]

Cromwell might have attained a greater influence at court than any of his peers, but in seeking to safeguard his position at court, it was clear that he would need to cultivate other allies besides his royal master. It may have been with this in mind that Cromwell had his secretary and confidant, Ralph Sadler, moved into the privy lodgings at court. From here, he could easily relay messages to and from his master, and generally keep his ear to the ground for any news or gossip that might prove of interest. Cromwell also used his protégé to curry favour with the king by delivering various gifts on his behalf. In January 1536, for example, Sadler reported that he had 'delivered unto his Grace your lock and opened unto him all the gins of the same, which his Grace liketh marvellously well and heartily thanked you for the same'.[45]

Sadler had continued to flourish under his master's tutelage, and by the middle of the 1530s his influence was widely recognised. It was almost certainly Sadler to whom Chapuys was referring in February 1536 as 'a secretary of his [Cromwell] who carries all the messages between the King and him'.[46] The fact that Sadler had assisted his master in the examinations of two of the most high-profile Catholic martyrs of the age, Fisher and More, brought him to the attention of the king himself. In the same year as their execution, he was appointed a clerk of the hanaper of chancery – a highly responsible post that involved the sealing of charters and patents, and issuing certain writs under the great seal. Proving equal to this task, in 1536 he was named a gentleman of the king's privy chamber, a position that propelled him to the heart of the court. He also began his parliamentary career that year, and was returned as MP for Hindon in Wiltshire thanks to Cromwell's patronage.

Cromwell had need of loyal servants such as Sadler, one of precious few men with whom he would entrust the many secrets associated with his position at court. After the humiliating episode with the king on 21 April, Cromwell had taken a leave of absence from court, but Sadler remained his eyes and ears there. He had much to report, for despite the king's apparent volte-face with regard to his wife and the Imperial alliance, his obsession with Jane Seymour was growing more intense by the day.

Jane herself was hardly a passive observer in the intrigues that now centred on her. For all her apparent placidness, she was every bit as ambitious as her brothers and had a streak of cold ruthlessness which gave her little sympathy for Anne. Almost from the moment the king had started paying her attention, she had begun sending messages to his daughter, Mary, urging her to have courage because her troubles would soon be over. With no less audacity than her arch-rival, Jane also plotted to ensnare the king for good, employing some of the same tactics that she had seen Anne put into such powerful effect. She knew that a mistress could become a queen and was determined to follow suit.

Gently rebuffing Henry's advances with a show of maidenly modesty, Jane steadfastly refused to yield her virginity. But she knew that she had to offer some encouragement, so she played the part of a woman who was constrained by propriety to give in to the passions that she secretly harboured. Thus when in April 1536 Henry sent her a purse of money with an accompanying declaration of love, Jane reverently kissed the letter before sending it back unopened, begging the king to consider that there was 'no treasure in the world that she valued as much as her honour, and on no account would she lose it, even if she were to die a thousand deaths'. She cunningly added that if her royal suitor wished to send her such a present in future, then he should wait 'for such a time as God would be pleased to send her some advantageous marriage'.[47] This drove Henry to distraction, and his attempts to win her heart grew increasingly passionate. Before long, his ardour for Jane had become so great that it was known throughout the court. In a striking repetition of history, courtiers now flocked to Mistress Seymour in the hope of advancement, just as they had to Anne. Henry appointed rooms for Jane next to his own in Greenwich Palace, and installed her brother Edward and sister-in-law Anne there so that they could act as chaperones whenever the couple met.

Still, Cromwell proceeded cautiously. Even though Jane's star appeared to be in the ascendant while Anne's was fading fast, he knew Henry well enough not to hazard his career – his life, even – on the king's notoriously fickle affections. Moreover, Anne was at her most dangerous when fighting for survival – like a deadly serpent cornered by predators. Her response to any threat had always been attack, not defence. And now she had Cromwell in her sights as her greatest adversary.

CHAPTER 12

'The Lady in the Tower'

ACCORDING TO CHAPUYS, what had made Cromwell resolve upon Anne's destruction was not the open declaration of war which the Passion Sunday sermon had constituted, but the humiliating exchange with the king and ambassador on 21 April. This had made it clear how fragile Cromwell's favour was, and how deftly Anne could still control her husband, urging him to favour a French alliance over an Imperial one. But Cromwell was not a man to act out of wounded pride alone. Although wracked with 'disapointment and anger' at the encounter with his royal master, he had 'suddenly recovered his wits, and said that the game was not entirely lost, and that he had still hopes of success.'[1] The ambassador soon learned of the game that Cromwell had in mind.

Cromwell had come to realise that an alliance with Charles V could be just as disastrous to his position as one with Francis I. The emperor hoped that his cousin Mary would inherit the throne of England, and he shrewdly observed to Chapuys that the best chance of achieving this would be to ensure Henry did not divorce Anne Boleyn: 'To make the King give up his concubine, he might marry another, whereas it is certain he could have no issue from the concubine to hinder the succession of the Princess.'[2] Perhaps it was his appreciation of this fact that motivated Cromwell to abandon his pro-Imperialist stance and work towards Anne's destruction. Much as he might favour an alliance between Henry and Charles, if Mary succeeded to the throne it would spell disaster for his career. Indeed, given the antipathy that existed between them, it might well cost him his life.

Chapuys was very clear that it was Cromwell, not the king, who was responsible for everything that happened next. He told his master that the Lord Privy Seal 'had planned and brought about the whole affair'.[3] According to his report, after suffering the 'unspeakable obstinacy of the King', Cromwell had retreated to his house at Stepney and 'taken to his bed from pure sorrow'.[4] True, it had been a mortifying experience, but Cromwell was a hard-bitten courtier who had lived through far worse than that. He was not such a sensitive soul that he would need to retreat from court to lick his wounds – particularly as it took him almost a week to 'recover'. More likely is that he used this time for an altogether darker purpose: to plot the queen's downfall. Cromwell knew that he had to construct a watertight case against her: the fact that she had failed to give Henry a son was insufficient basis for a divorce. Neither could he find some religious justification to prove her marriage to the king had been invalid. This had worked (just) for Catherine, but it would make a mockery of those tortuous divorce negotiations if the king's second marriage had been dissolved on similar grounds. Besides, an annulment was not enough: to be sure of his own survival, Cromwell had to destroy Anne and her faction totally. She had proved too many times in the past how skilful she was at wheedling her way back into the king's favour. What Cromwell needed was incontrovertible proof that she was a traitor.

The queen herself provided the perfect inspiration. Anne had always been known for her flirtatious manner, and she loved to surround herself with a coterie of male admirers. Principal among them was her own brother, George, Viscount Rochford. Thanks to the favour that his father and two sisters had enjoyed with the king, George Boleyn had been able to carve out a very lucrative career for himself at court, ever since his first appearance there at the age of just twelve. Like the rest of the Boleyns, he had become an adversary of Wolsey, but the cardinal had – too late – tried to curry favour with him when it was obvious that his grip on power was weakening. The gift that Cromwell had arranged on Wolsey's behalf from the lands of the bishopric of Winchester had not had the effect that the cardinal had hoped for, but it had paved the way for a rapprochement between Cromwell and Boleyn. The pair may have later collaborated to secure the divorce from Catherine of Aragon. Boleyn was genuinely committed to the cause of reform, and he had been active in securing the submission of the clergy. While he and Cromwell may have been aligned in policy, however, there is no evidence to suggest that there was any love lost between them.

There is no doubt that Lord Rochford enjoyed a close relationship with his sister. He was often in her presence, and they held many private meetings and conversations. The sources hint that his marriage to Jane Parker, who had been appointed a lady-in-waiting to Anne, was not a happy one, and he seemed to find far more solace in the company of his sister than of his wife. The fact that the couple had no children has cast doubts on his sexuality – or at least his fidelity. Another George Boleyn, who became Dean of Lichfield in the reign of Elizabeth I, is often said to have been their son, but the evidence for this is questionable and he may have been illegitimate. Lord Rochford's inquisition post mortem made no mention of him and instead named Rochford's sister, Mary Boleyn, as his heir. In any case, her husband's obvious preference for the company of his sister fostered in Jane a dangerous resentment that was soon to find full expression.

Among the queen's other favourites was Francis Weston. Weston had begun his court service in 1526, aged fifteen, when he had been appointed a page. His rise to favour was due as much to his natural charm and charisma as to the connections of his father, who had been a favoured courtier of Henry VII. The king had always liked to surround himself with such men, and in 1532 he had made Weston a gentleman of the privy chamber. It was not an appointment that Cromwell had approved of, for Weston had associated himself with a number of his enemies. But Weston was as popular with the ladies at court as he was with the king. Cavendish claimed that he 'wantonly lyved without feare and dreade . . . Followyng his fantzy and his wanton lust.'[5] In May 1535 the queen had admonished him for neglecting his wife and flirting with Margaret Shelton, who was then being pursued by Henry Norris. Weston promptly retorted that Norris visited the queen's chamber so often not because of Margaret, but Anne herself. He added that he himself loved someone in her household better than either his wife or Mistress Shelton. When Anne challenged him to name his inamorata, he replied 'it ys your self.' The queen had 'defyed him' and upbraided his impudence.[6] But the exchange had not been forgotten.

Another of the men who played the dangerous game of courtly love, although with rather less skill, was Mark Smeaton, a handsome young musician renowned for his beautiful singing voice. Of obscure birth, he was talent-spotted by Wolsey, who had appointed him to his choir. After the cardinal's fall, Smeaton was transferred to the Chapel Royal and soon attracted the notice of Anne Boleyn, who loved music and dancing. Anne appointed the young musician to her household, and he (perhaps misreading her flirtatious manner) seems to have developed something of a crush on his royal mistress. The queen may have been flattered by the obvious admiration of her young musician, but scorned the idea that they might converse as equals.

Anne showed rather more favour towards Sir Thomas Wyatt, the foremost poet of her husband's court. The Wyatts had long enjoyed royal favour and appointments, and were also close in geography and allegiance to the Boleyns. The queen enjoyed Sir Thomas's company not just because of his skill in poetry, but because he shared her passion for France. He had held the office of High Marshall of Calais from 1529 to 1530, during which time he had developed an interest in French verse forms. He also harboured evangelical religious views and had a reputation for loose sexual mores. Although he courted the queen's favour, Wyatt became closely acquainted with Cromwell too, who was executor to his father's will. Cromwell was said to be 'very fond of Master Wyatt', and the two men shared a close and often humorous correspondence.[7]

The same was not true of Henry Norris, who had been a favourite of the king ever since his accession and had served as groom of the stool for the past ten years. This gave him unparalleled access to his royal master, and he became the king's most intimate servant and confidant – perhaps the closest thing Henry had to a friend. Norris also had considerable control over court patronage because he could choose just the right (or wrong) moment to secure the king's signature to a grant. Although widely acknowledged as a gentle, likeable man, he did not flinch from using his position to enhance his own power at court. He therefore became the focus of a wide network of supplicants for royal favour. As such, Norris had long been a thorn in Cromwell's side because he wanted to control royal patronage himself. The nature of Norris's position as groom of the stool meant that there was little Cromwell could do to overcome this obstacle. He did, though, wrest back financial control from Norris, who as Keeper of the Privy Purse had gradually encroached upon the treasurer's responsibilities.

Although Norris had begun as the king's favourite, he soon enjoyed a similar status with Anne. He had probably been among the small body of witnesses at their wedding in January 1533, and he made no secret of his admiration for the new queen. He played the game of courtly love to perfection, showering Anne with compliments but never stepping beyond the bounds of propriety. Their friendship had a more solid basis than mere flattery, however, for Norris shared Anne's reformist religious views, and the two would often converse on such matters. This did not make them immune to disagreements, however – a fact that would have fatal consequences.

Flirtatious and intimate though they were, there is no reliable evidence to suggest that the queen's relations with her coterie of male favourites ever strayed into the realms of infidelity. She had far too much to lose to risk adultery. Besides, her ability to keep Henry at bay for the seven years of their courtship had proved that she was not lacking in self-control. But Anne had always enjoyed the game of courtly love, and now that her husband's passion for her had cooled, her need for admiration and flattery took on a desperate new edge. Cromwell knew it, and it gave him the perfect opportunity to oust the woman who had become his deadliest enemy at court. Quite when he conceived the idea of framing the queen for adultery is not clear. Indeed, he was careful to cover his tracks enough for some doubt to have been cast about his role in the controversy. But the evidence is compelling. Among all Anne's enemies at court, Cromwell had the greatest incentive to get rid of her. Neither is it any coincidence that almost all the men who would be implicated in the scandal were troublesome opponents of the king's chief minister.

Having resolved upon the means of securing Anne's downfall, Cromwell began quietly to gather evidence. It is likely that he either bribed some of the queen's ladies, or placed spies in her household. The tales they reported, most of which were innocent enough in themselves, were soon twisted into damning evidence. All this was conducted with the greatest discretion. Anne knew nothing of the horror that was about to unfold, and even the king seems to have been kept in ignorance until Cromwell judged that he had a suitably persuasive case to take to him.

Then, in the last days of April 1536, events suddenly accelerated. Cromwell returned to court after his week's absence and at once sought an audience with the king. There is no record of what passed between them, but the chief minister – perhaps with Carew and others of his faction – must have imparted his suspicions (and evidence) of the queen's infidelity. The king, whose attitude towards his wife had until now vacillated between hostility and passion, turned swiftly and irrevocably against her. At the annual chapter meeting of the Order of the Garter that took place in Greenwich the same day, he announced with great flourish that the queen's most prominent adversary, Sir Nicholas Carew, was to be elected a Knight of the Garter in preference to her brother. George Boleyn's exclusion from the most prestigious brethren of the court was a deliberate snub. That Cromwell had been behind this is suggested by the fact that his new ally was the beneficiary.

The very next day, the Lord Chancellor, Sir Thomas Audley – 'Cromwell's creature' – appointed two special commissions of oyer and terminer at Winchester.[8] This was a legal procedure for hearing and judging pleas of the crown. Although it dated back to the thirteenth century, it was rarely used and only for the most serious cases. The procedure required the setting up of courts in the counties where the crimes had allegedly taken place. It had not been made clear what the commissions had been appointed to investigate, but the fact that the courts were established in Middlesex and Kent, where Anne's infidelities were supposed to have been committed, makes it clear that this was the official investigation into her alleged crimes. The sheriff of each county was responsible for selecting the jurors, but the list of those chosen – which included the dukes of Suffolk, Norfolk, William FitzWilliam and others hostile to Anne – smacks of Cromwell's influence. Moreover, in cases of oyer and terminer, it was rare for a commission to be issued before the accused was arrested. But Cromwell wished to avoid the usual delay of about eleven days in setting up the commissions, fearing – with good reason – that if Anne knew of them, she would use the time to win back the king's affections.[9]

Armed with his commissions, Cromwell wasted no time in beginning his assault on the queen. Discreet enquiries were conducted with members of her household, and of the wider court. 'In most secret sort, certain persons of the Privy Chamber and others of [the queen's side] were examined,' it was reported. Meanwhile, Cromwell's spies continued to cajole Anne's ladies into confiding titbits of gossip. Realising that these ladies might fear the repercussions of divulging such information, they assured them 'that the King hates the Queen because she has not presented him with an heir to the realm, nor was there any prospect of her so doing'.[10] It was not long before the ladies were tempted into complicity.

On 29 April, it was reported, an apparently irritable Anne had a minor altercation with her musician, Mark Smeaton. According to her later confession, 'I found him standing in the round window in my chamber of presence. And I asked him why he was so sad, and he answered and said it was no matter.' The queen cruelly retorted: 'You may not look to have me speak to you as I should do to a nobleman, because you are an inferior person.' Knowing the truth of her words, Smeaton miserably replied, 'No, no, Madam. A look sufficeth, thus fare you well.'[11] The conversation – innocent enough in itself – was immediately reported to Cromwell, possibly by one of the queen's ladies in his pay.

Around the same time, and possibly on the same day, a row erupted between the queen and Henry Norris. The source of the dispute was the matter of who Norris, a widower, should marry. Anne's favoured candidate was her kinswoman and lady-in-waiting,

Margaret Shelton. Margaret was rumoured to have become a mistress of the king the previous year, which may have prompted Anne's eagerness for the match with Norris. When the latter proved reluctant, Anne flew into a rage and admonished him: 'You loke for ded mens showys; for yf owth came to the king but good, you wold loke to have me.' Norris quickly retorted that 'Yf he should have ony [any] soche thought he wold hys hed wer of.'[12]

Cromwell decided that, taken together, these two tiffs constituted sufficient justification for him to act. On 30 April he had Smeaton arrested and brought to his house in Stepney, where he subjected him to intensive questioning about his relationship with the queen. The Spanish Chronicle claims that when Smeaton proved reluctant to confess anything of worth, Cromwell had him tortured. 'Then he called two stout young fellows of his, and asked for a rope and a cudgel, and ordered them to put the rope, which was full of knots, around Mark's head, and twisted it with the cudgel until Mark cried out, "Sir Secretary, no more, I will tell the truth".' But when he failed to say what Cromwell wanted to hear, the latter 'ordered him a few more twists of the cord, and poor Mark, overcome by the torment, cried out, "No more, Sir, I will tell you everything that has happened." And then he confessed all.'[13]

It is likely that Cromwell had brought considerable pressure to bear upon Smeaton, who among all the men of the queen's entourage was the youngest and least experienced in the politics of the court. Moreover, Smeaton's arrest constituted Cromwell's first move against the queen, and if he failed to secure any evidence from it, then he might find himself on the wrong side of an indictment for treason. But Mark may not have taken much persuading. He was no doubt overawed by the presence of the king's chief minister and eager to say whatever would secure his release. This naive, frightened and possibly lovestruck young musician was no match for the man who had already proved himself as highly skilled in politics as he was in law. A confession soon followed. As well as admitting to having had sex with the queen, Smeaton also dutifully provided Cromwell with the names of other members of her circle with whom she had conducted illicit liaisons. Smeaton's confession may have given Cromwell everything he needed to put his plan into action, but it by no means secured the young man's liberty. Cromwell detained him at his house overnight, and the following day – one of the most momentous in English history – he had him thrown into the Tower.

According to the Spanish Chronicle, Cromwell wrote at once to the king, enclosing Mark's confession, and entrusted the task of delivering it to his nephew, Richard. When Henry opened the letter, he read:

> Your Majesty will understand that, jealous of your honour, and seeing certain things passing in your palace, I determined to investigate and discover the truth. Your Majesty will recollect that Mark has hardly been in your service four months and only has £100 salary, and yet all the Court notices his splendour, and that he has spent a large sum for these jousts, all of which has aroused suspicions in the minds of certain gentlemen, and I have examined Mark who has made the confession which I enclose to your Majesty in this letter.[14]

The King was greatly agitated on reading this, but kept his composure and ordered that everything should proceed as normal for the traditional May Day tournament, which was to be held at Greenwich Palace. Nevertheless, he immediately cancelled the trip to Calais that he and Anne had been due to embark upon directly after the tournament.

The first day of May 1536 began like any other for Queen Anne. She had not been informed of her musician's arrest, and had apparently not yet noticed his absence. Her mind was no doubt preoccupied by preparations for the tournament. It was a beautiful late spring day as Anne entered the arena with great ceremony and took her place on the royal viewing platform. The king, ever the master of dissimulation, showed no hint of his inner turmoil and apparently 'gave himself up to enjoyment'.[15] Halfway through the jousts, in which the queen's beloved brother was participating, a message was passed to Henry who, to everyone's astonishment, left the tournament in great haste, accompanied by a handful of courtiers. Everything now happened with bewildering speed. Henry Norris, who was leading one of the teams in the jousts, was told to accompany the king to London at once. As they rode towards Westminster, a horror-struck Norris was accused of committing adultery with the queen. He fiercely denied the charge, even though Henry – who still cherished some affection for his long-standing friend and servant – offered him a full pardon if he confessed. He was duly taken to the Tower, where he joined Mark Smeaton. Meanwhile, Cromwell had taken the precaution of blocking access to the king so that none of Anne's supporters could plead on her behalf – or, indeed, their own. A seasoned courtier, he knew that the only chance anyone stood of regaining favour was to petition the king in person. For the next few days, he therefore ensured that Henry was a virtual recluse, being seen only 'in the garden and in his boat at night, at which times it may become no man to prevent him'.[16]

In constructing a case against Norris, Cromwell had been assisted by the prominent courtier William FitzWilliam, Earl of Southampton. FitzWilliam's alliance with Cromwell was a fragile one. He was notoriously fickle and chose his allies by power rather than principle. As soon as they lost the former, he would abandon them. Thus, although he had been a protégé of Wolsey and benefited greatly from the connection, he had displayed no qualms about signing the House of Lords articles against the cardinal when he fell from grace. Likewise, while in theory an adherent of the traditional faith, he had thrown his weight behind the divorce and Cromwell's subsequent reforms when it was obvious how high the latter had risen in royal favour. Cromwell was well aware of FitzWilliam's failings but cared little for them. When it came to court (rather than personal) alliances, he too was governed by pragmatism rather than principle. In plotting Anne's downfall, Cromwell had realised that FitzWilliam could be of use to him because his half-sister, Lady Worcester, was a member of the queen's household and apparently felt little allegiance towards her. Consequently, she was only too happy to provide Cromwell with evidence that would raise the king's suspicions about his wife's relationship with Norris. FitzWilliam assisted in the latter's interrogation, and Norris accused the earl of tricking him into a confession.

Other arrests soon followed – including that of the queen herself, who was taken to the Tower on 2 May. According to Wriothesley's chronicle, written shortly after the event, Cromwell himself had accompanied her there, along with Norfolk and Audley.[17] Another source claims that Archbishop Cranmer joined them in this grim task. They had only just begun their interrogations when Anne interrupted them. 'Waste no more time,' she told them, 'I have never wronged the King, but I know well that he is tired of me, as he was before of the good lady Katharine.' When Cranmer protested that her 'evil courses' had been discovered, she flew into a rage and cried: 'Go to! It has all been done as I say, because the King has fallen in love, as I know, with Jane Seymour, and does not know how to get rid of me.'[18] Realising that it was futile to question her further, Cromwell and his companions retreated.

Anne was joined on the same day by her brother George, who faced charges of committing adultery with his sister the queen, an act 'most detestable against the law of God and nature also', and of conspiring to cause the king's death. The next arrest came two days later and was altogether unexpected. William Brereton was, like Norris and Weston, one of the king's personal servants, being a groom of the privy chamber. His royal ties were strengthened still further in 1529, when he married the daughter of Henry's cousin, the Earl of Worcester. But Brereton had no connection to the queen, and by the time of the other arrests he was spending most of his time at his family estates in Cheshire. The fact that he became implicated in the scandal that was unfolding at court is one of the clearest indications that Cromwell was its architect. Brereton was keenly aware of his own status and ran his affairs in a high-handed manner. He dominated the monasteries in Cheshire and had blocked Cromwell's attempts at reform in the region. He also covered up, and may even have encouraged, lawlessness among the marcher lordships where he was steward. Matters had come to a head in 1534, when Brereton had ordered the judicial murder of John ap Gruffith Eyton, his former deputy, on trumped-up charges of killing one of his retainers. Cromwell was determined to bring this troublesome subject to heel, and his plot against the queen presented him with the perfect opportunity.

Brereton's arrest on 4 May 1536 occasioned great surprise at court. As part of the group accused of adulterous relations with the queen, he was very obviously the odd one out. Not only had he never been part of Anne's circle but, aged almost fifty, he was also considerably older than the rest. Thomas Wyatt, who had been a close associate of the queen for many years, described him as 'one that least I knew'.[19] Anne herself showed no reaction to his arrival at the Tower. By contrast, she (perhaps inadvertently) implicated one of her favourites, Francis Weston, by talking of his open flirtation the previous year. The fact that she made these remarks in the hearing of Sir William Kingston, constable of the Tower, meant that they were admissible as evidence, and Weston was duly arrested on 5 May. Sir Thomas Wyatt joined him in the Tower on the same day. Chapuys was quick to report that Wyatt had been detained because of his relationship with Anne. Other sources claimed that he had been one of Anne's lovers before her accession, and that he had warned Henry not to marry her. However, all these accounts were written by anti-reformist men who had a vested interest in Wyatt's downfall.

In fact, Wyatt was not formally charged with adultery, and Cromwell had almost certainly not been responsible for his arrest, or that of Sir Richard Page who was committed to the Tower three days later. Both men had been his associates for some time, and it would hardly have been in his interests to have them implicated in the plot.[20] Wyatt himself later claimed that his imprisonment had been the result of the 'undeservyd evyll will' of the Duke of Suffolk.[21] Subsequent events bear this out. The Spanish Chronicle describes how Cromwell had managed to intercept Wyatt before he was taken to the Tower. He sent his nephew Richard to tell Wyatt to meet Cromwell in London – presumably at Stepney or Austin Friars. 'Cromwell took Master Wyatt apart, and said to him, "Master Wyatt, you well know the great love I have always borne you, and I must tell you that it would cut me to the heart if you were guilty in the matter of which I wish to speak." Then he told him all that had passed; and Master Wyatt was astounded.' He denied that he had ever wronged the king 'even in thought', and Cromwell assured him that although he would be taken to the Tower, 'he would promise to stand his friend.' His nephew then escorted Wyatt to the Tower, and upon arriving addressed the constable: 'Secretary Cromwell sends to beg you to do all honour to Master Wyatt.'[22]

There is no reason to doubt this account, for it is corroborated by the events that followed. Wyatt's father wrote to Cromwell on 11 May, thanking him for his efforts on his son's behalf and evidently believing that he would be released shortly. Wyatt was indeed released without charge in mid-June, almost certainly at Cromwell's instigation.[23] Page had to wait another month before he too was released. That both men escaped reprisal proves not just their association with Cromwell, but the extent to which he dictated the course of Anne's downfall and that of her followers.

Another courtier who looked set to be trapped in the net of the conspiracy was Sir Francis Bryan. The son of Lady Margaret Bryan, half-sister of Anne Boleyn's mother and governess of her daughter, Princess Elizabeth, he had been active in the promotion of the annulment of the king's first marriage and was therefore firmly in the Boleyn camp. He was no less favoured by Henry. Having been appointed a gentleman of the privy chamber in 1518, he had quickly become one of the king's closest companions and had gained a reputation for gambling, drinking and 'vices'. But he also had strong conservative religious convictions, and his rather wry motto was 'ja tens grace' ('I hope for salvation'). Cromwell later nicknamed him the 'Vicar of Hell'. When it became obvious that Anne was falling from favour, Bryan had attempted to distance himself from her faction by staging a well-publicised quarrel with her brother. But it was not enough to save him from implication in the scandal that now surrounded her. Shortly after the main arrests, Bryan was suddenly sent for 'upon his allegiance' to court, where he was informally interrogated by Cromwell. No charges were made and he was released shortly afterwards.

Meanwhile, the evidence that Cromwell and his fellow interrogators gathered against the remaining five men was embarrassingly weak. Mark Smeaton had been the only one to confess: all the others steadfastly denied having had any improper relations with the queen. A simple review of the dates on which they were claimed to have committed adultery proves that they were in different places to Anne on almost every occasion. Smeaton could not, as he claimed, have had sex with Anne at Greenwich on 13 May because she had been in Richmond on that day. Likewise, on at least two of the four dates cited for Anne's adulterous relations with Brereton, she had not been in the location claimed. The rest was little more than hearsay.

The evidence Cromwell had secured from the queen's ladies became more salacious after her arrest, when they could be more certain of escaping reprisals. One of the most damning testimonies was provided by Anne's own sister-in-law, Jane. Evidently rejoicing in the chance to take revenge on her husband, she not only gave lurid accounts of his incestuous relationship with the queen, but claimed that the latter had made fun of the king's declining sexual capacity in front of her ladies. Worse still, it may have been Jane who had inspired Cromwell with the idea that Anne sought more than sexual satisfaction from her lovers: together, they had plotted her husband's death. He later reflected: 'In whiche examynacions the matier appered soo evident, that besides that cryme, with the accidentes, there brake out a certain conspiracye of the kinges deathe, which extended soo farre that all we that had thexamynacion of it quaked at the daunger his grace was in.'[24]

In order to bolster such evidence, Cromwell had taken care to appoint ladies to attend Anne in the Tower who would actively spy on her there. He had also instructed the constable, Sir William Kingston, to send regular reports of her conduct. These form one of the most reliable sources for what Anne said during her imprisonment, and in particular her views about the charges against her – all of which she utterly (and convincingly) refuted. She not only protested her own innocence, but that of the men with whom she stood accused, and she seemed genuinely distressed on their behalf. Cromwell was left with virtually nothing with which to construct a case. Only one of Kingston's letters contained anything of use.

In describing Anne's arrival at the Tower, he said she had asked if she was to be placed in a dungeon. When Kingston replied that she was to have the lodgings she occupied before her coronation, she cried: 'It ys to[o] gu[de] for me,' and fell to weeping.[25] This has been taken as an admission that she had done wrong and therefore did not deserve the fine lodgings she had been given. But it was more likely to have been a hysterical outburst by a terrified woman who had fallen so suddenly and shockingly from grace.

Among Cromwell's papers was found a letter from Anne to Henry, written from the Tower four days after her arrest. Its authenticity has been called into question, partly because it is not in Anne's handwriting, and partly because the style was not in keeping with her other letters. It is a bold statement of her innocence in which she upbraids her husband for bringing her to this state. Although Anne was always outspoken with the king, she might have been expected to show more deference and humility in a letter pleading for her life. Instead, she ranted against Henry's 'unprincely and cruel usage of me', and declared that if he persisted in this 'infamous slander' then she hoped God would pardon his 'great sin'. Cromwell endorsed the letter: 'To the King from the Lady in the Tower'.[26] Whether he ever showed it to his royal master is not known. He might have judged that, inflammatory though it was, it was better to keep such a heartfelt avowal of innocence from the king.

Although the evidence against Anne was unsubstantiated, it was enough to convince the king, and that was all that mattered. Upon hearing of his wife's alleged infidelities, Henry made a show of outrage and dismay, but was suspiciously quick to believe them. While he hated to play the part of a cuckolded husband, he appreciated the convenience of the charges. His marriage to Anne had soon turned sour, and her failure to produce a son had made him as desperate to escape it as he had been his first marriage. Cromwell had cleverly presented him with a quick and relatively painless (albeit humiliating) way of doing so. But did Henry really believe the accusations against the queen? It is possible that he did. When Anne had finally given way to his sexual advances, he was said to have been shocked by the level of experience that this apparently virginal woman seemed to have. Had she – like her sister Mary – learned more than French manners at the court of Francis I? His suspicions now hardened into certainty. According to Chapuys, the king, perhaps to save face, claimed that he had been bewitched into marriage by Anne. The fact that she was alleged to have a sixth finger on one hand added weight to his claims, and the people of England needed little encouragement to believe the very worst of this hated queen.

To what extent Henry himself directed, rather than simply reacted to, the arrest of his wife and her alleged lovers has been the subject of intense debate ever since. A remark made by Cromwell to the Imperial ambassador and relayed in a letter to Charles V shortly after the controversy, has been taken to mean that the principal secretary was simply carrying out the king's orders. Cromwell told Chapuys that 'He, himself, had been authorised and commissioned by the King to prosecute and bring to an end the mistress's trial, to do which he had taken considerable trouble.'[27] It is possible that Henry had instructed Cromwell to find a means of getting rid of her – perhaps after Anne's last miscarriage in January that year. If he had, though, there is no evidence that he devised the 'Boleyn catastrophe': indeed, it seems unlikely that he would, given that he would inevitably suffer considerable humiliation as a result.[28] Even if Jane Rochford had not made it explicit, the fact that his wife had sought sexual gratification outside the marital bed did not say much for his own prowess as a lover. In fact, Cromwell's remark makes it clear that the king had instructed him to ensure that Anne's trial would achieve the hoped-for conclusion – not that he had thought up the whole affair to begin with.

The letter that Cromwell wrote to Gardiner and Wallop in France, informing them of the queen's arrest, provides further evidence that he had masterminded it. The dispatch is a blatant attempt not only to blacken Anne's character, but also to distance himself from bringing her alleged crimes to light. He reports it as a shocked bystander at court, rather than the orchestrator of the whole, and insists that everything was done at his royal master's command. 'The kinges highnes thought convenient that I should advertise you of a chance, as most detestably and abominably devised contrived, imagined, done and continued, so most happily and graciously by the ordnance of God reveled, manifested and notoriously known to all men,' he began.

Cromwell went on to describe, in horrified and sententious language, the crimes of which Anne stood accused. 'The Queen's abhomination both in incontinent living, and other offences towardes the king's highness, was so rank and common, that her ladies of her privy chamber . . . could not contain it within their breasts . . . at the last it came so plainly to the ears of some of his grace's council that with their duty to his Majesty they could not conceal it from him.' Only then, said Cromwell, were the ladies questioned – but here again, he implies that the responsibility for this had not been his alone, or even primarily. When they divulged evidence of a plot against the king's life, Cromwell and his colleagues 'on our knees gave him [God] laude and praise that he had preserved him [the king] so long from it, and now manifested the most wretched and detestable determination of the same'. The wicked conspiracy thus discovered, 'certain men [were] committed to the Tower for this cause, that is Mark Smeaton and Norris, and her brother, then was she apprehended, and conveyed to the same place, after her was sent thither for the crimes specefied, Sir Frances Weston and William Brereton.'[29]

In a rather unconvincing show of sensitivity, Cromwell pretended to flinch from disclosing any further details of the case because they were so shocking. 'I write no particularities, the things be so abhominable, that I think the like was never heard.' Even after Anne's trial, when all the lurid details had been revealed, he claimed that there was still more that had remained hidden. 'In good faith I wrote as much and as plainly of the matters that chanced here as I could desire unless I should have sent you the very confessions, which were so abhominable that a great part of them were never given in evidence but clearly kept secret.'[30]

The first trial took place at Westminster Hall on 12 May. Brereton, Norris, Smeaton and Weston were called to answer the charges against them. All except Smeaton steadfastly protested their innocence. Brereton had confided to an old schoolfriend, George

Constantine, before the trial that he was entirely blameless of the charges against him. Even at the moment of death, he continued to insist upon his innocence, prompting Constantine to declare: 'If he were gyltie, I saye therefore that he dyed worst of them all.'[31] Their protestations counted for nothing. Cromwell reported: 'Norres Weston Brereton and Markes be already condempned to deathe, uppon arraynement in Westminster hal on Friday last.'[32]

Three days later, the queen herself was tried, along with her brother George. The fact that the latter was afforded a separate trial from the other men may have been out of respect for his rank as a viscount and the queen's brother. The only formal charges that Cromwell had managed to gather against him were that on one occasion he had spent a long time in his sister's room, and on another he had claimed that the king was not Elizabeth's father. George denied both of these, and presented such a dignified, energetic and well-reasoned defence that he won the admiration of many. It was said that people on the streets offered long odds against his conviction. But he, like the others, stood no chance against what was a predetermined outcome. The day before the trial, Cromwell had confidently predicted: 'She and her brother shalbe arayned tomorowe, and wil undoubtedlie goo the same waye [as Norris et al.].'[33]

For all his pretence at prudishness, Cromwell reserved the most sensational and shocking details for the trial that he knew would attract most attention: that of the queen herself. Soon after entering the great hall of the Tower of London, which was crammed full of officials and courtiers who had come to witness the downfall of the queen, Anne was obliged to listen as the charges against her were read out. Her crime, said her accusers, was not just adultery, but incest and perversion. Driven by her 'frail and carnal lust', she had kissed her brother by 'inserting her tongue in his mouth, and he in hers', and had incited others in her entourage to yield to her 'vile provocations'.[34] So crazed was she with lust, that she had taken Henry Norris to her bed just six weeks after giving birth to Elizabeth.

As the details of her supposed crimes grew ever more explicit, Anne remained impassive. When the time came for her to speak, however, she gave 'so wise and discreet aunswers to all thinges layde against her, excusinge herselfe with her wordes so clearlie as thoughe she had never bene faultie to the same'.[35] But it did nothing to alter the resolve either of her accusers or the king himself who, upon hearing of her bravery, remarked: 'She hath a stout heart, but she shall pay for it!' Chapuys shrewdly observed that even if his wife had been found innocent, the king had already decided to abandon her.[36]

The jury knew what was expected of them, and they did not disappoint. Anne was convicted of high treason and sentenced to death. When she was escorted back to her rooms in the Tower, her courage gave way to hysteria. She told Sir William Kingston: 'I heard say the excutor was very gud, and I have a lytel neck,' before putting her hands around it and 'lawynge [laughing] hartelye'. Aghast, Sir William exclaimed that 'this lady hasse mech joy and plesure in dethe.' Even on the night before her execution, Anne was reported to have chattered and joked endlessly, telling her astonished companions that it would not be hard for her enemies to think of a nickname for her when she was dead, for they could call her 'la Royne Anne sans teste [tête]'. She then 'laughed heartily, though she knew she must die the next day'.[37]

Anne may have witnessed the five men who had been 'proven' to be her lovers being led to their place of execution on 17 May 1536. As convicted traitors, they should have met the horrific death of hanging, drawing and quartering, but their sentences had been commuted to beheading. As Smeaton was led to his execution, he stumbled back from the scaffold, which was covered with the blood of those who had been executed before him. Collecting himself, he cried: 'Masters, I pray you all pray for me, for I have deserved the death.' His words were taken as a convenient confirmation of guilt, rather than the terrified ramblings of a man who was about to meet his death.

On the same day, Cranmer declared the king's marriage to Anne invalid. He did so with some reluctance, having previously defended her to his royal master, telling him that he could not believe Anne to be guilty of the charges against her because 'I had never better opinion of woman.'[38] But he soon realised that he was swimming against the tide, and it may have been Cromwell who persuaded him to change his course or risk losing his position – or worse. The grounds for the annulment were shaky, to say the least: Henry Percy was pressured into admitting that he and Anne had been pre-contracted. It is ironic that it should be so swiftly achieved, given the years of wrangling to extract the king from his first marriage. That he should seek an annulment at all, given the queen's impending death, might seem strange. The main motivation seems to have been to render the Princess Elizabeth illegitimate, and thus remove her from the line of succession.

Anne met her own death two days later. She conducted herself with immense dignity throughout, winning great respect from the crowds that had gathered to witness the final moments of the 'Great Whore'. Cromwell himself was among them. A highly skilled executioner had been brought over from Calais and used a sword in the French fashion, rather than the traditional axe – the only mercy that Henry showed towards his estranged wife. The fact that he had sent orders for the executioner to be enlisted for this task well before his wife had even been tried proves how certain he had been of the outcome. It was worth the trouble. With a clean strike, Anne's head was severed from her body. The sombre crowd looked on aghast as her eyes and lips continued to move, as if in silent prayer, when the head was held aloft. When the spectators had finally dispersed, Anne's weeping ladies sought in vain for a coffin in which to lay their mistress's body. In one final indignity, they were compelled to use an old arrow chest, and it was in this that Henry's second queen was laid to rest in the Tower Chapel of St Peter ad Vincula.

Cromwell's triumph was complete.

CHAPTER 13

Rebellion

THE POLITICAL LANDSCAPE changed dramatically in the wake of Anne Boleyn's execution. Her family had dominated court for the past ten years, but they were replaced almost as quickly as Anne's head had been struck off. The Seymours were now in the ascendancy. Henry was betrothed to Jane the very day after his second wife had been put to death, and they were married ten days later, on 30 May 1536. The carpenters at Hampton Court and the other royal palaces now hastily set about removing the carved 'HA's and replacing them with 'HJ's.[1] Equally anxious to remove all trace of his former alliance with the executed queen, Cromwell was now full of praise for the king's new wife, claiming that Jane was 'the vetuost lady and the veriest gentlewoman that lyveth and oon that variethe asmoche from the conditions of thother as the daye variethe from the night.'[2] His reference to her virtue is interesting. Although Jane's conduct had apparently always been above reproach, Cromwell was the first person to emphasise her purity in this way. His aim was undoubtedly to hammer a final nail in Anne's coffin: praising the morals of the new queen was a certain way of condemning those of her late predecessor.

There is evidence to suggest that Cromwell also tasked his most trusted servants with blackening the name of the fallen queen. Alexander Ales, who was in London at the time of Anne's execution, was dining with members of the court when a servant of Cromwell's arrived, 'exceedingly hungry' and demanding something to eat from the landlord. The other guests immediately started questioning him about the latest news from court and whether he felt sorry for the queen. 'He answered by asking why should he be sorry for her? As she had already betrayed him [Henry] in secrecy, so now was he openly insulting her. For just as she, while the King was oppressed with heavy cares of state, was enjoying herself with others, so he, when the Queen was being beheaded, was enjoying himself with another woman.' When the shocked gathering ordered him to hold his tongue, he retorted: 'You yourselves will speedily learn from other persons the truth of what I have been saying.'[3]

It is interesting to note that the newly widowed Jane Rochford, who had been so useful to Cromwell in providing evidence against her sister-in-law, was back at court very soon after the executions. It might be expected that with her close ties to the fallen Boleyns, together with her testimony casting doubt upon the king's virility, she might never have been seen at court again. But, far from sharing in her husband's disgrace, she was now appointed a lady of the bedchamber to the new queen. This was almost certainly thanks to Cromwell's influence: he was always careful to reward those who had done him a good turn.

Meanwhile, Sir Nicholas Carew and his conservative faction attempted to push home their advantage by having the king's elder daughter, Mary (now aged twenty), restored to legitimacy. But Cromwell had no intention of letting this happen. He had successfully withheld the Imperial ambassador's attempts to bring this about for the past three years, on one occasion admonishing him that Charles V's agents were 'like hawks; they rose very high to come down on their prey with greater rapidity; and that he fancied the one object of all our exertions was to have the Princess declared heir and successor to this crown; but if so, Cromwell added, I may tell you that the thing is quite impossible.'[4] Mary symbolised not just the king's first marriage but the old religion. A staunch Roman Catholic, she despised Cromwell's reforms and fervently prayed that England would soon be returned to the papal fold. If she was made legitimate, it would at a stroke undermine everything that Cromwell had fought so hard to achieve. Besides, he no longer had any interest in furthering Carew's cause: that had served its purpose in getting rid of Anne Boleyn. Their fragile alliance collapsed soon after her execution and they were once more on opposing sides.

Cromwell must have been alarmed when Lady Mary was invited back to court by her father, who 'made much of her' and gave her 'many jewels belonging to the unjust Queen'.[5] By contrast, her half-sister Elizabeth was confined to her rooms. It was an ominous sign. But Cromwell was always quick to act when he was under threat. If the king had entertained any thoughts of restoring his elder daughter, his chief minister soon persuaded him how unwise this would be. After all, the king would not wish to appear a fool in front of Catholic Europe by backtracking on the 'Great Matter' that had wrought such turmoil in his kingdom and established him as head of its Church. Rather, Cromwell urged his royal master that Mary must be made finally to acknowledge her father's supremacy. He added a side-swipe at his rivals by persuading Henry that Carew and his supporters were to blame for encouraging Mary's stubborn refusal to submit.

At first, Mary refused to give in, determined to honour her mother's memory. The king soon lost patience with her, and ordered Cromwell to make her see reason. The pair exchanged a series of apparently cordial letters, Mary thanking the minister for his 'gentle and friendly' dispatches, assuring him that she was 'much bound unto you for the great pain and labour that you have taken for me', and that she had 'great hope in your goodness'. She ended with a pitiful plea to be forgiven for her 'evil written letter', which she excused on account of the 'rheum in my head'.[6] When Mary continued to hold firm, though, the exasperated minister dispensed with all niceties and bluntly told her that 'howe gr[eat] your discomfort is', it was no excuse for such 'full obstinacy'. He went on: 'To be plain with you, I think you the most obstinate woman that ever was,' and vowed that if she did not conform to her father's will, 'I will never think you other than the most ungrateful, unnatural, and most obstinate person living.' He added a warning that not only ought she to be 'moche ashamed' but 'likewise afrayed'.[7]

The gloves, at last, were off. Realising that this recalcitrant young woman would never listen to a man so diametrically opposed to her in every respect, Cromwell dispatched the dukes of Norfolk and Sussex to intimidate her into submission. When she continued to resist, they brutally told her that 'if she was their daughter, they would beat her and knock her head so violently against the wall that they would make it as soft as baked apples.'[8]

Stubborn and principled though she was, Mary was not entirely devoid of political awareness. She was also influenced by Ambassador Chapuys, her friend and confidant for almost seven years, who urged that her cause would be best served in the long term by sacrificing her principles now. On 15 June 1536 Mary finally, and with great reluctance, announced her submission. In a letter drafted by Cromwell and copied by Mary 'word for word', which was full of humble deference and pleas for forgiveness, she even apologised for her refusal to acknowledge her half-sister's status. 'Concerning the Princess (so, I think, I must call her yet, for I would be loth to offend), I offered at her entry to that name and honour to call her sister, but it was refused unless I would also add the other title unto it; which I denied not then more obstinately than I am now sorry for it, for that I did therein offend my most gracious father and his just laws; and now that you think it meet, I shall never call her by other name than sister.'[9] It was with some satisfaction that Cromwell reported: 'My lady Mary is also a most obedient child to the kinges highnes, and as conformable as any living faithfull subgiet canne be.'[10]

In the wake of Mary's capitulation, there did seem to be a rapprochement between her and Cromwell. It was even rumoured that the king's chief minister harboured secret plans to marry her so that his heirs might inherit the crown of England. The rumour had been started by some of the princess's household servants, who told her mother's former physician that they feared the king would force her to marry an Englishman. The physician reported this to Chapuys, who told his master: 'They even apprehend that he [Henry] intends marrying her to Master Cromwell.' The ambassador was sceptical: 'I cannot in any wise believe [it]; indeed, I take it that had the offer of her hand been made, he [Cromwell] would not accept it.' He added: 'The apprehensions and fears of the Princess' servants are, in my opinion, founded only upon the very great favour the King has shown to his Secretary ever since his return from the visit he paid her.'[11]

But two weeks later, Chapuys appeared to have changed his mind. He reported that Cromwell had had a gold ring made for the princess, upon which was carved her likeness, together with that of her father and his new queen. A Latin inscription was carved around the whole. 'Cromwell meant to make a present of it to the Princess,' the ambassador claimed, 'but the King wishes to have the honour of it himself, and Cromwell will have to find other presents.'[12] That Cromwell should have chosen a ring, rather than a more innocuous piece of jewellery, was enough to arouse Chapuys's suspicions. But the Latin inscription suggests that he intended it more as a reward for her submission than as a declaration of love because it urges Mary to show all due obedience to her father. He followed it up with another gift a month later. On 20 August Mary wrote to thank him for 'the well-favoured horse that you have given me, with a very goodly saddle, for the which I do thank you with all my heart.'[13]

There is no other reliable proof that Cromwell ever presumed so far as to countenance marriage to his sovereign's daughter. Ruthless and ambitious though he undoubtedly was, he was above all a realist. Even if he had harboured hopes of such a marriage, it is highly unlikely that the king would have sanctioned it: no matter how high he had risen at court, Cromwell was still a commoner. The fact that Henry had prevented him from even giving his daughter a gift suggests that he would hardly have welcomed the minister as a potential son-in-law. Moreover, the court had only days before been rocked by the scandal of Lord Thomas Howard's engagement to Lady Margaret Douglas. Howard, a younger brother of the Duke of Norfolk, had begun a secret courtship with Lady Margaret, the king's niece, when she served as a lady-in-waiting to his own niece, Anne Boleyn. It was unlawful for a person of royal blood to contract a marriage without the monarch's consent, so when the news had broken in early July it had caused an uproar at court. Henry had been so incensed that he had ordered a clause to be added to the 1536 Act of Succession, making it treason to 'espouse, marry or deflower being unmarried' any of the king's female relations.[14] In such a political climate, Cromwell would hardly have risked provoking his sovereign's ire by plotting to marry his daughter.

Besides, Mary herself would never have agreed to it. The pair were diametrically opposed in every way that mattered. She was a staunch Roman Catholic: he a reformist who masterminded the destruction of the monasteries and England's break from Rome; she was the daughter of Henry VIII's first queen: he had helped the king to replace her with Anne Boleyn. Thanks to Cromwell, Mary had suffered the misery and humiliation of being demoted from heir to the throne to illegitimate outcast. His antipathy towards her had been such that he had not flinched from inflicting petty and sometimes cruel punishments for what he saw as her stubborn intransigence. He had denied Mary and her mother the comfort of seeing each other before the latter's death in January 1536. The following month, he had deprived the grief-stricken Mary of the small comfort that Catherine had intended for her daughter, as Chapuys reported: 'The Princess has just sent to me to say that since Cromwell spoke with me he had sent to her, on the part of the King, for a little cross which the Queen had ordered to be taken to the said Princess after her death. I think there are not 10 crowns worth of gold in the said cross nor any jewellery, but within is a portion of the true Cross, towards which the Princess felt great devotion.'[15]

Nevertheless, according to his own account, Cromwell had worked quietly and consistently behind the scenes to restore Mary to her father's favour. In February 1536 he had assured Chapuys that he had already achieved a great deal for Mary, 'for whose service he offered to do all that was possible'. Mary herself acknowledged 'Cromwell's good intentions towards her, and that he has been, and is still, working for her welfare and the settlement of her affairs'. Such was Cromwell's sympathy for Mary, indeed, that it brought upon him the wrath of his royal master. On 1 July 1536 Chapuys reported: 'The King has been all the time furious, and Cromwell himself in some danger of his life, owing to his having communicated with me respecting the Princess' affairs, and having shown sympathy for her. Indeed, as Cromwell himself has since told me, for four or five days after that, he considered himself a dead man.' Suitably chastened, the principal secretary subsequently refrained from referring to Mary as princess in his conversations with Chapuys, and 'requested me not to use it when alluding to her'.[16] Cromwell may have exaggerated, or even invented Henry's ire for Chapuys's benefit, because all the while he had been working with his royal master to counteract any ill-feeling among the English subjects as a result of Mary's ill-treatment.

The most that could be said about Cromwell's intercession on behalf of the king's elder daughter was that he had worked hard to secure her submission. But that had been in the interests of pushing forward his reforms, rather than safeguarding Mary's own position. He might have harboured some genuine sympathy for this sickly, motherless young woman, but this had never blinded him to the harsh political realities of Henry's court. The notion that he planned to marry her remains unlikely in the extreme. But the very fact that a betrothal was rumoured is an indication of how great Cromwell's standing at court was perceived to be.

A note in Cromwell's accounts dated February 1537 suggests that he was fully aware of the rumours, and made a joke of them. A payment of fifteen pounds was made to Thomas Wriothesley, who had occasionally acted as an intermediary between Cromwell and Mary, 'because my Lord was her valentine'.[17]

If a truce had been declared with the elder of Henry's daughters, Cromwell was now called upon to attend to the younger. The annulment of her parents' marriage had rendered Elizabeth a bastard in the eyes of the law, and Cromwell set about formalising this. In the first week of July, parliament repealed the statute declaring Elizabeth the king's lawful heir, and Cromwell reported to Gardiner soon afterwards: 'The late princesse the lady Elizabethe is by parliament pronounced also Illegitimate.'[18] The precocious young girl, still two months shy of her third birthday, was quick to recognise the change in her status. 'Why Governor,' she famously demanded of Sir John Shelton, 'how happs it yesterday Lady Princess and to-day but Lady Elsabeth?'[19] Her father, who hated to be reminded of Anne Boleyn, had apparently resolved to put their daughter firmly out of his mind, as well as out of the line of succession.

But Elizabeth was not entirely devoid of supporters, and Cromwell himself seems to have had some sympathy with the motherless child. As soon as she heard that the young girl had been rendered illegitimate, her lady mistress, Lady Margaret Bryan, wrote a furious letter to the chief minister. She complained bitterly that nobody had thought to inform her of Elizabeth's new status, and that she had been left to get on with the important business of managing the poor girl's affairs without any guidance from the council. She had a point. Although Elizabeth's attendants were responsible for her upbringing, they had received regular instructions from the council on everything from how she should be served to what age she should be weaned. That Cromwell should concern himself with such matters is a testament to the control he exerted over every aspect of court business. While the upbringing of a royal heir had justified his attention, however, that of an illegitimate child did not.

But Lady Bryan was not a woman to be gainsaid. 'Now as my Lady Elizabeth is put from that degree she was in, and what degree she is at now, I know not but by hearsay,' she began. 'I know not how to order her or myself, or her women or grooms.' With more than eight years' experience in charge of the king's children, Lady Margaret cannot have been so uncertain about how to proceed. But she was determined to make a point: no matter how distasteful she might now be to her father, Elizabeth could not simply be ignored. Warming to her theme, Lady Bryan went on to complain that her young mistress had barely any clothes to wear. In the past, this need had been more than adequately supplied by the regular parcels of lavish, made-to-measure dresses and accessories sent by her mother. But this supply had now ended for ever. Lady Bryan therefore implored Cromwell: 'I beg you to be good to her and hers, and that she may have raiment, for she has neither gown nor kirtle nor petticoat, nor linen for smocks, nor kerchiefs, sleeves, rails [nightdresses], body stitchets [corsets], handkerchiefs, mufflers, nor begins [nightcaps]. All thys her Graces mostake I have dreven of as long as I can, that, be my trothe, I cannot drive it any lenger.'[20] It is hard to believe that in less than two months Elizabeth had already outgrown all her clothes. But her lady mistress was determined to make her point.

The rest of the letter contained a string of other complaints, including that Elizabeth's household had fallen into disorder. Meals were not being served in the appropriate manner, and the young girl's diet was no longer strictly supervised, so that she was even able to help herself to wine at the dinner table. Lady Bryan ended the letter on a softer note, perhaps hoping to appeal to Cromwell's empathy as a father, not just an official. 'My Lady has great pain with her teeth,' she wrote, 'which come very slowly.' She went on to praise Elizabeth's character and precociousness, saying that she was 'as toward a child and as gentle of conditions as ever I knew in my life'. She promised that if the child might be 'set abroad' (be seen in public) on special occasions, 'she shall so do as shall be to the King's honour and hers'. Lady Bryan signed off with a rather insincere apology for her 'boldness in writing thus'.[21]

Any irritation that Cromwell might have felt at having to involve himself in such petty affairs was soon set aside. With his customary efficiency, he soon resolved all the issues that Lady Bryan had raised. The records contain no further requests for clothing, which suggests that this need had been supplied. Cromwell also admonished Sir John Shelton for allowing such a breach of etiquette at mealtimes, and from thenceforth Elizabeth ate in private, as Lady Bryan had requested. That he should take such trouble at a time when there were far more pressing matters to deal with may be more than an indication of his interest in even the smallest points of detail. It is possible that Cromwell felt some sympathy for Elizabeth, and perhaps even guilt that he was largely to blame for the miserable condition in which she now found herself, having lost her mother, become estranged from her father, and apparently entirely forgotten by the rest of the court.

But Cromwell soon had more important affairs to address. Principal among them was to destroy the influence of Carew and his supporters, who were threatening to undermine his reforms – and, thereby, his position. He had William FitzWilliam and the Marquess of Exeter expelled from the council, along with other members of the conservative faction. Carew was harder to extract because of his enduring favour with the king, but Cromwell was content to play the long game. He began by gradually encroaching upon Carew's predominance in the privy chamber, appointing members of his own circle – notably Ralph Sadler, Philip Hoby, Peter Mewtis and Anthony Denny – to the positions left vacant by those men who had been implicated in Anne Boleyn's disgrace. As well as having served Cromwell in various capacities at court for some time, these men were also committed evangelicals, even radicals. Their appointment was therefore a deliberate attempt by Cromwell to surround the king with men who would promote his reforms.

The other telling characteristic of Cromwell's new appointees was their birth. Whereas their predecessors had been of noble birth or connection, their origins were not at all 'courtly'. They were, like their patron, self-made men who had risen through their own merits and hard work, rather than their blue blood. Cromwell, it seemed, was attempting to start a social revolution at court. In so doing, he infuriated Carew, Norfolk and the other leading conservatives, who already deeply resented the presence of one lowly born member of the court and were now faced with a whole army of them.

The king himself was apparently content to welcome this strange new breed of attendant into his court. But his goodwill was not inexhaustible. When Cromwell attempted to appoint another of his protégés, Richard Morison, to a privy chamber office, Henry objected. A gifted scholar, Morison had been admitted to Wolsey's foundation at Oxford, Cardinal College, and had subsequently studied at the University of Padua, where he became a dedicatee of Machiavelli and Lutheran teachings. Cromwell had spotted his potential and had enlisted him as an agent in Italy, from where he sent news reports and intelligence. Glad though he was to be in Cromwell's service, it brought him little material reward and he wrote to ask for a return to England, pleading: 'He who has saved all England from papal tyranny has promised to free Morison from the tyranny of poverty.'[22] Cromwell duly summoned him back to court in May 1536, judging that the time was right to introduce him to the king and secure a position in the privy chamber. But Henry did not like Cromwell's latest recruit. Although he was prepared to tolerate men of low birth, they must at least be good company. Morison, it seems, was not. 'I blush as long as I am at the court,' he complained to his patron.[23] Unnerved by the king's rebuff to one of his loyal servants, Cromwell eventually succeeded in persuading Henry of the young man's merits and he was admitted to the privy chamber. Cromwell's triumph was complete when he himself assumed the headship of the privy chamber three years later.

Cromwell emerged from the testing weeks that followed Anne's execution stronger than ever. 'Cromwell rules all,' observed Reginald Pole on 8 June.[24] On 18 June Anne's beleaguered father, Sir Thomas, surrendered the office of Lord Privy Seal and Cromwell inherited it two weeks later. Then, on 6 July, he was made Baron Cromwell of Wimbledon and was knighted twelve days later. Being raised to the peerage must have been a cause of great satisfaction for this blacksmith's son from Putney. No matter how much influence he had won at court, until now his lack of a title had made him vulnerable to the machinations, as well as the scorn, of his noble adversaries in the council. Now he could deal with them on a footing that was equal on paper, if not by birth. With titles came property. Although Cromwell already owned a magnificent new residence at Austin Friars, together with his property on Chancery Lane and another lodging close to the Thames, between Greenwich and Westminster,[25] in April 1536 Chapuys reported that the king had given him 'a very fine house . . . well furnished', and that the chief minister was already receiving important guests there. The ambassador reflected, with uncharacteristic good grace: 'Certainly the great services which Cromwell has hitherto rendered well deserve that, besides the title of lord, he should have also the property and domain of the place.'[26]

It seemed that Cromwell held all before him. Forgetting his earlier benevolence, Ambassador Chapuys complained that the secretary now controlled all access to the king, and that he would deliberately withhold or misinterpret messages if they did not tally with his own objectives. On 23 July he confided to Charles V that he feared 'Cromwell might not have let him [Henry] know all the urgency I had made in soliciting audiences.'[27] Cromwell also relayed verbal messages from the king to those who sought an audience, and no doubt put his own spin on them to suit his ends. So great was his power that the Spanish Chronicle claimed: 'This Cromwell had more command even than the Cardinal had had, and the gentleman [i.e. the council] obeyed him as if he were the King.'[28]

Coming so soon after his move to oust his opponents from power, Cromwell's newfound power and promotions merely served to stoke the flames of their resentment. 'The grace and favour he had with the king/Hath caused him [to] have so many enemies,' observed the author of the play about Cromwell's life.[29] There was now a growing body of conservatives at court who were determined to get rid of the man whom they regarded as the architect of all their troubles. Cromwell was well aware of their antagonism, and as ever his response was to go on the offensive. Not content with the enormous religious change he had orchestrated during the past three years, he now resolved upon even more ambitious reform.

The parliament that had opened on 8 June 1536 had little business except to pass the second Act of Succession, which recognised the rights of Queen Jane's heirs to the throne. It was followed by convocation, which by contrast was a hive of activity. Cromwell attended in person several times during the session, and his lay representative, Dr William Petre, worked with Cranmer to emphasise the validity of the royal supremacy. Meanwhile, Dr Edward Fox (now a bishop), who had led the team of scholars assigned to find the justification for the king's divorce among the scriptures, had been conducting an embassy to the Lutheran princes of Saxony with the aim of forging a religious and political alliance. Although negotiations had collapsed, they inspired a set of evangelical proposals (known as the Wittenberg Articles) which Fox presented to convocation upon his return. These had the strong backing of

Cromwell and Cranmer, but they were too radical for most of those present and met with fierce opposition.

The king did little to help matters. He had been content to support Cromwell's reforms when they had served his purpose of divorcing Catherine and marrying Anne, but he had never taken them fully to heart and still veered towards conservatism. His attempts to find a middle ground merely served to create confusion and give hope to both sides. Eventually, after much persuasion by Cromwell, he agreed to endorse ten articles of religion. These were at best mildly evangelical. To satisfy radicals such as Cromwell, they cast doubt on some of the long-cherished Catholic doctrines, such as purgatory, promoted only three out of the traditional seven sacraments as being essential for salvation, and included the words 'justification' and 'faith' in close proximity.[30] But they encouraged the use of the images and ceremonies that were synonymous with the 'old religion', and continued to assert that the body and blood of Christ were really present at the Eucharist. It may have been at the insistence of a frustrated Cromwell that a few days after the articles had been agreed convocation enacted a law that abolished a number of saints' days.

The articles were published in August 1536. They were followed by injunctions for their enforcement, which Cromwell was quick to circulate. He used these to stipulate that the clergy must enforce all convocation's decisions and 'faithfully kepe and obserue . . . all and singular Lawes & statutes of this Realme made for thabolisshing and extirpation of the busshop of Romes pretensed power and Jurisdiction within this Realme. And for thestablishment and confirmacion of the kinges Authoritie and Jurisdiction within the same, as the supreme hedd of the churche of England.' The preamble made clear the extent of Cromwell's own powers, for it referred to himself as: 'Thomas Crumwell knyght Lorde Crumwell keper of the privey Seale of our said soueraigne Lorde the king and vitzgerent [stet] to the same for and concernyng all his Jurisdiction ecclesiasticall within this Realme'.

In order to strengthen those who favoured the new religion and opposed papal authority, Cromwell put in place certain measures for the advancement of learning. Among the injunctions he issued to the clergy in 1536 was one that provided for an increased number of scholarships at schools and universities 'to thintent that lerned men maye hereafter spring the more'.[31] He even stipulated the manner in which young children should be educated in religion, urging that 'parentes Maisters and gouernours of youthe being within their cure to teache or cause to be taught their children evyn from their infancie their pater noster, tharticles of our faithe, and the x commaundementes in their mothers toong, and the same so taught shall cause the said youthe ofte to repete and undrestande.' His attention to detail is astonishing. Perhaps drawing upon his own experience of educating children, he advised curates to 'planely recite one clause of the said pater noster, articles or commaundementes one daye and a nother a nother daie till the hole be taught and lerned by Litle & Litle'. This, he claimed, would help to ensure that the children would grow into honest and industrious adults, keen to work hard in order to make their own way in the world – much as he himself had done.

In pushing forward his reforms, Cromwell seemed to be genuinely concerned to root out corruption and abuse within the Church. He had evidently seen enough evidence to the contrary during his campaign against the monasteries to inspire him to create a new Church of England that was pure and godly. He exhorted members of the clergy not to 'haunte or reasorte to any tavernes or alehouses', but rather when they found themselves at leisure they should 'reade or here somewhat of holyscripture, or shall occupie theymself with some other like honest exercise . . . Having allweys in mynde howe they ought to excelle all other in puritie of lif, and shuld be example to all other to live well and christianely.'[32] The Reformation had become more than a means to power for Cromwell: it was an expression of his personal piety and values.

Cromwell then proceeded to overstep his authority by ordering that every parish church should provide copies of the Bible in both English and Latin – even though convocation had not agreed to this. He also used much harsher language to attack the cult of saints and the use of images than had been employed by the ten articles.

The result was to inflame, rather than subdue, popular resistance to his reforms. Cromwell knew it, but was unrelenting. He complained to Chapuys of 'the great hatred which all this English priesthood, as he called them, bore him, for his having attempted to put down the tyranny of the Church and reform the Clergy'.[33] He was becoming increasingly outspoken in his criticism of the Roman Catholic Church, and on another occasion surprised the ambassador with an uncharacteristically passionate outburst: 'He began to rage against all these popes and cardinals, saying that he hoped the race would soon become extinct so that people might rid themselves of their abomination and tyranny.'[34]

Determined to stamp out any opposition, Cromwell did not flinch from using torture in order to wring confessions from those whom his spies discovered were still loyal to Rome. In September 1536 he wrote detailed instructions to his agents, Sir Gilbert Talbot and John Russell, who had reported the 'lewd communication' of the vicar of Crowle in Worcestershire. Suspecting that he might be part of a wider network of 'papists', Cromwell urged: 'Using all the wayes ye canne possibly deuise to fishe out of him whither he knowe any man mynded or disposed if he might get suche opportunytie to suche purpose not sparing for the knowleage hereof to pynche him with paynes to the declaracion of it in case good aduertisement will not serue the same.'[35] It was a time of suspicion and paranoia, but Cromwell was right to be afraid. As well as persecuting – and, it seems, torturing – known dissenters, he also strengthened his networks so that any whiff of rebellion might be quickly discovered and dealt with. The following month he wrote to Sir Thomas Butler: 'desiring you to be vigilant nowe in this queysie tyme'.[36]

At the same time, Cromwell's systematic dissolution of the smaller monastic houses was continuing. Although their inhabitants were in theory moved to another religious house or given a pension to sustain them, if they chose not to stay in the religious life then the latter was withdrawn. Neither was there enough space at other houses to accommodate all of them. Many former monks and nuns therefore found themselves destitute. In a letter written in July 1536 Chapuys painted a pitiful picture of their fate: 'It is a lamentable thing to see a legion of monks and nuns, who have been chased from their monasteries, wandering miserably hither and thither, seeking means to live, and several honest men have told me, that what with monks, nuns, and persons dependent on the monasteries suppressed, there were over 20,000 who knew not how to live.'[37]

By contrast, Cromwell was continuing to profit from the dissolution. Just as he had when undertaking his first such commission for Wolsey in the previous decade, so he upheld his strategy of promising to save certain religious houses from destruction if their prior paid him an appropriate fee. Thus, in September 1536 he wrote to the prior of St Faith's in Norfolk, pointing out that although his priory had been on the list of those that the king had chosen to suppress, it had been saved by Cromwell's 'dyllygens'. He therefore asked the prior to consider how much trouble he had gone to on his behalf, and hinted that a reward would be appreciated. The following year he wrote in a similar vein to the prior of Coxford in Norfolk, asking him to lend him forty pounds, in return for which: 'I shallbe Redy to kepe yow owtt off danger.'[38]

Aware of the increasingly vociferous complaints against such practices, and of the widespread sympathy for the monks who had lost their homes and livelihood as a result, Cromwell made a rather unconvincing attempt to present the dissolution as a consultative exercise. In a letter to an unnamed abbot, he insisted that the king had no intention of suppressing any monastery unless the inmates willingly agreed to it:

> Whereas certeyn Governours and Companies of a few Religious houses have lately made fre and voluntary surrendres, into his graces handes, his graces highnes hathe commanded me for your reposes, quytes, and for the causes specified on his graces behalff to advertise you that onlesse there had ben ofertures made by the seid howses that have resigned, his grace wolde never have receyved the same And that his maiestie entendeth not in any wise to trouble you or to devise for the Suppression of any Religious howse that standeth Except thei shall either desire of themselffes with one hoole consent to resiste and forsake the same.

He added, though, that if the inhabitants of a house did unanimously resist, 'thei shall deserve the losse of moche more then theire howses and possessions, that is the losse also of their lyves.'[39]

Resistance soon broke out into open rebellion. Its focus was not the king, but the architect of the new reforms: Cromwell. The fact that a mere commoner could wield such power, and use it to such devastating effect, fanned the flames of their discontent. A popular ballad decried 'Crim crame and riche' [Cromwell, Cranmer and Richard Rich] and prayed that 'god theym amend.'[40] Although Cranmer and Rich were also implicated, it was Cromwell upon whom the popular hatred was centred. Some rebels called for the restoration of the monasteries; others for an end to exorbitant taxes; but all united in demanding the death of Cromwell, whom they believed was solely responsible for their misery. A proclamation was issued that urged the common men in every shire to 'rise on pain of death' and 'put down the lord Cromwell, that heretic.'[41]

On 1 October 1536 Thomas Kendall, vicar of Louth in Lincolnshire, used his weekly sermon to speak out against Cromwell's agents, who were expected in the town the following day. It was rumoured that these men were planning to raid all the local churches, as well as the monasteries, seizing their treasures and laying waste to their adornments. The rumours spread like wildfire, and within days almost all of northern Lincolnshire was up in arms. It was reported that the cook of one of Cromwell's commissioners had been hanged, while another commissioner had been murdered in a particularly barbaric manner: 'Because a servant of my lord Privy Seal reproved them for the execution of the said cook they took the said servant, wrapped him in the hide of a cow newly killed and caused him to be attacked and eaten by dogs, threatening to do the like to his master.' On 7 October Chapuys reported that 'a great multitude of people rose against the King's commissioners' and that 'their numbers are reckoned by some at 10,000; by some more, by others less; but, to judge by the preparations made against them, the numbers must be very great and apparently increasing, for there is not a gentleman or man of influence whom the King has not ordered to be ready with his power.'[42]

Henry was indeed swift to act. He ordered his nobles to provide men and arms to suppress the rebellion, and dispatched the Duke of Suffolk to bring order to the county. Cromwell, meanwhile, ordered his nephew Richard to gather up arrows and other weapons from the Tower of London, and sent a consignment of men to Lincolnshire. It is a testament to the panic that had taken hold at court that Henry also recalled the Duke of Norfolk. According to Chapuys, he had been sent away from court a short time before – thanks, apparently, to Cromwell's influence. 'He has sent for the duke of Norfolk, although it was rather against the grain, for he has been somewhat angry with him at Cromwell's suggestion, and it was said that he was half banished the Court but urgent necessity has caused him to be recalled.' Although eager to regain the king's favour by throwing his weight behind the counter-attack, Norfolk was secretly sympathetic to the rebels and delighted at the damage that their uprising would do to his chief rival. Chapuys reported:

> The bishop [of Carlisle] tells me the duke does not think much of the said commotion and believes it will be easily remedied, saying that the rebels cannot exceed 5,000 men. The bishop also has sent to me to say that he never saw the duke so happy as he was today, which I attribute either to his reconciliation with the King, or to the pleasure this report itself has given him, thinking that it will be the ruin of his rival Cromwell, to whom the blame of everything is attached, and whose head the rebels demand; also that it may be the means of stopping the demolition of the churches and the change in matters of religion, which is not to his mind. It was because he declared a part of his wishes in these matters that he incurred the King's displeasure.

The wily ambassador realised, however, that Norfolk's preference for the old religion would not override his political ambitions: 'The duke was one of those whom the good lord [Lord Clinton] of whom I formerly wrote, counted as willing, when occasion required, to defend the cause of the Church, though he did not rely much upon him, considering his inconstancy.'[43]

Alarmed though he was at the reports of the uprising, Cromwell had no intention of letting his rival capitalise on it. He therefore persuaded the king that the duke should remain in Norfolk, rather than coming to court. A letter was duly dispatched to the duke's country residence, ordering him to send his son to court instead. Norfolk was furious. He railed against the king's letter, describing it as 'the most discomfortable that ever came to his hands', and protested that he could 'do no service in repressing the people here, nor come to the King when commanded'. In a pointed insult to Cromwell, he insisted that he had no desire 'to sit still like a man of law while other noblemen either come to the King or go towards his enemies. Unless he hears again by Tuesday night, will rather set forward to the enemy, though he has only 40 horses with him, than remain at home with so much shame.'[44]

The threat in Lincolnshire was swiftly dealt with, but fresh revolts soon broke out in the six northern counties, which – at the greatest distance from the court in London – had always proved the hardest to control. The ringleader, a one-eyed Yorkshire lawyer named Robert Aske, quickly amassed a huge body of supporters and one report claimed that as many as 50,000 men had taken arms against the king.[45] Before long, members of the northern nobility, most prominent among whom was Thomas, Lord Darcy, had joined the uprisings, which became known collectively as the Pilgrimage of Grace.

This was the greatest threat to his authority that Henry VIII had faced during his twenty-seven years on the throne. But it seems that the king underestimated the danger. Recalling the Duke of Norfolk at last, he ordered him to hasten to Yorkshire and crush the rebels by force. The duke, however, realised what his sovereign did not: the royal troops were significantly outnumbered by those of the rebels. He therefore negotiated a truce, promising that the king would listen to their grievances. There followed an uneasy peace, but it was very much on the rebels' terms and over the winter the north remained under their control.

Throughout the rebellion, Cromwell remained firmly at court. There was no question that he would venture north with his fellow councillors: given that he was the focus of the rebels' ire, they would not have hesitated to murder him on the spot. Even at court, Cromwell seemed to keep a low profile, and very little of his correspondence refers to the rebellion. There was just one letter to Sir Ralph Eure (or Evers), deputy constable of Scarborough Castle, in which he uses warlike language to inspire loyalty to the king. Thanking Eure for his faithful service thus far, Cromwell assured him: 'His highnes haith putt every thyng nowe in suche parfitt order [that] if thes rebelles doo contynue eny lengar in their rebellyon Doubt you not but ye shall see theym so subdued as their example shalbe fearfull to all subgiettes whilles the woorld dooith endure.' But for all its brave sentiments, this letter, written from the safe confines of Westminster, lacks conviction. Likewise, when Cromwell tried to stop rumours circulating in France that the king's forces had been weak and disloyal, and had only quelled the rebellion thanks to a dishonourable treaty, his words fell upon deaf ears.[46] Neither was Cromwell redeemed by his nephew, Richard, who had struggled to obtain the arms and men from the Tower as instructed because of sympathy for the revolt among the people of London. It was left to the warlike dukes of Norfolk and Suffolk to seize the initiative – and the glory.

As part of the truce negotiated by Norfolk, Robert Aske had been promised safe passage to London so that he might present their grievances in person to the king and seek pardon. The Spanish Chronicle describes the meeting that took place between the rebel and his sovereign. 'As soon as the King saw him he rose up, and throwing his arms around him said aloud that all might hear: "Be ye welcome my good Aske; it is my wish that here, before my Council, you ask what you desire, and I will grant it." Aske answered, "Sir, your Majesty allows yourself to be governed by a tyrant named Cromwell. Everyone knows if it had not been for him the seven thousand poor priests I have in my company would not be ruined wanderers as they are now."'[47] The king promised Aske full redress for their complaints and sent him away in good cheer. But when news reached court of renewed fighting in the north early in 1537, Henry changed his mind and had Aske seized and brought to the Tower of London for interrogation. He was convicted of high treason and taken to York, where he was hanged from the city walls.

The new rebellion had been led by Sir Francis Bigod, a well-born man who may have grown up in Wolsey's household. This time, the king's orders to quash it were successfully followed. Henry then used Bigod's betrayal as an excuse to wreak vengeance on the rebels. Forgetting his promise to listen to their grievances, he made an example of the rebels by ordering the execution of more than 200 of their members. He also had the leaders brought to London for interrogation.

When subjected to questioning, the rebels voiced wide-ranging grievances. Among their most vociferous complaints was that against the Statute of Uses, which Cromwell had forced through parliament in early 1536, and which protected the crown's feudal rights by redefining the terms on which settlements of land were made. This statute, which had wide-reaching repercussions (none of which particularly favoured the common man) had almost certainly been Cromwell's brainchild: mention of it is made in one of his remembrances the previous year.[48]

The rebels' greatest complaint, though, was about dissolution of the monasteries, and they were in no doubt who was to blame: the king's 'evil counsellors', foremost among whom was Cromwell. The extent of the hatred felt for Cromwell was remarkable. He had destroyed their beloved monasteries, deprived them of the comforting rituals and ceremonies of the old religion, and threatened – so it seemed – everything they had held dear. Lord Darcy articulated their fury during his interrogation on 19 April 1537, telling Cromwell to his face: 'It is thou that art the very original and chief causer of all this rebellion and mischief, and art likewise causer of the apprehension of us that be noble men and dost daily earnestly travail to bring us to our end and to strike off our heads, and I trust that or thou die, though thou wouldest procure all the noblemen's heads within the realm to be stricken off, yet shall there one head remain that shall strike off thy head.'[49]

In this one short speech was expressed the depth of popular anger and hatred for the king's chief minister. He, not Henry, was responsible for destroying the very fabric of England. He was a despot who struck off the head of any who dared to oppose him. And –

perhaps worst of all – he was a commoner who had risen far beyond his rightful station in life. Darcy had made this clear: there were those 'of us that be noble men' (and thus entitled to power), and there were the likes of Cromwell, who should stay in the gutter. Cromwell was, by now, well used to such jibes and would no doubt have shrugged off this latest one with no greater concern than as if batting away an irritating fly. But Darcy's last remark must have caused him a moment of cold terror, for he knew the truth of it all too well. He had seen how ruthlessly his royal master had dispatched those closest to him, whose position had seemed unassailable: Cardinal Wolsey, Sir Henry Norris, Anne Boleyn. Favour, titles and promotion counted for nothing. The king might slap you on the back one day and cut off your head the next. Cromwell knew it, perhaps better than anyone, but it made no difference: his fate was by now inextricably bound to that of his master.

Even though he had been instrumental in putting down the rebellion, the Duke of Norfolk hoped that it would succeed in one respect. He confidently anticipated that it would prove the end of Cromwell. According to Chapuys, the duke expected that the rebellion 'will ultimately work the ruin and destruction of his competitor and enemy, Cromwell'.[50] The Spanish Chronicle, however, described how Henry stood by his chief minister. 'When it was all over, the King said to Cromwell, "It seems, Cromwell, that the country does not know thee as I know thee. Whoever harms thee shall harm me."' A grateful Cromwell then knelt and kissed his sovereign's hand. That he was as high in favour with Henry as ever, despite the recent troubles, was reported by Charles V, who in February 1537 remarked that 'councillor Cromwell' was 'most in favour now and has greatest influence with his master'.[51]

full maieste', for which there could have been no other punishment. 'Seing their cankred recidive hert he [Henry] could no lesse doo then to suffer them to have his laws.'[1]

The death of the Percy brothers provided Cromwell with a further opportunity to assert royal control. The sixth earl had died with no natural heirs, and because he was in dispute with his brothers, he had left most of his estates to the crown. Cromwell made the most of this good fortune, appointing able and loyal men from the local gentry to act as deputy wardens of the east, middle and west marches. He also secured grants of pensions from the king to buy further loyalty in the border region. Sadler, meanwhile, was rewarded for his loyal service with a promotion to the position of protonotary (or chief clerk) of chancery, and took his place on the Privy Council.

Sadler's mission had no doubt been intended to undermine the authority of the Duke of Norfolk, as much as to root out continuing opposition in the north in the wake of the rebellion. Cromwell was determined that the duke should not be able to capitalise on this position of great responsibility: he had already gained too much ground over his rival as a result of the rebellion. He therefore made a show of directing Norfolk's actions there, sending him a long and detailed memo in May 1537. Anxious to prove that he was no less ruthless than the duke, despite his absence from the king's forces, Cromwell instructed him to carry out a particularly cruel and brutal punishment against the rebels' families and supporters. He ordered that the wives, mothers and sisters of the traitors should desist from cutting down and burying the bodies of their loved ones, which were displayed as a warning to other would-be traitors. He added: 'Considering, that suche a misbehaviour is not to be passed over without some convenyent punishment, his highnes requireth you . . . to trye and serche out the princypall doers and occasioners of the same, whiche oons done, and they apprehended, punishment shalbe devised for them according to the qualities of their offences.'[2]

Although on the surface Cromwell was unrelenting in punishing dissenters and driving through his reforms, in private he was suffering from increasing bouts of ill health, perhaps exacerbated by the stress of the recent events. Between February 1537 and July 1538 he received five visits from surgeons, 'doctors of physic' and apothecaries, running up considerable expense in the process. Like his royal master, he was also increasingly troubled by pain in one of his legs, no doubt aggravated by his expanding girth, and was observed to walk with a rolling, awkward gait. His accounts attest that he was eventually obliged to invest in two stools 'to set my lord's leg on'.[3]

Despite the fact that Cromwell must have been in frequent discomfort, none of his physical infirmities caused him to slacken the pace of his work. In 1538 he set about reforming the Council of the North, an administrative body set up by Edward IV as a means of exerting greater authority over that part of the kingdom. Its effectiveness had waned under the Tudors and had been no match for the overmighty northern nobles. But Cromwell realised the potential of the council as a symbol of royal power in the north, and he therefore filled it with men known to be loyal to his master. Thwarting the Duke of Norfolk's attempts to build up his own powerbase there, he ensured that the majority of the council comprised men of low birth. The king had, apparently, been convinced by Cromwell's example that he could be as well served by 'base-born' councillors as by men at the peak of society who had traditionally composed his government, both local and central. Norfolk was disgusted by the move. 'More arraunt theves and murderers be not in no Realme,' he scoffed. 'The same shall not only cause Light persounes to saye and beleve that the Kinges Highnes is fayne to Hire with Fees the moost malefactors to syt in rest, but also not to Loke uppon theire most detestable offences.' He concluded: 'Borders cannot be restrained by such mean men, but that some man of great nobility should have the rule.'[4]

Undeterred, Cromwell also reconstituted the council as a permanent institution and made sure that he maintained regular contact with each of its members. In so doing, he successfully transformed the body into an effective enforcer of royal justice and religious reform. Norfolk continued to grumble, and a bitter dispute raged between him and Cromwell for months afterwards. In the end, the king brought an end to it. He told Norfolk: 'We doubt not but you woll both conforme your owne mynde to fynde out the good order whiche we have therin determyned and cause other by your good meane to perceyve the same. For surely we woll not be bounde of a necessitie to be served there with lordes, But we wolbe served with such men what degre soever they be of as we shall appoint the same.'[5] Cromwell must have triumphed in receiving such a clear sign of his royal master's favour – which was all the sweeter because it had been at the expense of his detested rival.

He enjoyed similar success elsewhere in the kingdom. In 1536 he had paved the way for parliament to pass an 'act for laws and justice to be ministered in Wales in like forms as it is in this realm'. This reinforced the traditional union of England and Wales, which dated back to Edward I's reign, and decreed that the Welsh should now enjoy the same legal rights as their English neighbours. The old marcher lordships were replaced by five new counties, each with parliamentary representation. At the same time, an exchequer and chancery were to be established at Brecon and Denbigh. However, this new Act proved difficult to implement – not least because the king himself decided to invoke certain powers of veto that had been written into it.[6] This was a warning to Cromwell (if he needed it) that his power was very much subject to that of his royal master. But if the Act was not fully realised until several years later, Cromwell had, in the meantime, achieved greater stability and conformity in that part of the kingdom.

Meanwhile, in Ireland Lord Leonard Grey, whose loyalty to the Henrician regime seemed assured, was appointed deputy after the death of Sir William Skeffington on 31 December 1535. Grey played an active part in the Irish Reformation Parliament which, by the time it concluded in December 1537, had enacted all the major English reform legislation. It had also attainted Offaly and his supporters, who suffered traitors' deaths at Tyburn that year. At the same time, Cromwell dispatched a group of high-ranking officials to assess and correct abuses in all areas of government. He maintained a regular correspondence with them to ensure that his instructions were carried out to the letter. But, as in Wales, achieving lasting control was a considerable challenge. The Irish lords continued to dominate their principalities, and only by a series of military campaigns and negotiations was any form of order maintained.[7] This did not deter Cromwell from attempting to extend royal authority to Calais, where in 1536 he had started to introduce a series of measures to make it like any other English borough, complete with parliamentary representation.

Neither did Cromwell's grip on foreign affairs loosen during this time, no matter how pressing the need to ensure the successful progress of his domestic reforms. As in England, his favoured approach was to appoint his protégés and allies to positions of responsibility. Among them was Thomas Wyatt, who owed his life to Cromwell and had not forgotten it. In March 1537 he was appointed ambassador to the court of the Emperor Charles V – a position he was to retain for the next two and a half years. His brief was to improve relations with the emperor, which had been predictably hostile since Henry's divorce from Charles's aunt, Catherine of Aragon. In order to cement the alliance, Wyatt was also to negotiate a marriage between the king's elder daughter, Mary, and the Infante of Portugal. But the hidden agenda of his embassy – and the one that counted above all others – was to make sure that the emperor did not form a league with the French king. Although this had appeared unlikely in the immediate aftermath of Catherine's death, when Henry had successfully played each power off against the other, this strategy was wearing thin and there had been worrying signs of a rapprochement between Charles and Francis. Cromwell urged his protégé not to be misled by amicable sentiments and false promises so typical of foreign diplomacy, but to find out Charles's true intentions – or, as he put it, 'fishe out the botom of his stomake'. He added that Wyatt 'must in all these things speak with the Emperor so frankly as to be able to feel the deepness of his heart'.[8] When it seemed that Wyatt was not fulfilling his brief with the assiduity expected of him, Cromwell swiftly chastised him: 'Ye have ben hitherto somwhat slak and negligent to write unto me and aduertise me from tyme to tyme of your occurrences and successes.'[9]

Although he would soon become embroiled in attempts to protect England's position in this dangerous new world order, for the time being Cromwell had once more become preoccupied with domestic matters. If he had enjoyed only limited success in the outlying parts of the kingdom, he was determined to drive home further reform in England. In February 1537 Cromwell convened a vicegerential synod of bishops and doctors, which was held in the king's vacant parliament house in Westminster. In his opening speech (which was made in the king's name) he called for a calm, considered debate about the current religious controversies. But he had no intention of compromising. During the ensuing debate, he steered the arguments along strictly evangelical lines. After its first few meetings, the synod became more like an informal committee, the aim of which was to carry out Cromwell's designs. Apparently content that it was moving in the right direction, he left it to Cranmer and Bishop Fox to oversee the meetings and ensure that the reformers remained in the ascendancy.

Together, the three men continued to push forward the evangelical cause during the months following the northern uprising. They were conscious enough of popular opinion to do so subtly much of the time, but this did not lessen the effectiveness of their measures. Although the conservatives had achieved a qualified acceptance of the seven medieval sacraments, Cromwell, Cranmer and Fox had succeeded in emphasising the role of faith, rather than good works (or behaviour), as the principal means of attaining salvation. They had also downplayed the traditional Catholic belief in the 'real' presence during the Eucharist. Most significantly, they edited and renumbered the Ten Commandments to conform with Protestant teachings, giving greater emphasis to God's prohibition of the making and worshipping of 'graven images'. All this was encapsulated in *The Institution of a Christian Man* (more commonly known as the Bishops' Book), which was published in October 1537.

The zeal with which, by now, Cromwell had driven forward religious reforms has often been cited as proof that he harboured genuine evangelical beliefs. But his personal faith is more of a conundrum. It is equally possible that he viewed the evangelical cause as the most effective route to power, as well as a means to defeat his enemies at court, the most dangerous of whom were sworn adherents of the old religion. Moreover, there are fragments of evidence to suggest that Cromwell privately preferred the traditional faith. Among them is the fact that he arranged the marriage of Jane Cromwell to one of the staunchest Catholic families in England at the height of his reforming policies.[10] By then one of the most powerful men in the country, Cromwell could have chosen any number of husbands for his (alleged) daughter. If he was as committed a reformer as he claimed, why did he choose a sworn religious conservative?

But this evidence is at best circumstantial, and the records that attest to a growing interest in, and alignment with, reformist beliefs are more compelling. Cromwell may not have been a Lutheran, but he did adhere to some of Luther's teachings, notably the truth of the scriptures and the need for these to be readily understood by the masses. He was, however, ambivalent on the central Lutheran doctrine of justification by faith alone. By contrast, he saw much to admire in the teachings of Erasmus and other more moderate evangelical teachers, and his active patronage of the latter suggests a genuine conviction. The zeal with which he approached his religious reforms, notably the spreading of God's word in English, and the extraordinary care and detail he took over the wording of each of the related Acts, were not the actions of a cynic who was promoting these reforms purely for his own ends.

Perhaps the word that best describes Cromwell's personal faith was neither reformist nor conservative but rationalist. He preferred arguments based upon evidence and reasoning, rather than tradition or dogma. That is why he himself spent so much time studying and promoting new translations of original texts, appreciating that this was a way of stripping back centuries of false interpretation and reconnecting with the purity of the original ideas. He was a pragmatist, rather than an idealist, and his preference for moderation laid the foundations of the 'middle way' so favoured by Henry's daughter Elizabeth when she became queen.

The fact that his son Gregory harboured strong reformist beliefs when he reached maturity suggests that he had been influenced by his father's outlook, and that of his carefully appointed tutors.

Cromwell's son seems to have completed his education and training by the beginning of 1537. He had matured into a young man who was widely admired by Cromwell's allies and enemies alike. Rowland Lee, with whom Gregory had resided for a time, wrote to Cromwell on 19 January 1536 to ask for assistance now that he had to 'learn a new school, to play with pen and counters, for the King's grace's money'. Referring to his reputation as the 'hanging judge', he asked Cromwell to 'please send me my lover Mr Gregory, for though the thieves have hanged me in imagination, I trust to be even with them shortly.'[11] On 5 August the Duke of Norfolk wrote from Kenninghall Lodge in Norfolk, where Gregory was staying, to assure Cromwell that his son was in good health, 'sparing no horseflesh to run after the deer and hounds'. He could not resist taunting his rival by adding: 'I trust you will not be discontent that I now cause him to forbear his book,' but admitted: 'Be sure you shall have in him a wise quick piece.'[12] Given their long-standing antipathy, Norfolk – who was always sparing in his praise – would not have complimented Cromwell on his son if Gregory had been slow-witted, as some recent commentators have suggested. This seems to have been based upon a chance remark in a letter written in February 1541 by the merchant Richard Hilles, who claimed that Gregory was 'almost a fool'.[13] There is no evidence to suggest that Gregory was in any way mentally deficient. He may not have been as intellectually gifted as his father, and his inability to master Latin frustrated his tutors, but his letters suggest a bright, articulate and perceptive young man. The fact that he did not measure up to his father's enormous intellectual abilities is hardly justification for criticism.

By autumn 1537, Cromwell had achieved significant progress in his religious reforms. By contrast, his position at court had suffered a series of worrying setbacks. During the Pilgrimage of Grace, a group of leading magnates had formed a special war council to bring the rebels under control. This had proved so effective that it had been developed, during the spring of 1537, into a permanent new 'privy council', dominated by Cromwell's conservative opponents. Norfolk was principal among them, and this could explain the friendly overtures that Cromwell had lately been making towards him. Not only had he entrusted his son to the duke's care, but he had also helped Norfolk to obtain some lucrative former monastic property that he had set his sights on.

But any alliance between Cromwell and Norfolk was bound to be tenuous at best. Although Cromwell remained Henry's chief minister, the fact that he was not part of this powerful new council made him more dependent than ever upon the king's favour and support. Henry demonstrated his support periodically – such as when, in May that year, he allowed Cromwell to write on his behalf to his sister Margaret, Dowager Queen of Scotland. This was a great honour, and Cromwell knew it. He addressed Margaret with all due deference, assuring her: 'I shall in all thinges wherin I maye convenyently doo your grace any sted or seruice, as willingly and gladly applie myself therunto.' He also sent her some cramp rings, which were believed to cure the 'falling sickness' (epilepsy). Cromwell could not resist adding a request, though, that Margaret might inform him 'from tyme to tyme' of affairs in Scotland.[14] He was no doubt keen to maintain such a prestigious correspondence.

A further sign of royal favour was given when the king elected Cromwell to the Order of the Garter on 5 August 1537. The oldest and most senior order of chivalry, it was founded by Edward III in 1348 to honour those who had served their king with particular distinction. Highly exclusive, it consisted of the king and twenty-five knights, their spiritual home being St George's Chapel in Windsor. Each knight was required to display a banner of his arms in the chapel, along with a helmet, crest and sword. It was the highest honour that Cromwell had yet received, and he accepted this with his usual charm and grace. It was even noted in the Register of the Garter, which usually provided only a cursory account of official proceedings, that he gave thanks 'with all the eloquence he was master of (and certainly he was master of the justest)'.[15]

Great though this honour was, Cromwell knew that his position at court had become much more vulnerable. He therefore resolved upon an audacious tactic that, if it succeeded, would tie him more closely to the king. Aged seventeen and having completed his education, Gregory Cromwell was not only ripe for a career, but for marriage. And his father had his eye on the perfect candidate. Elizabeth, Lady Ughtred, was the widow of Sir Anthony Ughtred, head of one of the most prominent families in Yorkshire and renowned for their loyal service to the crown. Elizabeth's importance, though, lay not in being the widow of a distinguished nobleman, but in her own family connections: she was the sister of Queen Jane. The man who became her next husband would therefore be related to the king by marriage – a tantalising prospect, and one that Cromwell could not resist. So great a prize was she, indeed, that Cromwell may even have contemplated marrying her himself. After all, his power and wealth made him one of the most eligible bachelors at court. Although the exact date of Lady Ughtred's birth is not known, it is commonly assumed to have been between 1500 and 1505, which would have made her Cromwell's junior by fifteen or twenty years – hardly a significant gap. By contrast, she would have been exactly the same number of years older than Cromwell's son, Gregory, and it was more unusual for wives to be older than their husbands, considering that most marriages were made to beget heirs. But either Cromwell had no taste for the match or he judged that Gregory would present the more alluring prospect, because it was his son who formed the basis of his negotiations.

Quite when Cromwell conceived the idea of a match with the Seymours is not certain. Perhaps it was prompted by Lady Ughtred herself, who wrote to Cromwell on 18 March 1537 pleading her reduced circumstances and asking for his help in acquiring one of the soon-to-be-dissolved Yorkshire monasteries. 'I beg your favour that I may be the King's farmer of one of those abbeys, if they go down, the names of which I enclose herein,' she wrote. Referring to herself as a 'poor woman alone', she pleaded: 'As my late husband ever bore his heart and service to your Lordship next to the King, I am the bolder to sue herein, and will sue to no other.' As an extra persuasion, she added: 'When I was last at Court you promised me your favour.'[16] This latter remark suggests that Cromwell had started to cultivate her goodwill some months before: indeed, he had arranged for Lady Ughtred to reside for a time at Leeds Castle. It is probable that he already had the match in mind then.

But Cromwell had lived to see two of the king's wives dispatched without ceremony, and it is likely that the wily minister would have hedged his bets for a while longer – at least until there was a sign of a new royal heir. Confirmation of this came in late May 1537, when the queen's pregnancy was formally announced at court and celebrated at a mass. The king was once more transported by hope and joy, convinced that now, at last, he would have a son. 'The kinges Maieste is in as good helth, and disposition as I saw hys grace of a long season,' reported Cromwell the following month, 'and the more bicause the Quenes grace is qwick with childe god by his grace sende her good deliuerance of suche aprince long to lyve according to his Maiestes graciouse desir and the common Joye and welth of all his Realme and good feithfull subiectes.'[17] If the king's new wife succeeded where the others had failed, then alliance with her family would be an excellent move indeed. But it seems that Cromwell was prepared to take a risk by cementing such an alliance before the child was born.

A reference made by one of Elizabeth's other suitors, Sir Arthur Darcy, on 15 June suggests that rumours of the match had already begun to circulate. The Yorkshire lord told her: 'If I do tarry here in the country, I would have been glad to have had you likewise, but sure it is, as I said, that some Southern lord shall make you forget the North.'[18] Cromwell negotiated with Elizabeth's brother Edward, and an agreement was reached by July. The wedding itself took place some time between 17 July and 3 August 1537 at the Seymour family home, Wolfhall.[19]

It proved to be a successful union for all parties. It certainly strengthened Cromwell's ties with the Seymour family. On 2 September Edward Seymour wrote to express his wish that Cromwell was with him so that he should have 'the best sport with bow, hounds, and hawks'. In a postscript, he sent his commendations to his sister and brother-in-law, adding: 'and I pray God to send me by them shortly a nephew.'[20] His prayers were soon answered, for Elizabeth proved a fertile wife to Gregory, giving him a son the year after their wedding and five more children (three sons and two daughters) in the years that followed.

Elizabeth was the very model of deference to her new father-in-law, who had generously given the couple one of his houses in which to establish their new family. In October 1537 she wrote: 'I cannot render unto your lordship the manifold thanks that I have cause, not only for your great pain taken to devise for my surety and health, but also for your liberal token to me, sent by your servant Worsley [Wriothesley]; and farther, which doth comfort me most in the world, that find your lordship is contented with me, and that you will be my good lord and father the which, I trust, never to deserve other, but rather to give cause for the continuance of the same.' Cromwell had evidently been generous to his new daughter-in-law, for she went on to thank him for giving her 'choice of your own houses as others'. She ended by assuring him: 'My trust is now only in you.'[21]

No matter how high Cromwell had risen in favour as a result of this marriage, as well as his own endeavours, he remained approachable to all – common people as well as courtiers – just as he had in the early years of his career. This is perhaps something he had learned from Wolsey's example, for the cardinal had been greatly criticised for the disregard he had shown to ordinary people, as well as to the nobility. By contrast, Cromwell was particularly sympathetic to poor women and widows, and the records attest that he intervened on their behalf in numerous cases during the late 1530s. They included Elizabeth Constable, who was left destitute after being abandoned by her husband and pleaded that she was too ashamed to turn to begging or prostitution. Dame Elizabeth Burgh, meanwhile, had been delivered of a premature son in late 1537. Her father-in-law claimed that his son was not the true father, and because her husband was too weak-willed to defend her, she entreated Cromwell to prevent the boy being disinherited. Another Elizabeth, Dame Whettyl, sought Cromwell's help because her son was refusing to honour his late father's will and provide for his mother. Alice Parker, a former member of Cromwell's household staff, asked for his assistance when two other servants refused to settle their debt to her.

Cromwell also came to the rescue of Mawde Carew, the frail and almost blind old widow of the courtier Nicholas's father Sir Richard, when thieves robbed or defrauded her of her savings. She was effusive in her gratitude, vowing that she felt 'most bounden' to him, and begging God to 'prosper and continue your good lordship, for the comfort of all poor widows'.[22]

Margaret Vernon had had good cause to seek Cromwell's help when she had visited him at the Rolls House in July 1536. Little Marlow, where she had been prioress, had been closed on 27 June that year. Although a letter from one of Cromwell's agents a few days before reported that the prioress had reacted 'like a wise woman' to the dissolution, her letter to Cromwell implies that this had been an act. Cromwell did not overlook her pleas. Three months later, Margaret was appointed abbess of the major Kentish house of Malling, upon the unexplained resignation of Abbess Rede. Given that Malling was valued at more than ten times her old priory of Marlow, this constituted a significant uplift in status. It would be only temporary, however: Malling, too, was dissolved in October 1538. But Cromwell negotiated a generous pension for Margaret and her fellow nuns. Her letter to Hugh Latimer, written shortly afterwards, in which she 'desires him to thank Cromwell for his goodness', suggests that she was well satisfied.[23]

Not all the women whom Cromwell assisted were poverty-stricken. Lady Elizabeth Hungerford wrote to him in 1536, bitterly complaining about her miserable marriage. 'So am I, your most woefullest and poorest beadswoman, left in worse case than ever I was, as a prisoner alone, and continually locked in one of my lord's towers of his castle in Hungerford, as I have been these three or four years past, without comfort of any creature.' Hungerford had apparently sought Cromwell's help in securing a divorce from his wife, claiming that she had dishonoured him – a claim that she furiously denied as a 'great slander'.[24] It seems she had cause. Her husband, who was almost certainly homosexual, had ill-treated all his previous wives and seemed to delight in inflicting cruelty upon them. Lady Hungerford therefore sought Cromwell's help in fighting the injustice of her husband's treatment.

Another woman whom Cromwell helped was – somewhat surprisingly – Elizabeth, Duchess of Norfolk. Her marriage to Cromwell's rival had never been a happy one, and it had taken a sharp downturn when Norfolk had moved his mistress, Bess Holland, into the family home and sent Elizabeth to live in Hertfordshire. In her distress, she wrote to Cromwell, begging him to intervene on her behalf. There is no record of his reply, but he must have provided some assistance because the grateful duchess soon wrote again to thank him for his kindness and sent him a pair of quality carving knives as a token of her gratitude. The couple remained estranged, however, and in June 1537 Elizabeth wrote again to Cromwell, lamenting that 'he [Norfolk] hath put me away four years and a quarter this Midsummer.'[25] But there was little that the minister could do to bridge the gap between the duke and countess. Cromwell seems to have flinched from involving himself too closely in Norfolk's personal affairs, perhaps honouring their newfound alliance, and it is to his credit that he did not use it as a means of creating mischief, such as whipping up a scandal about it at court.

Nevertheless, the following year another member of the Norfolk family sought Cromwell's aid: the duke's daughter, Mary. The king had arranged her marriage to his illegitimate son, Henry Fitzroy, but on the latter's premature death in July 1536 he refused to grant her the jointure that had been assigned to her. Mary appealed first to her father, but 'he made me so short an answer, that I am more than half in despair to obtain by his suit', she confided to Cromwell. 'Alas! good my lord, you that do many deeds, help me, the poorest widow of the realm.' Shortly afterwards, she was writing to thank him for 'how painfully you daily use you in labouring to the king's majesty for my matter', which suggests he did all he could for her, whether or not he was able to obtain the jointure.[26]

Undoubtedly the most distinguished female supplicant for Cromwell's assistance was Lady Margaret Douglas, the king's niece. Although born in Scotland to Henry's elder sister Margaret and Archibald Douglas, sixth Earl of Angus, she had come to England in 1530 and had become a firm favourite with the English king, who called her 'our dearest niece'.[27] Margaret's subsequent career at court had been marked by extreme highs and lows. A shrewd politician, she had succeeded in winning favour with each of Henry's queens, whom she had served in turn. But she had been reckless in her personal life. Described by one contemporary as 'beautiful and highly esteemed', she had attracted a great deal of attention among Henry's male courtiers.[28]

When Lady Margaret had been arrested on the discovery of her secret betrothal to Thomas Howard in 1536, the king had ordered Cromwell to arrange her imprisonment at Sion Abbey. An apparently contrite Lady Margaret had written to the minister from there shortly afterwards. Denying that she had brought too many servants with her, she nevertheless agreed, according to Cromwell's orders, to dismiss any from Thomas Howard's household. She also begged him to settle the wages of those servants who had been allowed to stay with her. Conscious that Cromwell was the means by which she could regain her uncle's favour, she exclaimed: 'What cause I have to give you thanks, and how much bound am I unto you, that by your means hath gotten me, as I trust, the king's grace's favour again!' Her thanks were premature. A year later, she was declared illegitimate by the king because her father, Archibald Douglas, had divorced her mother after finding evidence of a precontract on her part. He had successfully argued that this rendered their marriage unlawful, and their daughter had been openly reputed a bastard in Scotland.[29]

These letters, and many others, can be found among Cromwell's correspondence throughout the 1530s.[30] They attest to his reputation for helping women in distress, as well as to the care and attention he gave to every plea for assistance. Although the outcome of some of the cases is not clear, the repeated expressions of thanks for his endeavours suggest that he was at least assiduous, if not always successful, on their behalf.

As autumn 1537 drew near, Cromwell was keen for his royal master to grant his full assent to the Bishops' Book. But by the time it appeared, Henry had more pressing concerns. His new wife, Jane, had recently entered her confinement. Jane's pregnancy had progressed without incident, and in the middle of September she was conveyed to Hampton Court for her lying-in. A little short of a month later, she went into labour. Henry and his courtiers waited anxiously for news as Jane's labour dragged on for two days and three nights. Finally, at about two o'clock in the morning of 12 October, came the joyous news that the queen had been safely delivered of 'the most beautiful boy that ever was seen'.[31] The king's long struggle for a male heir was over at last. Surely now, the Tudor dynasty was secure.

Cromwell wrote at once to Sir Thomas Wyatt at the Imperial court: 'It hath pleased allmyghty god of his goodnes to sende unto the Quenes grace delyvraunce of a goodly prince to the grete confort Reioysse and consolacion of the Kinges Maieste and of all us his most humble loving and obedient subiectes . . . we have veray grete cause to thancke our most benigne and graciouse creatour, who after so long expectacion hath exalced our prayours and desyres.'[32] The letter was more than a joyful conveyance of news, however. Cromwell urged Wyatt to let the emperor know straight away so that he, and the other princes of Europe, might share in his 'grete Joye and confort' – or, in other words, that he might gloat that the King of England now had a son to secure his dynasty, and was thus in a much stronger bargaining position in foreign affairs.

A lavish christening was held for the young prince three days later. Cromwell's adversary, Carew, was given a place of honour at the ceremony. Edward's birth marked the triumph of his patient support for the Seymours, and the king was only too glad to recognise the fact. But the king's happiness was marred by news that his beloved Jane had fallen gravely ill. Twelve days after giving her husband what he most desired in the world, she was dead. Having never recovered from the birth, it is likely that Jane contracted puerperal fever, a bacterial infection caused by lack of proper hygiene in the delivery room. Such illnesses were not understood at the time, however, and Cromwell was quick to blame others for her death. He told Gardiner and Lord Howard that it was 'the faulte of them that were about her which suffred her to take greate cold and to eat thinges that her fantazie in syknes called for'.[33]

'Divine Providence has mingled my joy with the bitterness of the death of her who brought me to this happiness,' Henry lamented.[34] By contrast, for all his expressed sorrow at Jane's passing, Cromwell was already planning for her successor. In a letter written just days after her death, he opined:

> Forasmoche as thoughe his Maieste is not anything disposed to mary again . . . Yet as sundry of his graces co[un]sail here have thought it mete for us to be most humble suters to his Maieste to consider the state of his realme and to enter eftsones in to an other Matrymonie in place for his highnes satisfaction convenient Soo his tendre zeale to Us his subgiettes hathe already so moche overcome his graces disposition And framed his mynde bothe to be indifferent to the thing and to thelection of any person from any parte that with deliberation shalbe thought mete for him.[35]

He then went on to note the candidates he had already shortlisted as being most suitable, and spent the next few months instructing Henry's ambassadors to make overtures to various potential foreign brides. With typical attention to detail, he even penned the speeches that they were to address to the ladies in question in order to flatter them into agreeing.[36]

For all his brisk, businesslike reaction to Jane's death, Cromwell also had genuine cause to lament her passing. His son Gregory had been the queen's brother-in-law for little over two months. He could, though, console himself with the fact that for as long as the young prince survived, the Seymours would remain a powerful force at court. It would prove an empty consolation.

CHAPTER 15

'These knaves which rule abowte the kyng'

CROMWELL MADE SURE that his family was well represented at the funeral of the late queen, which took place on the morning of 12 November in St George's Chapel, Windsor. Her sister Elizabeth naturally took a prominent place in the funeral procession, as did her new husband Gregory and his cousin Richard, both of whom carried banners. Cromwell himself was there, leading the procession of councillors and diplomats, and accompanied by the French ambassador. After the service, the mourners made their way to the castle, where they were 'sumptuously provided for'. It was all over by midday, and Cromwell – apparently eager to be back to work – returned immediately to London, where he wrote and received a flurry of letters relating to matters of state and private legal affairs.

Despite the long-awaited arrival of a Tudor prince, the year 1537 had not been a happy one for either Cromwell or his master. The king had lost the only wife whom he claimed to have truly loved. He had also become increasingly aware that the reforms that were being carried out in his name were deeply unpopular with many (if not most) of his subjects. Cromwell, meanwhile, had been outplayed by the conservative faction at court, who had forged a dangerous new coalition against him. His antipathy towards Gardiner had now boiled over into open warfare. In a letter written shortly after Queen Jane's death, Cromwell lashed out at the bishop for accusing him of not fulfilling his promises: 'Whatsoever your opinion be of me I mervayl that you knowing the wisedom of our Maister canne thinke any man hable to obteyne thinges soo at his hande.' His rivalry with Norfolk had also resumed with a new intensity, and it was with some justification that one contemporary observed:

'The Duke of Norfolk was always on bad terms with this secretary.'[1] Furthermore, no matter how defiant he might have appeared in the face of growing opposition to his evangelical reforms, the knowledge that he was by now the most hated man in England must have caused him profound unease.

Neither did the situation on the Continent give any cause for comfort. Sensing that he was being outmanoeuvred by his rivals, Charles V and Francis I, who had become increasingly aligned, Henry desperately instructed Cromwell to seek marriage alliances for himself and his daughters. This was not an easy task, for the king's marital escapades had scandalised the whole of Europe. An Italian gentleman summed up the scorn felt by many when he reflected in 1546: 'And not his first wife, but three or four more, did he not chop, change, and behead them, as his horse coveted new pasture, to satisfy the inordinate appetite of his lecherous will?'[2]

Even if his royal master was becoming a laughing stock among foreign observers, Cromwell had little choice but to accede to his orders. He duly rattled off a series of confusing and contradictory letters to his friend Philip Hoby, an enthusiastic supporter of the Protestant Reformation, who now served as the king's envoy on various diplomatic missions. He instructed Hoby to negotiate for possible marriages with the younger sister of Mary of Guise, who had recently married James V of Scotland, as well as with the Duchess of Milan and the daughter of the Duke of Lorraine. Hoby arranged for Hans Holbein to paint the portraits of some of these ladies. Henry was delighted with the likeness he received of the Duchess of Milan. The lady herself was somewhat less enraptured with the idea of marrying the English king, however, and was reputed to have sent word that if she had two heads, one should be at his disposal.

When all Cromwell's efforts to secure a suitable wife for his royal master resulted in failure, Henry ordered him to focus on his two daughters. Keen to regain the delicate balance of relations with France and the empire, Henry proposed the Duke of Orleans and the son of the King of Portugal for his elder daughter Mary. Cromwell struck up negotiations with both courts, and also seized the opportunity to stir up trouble for his rival, Gardiner, who was on an embassy to the French court. He gleefully told Chapuys that 'Henry was much annoyed with the bishop of Winchester, his ambassador in France, who had written to him about marrying the princess Mary to some Frenchman, although he knew that the king was negotiating to marry her to Dom Luiz.'[3] But Cromwell soon found himself at the receiving end of his master's ire. The French ambassador, Castillon, claimed that the minister had a 'great Spanish passion' and complained that he was favouring the Portuguese match. This prompted a furious reprimand from the king, who admonished Cromwell as 'not fit to intermeddle in the affairs of kings' and summoned Norfolk to deal in his place.[4] All Henry and Cromwell's attempts at a match proved in vain, and in July 1538 the unpalatable news reached England that a truce had been signed between Charles and Francis.

If Cromwell could not control the course of diplomatic affairs, he could at least try to prevent the spread of England's religious enemies on the Continent. There is a hint of increasing paranoia, as well as of ruthlessness, in the many dispatches he issued at this time, ordering the investigation of known and suspected dissenters abroad. Thanks to his network of informants overseas, he uncovered a 'nest of Traytours' on board a French ship that had been blown ashore off the north-east coast of England. He reported to his royal master that they had been carrying 'sediciouse and Trayterouse lettres agenst your grace directed to the bishop of Rome and to the traytour Pole'.[5] Cardinal Reginald Pole was one of the most dangerous and outspoken objectors to Cromwell's regime. A highly gifted scholar and theologian, he had royal blood coursing through his veins. He was the grandson of George, Duke of Clarence, brother of Edward IV and Richard III, and son of the formidable Margaret Pole, Countess of Salisbury, former governess of the Princess Mary and a staunch adherent of the Roman Catholic faith. Henry had sought to keep her son on side by offering him the archbishopric of York or the diocese of Winchester if he agreed to support his divorce from Catherine of Aragon. Pole had refused and had gone into self-imposed exile in France and Italy. After a brief return to England he had definitively broken with the king and urged the princes of Europe to depose him. The Pope was delighted with this faithful son of England, rewarding Pole with a cardinalship in 1537, and incited him to generate support for numerous plots and rebellions against the 'heretical' king.

Pole had thus become a thorn in Henry's side, and Cromwell made it his business to eliminate him and all his associates. He had started two years previously by cajoling him – via his agent, Thomas Starkey – to return to England so that he could satisfy the king of his loyalty. Starkey assured Pole of 'Cromwell's goodness, even though he does not know you', and promised that his return would greatly advance his family and friends.[6] But Pole refused to acquiesce, and in September 1537 Cromwell was obliged to send two more envoys, Dr Wilson and Dr Heath, to negotiate with Pole and urge him to return home to be reconciled with the king – or, more likely, be put to death on charges of treason. Cromwell's instructions were aimed at whipping up a fierce hatred and suspicion of the cardinal on the part of the envoys. He referred to Pole as 'a most Unkynde deuiser and Worker of thinges most detestable and traytorous against hys sayd Souereigne lorde' and instructed Wilson and Heath to address him in the most simple terms, making no reference to his 'vayn title' of cardinal. Further, they should 'playnely and in a Franke sorte declare unto the sayd Pole his miserable state and condytyon, and [on] thother syde the greate clemencye and benignyte that is in the Prince'. He also urged them to frighten Pole into obedience: 'advising him as moche as they maye . . . what thende is lyke to be yf he persyst in his madnes'.[7]

Perhaps not surprisingly, Pole defied the summons to England. When he continued to whip up opposition to the king among his continental allies, it was rumoured that Henry's advisers plotted to have him assassinated. Cromwell was instrumental in this, thanks to his knowledge of Italian affairs gained during his youth and the contacts he still maintained there. He issued the following thinly veiled warning: 'There maye be founde wayes ynow in Italy, to rydd a trayterous subiect. Surely let hym not thinke, but where Justice can take no place by processe of Lawe at home, some tymes she may be enforced to seke new meanes abrode.'[8]

Although Pole himself survived, the English king wreaked a terrible vengeance on his family. His brother Geoffrey was arrested in August 1538 on charges of conspiracy. Three months later, his eldest brother Henry was thrown into the Tower and executed the following January. Meanwhile, their mother had also been arrested and attainted, which meant that she lost her considerable lands and titles. She languished in the Tower for almost three years, until she was condemned to death and suffered a horrifying, botched execution. It was said that it took eleven blows of the axe before her head was finally severed from her body.

Brutal though it was, the punishment of the Pole family was at least partially justified by the danger they had constituted. The evidence suggests that Cromwell had been deeply disturbed by the extent of their conspiracy – particularly when he discovered that it included a man whom he had trusted as a loyal informant. Michael Throckmorton was an agent of Pole, but it seems he had convinced Cromwell that his true loyalty lay with King Henry. When Cromwell discovered that Throckmorton had all the while been actively involved in Pole's endless plotting, he was shocked. The anger he unleashed upon the agent seems to have been as much directed against himself for being so deceived. 'Yow have bleared myn yee [eyes] ones,' he told him: 'Your credite shall nevermore serve youe so farr, to deceyve me the second tyme.' He went on to accuse Throckmorton of having forged letters in order to trick Cromwell into thinking that he was acting on his royal master's behalf. 'Loyaltie and treason dwell seldome together,' he observed bitterly. Pole wrote to taunt him for his uncharacteristic lapse of judgement, and scorned his angry threats, saying: 'You attack me violently but in a pompous and empty fashion . . . the milder I am, the angrier you become, although you never say anything new.' This made Cromwell even more determined to regain the upper hand, and he gloated that the 'braynesick', 'witles foole' whom Throckmorton served 'shuld be the Ruyn of so gre[at] a famylie'. He also extended the same threat of assassination that he had served upon Pole and ended the letter by assuring him: 'Ye maye perchaunce be as evyll delt with in Rome itself, as ye have deserved to be in Englond . . . I have done what I may, to save youe. I must I thinke do what I can to se youe condigly punysshed.'[9]

Cromwell's ruthlessness was, like the king's, born of increasing paranoia. That he was feeling vulnerable around this time is suggested by the fact that in 1538 he took steps to secure the future of his dependants. Thomas Avery was appointed master of the hunt in Bushley Park, Worcestershire, an office that carried with it a cottage and some land. It may be significant that Cromwell was helping him to establish himself away from court. Did he fear that he could no longer protect those closest to him? This may have been why he also paved the way for his beloved son Gregory's independence. By now, Gregory was in his father's service, and being trained in both the law and statecraft. He would have spent a great deal of time with his father at court during this period. Gregory evidently proved competent because in April 1538 Cromwell decided the moment had come to secure him his first official position. The dissolution was now in full swing, and among its architect's recent acquisitions was the former Cluniac priory of St Pancras in Lewes. One of the oldest and largest monastic houses in the land, its destruction the previous year had proved an enormously symbolic event in the progress of Cromwell's reforms. He had appointed a specialist demolition team under the direction of the renowned Italian architect Giovanni Portinari, who undertook the commission with meticulous care and thoroughness. Cromwell leased out the site but retained the prior's lodgings and had them extended as a house, which became known as the Lord's Place. He would not usually have taken such care over the conversion of a monastic building, but he planned to give this one to his son and daughter-in-law.

Gregory and Elizabeth moved to Lewes in great state in April 1538, accompanied by a large retinue. Shortly afterwards, Gregory was appointed a Justice of the Peace. If there was any resentment among the local population against the son of the minister who had ordered the destruction of the jewel in Sussex's monastic crown, they were careful not to show it. Gregory wrote to his father that he and his wife had received a warm reception from the families of the neighbourhood, who had given gifts to welcome them.[10] They did not stay long, however, because the town was hit by an outbreak of plague soon after their arrival. Cromwell had heard of the outbreak and had written in some alarm to two of his servants there, instructing them to prevent the burial of any plague victims within the grounds of the house where his son and daughter-in-law were staying. Three days later, on 24 May, William Cholmeley wrote to assure him that his orders had been carried out. While most of the other inhabitants of the town would have had little choice but to stay in their homes and hope to avoid infection, Cromwell owned several other properties in the area that Gregory and Elizabeth could choose from. They moved to one called the Motte, described as a 'pretty house' four miles from Lewes, which Gregory 'likes . . . right well'. Cholmeley assured him: 'Your bakehouse, brewhouse, slaughterhouse, and pullitrie may be continued,' so that Cromwell's son and daughter-in-law would be well provided with victuals. It is an indication of the style in which Gregory and Elizabeth were now living that another nearby house, called Swanborough, was rejected because it was 'thought too little for Mr. Gregory's company'.[11]

The plague had still not abated by late June, when Gregory wrote to warn his father that the king might wish to consider visiting the town on his summer progress.[12] Gregory and Elizabeth were still living in or near Lewes when their first child – a boy – was born, later in 1538. He was named Henry, to flatter the king. A second son, Edward (after Elizabeth's nephew, the young prince), was born the following year, but it is likely that they had already left Lewes by then – or if not shortly afterwards. Their correspondence hints at a loving and harmonious relationship. When business called him to Calais in December 1539, Gregory wrote to his wife, addressing her as his 'loving bedfellow' and assuring her: 'I am, thanks be to God, in good health, trusting shortly to hear from you like news, as well of yourself as also my little boys, of whose increase and towardness be you assured I am not a little desirous to be advertised.' Cromwell was also closely involved with his grandchildren's upbringing, and his accounts for the year 1539 include a payment to the launderer at court for washing '100 dozen . . . clottes for my

Lord's issue'.[13] These 'clottes' were cloths used as an early precursor to nappies.

Delighted though Cromwell no doubt was on hearing the news of his first grandson's arrival, there was no question of visiting him. His business and political affairs had become so demanding that they would have defeated a man with less ability and capacity for hard work. And, with his enemies at court increasing on an almost daily basis, there were few men Cromwell could trust to delegate his affairs to. Although his reforms were deeply unpopular, Cromwell had by now ventured too far to retreat. He had started a revolution in government and religion that could not be undone, and his only option was to stake everything he had on its success. He therefore pushed on relentlessly with his reforms and urged the king to ever more radical measures.

In January 1538 Cromwell launched a fresh attack against all forms of idolatry, ordering that statues, roods and images be destroyed in churches and religious houses across the land. His commissioners were to scour the country for relics, shrines and other traces of the old religion. Determined to pour scorn on such adornments, he ordered his men to bring some of the more notorious examples to London so that he might show them to be fakes. Thus, the famous 'Rood of Grace' at Boxley Abbey in Kent, which comprised a 'miraculous' talking crucifix, was revealed to be a puppet, operated by 'certain engines and old wire, with old rotten sticks in the back of the same'. Cromwell's campaign rapidly got out of hand, and during the summer of 1538 an attack was launched against some of the greatest shrines in the country. The shrines of Our Lady of Walsingham and Ipswich were brought to London, along with 'divers other images . . . that were used for common pilgrimages, because the people should use noe more idolatrye unto them, and they were burnt at Chelsey by my Lord Privie Seale'.[14] This wholesale destruction of Roman Catholic shrines culminated in the dismantling of the most sacred of them all, that of St Thomas Becket at Canterbury.

It was also in this year that the Austin Friars, next to which Cromwell had made his home for almost two decades, was dissolved. Cromwell clearly did not – or could not – allow any room for sentiment in driving forward his reforms. Indeed, it may have been the behaviour of the monks there that had inspired some of his reforms in the first place. Four years earlier, a group of anonymous disaffected members of the friary had complained of various abuses, such as drinking alcohol, dining alone rather than communally, neglecting services and failing to adhere to monastic rules. Although he had apparently failed to correct these abuses, the prior, George Brown, had become a useful ally to Cromwell and had preached sermons in support of the king's divorce from Catherine of Aragon. Cromwell's reward had been to appoint him as one of the commissioners whose job it was to visit all the monastic houses in the kingdom and assess their piety and wealth prior to the dissolution. Now that Austin Friars itself had been dissolved, it is not clear what happened to Brown, but it is possible that Cromwell kept him in gainful employment as a commissioner.

With the dissolution at its height, Cromwell was becoming ever more despised. 'Noo lorde or gentilman in Englande berith love or favor to my Lorde Pryvee Seale,' alleged George Paulet during his imprisonment in 1538, 'by cause he is soo great a taker of money, for he woll speke, solicite, or doo for noo man, but all for money.'[15] If Cromwell knew that such criticism was being levelled at him – and with his considerable network of informants, it is safe to assume that he did – then it did not deter him. At the same time as his commissioners were destroying relics and shrines across the land, a new delegation from the Schmalkaldic League, a defensive alliance of Lutheran princes from north Germany, arrived at court in May 1538. Cromwell had arranged the visit, and he was heartened when his royal master expressed his desire to conclude a formal treaty or agreement with them. Cranmer and a team of theologians were entrusted to conduct the talks, but they had been well briefed by Cromwell.

Throughout this time, Cromwell had relied increasingly on his old friend Stephen Vaughan as a trusted agent on the Continent. It was probably through his influence that Vaughan was appointed Henry VIII's ambassador to the Low Countries in 1538, as well as succeeding to the governorship of the Merchant Adventurers. From then on, his role as a diplomat in Cromwell's service became ever more active, and he also undertook an increasing range of duties for the crown.

Early in September 1538 Cromwell completed a new set of vice-gerential injunctions that significantly intensified his reformist drive. These declared open war on 'pilgremages, reliques or Images or any suche superstition', and emphasised the virtue of the scriptures as 'the very lyvely worde of god, that every christen person is bounde to embrace, beleve and followe, if they loke to be saved'.[16] His instruction, two years previously, that every church should have a copy of the Bible in English had been only partially carried out. This had not been solely due to popular resistance. The king had licensed a translation known as 'Thomas Matthew's Bible', which Cranmer had first brought to Cromwell's attention in August 1537. Cromwell had duly ordered it to be distributed to churches across the country, but only 1,500 had been printed and there were almost 8,500 parishes in England. He therefore commissioned his friend Miles Coverdale to revise Matthew's Bible so that it was more scholarly. Coverdale was to work in Paris, where the printing presses were superior to any that could be found in England. Cromwell's associate, Hans Holbein, who by now had produced a number of works promoting the English Reformation, was commissioned to produce the title page. But when the book was in the final stages of production, disaster struck. One of the English team working on it was accused of heresy, and it was reported that some English bishops were campaigning at the French court to have the printing stopped. Coverdale himself informed Cromwell that some of the 2,500 finished copies had been confiscated by the Inquisition. When work ground to a halt, Cromwell wrote to the King of France, begging him to release the unfinished books so that printing could be transferred to England. Francis agreed, and the project resumed in February 1539 at Grey Friars in London, which was in Cromwell's hands. By the end of April, 3,000 copies were ready for distribution.

Cromwell was determined that this time he would succeed. He therefore ordered that 'one book of the whole Bible of the largest volume in English' should be set up in every church, 'that every man having free accesse to it by reading of the same may bothe be the more apte to understande the declaration of it att the preachars mowthe, and also the more hable to teache and instructe his wif, chuldern and famylye att home.'[17] Taking a dim view of the lack of refinement among the masses who would now have ready access to the word of God, he issued a set of injunctions to curates, urging that:

> If at any tyme by reading any doubt shall come to any of you touching the sense and meanyng of any parte thereof, That thenne not geving to moche to your owne myndes fantazies and opinions nor having thereof any open reasonyngin your open Tavernes or Alehowses, ye shall have recourse to suche lerned men as be or shal be auctorised to preache and declare the same, Soo that . . . His grace may wel perceyve that you use this most hiegh benefyte quietly and charitably every of you to the edefying of himself his wief and famylye in al thinges.[18]

Cromwell added a further instruction that every clergyman should 'keep one book or register, wherein ye shall write the day and year of every wedding, christening and burying, made within your parish for your time'.[19] This would have enormous significance for local historians of the future, who ever since that time have had cause to be extremely grateful for Cromwell's assiduity. His main concern, though, was to ensure the 'Great Bible' was distributed effectively. So committed was he to the project, that, as he admitted to the French ambassador, he had contributed 400 pounds of his own money to bring it to fruition. A further 3,000 copies were printed in England in April 1540, which meant that there were enough for every parish in the country. This in turn made God's word readily accessible to almost everyone who wished to hear it. As such, it was one of Cromwell's greatest achievements. How active he had been in bringing it to pass was still recognised a century later. The historian John Strype gave him full credit: 'It appears how instrumental Crumwel was, when the Bible was printed, to procure the setting it forth by the King's authority.'[20]

Cromwell's triumph seemed complete when the king then gave

his assent to a measure inviting the larger monasteries to surrender. Although the truth was rather more complex than this, the king was strongly motivated by the prospect of financial gain, and Cromwell no doubt set out just how considerable this could be. Henry's conscience (such as it was) was partially salved by the fact that many monks and friars had been involved in the Pilgrimage of Grace. Cromwell's envoys had already started to visit the larger houses in 1537, using the rebellion as an excuse to interrogate them closely. John Pasleu, Abbot of Whalley Abbey in Lancashire, had been executed for taking part in the rebellion, and the king had urged the Earl of Sussex to 'laye unto the charges of all the monkes there their grevous offences . . . and therwith assaye their myndes, whither they woll conforme themselfes gladly for the redubbing of their former trespaces to goo to other houses of their cote . . . or rather take capacities and soo receyve seculer habite.'[21]

Cromwell's men were also instructed to hunt down any evidence of superstitious practices among the monks and nuns, notably the keeping of relics. They soon returned stories of a host of fake relics being used to impress or intimidate the occupants of the houses. A phial of liquid believed to be the blood of Christ was proven to contain only the blood of a duck, while a bottle containing 'Our Ladies milke' was 'broken and founde but a peece of chalke'.[22] Cromwell made sure that stories such as these were well publicised in order to pour scorn on the monasteries, and thus help to justify their dissolution.

The dissolution of the larger houses was legitimised by parliament in the spring of 1539. By the end of that year, only a handful of monasteries had been left untouched by Cromwell and his commissioners. Most had been intimidated into submission, but a few had made a stand – and paid a dreadful price. The abbots of Glastonbury and Reading were attainted for refusing to surrender. That the outcome of their trial was preordained is suggested by Cromwell's order that they should be 'tryed and executyd'.[23] Devastating and unjust though the process undoubtedly was, it generated enormous wealth for the crown. Although the king promised to use his newly won gains to build many new churches and cathedrals, there is only evidence that he erected six. Instead, most of the lands from the dissolved monasteries were sold off to the nobles as a way of securing their loyalty and generating more funds.

But Cromwell did not long savour his victory, for the king was showing signs of being increasingly reticent about his reforms. There was a fundamental (and dangerous) difference between the king's stance on the religious changes and that of his minister. Although both men were keen to enforce the royal supremacy over the Church, Henry was motivated by a desire to rid England of papal authority, whereas Cromwell was more interested in advancing evangelical reform. Furthermore, while Cromwell planned to use the funds from the dissolution of the monasteries to create a permanent landed endowment for the crown, Henry preferred to sell the land in order to finance campaigns against France and Scotland. This difference would become ever more pronounced in the years to come.

In January 1538 the king had drawn up no fewer than 250 amendments to the Bishops' Book. An even clearer indication of his growing aversion to Cromwell's reforms was his invitation to Cuthbert Tunstall, the conservative Bishop of Durham, to accompany him on his progress that summer. It was a move that made Cromwell aware of just how vulnerable his position was because this progress was both more isolated and peripatetic than usual, which made it much harder for the chief minister to contact his royal master. Contemporaries were quick to grasp the significance. George Constantine, a former servant of Henry Norris, observed that Tunstall and Gardiner together presented a real threat to Cromwell's power. 'I wold not cownceill my Lorde Privey Seale to trust them to moch,' he told a confidant. 'For I dare saye this, that they will do the best they can to have hym owte, if they can se hym at an advantage.'[24]

Worse was to come. In August 1538 the Lutheran delegation wrote to Henry asking him to stipulate his views on the key issues of theological dispute, as outlined in Philipp Melanchthon's *Apologia*. They argued that this would help them to reach a conclusion more speedily. But it was the end of September when the king presented his objections, by which time the talks had already fizzled out. The

Lutherans went home in October, having achieved little. A disappointed Cromwell explained to them that although he inclined to their faith, 'as the world stood, [he] would believe even as his master the king believed'.[25] This short remark reveals much – not just about the divergence between Cromwell's faith and that of his master, but about the depth of his loyalty. No matter how strongly he might espouse the evangelical cause, this would never take priority over his service to the king. But this did not stop him trying to win Henry over to his point of view.

The king's concerns about the justice and effectiveness of Cromwell's reforms were heightened still further by an ill-advised letter from Hesse, a heartland of the evangelical German states, which was sent on 25 September. It drew the king's attention to the prevalence of Anabaptism in his country. This was a radical form of Protestantism that forbade its followers to hold office in government and advocated only loose obedience to secular authority. As such, it posed the danger of insurrection. Cromwell was swift to act. On 1 October he issued a commission to root out Anabaptists and sacramentaries (those who deny the real presence of Christ in the Eucharist). But the damage could not be undone: Henry was now convinced that his minister's evangelical reforms had created the conditions for radicals and heretics to thrive in his kingdom. The Spanish diplomat Mendoza reported meeting a 'fearful' Cromwell in September 1538, and although he knew from his compatriot Chapuys that the minister was a master of dissimulation, he believed 'that there was no reason to suppose that sentiment to be feigned'. Chapuys, meanwhile, reported that Cromwell had lately 'passed many sleepless nights, and met with a thousand reproaches and objurgations' from his royal master.[26]

Seizing the initiative, the conservative faction at court grew in strength and cohesion. Gardiner, newly returned from France, had wheedled his way into favour with Henry. Strype recounts: 'About this time Crumwel's interest was not so absolute, but Winchester sometimes got the ascendant of him with the King.'[27] Realising the danger, Cromwell went on the attack. In a ruthless and largely ill-founded campaign, he had several high-profile conservatives indicted for treason. Among them was Henry Courtenay, Marquess of Exeter. Courtenay was of royal blood, being the grandson of Edward IV and Elizabeth Woodville, whose second youngest daughter Katherine had married William Courtenay, Earl of Devon. This royal blood proved both a blessing and a curse. On the one hand, it afforded him a prominent place at court, and although his estates were in the West Country, he chose to live at the centre of royal power. Having spent most of his childhood at court, he became a close companion of the king and in 1520 was appointed to positions in both the council and privy chamber. It was in the latter that he was predominant, which set him on a collision course with Cromwell, who dominated the council. This, and their difference in birth, made the two men natural enemies. They had allied for a time in order to bring down Anne Boleyn, but as soon as she was out of the way, Cromwell had accused Courtenay (along with Carew) of promoting the Lady Mary's cause too zealously. Relations between them had reached such a nadir by 1537 that a rumour began to circulate that Courtenay had been sent to the Tower for stabbing Cromwell with a dagger.

Although Henry had believed enough of Cromwell's complaints to force Courtenay into a public display of loyalty by dispatching him to help deal with the northern insurgents the previous year, he was soon back in favour. His wife had carried the cherished Prince Edward to his christening in October 1537, and Courtenay himself had been afforded a place of honour at the ceremony. Realising the strength of the bond between Courtenay and his royal master, Cromwell changed tack. Courtenay and his circle still clung to the old religion, as did swathes of their fellow West Countrymen. Cromwell used this as the basis of an indictment against him in 1538, in which he was accused of conspiring with Reginald Pole, whose brother Geoffrey had informed on them during his interrogation at the Tower shortly before. Their co-conspirators were Sir Edward Neville and another Pole brother, Henry, Lord Montague. Together, it was claimed, this 'White Rose faction' had desired the king's death, sought to deprive him of his title as supreme head of the Church, and plotted to reclaim England for the Pope. Cromwell condemned their 'miserable wretchednes and trayterouse malice' as an 'abhominacion'.[28]

Shortly after Courtenay's incarceration, Cromwell took the precaution of having his wife, Gertrude, Marchioness of Exeter, arrested and placed in the Tower. The marchioness had been a devotee of Catherine of Aragon and her conservative religious stance was well known. Cromwell assured his royal master that, despite her intransigence, 'I shall assaye to the uttermost of my power, and never cesse tyll the botom of her stomacke may be clerely opened and disclosed, and to that shal I not be slack, to thintent that If I may pycke oute the same and be as helthy as I trust to make meself, I shall on mondaye next by mouth declare the same unto your highnes more then I could by any writing.' He added his earnest hope that 'allmyghty god shall bringe all thinges to lyght that any ungodly and untrue persons have conspired agenste your grace.'[29] Gertrude was attainted for treason in July 1539 but was later released. Her husband would not be so fortunate.

Throughout November 1538 Cromwell and his associates conducted multiple interrogations of the alleged traitors and their households. Among the evidence gathered was a record of a private conversation between Courtenay and Montague in August 1536, in which the former had confidently predicted: 'I trust ones to have a faire day upon these knaves which rule abowte the kyng; and I trust to se a mery woreld oone day.'[30] Principal among the 'knaves' to whom he had been referring was Cromwell, whom he recognised – and despised – as his deadliest enemy. Even though this had been a private conversation, it was still admissible as evidence thanks to the passing of the Treasons Act in 1534. The interrogators made much of the fact that in 1531 Courtenay and his supporters had whispered that he was heir-apparent to the throne – a claim that had prompted the king to eject him from the privy chamber that year. He had soon returned to favour, but Cromwell now used this as a means to seal his doom. He commissioned the religious radical Richard Morison, one of his favourite propagandists, to chronicle the conspiracy as *An Invective Ayenste the Great and Detestable Vice, Treason* in 1539.

The case against Courtenay and his fellow 'conspirators' was almost entirely groundless. True, they were devotees of the old religion, but there is little evidence that they were planning an armed insurrection in the west. The fact that Courtenay hardly spent any time there and so had precious few contacts among the local population was swept aside in a wave of devastatingly effective propaganda orchestrated by Cromwell. So too was the fact that, as the contemporary records prove, Courtenay harboured a genuine and enduring sense of loyalty to his sovereign. His real crime was in opposing Cromwell and his reforms. Cromwell had chosen the most apposite moment to strike. Although Henry was growing increasingly anxious about the nature and pace of reform, he was also threatened by the alliance between the kingdom's traditional adversaries, Charles V and Francis I, which might result in an invasion of 'heretic' England. Any hint of insurrection by Henry's courtiers in support of such an invasion would therefore spark great alarm. Courtenay and his associates were duly condemned at Westminster Hall on 3 December 1538, and he and Montague were beheaded on Tower Hill six days later.

Their execution was quickly followed by that of another of Cromwell's most dangerous adversaries, Sir Nicholas Carew. Like that against Courtenay and Montague, the evidence upon which the charges against him were based had been gathered from the confession of Sir Geoffrey Pole during his interrogation in the Tower in late October 1538. Carew, whose arrest came on the last day of the year, was accused of plotting with the Poles, whose royal blood and staunch papist beliefs rendered them a dangerous threat to the crown. He was tried and convicted on 14 February 1539, and beheaded on Tower Hill on 8 March. Ironically, although they had been sworn enemies for most of their lives, Carew apparently converted to Cromwell's faith at the last. According to a contemporary chronicler, he 'made a goodly confession, both of his folie and supersticious faith, geuyng God most hartie thankes that euer he came in the prison of the tower, where he first sauored the life & swetenes of Gods most holy word meaning the Bible in English'.[31]

Although he had been preoccupied with ridding the court of

some of his most deadly enemies, Cromwell had continued to take a close interest in more domestic matters. In October 1538 he had arranged for Sybil Penn to be appointed as dry nurse to Prince Edward. He also demanded regular reports on the boy's welfare from the indomitable Lady Margaret Bryan, who had transferred her services to the prince's household. When a distinguished visitor was expected at Edward's residence in Havering, Essex, in 1539, Cromwell instructed Lady Bryan to ensure that the prince was well presented. Ever one to spy an opportunity for more funds, she insisted: 'He [Edward] hath never a good jewel to set on his cap; howbeit I shall order all things for my lord's honour the best I can.' She could not resist adding that 'my lord prince's grace is in good health and merry, and his grace hath four teeth; three full out, and the fourth appeareth.' In another report, she proudly described the success of the visit: 'The minstrels played, and his grace danced and played so wantonly that he could not stand still, and was as full of pretty toys as ever I saw child in my life.'[32]

Cromwell's interest in the young prince was, of course, more than just domestic. He needed to ensure that the boy received the best possible care, given that he was the king's sole male heir. Likewise, Lady Bryan – a shrewd operator in court affairs – used her communications with the king's chief minister to further the cause of her family. They included her daughter, Elizabeth, who was the widow of Sir Nicholas Carew. His property had been confiscated on his death, and his widow had written to plead for Cromwell's assistance. He had apparently been helpful, for Lady Bryan thanked him 'for the great goodness you shew upon my poor daughter Carew, which bindeth me to owe you my true heart and faithful service while I live'.[33] His action demonstrates Cromwell's capacity to be merciful towards his enemies – or those connected with them.

Shortly after this exchange with Lady Bryan, Cromwell was again obliged to focus his attention on the continuing campaign to enforce his religious reforms in all parts of the country. The whiff of insurrection in the western counties, which had been enough to help seal Courtenay's doom, gave Cromwell the premise he needed to establish a Council of the West in March 1539. Analogous in form to the Council of the North, its aim was to bring order to the counties of Somerset, Dorset, Devon and Cornwall. The Dorset-born John Russell, first Earl of Bedford, was appointed its Lord President. Russell was the same age as Cromwell and, like him, had been in royal service for many years. His assiduity in helping to suppress the Pilgrimage of Grace in 1536 had won royal approval, although by then he was already one of Henry's closest associates. Russell's loyalty was no guarantee of success, however, and the council was dissolved a year after its inauguration.

In the same month that the Council of the West had been established, Cromwell had planned 'a device in the Parliament for the unity in religion'.[34] Aware of the likely resistance, Cromwell resolved to swell the ranks of his allies. As it stood, there were only four men who could be described as being of his party by this time. They were Thomas Cranmer, Archbishop of Canterbury, William FitzWilliam, now Lord Admiral, Thomas Wyatt and Thomas Wriothesley. His former ally Thomas Audley had proved false by casting doubt on Cromwell's loyalty to the king. Audley had been tasked with helping to collect a new tax in April 1535, which was proving extremely unpopular among Henry's subjects. Chapuys reported that on returning to London, 'he had high words with Cromwell, accusing him of being the promoter and inventor of a tax which might be the cause of most dangerous riots throughout this kingdom, and that it was advisable to put a stop to it.' But, according to this report, Cromwell retorted that 'the idea was not his but the King's, whose avarice and cupidity were well known to him [Audley].'[35] It would have been entirely out of character for Cromwell to criticise the king in this manner: even his enemies admitted that he served Henry with utter constancy and dedication. Audley's loyalty to Cromwell had been a good deal less constant, as this attempt to shift the blame suggests, and although many courtiers believed them to be allies, Cromwell had been unable to trust him from that day forward.

Although Cranmer's allegiance with Cromwell was born of genuine principles and friendship, he was not a man to sacrifice everything for the sake of his allies. His attempts to defend Anne

Boleyn to the king had been both short-lived and somewhat half-hearted. FitzWilliam, meanwhile, was one of the most notoriously fickle men at court. Wyatt's loyalty to Cromwell was strong, given that the latter had been his chief protector at court since his near fatal brush with the Anne Boleyn controversy. Their correspondence suggests that the two men struck up a genuine and trusting friendship, and Cromwell had assumed an almost fatherly affection for Wyatt, often gently chiding him for his inability to stay solvent. 'I thinke your gentil franck hert doth moche empovrishe you,' he told him on one occasion, 'whan ye have money ye are content to departe with it.' He always addressed Wyatt as 'my very loving freend'.[36] But Wyatt had only ever been grudgingly accepted by the king, so he could offer Cromwell little assistance or protection in return. More reliable – at least in theory – was Thomas Wriothesley, described as 'the most successful civil servant of his day'.[37] Although he served as a clerk under Stephen Gardiner, Wriothesley's reformist beliefs had alienated his master, and by 1538 he was providing Cromwell with inside information on the bishop's household aimed at discrediting him. Apparently sufficiently convinced of his loyalty, Cromwell had him elected to the House of Commons as a knight of the shire for Hampshire in March 1539.

But these men were hardly enough to keep the likes of Norfolk and his increasingly coherent body of supporters at bay. Cromwell therefore looked for allies closer to home. In January 1539 he had been appointed constable of Leeds Castle in Kent. His son Gregory moved to the castle that year, followed a short time later by Elizabeth. They lived at Cromwell's expense, but this was more than mere generosity on his part. He knew that residing at the castle would qualify his son for election as one of the knights of the shire for Kent in the next parliament, scheduled for April. Technically, though, Gregory should not have qualified for election because he was not yet twenty-one years old. But his father had corralled the influential Thomas Cheyney, Lord Warden of the Cinque Ports, to ensure Gregory's successful return.

For all Cromwell's careful planning, the parliament went against him – largely thanks to his royal master. He had been confident enough of Henry's favour to discuss its preparations with him. But the king proved false. Even as Cromwell was routing his enemies at court and in the provinces, his royal master was conducting a similar purge of evangelicals. On 16 November 1538 Henry had personally presided over the trial of John Lambert. The king, who was dressed in white to emphasise his purity, delivered a powerful speech defending the doctrine of transubstantiation, whereby the bread and wine become the body and blood of Christ during the Eucharist. In order to make a point, he ordered Cromwell to read out the sentence condemning Lambert. According to John Foxe: 'This vndoubtedly was the malityous and crafty subtilty of the bishoppe of Wynchester [Gardiner], whiche desired rather that the sentence should be reade by Cromewell then by anye other, so that if he should refuse to doo it, he should likewise haue incurred the like daunger.' But Cromwell refused to be goaded into saying anything that might implicate himself and, though the words must have stuck in his throat, he read out the condemnation: 'wherein was conteined the burninge of heretickes, whiche eyther spake or wrote anye thinge, or had anye bokes by them repugnaunte or disagreinge from the Papisticall churche'.[38]

On the same day that Lambert was consigned to the flames, Henry issued a proclamation defending transubstantiation and another linchpin of the conservative religion: clerical celibacy. He also banned heretical books. Then, during Holy Week and Easter 1539, the king made a show of performing traditional ceremonies, and he celebrated Ascension Day (one of the most important observances of the Roman Catholic faith) in extravagant style. There could have been no clearer signal to Cromwell and his fellow evangelicals that in pushing forward reform, they were now acting in direct opposition to the king's own wishes. One of Cromwell's critics later accused him of 'secretly and indirectly advancing one of the extremes [i.e. Lutheranism], and leaving the mean indifferent true and virtuous way, which his Majesty sought and so entirely desired'.[39]

Cromwell was on the back foot and he knew it. When an opportunity arose to undermine Norfolk, he therefore seized upon it. It was a comparatively trivial matter, but Cromwell made the best of it. A gentleman of the duke's household named Anthony Rouse had his sights set on the daughter and heiress of the late Sir Edward Inchingham, who was a ward of the king. But Norfolk's steward, Robert Holditch, abducted the girl with the intention of marrying her to his own son. Rouse appealed directly to Cromwell who, with Norfolk away in the north, was able to act in the way he judged would most annoy his rival. Concluding that the duke would have supported the actions of his steward, Cromwell decided in favour of Rouse and ordered Holditch to hand the girl over. When the duke returned and discovered what had happened, he fired off a series of furious letters. An apparently guileless Cromwell showed these letters to the king, expressing his sorrow that Norfolk 'taketh the matter so much to heart'.[40]

It was a satisfying victory, but a minor one and did nothing to turn the tide. Events now seemed to conspire rapidly against Cromwell. In April 1539 he was struck down by a fever. Overcoming his discomfort, on the 23rd he wrote to the king, excusing his absence from court: 'To my great regret sorrow and displeasure, by reason of certain excess of a fever tertian that is come upon me, I am compelled to be now absent and to forbear such mine attendance upon your Royal highness.' He explained that he had prepared to leave for court the morning before, but that 'my fit of the ague cast me down and held me in a great heat [for] aboute ten howres.'

Cromwell's frustration at being away from court at such a crucial time was obvious. 'The pain of the disease grieveth me nothing so much as that . . . I cannot be . . . present and employ my power to your grace's affairs and service as my heart desireth to do,' but he assured Henry, 'I trust so to withstand mine enemy the fever in the very begynning and before ever it shall have more hold upon me that I trust shortly to overcome it. In the meantime, I doubte not but your bounteous and benign grace of his accustumed clemency will hold me for excused, and thereof I beseech your Majesty most humbly.'[41]

No doubt Cromwell would have forced himself to attend court, despite his enfeebled state, had he not been conscious of the king's morbid fear of illness. Whenever there was the slightest chance of infection, Henry would hasten away with all speed. Cromwell could therefore only return to his presence when he was fully recovered. Henry was quick to pardon his absence from court, and although Cromwell expressed his gratitude, he was clearly desperate to return. But he was obliged to make the best of it and so conducted as much business as he could from his sickbed. He received numerous visitors and fired off a series of letters to the English ambassadors on the Continent. Determined that his adversaries should not capitalise on his absence, Cromwell also arranged for the ever faithful Ralph Sadler to represent him at court and issued him with a set of detailed instructions. He wrote again to Henry – an impressively long and coherent letter that must have taken some effort to compose – conveying every scrap of news he could gather from his home, and apologising once more for his prolonged absence. 'I am sory that I am not in the cace that I myght attende and do service to your Maiestie as my duetie and desire is,' he wrote. 'This night I have had evill rest, this is the daye of thaccesse of my fytt. If I cam [can] scape it I hope to be sone recovr[ed]. If it shal contynue then yet will I do my best to overcome it the sonest I cam [can] For I thinke the tyme very long, tyll I be better hable to serve your Maieste.'[42]

Cromwell's hopes would not be answered. His sickness lingered on for several weeks. He was forced to miss the opening of parliament on 28 April, and by 10 May he still was not well enough to sit in the Lords. His enemies had taken full advantage in the meantime. On 5 May the Lord Chancellor, Audley, delivered a speech in the Lords that reiterated the king's desire to control 'diversity of opinions'. A committee was duly established to examine doctrine. If he had been present, Cromwell would surely have fought hard to prevent this. Opening up religious issues to debate gave his opponents just the chance they had been looking for to cast doubt on the validity of his reforms, not least in the mind of their royal master. Worse was to come. On 16 May the Duke of Norfolk seized the initiative by announcing that the committee was unable to reach a decision. He then presented six questions for the house to consider – each of them arguing the case for a return to conservative religious observance. They included an orthodox understanding of the mass, whereby the bread and wine became the body and blood of Christ, and promoted the value of private masses and confession. Others condemned the practice of communion in both kinds (both the consecrated bread and wine) for the laity, criticised clerical marriage and called for the vows of chastity to be upheld. In short, the six arguments promoted a traditional view of the priesthood and unpicked some of the most significant reforms that had been achieved during the previous seven years. On 20 May Norfolk cleverly proposed that parliament be prorogued for a week so that its members could take time to consider the arguments. In truth, however, the break was to enable the duke and his allies to lobby support for their cause.

In the meantime, Henry seemed set on a policy of conciliation with the Catholic powers of Europe. Much as he exalted in the title of Supreme Head of the Church in England, the role of reformist monarch was not one that had ever sat easily with him. On 7 June he made positive overtures to Charles V by declaring two days of official mourning for Isabella, the emperor's wife and the niece of Catherine of Aragon. This sparked unease among the reformist community and prompted Franz Burchard, who had led another Lutheran delegation to England, to return home on the very same day.

The situation in Calais had also started to unravel. The English outpost was governed by Lord Lisle who, like his wife, was an ardent conservative and staunchly opposed to Cromwell's religious reforms. The two men had clashed several times in the past. In July 1537, for example, Cromwell had written a letter of sharp reproof upon hearing of 'the papisticall facion that is mayntained in that towne and by you chiefly that be of his graces counsail'. He added a side-swipe against Lisle's wife: 'It is thought against all reason that the prayers of women and there fonde flikeringes shuld move any of you to doo that thing, that shuld in any wise displease the prince and soueraign lord or offende his iust lawes.'[43] This controversy had soon blown over, but matters now came to a head as a result of Cromwell having moved some evangelical ministers there from

England in the interests of their safety.[44] They included Archbishop Cranmer's evangelical commissary John Butler, to whom Lord Lisle took particular exception. When the late Queen Jane's brother, the Earl of Hertford, had visited Calais earlier in the year 1539 on the premise of inspecting the defences, Lisle had seized the opportunity to voice his displeasure. Hertford, who had been content enough to align himself with Cromwell when seeking to place his sister on the throne, felt no loyalty towards him and soon spread the news throughout the court.

Although he was still at home convalescing, Cromwell soon heard the rumours and was alarmed enough to write at once to Lisle, on 6 May, asking him to look into the matter. But while Cromwell had envisaged a discreet, local investigation, Lisle had other ideas. The deputy was evidently well informed of developments in parliament because he took the bold step of rounding up the reformists and sending them to London for interrogation. This was little short of a witch hunt. Incensed, Cromwell demanded that Lisle halt the exodus immediately. But the deputy chose to ignore his instructions. That he was confident in doing so is an indication of how far Cromwell had fallen – and how fast. Just a few months before, his word had been as good as the king's and no man had dared oppose him. Now even the deputy of an English outpost could ignore his direct order as if it had been issued by a junior clerk.

Cromwell's supporters suffered a similarly dramatic loss of influence. When Thomas Broke, one of the members of parliament for Calais, made an impassioned speech against the Six Articles on 12 June, he joined the others from that city who were under investigation. By now, Cromwell had recovered enough to join the parliament when it reconvened on 30 May. He wasted no time in trying to turn the tide back in favour of reform. It is a sign of his tenacity and skill in the face of opposition that he was able to secure assent for the contentious Statute of Proclamations, which gave decrees issued by the king or council the same legal status as an Act of parliament. This removed the often frustrating wait for important decisions to be ratified by parliament, and meant that policy could be forged much more quickly. Cromwell no doubt had in mind further religious reforms when forcing through this statute, which suggests that he was confident of wresting back the initiative in council – and, crucially, his favour with the king. He quickly built on his advantage by securing the agreement of both houses of parliament to relax Norfolk's strictures about clerical marriage and celibacy, thus taking the sting out of the six proposed articles.

Cromwell's buoyancy was ill-founded. The six arguments and accompanying penalties for failure to conform were enacted into law as the Act of Six Articles on 16 June 1539. This included a justification that enabled the king to save face, in case he should seem to be backtracking on the earlier reforms: 'The King's most royal Majesty, most prudently pondering and considering, that by occasion of variable and sundry opinions and judgements of the said articles, great discord and variance has arisen, as well amongst the clergy of this his realm, as amongst a great number of vulgar people, his loving subjects of the same, and being in a full hope and trust that a full and perfect resolution of the said articles should make a perfect concord and unity generally amongst all his loving and obedient subjects.' The Act received royal assent on 28 June. The reformists were outraged and condemned it as 'the bloody whip with six strings'.[45] Bishops Latimer and Shaxton – who had vociferously opposed the articles – immediately resigned, realising that their positions were untenable. Both men had been among Cromwell's most valuable allies in pushing forward reform, and their loss was a real blow to the king's chief minister.

But about Shaxton at least he can hardly have been surprised, for the bishop had plagued him with complaints for many months. In March 1538 Cromwell had written to upbraid him for his constant griping. 'If ye be offended with my sharpe letters,' he demanded, 'how can your testie wordes, I had almost gyven them another name, delite me?' After many more chastisements, he supplied Shaxton with a vociferous justification of his actions: 'God gyve me no longer lyfe, then I shall be gladde to use myn office in edificatione, and not in destructione, as ye beare me in hand I do. God, ye say, woll Judge such using of authorite, meanyng flattely, that I do abuse such power, as hath pleased God and the Kinges hyghenes to setle me in . . . I may erre in my dolinges for wante of knowlege, I willingly beare no misdoers. I willingly hurte none, whom honestie and the kinges lawes do not refuse.' Shaxton, it seems, had touched a raw nerve. For all his sangfroid and easy good humour, Cromwell was becoming increasingly sensitive to the constant vitriol that was hurled against him and his reforms. His justification to Shaxton could have been to the world at large. He ended, though, with an obvious threat to the bishop: 'Ye shall do well to do your duetie, if yow so do, ye have no cause to mistruste my frendshyp. Yf ye do not, I must tell it yow and that somewhat after the playnist sorte.'[46]

Shaxton had clearly not heeded this warning and he now faced the consequences. Shortly after his resignation, he wrote to Cromwell to ask whether he should dress like a bishop or a priest. In early July he was seen wearing priest's clothing while in company with Cranmer, who continued in close confederacy with him. But neither he nor Cromwell could do anything to prevent his arrest on 7 July; indeed, given their earlier exchange, the latter may have actively promoted it.[47]

To the outside world, Cromwell was still at the height of his powers. His account books attest that there was no diminution in the bribes pressed into his hands by ambitious courtiers hoping for his intercession with the king.[48] But the passing of the Six Articles had marked the lowest point of his career to date. Norfolk and his faction had won a significant victory. The potency of the reforms for which he had worked so hard had been seriously undermined, and unless something was done to prevent it, they looked set to crumble into the dust.

But according to John Foxe, it was at this moment that the king suddenly changed tack and decided to hold a reconciliatory dinner in Cranmer's honour at Lambeth Palace on 29 June 1539. Both Cromwell and Norfolk were among the guests, and Henry apparently hoped that they would agree to settle their differences in this informal setting. This was soon proved to be wildly optimistic. Foxe claims that when a leading noble (probably Norfolk) made a disparaging remark about Cardinal Wolsey, Cromwell was so incensed that he became embroiled in a bitter argument to defend his old master's honour. He accused Norfolk of disloyalty and the duke retaliated by calling him a liar. The account is not substantiated by any other source, but it is commensurate with Cromwell's strong sense of loyalty, and it is easy to imagine Norfolk provoking him in this way. The simmering resentment between the two men had been stoked by the recent parliament, as well as by the Calais controversy, and it looked increasingly likely to reach boiling point.

The conservatives wasted no time in exploiting the new legislation to bring the reformists to heel. During the first half of July, a stream of evangelicals was reported to Cranmer for investigation, many of them put forward by Lisle. Even though he was sympathetic to their cause, the archbishop had little choice but to imprison most of the accused. By 12 July, the French ambassador Marillac was able to report to his master Francis I that the English king had 'taken up again all the old opinions and constitutions, excepting only papal obedience and destruction of abbeys and churches of which he has taken the revenue'.[49] Norfolk and his supporters rejoiced at the prospect of victory.

But then the pendulum swung back in Cromwell's favour. His royal master seemed as uncomfortable with a return to more conservative doctrine as he had been with the more radical of Cromwell's reforms. He therefore took Cromwell back into his favour and once more lent a willing ear to his reformist ideas. The situation was helped by the fact that after parliament had been dissolved, the conservative bishops had begun to return to their dioceses. In August their most influential member, Stephen Gardiner, had an ill-advised and very public rant against the evangelical Robert Barnes, in which he accused him of heresy. Cromwell wasted no time in having him expelled from the Privy Council. This deprived Norfolk of his most powerful ecclesiastical ally, for Gardiner had been active in his support of the Six Articles and had been busily drafting the penalty clause. The fact that Henry sanctioned his expulsion was an indication that events were at last turning back Cromwell's way.

Another encouraging sign came in the autumn of 1539, with the return of the Lutheran, Franz Burchard. Ever one to push home

CHAPTER 16

The Flanders Mare

Anne, sister of Duke Wilhelm of Cleves, a state of the Holy Roman Empire situated in the northern Rhineland, had first been proposed as a fourth wife for Henry in the closing weeks of 1537, very soon after the death of Jane Seymour.[1] She was then twenty-two years of age, and had already been used as a pawn in the international marriage market when she had been betrothed to François, heir to the duchy of Lorraine, in 1527. This had come to nothing, leaving her free to marry elsewhere. John Hutton, ambassador to Mary of Hungary, regent of the Netherlands, had originally made the suggestion, although he admitted he had heard no great praise of her beauty. Such a recommendation hardly motivated the English king, who was still in mourning for Jane, to pursue the scheme any further, and it was not until early 1539 that the idea was mooted again. This time Henry gave it more credence because he desperately needed new allies. By the terms of their peace treaty of January 1539, Charles V and Francis I had sworn not to make any alliance with Henry without each other's consent. To make matters worse, a short while later Pope Paul III had reissued the bull of excommunication against the King of England. Although the then Duke of Cleves, Johann (Anne's father), was no Protestant, he – like Henry – had expelled papal authority from his domain some time before. His eldest daughter, Sibylle, was married to the Elector of Saxony, who was head of the Schmalkaldic League. An alliance with Cleves would therefore provide a major boost to the Reformation in England, and it may have been at least partly for this reason that Cromwell championed it so enthusiastically.

In March 1539 Henry had finally agreed that negotiations could begin – both for his own marriage to Anne and that of his daughter Mary to Anne's brother. But he made it very clear that this would be a purely political alliance. He was becoming increasingly uncomfortable with Cromwell's religious reforms in England and had no wish to align himself with what he saw as the radical reformists on the Continent. The king also made it clear, in distancing himself from the negotiations, that responsibility for the proposed alliance would rest entirely upon his minister's shoulders, thus making it easier to extract himself from it if necessary. This spelled danger for Cromwell, but having advanced this far he had little choice other than to proceed with negotiations. There is no evidence, though, that he was anything other than enthusiastic about the match. Not only did it align England with a key reformist power, it also prevented Henry taking a blue-blooded English bride, and thus kept aristocratic influence at bay in the court. He therefore dispatched two agents, Nicholas Wotton and Richard Beard, to Cleves to begin the task.

Both men could be trusted to further the marriage. Wotton had helped to draw up the so-called Bishops' Book two years previously, and Beard was among Cromwell's allies in the privy chamber. Their commission did not begin well, however, for Wilhelm was at that time attempting to conciliate the emperor and knew that an alliance with England would be seen as an impediment. There was also reluctance on the part of the English king, who saw the alliance as somewhat beneath him. Even Cromwell seemed to believe that his master deserved better. In a letter to his envoy in the Electorate of Saxony, he instructed him to confer with Vice-Chancellor Burckhard about Anne of Cleves, 'not as demaunding her, but as geving them a prick to stirr them to offre her, as the noblest and highest honour that could come into that noble house of Cleves, if they could bring it to passe'.[2] But with France and Spain in league, there was little other choice.

That the negotiations were being led by Cromwell, not Henry, was made painfully clear by the assurance Cromwell gave the Elector of Saxony about the proposed match for the Lady Mary, claiming that when he spoke of it to his master, he perceived 'the kinges hieghnes . . . by his graces countenaunce and exterior Visage . . .

to be of good Inclinacion'.[3] This was hardly a ringing endorsement. Cromwell had drawn up instructions for Christopher Mont, the king's envoy in Saxony and a long-standing agent of Cromwell, to smooth over any objections to the match in January – before Henry had given his sanction that negotiations might begin. Cromwell's praise for the Lady Mary lacked conviction. He urged Mont to assure the Elector of Saxony that 'she is indewed and adornate as all the world knoweth, aswell of suche grace of beautie and excellent proportion of her personage as of moost excellent lerning, honorable bihavour and of all honest vertues and good qualities.' But he also insisted that it was not necessary for her portrait to be sent abroad in order to justify such praise.[4] Although the king's elder daughter had been praised for her beauty when a child, and was still referred to by her supporters as 'one of the fairest, the most virtuous, and one of the gentlest creatures in all the world', since growing into adulthood she had been worn down by anxiety and poor health, which had taken their toll on her appearance.[5]

At the same time as Cromwell was working hard to bring the alliance to pass, his master was busy courting France. The arrival at the English court of Charles de Marillac, the long promised replacement for Ambassador Castillon, on 28 March 1539 gave the king great hope that Francis I would throw off his alliance with Charles and strike up an accord with England. The entire court seemed 'to wear a new aspect and to be quite delighted'.[6] Cromwell alone was aghast at this turn of events. But he forged ahead with the Cleves project, apparently undeterred.

The plans for the Lady Mary's marriage seem to have been abandoned at an early stage of the proceedings. Cromwell would later be accused of having deliberately disrupted them so that he could marry the king's daughter himself. Given the importance of the Cleves alliance to his survival, this is likely to have been nothing but hearsay, inspired by the earlier rumours of Cromwell's intentions towards Mary.

By late summer, Cromwell's envoys had secured a provisional agreement for Henry's marriage. Anne would be the only one of Henry's brides whom he had agreed to marry without ever having set eyes on her. For all its political advantage, he was not about to enter into the marriage without anything other than second-hand reports of the lady's appearance. At the beginning of the year, Cromwell had instructed Mont to 'diligently but secretly Inquere of the beautie and qualities of the Lady . . . Aswell what shapp, stature, proportion and complexion she is of As of her lerning actyvitie, bihavour and honest qualities.' Mont evidently sent back a favourable report, for Cromwell subsequently reported to his master: 'Every man prayseth the beawtie of the same lady aswell for the face as for the hole body above all other ladys excellent . . . she excelleth as ferre the duchesse as the golden son excelleth the sylveryn mone. Every man prayseth her good vertues and honeste with shamfastnes, which appereth playnley in the gravite of her face. Thus saye they that have seen them both.'[7]

But Henry was not content to take Cromwell at his word. Already reticent about the match, he dispatched his favourite painter, Hans Holbein, to Cleves so that he might capture her likeness. Wotton had been one of many who had praised Anne's beauty, describing her as 'verye lyvelye', and he attested that Holbein's portrait was an accurate representation. Cromwell ordered it to be shown to him before his royal master. He was not disappointed. 'When Cromwell saw the portrait, and found the lady was pretty, he was very glad,' recorded the Spanish Chronicle.[8] According to this same account, the Lord Privy Seal waited until the king was in a 'very merry' mood and then presented the portrait to him. Henry was said to have been delighted as he surveyed Anne's pretty, doll-like face, her fair hair, dark eyes, delicate mouth and chin, and demure, maidenly expression. With rather more enthusiasm than he had hitherto shown, he duly instructed Cromwell to bring the negotiations to a speedy conclusion.

Cromwell entrusted the matter to his old friend Stephen Vaughan, who was dispatched to Cleves at once. Vaughan was shown every honour by the Duke of Cleves, who 'gave him a great feast' on his arrival.[9] Under the direction of this seasoned envoy, the negotiations reached a swift and satisfactory conclusion. According to the custom when a king took a foreign bride, the betrothal was to be concluded by proxy. In late September a group of ambassadors from Cleves arrived at the court in London. On 4 October they signed the marriage treaty which had almost certainly been drawn up by Cromwell – or at least directed by him. According to its terms, the king would receive no less than 100,000 gold florins (25,000 English marks sterling). However, in a magnanimous gesture – one that perhaps displayed his eagerness for his new bride – Henry waived this sum, realising that Wilhelm could ill afford it. As a result, on the very next day the ambassadors signed a contract that completed an indissoluble union between Anne and Henry. Cromwell was quick to send 'lettres of congratulacion to my ladie Anne's grace', expressing his delight that her marriage would promote 'amytie' between their two countries. The Spanish Chronicle concurs that his 'pleasure cannot be described at having arranged this match', but added: 'it turned out wrong for him.'[10]

While Anne of Cleves prepared to embark for England, Cromwell turned his attention to religious matters. Capitalising on the king's renewed favour, he stoked Henry's enthusiasm for Coverdale's Great Bible. Inspired by his chief minister, Henry duly commissioned Cranmer to compose an official preface to the second edition, and on 14 November he issued a proclamation granting Cromwell responsibility for licensing all Bible translations for the next five years. This was a significant step forward for Cromwell, and seemed to indicate a genuine commitment on the king's part to the cause of reform. The demand for the Bible was such that it soon outstripped supply, and several new editions had to be commissioned during the following two years.

At the same time, Cromwell won a major victory for the Calais evangelicals, who had been languishing in captivity for several months. The death in September 1539 of their custodian, Bishop Stokesley of London, who had been one of the staunchest opponents to reform, enabled Cromwell to begin proceedings for their release. In mid-November, he and Cranmer secured the freedom of the vast majority of them, and successfully delayed proceedings against the rest.

That Cromwell was feeling more secure is suggested by a case of dissent that was reported by the Bishop of Lincoln in November 1539. A parish priest in Horncastle had been accused of 'preaching rashely and incenserely the worde of god', which had caused 'the people [to be] gretely offended'. The man had been interrogated and charged, but when his case was referred to Cromwell, the latter took a surprisingly benevolent view. He advised the bishop that in his opinion the priest's behaviour had rather 'proceded of simplicite and Ignorance than of any malice or arrogancie'.[11] His verdict was therefore that the man ought to be absolved. Such clemency on Cromwell's part was rare, particularly in matters of religion. But he evidently felt confident enough to be magnanimous on this occasion.

Just as the consolidation of Cromwell's reforms seemed assured, however, the king's notoriously fickle favour was withdrawn once more. The cause was the same woman who, just a few months earlier, had seemed his salvation. Anne of Cleves had set out for England on 26 November. Travelling in a horse-drawn chariot befitting her status as the new Queen of England, she and her entourage made their way towards Calais. Stephen Vaughan was among those appointed to welcome England's future queen, and Cromwell had dispatched his son Gregory to meet her there. Gregory had had a much less adventurous youth than his father, so this was probably the first time he had ever left England's shores. The voyage was not an easy one, and Gregory reported that many of the gentlemen on board had been 'extremely vexed with sickness' – although he himself proved to be of stronger stomach.[12]

The welcoming party arrived more than a week before Anne, and amused themselves with feasting and tournaments. Early in the morning of 11 December, the king's prospective wife at last reached the environs of Calais. Gregory rode out to meet her with the rest of the entourage, who 'wore three collars of cloth of gold and purple velvet and chains of gold, and 200 yeomen, &c., in the King's colours, red and blue cloth'. There were also eighty gentlemen in attendance dressed 'in coats of satin damask and velvet'. They escorted her for the last mile or so to the centre of the town. As Lady Anne rode past the king's ships, which were 'decked with 100 banners of silk and gold', they fired off 200 cannon shots, 'after which the town of Calais shot 300 pieces of ordnance'. According to one contemporary account, there was 'such a smoke that one of her train could not see another'.[13] It was a welcome as extravagant as it was deafening.

Gregory had ample opportunity to get to know his new queen because their onward voyage was delayed by bad weather, so Anne and her retinue remained in Calais for more than two weeks. His father reported that her gallant fiancé, though impatient to meet her, had instructed the English retinue there 'hartely soe to chere my lady and her trayne as they may think the tyme as short as the tediousnes of it woll suffer'. Gregory was at the heart of these entertainments. If he found his future queen less appealing than Holbein's portrait suggested, he was discreet enough not to mention it, and merely reported to his father that she was 'in good health'.[14] Neither did the other members of the welcoming party make any disparaging comments. Their reports were filled instead with descriptions of the jousts, banquets and other entertainments that were staged for the new queen during her prolonged stay in the town.

By 27 December the weather had finally improved enough for Anne and her attendants to set sail across the Channel. Having safely reached England's shores, she disembarked at Deal in Kent and then moved to Dover, where she was greeted by lavish celebrations. Battered by storms, her cavalcade reached Rochester on New Year's Eve. Eager to meet her, Henry braved the elements and rode south with his attendants. Following the custom favoured by Renaissance monarchs who were betrothed to foreign brides with whom they were unacquainted, Henry hastened to greet her in disguise, accompanied by a few trusted advisers – Cromwell included – in order to 'norishe love'. But his romantic escapade came to an abrupt end when he first set eyes on his new wife. Anne had apparently been rather flattered by her portrait. In contrast to the petite stature of his first three wives, she was tall and big-boned. She had a large nose which had been cleverly disguised by the angle of Holbein's portrait, and her skin was pitted with the marks of smallpox. Her body odour was so strong that it was remarked upon by several members of the court at a time when personal hygiene was by no means fastidious. The king was horrified. 'I like her not! I like her not!' he shouted at a dismayed Cromwell when the meeting was over. He went on to complain 'hevelye And not plesantlye' that Anne was 'nothing so well as She was spokyn of', adding that if he had known what she would be like, 'she shold not have Commen within this Realme'. He demanded of Cromwell 'what remedye', to which the beleaguered minister admitted he 'knew none but was veraye Sory therffore'.[15]

To be fair to Anne, until Henry expressed such a strong dislike of her, there had been no other disparaging accounts of her appearance. The famous nickname of 'Flanders mare' was only coined by Bishop Gilbert Burnet in the late seventeenth century. All the contemporary accounts before her marriage had been complimentary. Even Henry was forced to admit that she was 'well and semelye', and Cromwell was at pains to point out that 'she had a quenlye manner.'[16] But the fact that her new husband found her abhorrent ensured that she would go down in history as the 'ugly wife'. Little matter that Henry could hardly have been described as an attractive prospect himself by the time of their marriage. Now aged forty-eight, he was increasingly incapacitated by an old jousting wound in his leg that had turned ulcerous. As a result, he had long since lost his sporting prowess and his girth had expanded at an alarming rate. When he became king he had been a trim thirty-two inches around the waist; by the time he met Anne of Cleves it was closer to fifty-two inches. A sketch by the Antwerp artist Cornelius Massys drawn four years later shows the king as a grotesque figure. His beady eyes and tiny, pursed mouth are almost lost in the layers of flesh that surround them. He appears to have no neck, and his enormous frame extends beyond the reaches of the canvas. A contemporary chronicler corroborated this portrait: 'The King was so stout that such a man has never been seen. Three of the biggest men that could be found could get inside his doublet.'[17] Although none would have dared even to whisper such a thing (predicting the king's death being tantamount to treason), many of his courtiers – Cromwell included – must have privately mused on how much longer he would live. On balance, Anne had far more reason for complaint than her prospective husband.

Henry continued to bully Cromwell into finding a way out of the marriage and demanded: 'Is ther none other Remedye but that I must nedes agenst my will put my nek in the yoke.'[18] But the minister, for once, was at a loss. Reluctantly, the king eventually conceded that, having concluded the betrothal by proxy, he had little choice but to go through with the formal ceremony of marriage. It would have caused a major diplomatic incident if he had reneged on the treaty, and England could ill afford to lose allies. Even now, the French king was celebrating the New Year in Paris with Charles V, and the two were making plans to invade England. Although their alliance would prove short-lived, it constituted a significant threat to the English king. Henry himself admitted: 'Yf it were not that she is com So Farre into my realme and the great preparacyons that my states & people hathe made For her and For Fere of makyng of a Ruffull in the woorlde that is to meane to dryve her brother into the handes of the emperowre and Frenche kynges handes being now to gether I woolde never have ne marye her.' Nevertheless, he wasted no time in ordering his chief minister to get him out of the marriage that he had orchestrated. As if Cromwell needed any further incitement to act, Thomas Wriothesley urged him: 'For Godde's sake, devyse for the relefe of the King; for if he remain in this gref and trouble, we shal al one day smart for it.'[19]

Evidently not trusting Cromwell to free him from a marriage that he had been so keen to arrange, Henry secretly instructed Vaughan to go back to Cleves and find out more about Anne's earlier betrothal to François of Lorraine. According to the Spanish Chronicle, Vaughan plied the duke's attendants with drink and they revealed that Anne had actually been married to François, but as soon as negotiations began for a betrothal with Henry, the duke had had him taken away. François had apparently 'died of grief' a short time later.[20] When Vaughan reported this to the king, he seized upon it as a drowning man might do a passing branch. If Anne had been married, rather than merely betrothed, to François of Lorraine, then their union must surely have been consummated. This was grounds enough for an annulment. But the ambassadors from Cleves had failed to bring a copy of the Lorraine contract with them, as they had promised, so this was impossible to prove.

Angry and frustrated, Henry was said to have summoned Cromwell to him and demanded: 'Why hast thou led me into such a great sin as to cause the death of a gentleman? If thou didst know that Anne of Cleves was married, why didst thou make me marry her?' Cromwell was greatly 'grieved' upon hearing this, but stood his ground. 'Your Majesty might well keep her as her first husband is dead,' he retorted, 'and besides, if your Majesty leaves her, everybody will be saying what a many wives you have.'[21] The king flew into a rage at such insolence and ordered Cromwell out of his presence. Whether this exchange took place in quite the way described by the Spanish Chronicle is debatable. Henry's fury is easy to imagine; Cromwell's insolence is not. By now, he had served his royal master for a decade and knew full well that his frequent bursts of temper were best handled in a placatory manner.

In the meantime, to the outside world it appeared that everything continued as normal. Having made their way to London, the king publicly greeted his bride on Blackheath Common on 3 January amid great ceremony. All the chief dignitaries of the realm were present, including Cromwell. Henry failed to disguise his displeasure among all this pomp. 'It was much noticed that the King came along with her, but showed in his face he was disappointed,' noted the Spanish Chronicle. 'It was noticed that from that day forward the King was not so gay as usual.'[22]

Even as Henry was putting on a show worthy of his new queen, he was privately instructing Cromwell to interrogate her ambassadors about the nature of her earlier betrothal, since Vaughan had received no satisfactory answer to his previous enquiry. Cromwell granted them a day to consider, and on 4 January they gave an emphatic response that Anne had never been the wife of Lorraine, promising to have a copy of the contract sent to England without delay. To make matters worse, the guileless Anne agreed to sign a notarial instrument swearing that she was free to marry. How unpalatable a task it was for Cromwell to communicate this news to his royal master can only be imagined. He himself later recorded that he had been 'sent to your highnes by my lordes of your said Counsayle to declare to your highnes what answere they hadde made . . . wherwith your grace was veray moch displeasyd Saying I am not well handelyd, insomoche that I mought well persayve that your highnes was Fully determenyd not to have goone thorow with the maryage.'[23] Perhaps Cromwell sweetened the pill by promising to secure an annulment as soon as the ceremony was over. He certainly resisted the temptation to delay the evil tidings, for on 5 January the king certified Anne's jointure of more than 4,000 marks sterling – a clear sign that he had conceded the inevitable. He also agreed to the appointment of her ladies-in-waiting, among whom was Cromwell's daughter-in-law, Elizabeth.

It was with great reluctance that, the following day, Henry made his way to Greenwich for his wedding to Anne of Cleves. So little thought had been given to the ceremony that even on the morning of the wedding it had not been arranged who would lead Anne down the aisle. The earls of Essex and Overstein were decided upon, but as Essex could not be found, Cromwell was appointed in his place. Far from being an honour, this was no doubt intended as a punishment by Henry, who was determined to pin all the blame for the union on his minister – and thus associate him with it at every opportunity. Cromwell was only spared from the task at the last minute. He had just arrived at Anne's chamber to collect her when Essex finally made an appearance. Relieved, Cromwell went back to tell the king that everything was now ready. Beckoning his minister closer, Henry whispered with malice: 'My lorde yf it were not to Satysfye the woorld and my Realme I woolde not doo that I must doo this day For none erthlye thing.'[24] Cranmer presided over the ensuing ceremony, and afterwards the bride and groom entered into the usual celebrations.

But if the king had done his duty by going through with the marriage, its consummation was another matter entirely. A detailed account of the wedding night exists among the records of Henry's reign. The king had run his hands all over his bride's body, which had so repelled him that he had found himself incapable of doing any more. The following morning, Cromwell had gone to his master's bedchamber and 'fynding your grace not so plesaunte as I trustyd to have done I was so bolde to aske your grace how ye lykyd the quene wherunto your grace Sobyrlye answeryd saying that I was not all men, Surlye my lorde as ye know I lykyd her beffor not well but now I lyke her moche woorse.' He complained that 'she is nothing fair, and have very evil smells about her', and went on to claim that there had been certain 'tokens' to suggest that she was no virgin: 'I have Felte her belye and her brestes and therby as I Can Judge She Sholde be noe mayde which Strake me So to the harte when I Felt them that I hadde nother will nor Corage to procede any Ferther in other matyers, Saying I have left her as good a mayde as I Founde her.'[25]

For her part, Anne, who was apparently entirely innocent in the ways of the world, confided to her ladies that she believed she might be pregnant. 'How can I be a mayd . . . and slepe every night with the King?' she demanded. 'Whan he comes to bed he kisses me, and taketh me by the hand, and byddeth me, Good night, swete hart: and in the morning kisses me, and byddeth me, Farewel, darlying. Is this not enough?' The Countess of Rutland retorted: 'Madam, there must be more than this, or it wil be long or [ere] we have a Duke of York, which al this realm most desireth.'[26]

Henry's inability to consummate the marriage has traditionally been assigned to his revulsion at his new bride. But it is at least equally possible that he was impotent. He was more than twice his young bride's age and had become increasingly incapacitated in recent years. Although he still liked to play the game of courtly love, there had been no talk of a mistress for some time. The situation might have been useful in securing an annulment, but it was not the sort of thing that he would have wished to be publicly known. Kings, even more than ordinary men, prided themselves on their sexual potency. It was, after all, vital for the continuation of their dynasty. Henry had been a little too eager to boast to his physician, Dr Butts, that although he could not bring himself to have sex with Anne, he had had 'two wet dreams'.[27] A case of protesting too much, perhaps.

Meanwhile, Anne soon realised something was seriously wrong and she was desperate for advice. Her first recourse was to Cromwell. He was cautious (and nervous) enough to seek his royal master's consent to oblige her. Although the king was angry with his chief minister for, as he saw it, getting him into the mess that was his fourth marriage, Henry still trusted him. He therefore gave him permission to discuss the matter with Anne. Cromwell, though, seems to have found the subject rather distasteful: putting his royal master's religious and political business in order was one thing; sorting out his sex life was quite another. Instead, he instructed Anne's lord chamberlain, Thomas Manners, Earl of Rutland, to encourage Anne to behave in a way that might please the king. He later reported to his royal master that he had urged Rutland 'to Fynde Som mean that the quene might be inducyd to order your grace plesantlye in her behaveour towardes yow thinkyng therebye for [to] have hade Some Fawtis [faults] Amendyd to your Magestyes Comffort'.[28] Rutland's wife served in her privy chamber, and later events suggest that Cromwell had also instructed her to report on the royal couple's sexual activity – or lack of it. At the same time, he quietly instructed Anthony Denny to whisper words of encouragement in his royal master's ear, taking 'evermore occasion to praise [Anne] to the King's highness'. This was an unenviable task, and the hapless Denny soon admitted defeat. Henry upbraided him: 'He would utter plainly to him, as to a servant whom he used secretly about him . . . that he could never . . . be provoked and stirred to know her carnally.'[29]

Nonetheless, the king was careful to keep up appearances with his new queen by being seen in public with her as often as possible. A few days after the wedding, a celebratory tournament was held in Greenwich. The contemporary chronicler Edward Hall recorded the event and praised the new queen so effusively that nobody would guess there was anything amiss: 'The sonday after [the wedding] there were kepte solempne Justes . . . On whiche daie she was appareiled after the Englishe fassion, with a Frenche whode, whiche so set furth her beautie and good visage, that every creature reioysed to behold her.'[30]

In February 1540 the royal couple sailed by barge to Westminster and were cheered by the Londoners who lined the route. Anne received gifts from her new subjects and entered into the court festivities with all due alacrity. But she fell well short of the grace and accomplishments of her predecessors. The education of noble ladies in Cleves was very different to that of English ladies. The English ambassador there described her as being of 'lowly and gentle conditions . . . She occupieth her time most with the needle . . . She canne reede and wryte her [own language but of] Frenche Latyn or other langaige she [knows no]ne, nor yet she canne not synge nor pleye . . . enye instrument, for they take it here in Germanye for a rebuke and an occasion of lightenesse, that great ladyes shuld be lernyd or have enye knowledge of musike.'[31] Anne clearly lacked the refinements that her new husband was used to, and no matter how affable and eager to please she might be, her awkwardness rendered her an embarrassment in the sophisticated world of the Tudor court. It was another excuse for the king to be rid of her.

Even though Henry was determined to extract himself from his unpalatable new bride, the marriage had given heart to the Lutheran princes of the Schmalkaldic League, who in January 1540 sent a representative to the English court with instructions to conclude a religious and political alliance. The envoy, Ludwig von Baumbach, was to express his sorrow to Henry about the passage of the Six Articles, and bring the English king back to the cause of reform. On arriving in London, Baumbach and the rest of his party made their way straight to Cromwell, perceiving him to be the leader of the reformist party and therefore their greatest hope of success. But, to their dismay, they received the coldest of welcomes from the Lord Privy Seal, who demanded to know whether they had the power to conclude a political alliance. When the ambassadors demurred, Cromwell dispatched them to his royal master, who repeated the same question. Exasperated, Baumbach sought help from Vice-Chancellor Burckhard, who had accompanied Anne to England. Both men paid Cromwell a visit and reiterated their desire to conclude an alliance with the English king. He told the ambassadors that the king wanted only a political alliance, and that the religious question could be settled at a later date. Not to be deterred, they insisted that this was impossible and that religion was at the heart of their mission.

Cromwell's response is one of the clearest indications that no matter how greatly he might cherish religious reform, this would always take second place to his service to the king. Throwing off the accustomed decorum of diplomatic negotiations, he turned to the ambassadors and told them with astonishing frankness that he knew full well what they wanted in terms of a religious settlement but that, as things stood, he had no choice but to conform to his master's faith, even if it cost him his life. Cromwell may have spent the past decade furthering the cause of reform, but only when it had chimed with his political ambitions. Now that the king was taking an increasingly conservative stance in religious matters, Cromwell was not about to become a prisoner of conscience like More or Fisher. He had already been forced to align himself too closely to the Cleves match and could ill afford to compound the situation by declaring himself for the Lutheran cause. Besides, his personal faith was more closely allied to that of the more moderate evangelicals and he found many elements of Luther's teachings abhorrent. Caution and ambiguity had been his bywords in both domestic and international policy, and he was now desperate to regain that stance.

Greatly disappointed by what they perceived as the inconstancy of the man who had spearheaded the English Reformation, Baumbach and Burckhard paid one last visit to the king before departing. By now, Henry had lost all patience with the matter and not only continued to reject their pressure for a religious alliance, but told them in no uncertain terms that they were useless to England as political allies. If, as the ambassadors had argued, France or Spain chose to invade, then he was quite able to repel them without assistance from the Lutheran princes. He then dismissed the two men, leaving Cromwell to bid them a formal farewell. The minister was no doubt glad to see them go: their presence was an uncomfortable reminder of how far he had strayed from the king's own stance – and favour. But even though he had refused to put his weight behind their mission, as he might have done at the height of his powers, he was already so closely associated with the Lutheran cause that his attempts to disassociate himself from it would prove too little, too late.

Throughout this time, Cromwell was beset by other pressing matters aside from the problem of the king's new marriage. The Anne of Cleves fiasco had given new heart to his enemies at court, principal among whom was the Duke of Norfolk. The Spanish Chronicle recounts that after Henry's angry exchange with Cromwell about the marriage, the king had sent for Norfolk and Edward Seymour, telling them: 'I am determined to get rid of Anne of Cleves, and Cromwell shall not deceive me again.' Norfolk was quick to grasp this opportunity. When the audience was over, he told Seymour: 'Duke, this is the time for us to get rid of common people from our midst; you see that the King has quarrelled with Cromwell, and asks our counsel. We will advise him to take affairs into his own hands, and not be ruled so much by Cromwell.'[32] This conversation, as many others contained within the chronicle, was probably imagined, but certain it was that Norfolk resolved to use the Cleves marriage to destroy his rival.

Norfolk had also been capitalising on foreign affairs to enhance his position. A meeting between Charles V and Francis I in January 1540 had provided an opportunity for the duke to exercise his diplomatic skills and stir up a quarrel between the two potentates, thus lessening the threat that their cordiality posed to his own sovereign. By February, he was able to report from Paris that the French king 'was not content with thEmperours wordes'.[33] Norfolk could not claim to have achieved this discord alone: there was already tension between Francis and Charles on account of the latter's refusal to fulfil the promises made in their treaty. But the fact that he stoked the flames of their resentment was the source of great satisfaction for Henry. And Cromwell had had no part of it. By now, he was so strongly identified with the German alliance that he was effectively prevented from having any involvement in treating with France or

Spain, which left his arch-rival free to claim all the glory. Worse still, the breach between those two powers had substantially weakened the usefulness of the Cleves alliance anyway.

Norfolk's victory was a significant one. But he was not acting alone. Gardiner had been seeking opportunities to undermine their despised adversary ever since his recall from France in 1538 and now, sensing victory, they plotted Cromwell's downfall. Aware of the danger, Cromwell struck at the heart of Norfolk's estate. In February 1540 he arranged the closure of Thetford Priory in Norfolk. As well as being one of the last monasteries to escape dissolution (probably thanks to the duke's protection), Thetford was also the family burial place for the dukes of Norfolk. The duke had fought hard to save it and planned to refound it as a college of priests who could sing masses for his family's souls in perpetuity. But Cromwell had other ideas. In a move that was at once the most aggressive and the most personally vindictive he had ever made against his chief rival, he made sure that the priory was completely destroyed. No college was founded in its place, and Norfolk suffered the gross indignity of having to arrange for his ancestors' bones to be moved some thirty-five miles to Framlingham in Suffolk. It was both a studied insult and a declaration of war. If Norfolk resented this base-born upstart before, he utterly despised him now and would be content with nothing other than his total destruction.

In a further desperate move, Cromwell tried to have the duke exiled from court on the pretext that there was a case of the sweating sickness at Kenninghall. Knowing that the king had a morbid fear of illness and was careful to avoid anyone who had the slightest symptoms of it, Cromwell felt sure that this would guarantee Norfolk's absence for a few weeks – long enough to regain the initiative. But Norfolk stoutly denied that there was any risk of infection, since he had not seen the afflicted man for a long time. He also made it clear that even if he was banned from court he would stay at his house in London rather than retreat to the country. Henry was sufficiently convinced that there was no danger, and Cromwell was obliged to admit defeat.

Following this setback, the Spanish Chronicle claims that around the same time Cromwell plotted to have Norfolk framed for high treason. According to this account, a relative of Norfolk, known as 'Master Dartnall', had been arrested on suspicion of trying to poison the king's cherished son and heir, Prince Edward. Cromwell was said to have visited Dartnall in secret at the Tower, and tried to persuade him to attest that Norfolk had made him do it. The shocked prisoner had refused, crying: 'I should be the blackest traitor in the world, and there were never traitors in my lineage!'[34] There is no evidence to corroborate this story, and it is likely that its author constructed the tale as a means of demonstrating the depth of the antipathy – and ruthlessness – between the two men.

Events now seemed to conspire rapidly against Cromwell. As well as battling his enemies at court, he was faced with continuing dissent among religious conservatives across the country. Desperate to achieve some success in order to regain a measure of credibility with the king, he dispatched Ralph Sadler to the Scottish court to promote the cause of religious reform there. But the run of luck was firmly against Cromwell, and the mission ended in failure. For all his shrewdness and political guile, Sadler was inexperienced in diplomatic matters and overstretched himself by promising the Scottish king a meeting with Henry. The meeting never materialised, and Sadler was obliged to make an ignominious return to court.

Meanwhile, the Calais controversy had been reignited on 9 March 1540, when the Duke of Norfolk (who had remained in close contact with Lisle) arranged for a fresh investigation of heretics there. The men selected for the task were all staunch conservatives, and by 5 April they had concluded that there was 'great division' in the area. Thirteen heretics were subsequently sent back to London, five of whom were protégés of Cromwell.

Also in March, Bishop Gardiner began a fresh offensive when he had Robert Barnes arrested. Barnes had taken violent exception to a sermon preached by Gardiner at St Paul's Cross, in which he had denounced various Protestant doctrines. Two weeks later, Barnes had preached in the same pulpit and had seized the opportunity not merely to refute Gardiner's arguments but openly to insult him. Barnes may have bargained on the protection of Cromwell, who had saved him from being prosecuted for heresy in the past, but if so then he fatally misjudged the situation. Gardiner appealed to the king, who ordered that the preacher be brought to him for interrogation. Barnes was outmanoeuvred by Gardiner in the ensuing theological discussion, and when he lashed out at his opponent he was arrested and thrown into the Tower, along with two other notorious evangelicals, Thomas Gerrard and William Jerome, both of whom had supported him.

Jerome was vicar of Stepney, the church where Cromwell and his family worshipped, so this was intended as a clear warning shot by Gardiner. Intense pressure had been brought to bear upon the three men, and they had been forced to recant publicly during Easter week. When Cromwell's son Gregory heard of Jerome's recantation, he was so distressed that he wrote to his former tutor, Henry Dowes, urging him to find out the details. Dowes replied in March: 'Your comaundemente hath fully persuaded me you be nott a litle desyrous to receyve knowledge after what sorte he [William Jerome] behaved himselfe, aswell concernyng his Recantation, as also the reste of thinges conteyned in his saide Sermon.'[35] The recantations were deemed unreliable, so proceedings against the three men continued. The French ambassador Marillac wryly observed that defending the heretics 'lately shook the credit of maistre Cramvel, so that he was very near coming to grief'.[36]

CHAPTER 17

'Cromwell is tottering'

CROMWELL WAS FLAILING, and the world knew it. On 10 April Marillac cheerfully predicted his imminent downfall and even speculated about who would take over his various offices. 'The farce of which I have already written has been still better played by those who, after encouraging the doctors at whose preaching they despoiled the abbeys, and took the wealth of the Church, now procure the ruin of the said doctors, who lay the blame upon them – amongst others upon Cromwell and the archbishop of Canterbury, who do not know where they are' he reported. 'Within few days there will be seen in this country a great change in many things; which this King begins to make in his ministers, recalling those he had rejected and degrading those he had raised.' The ambassador declared:

> Cromwell is tottering, for all those recalled, who were dismissed by his means, reserve 'une bonne pensee' for him; among others the bishops of Hoyncester, Durans and Belde [Barnes, Gerrard and Jerome], men of great learning and experience, who are now summoned to the Privy Council. It is said on good authority that Tonstallus, bishop of Durans, a person in great esteem with the learned, shall be vicar general of the spiritualty, and that the bp. of Belde [Bath] shall be keeper of the Privy Seal, which are Cromwell's two principal titles. In any case, the name of vicar general will not remain to him, as even his own people assert.

Marillac's concluding remark was telling: 'If he remains in his former credit and authority it will only be because he is very assiduous in affairs, although rough in his management of them, and that he

Edward VI (1537-1553) as a child by Hans Holbein, c.1538. Edward's birth in October 1537 was met with great rejoicing. Cromwell's son Gregory married the boy's aunt, Elizabeth Seymour.

Jane Seymour (c.1508/9-1537) by Hans Holbein, 1536. This was painted to commemorate the marriage of Henry VIII to his third wife, which took place just days after the execution of his second.

The family of Henry VIII, c.1545. This portrait was probably commissioned to mark the restoration to the order of succession of the King's two daughters, Mary and Elizabeth (on the left and right respectively). Henry's son and heir, Edward, sits on his right and Jane Seymour (who had died eight years before) on his left.

Thomas Cranmer (1489-1556) by Gerlach Flicke, 1545. As Archbishop of Canterbury, Cranmer was an important ally for Cromwell in pushing forward his religious reforms.

Title page of The Great Bib c.1539. First printed in 1539, i ran into six further editions and by 1541 9,000 copies had been distributed across the kingdom. This copy may ha belonged to Henry VIII, wh is shown handing the Bible to Cranmer on his right and Cromwell on his left.

Sir Thomas Wyatt (c.1503-1542) by Hans Holbein, c.1535-37. A renowned poet and ambassador, Wyatt was said to be 'devoted' to Cromwell. He remained his faithful friend and protégé throughout his career at court.

rtrait of a Man (possibly Sir Ralph dler, 1507-1587), workshop of Hans ılbein, 1535. Sadler was Cromwell's cretary for almost twenty years. His yalty was richly rewarded, and in 1535 built a new residence for himself, tton House in Hackney (interior own below).

Charles V (1500-58). As Holy Roman Emperor and ruler of Spain, Charles commanded an enormous territory. He was also the nephew of Catherine of Aragon, which made his relations with Henry VIII increasingly strained.

Francis I (1494-1547). The King of France was Henry's greatest rival, both personally and politically. Their lust for military glory, combined with the proximity of their kingdoms, was a constant source of friction.

The Solemn Entrance of Emperor Charles V, Francis I and Alessandro Farnese (Pope Paul III) to Paris in 1540. Henry VIII was deeply troubled when his two great continental rivals forged an alliance in 1539, supported by the Pope.

Anne of Cleves (1515-1557) by Hans Holbein, 1539. Henry VIII insisted upon seeing a portrait of his prospective fourth wife before agreeing to marry her. Holbein may have flattered her in this painting, for when the King saw her in the flesh, he was bitterly disappointed.

Henry VIII by Cornelis Massys, 1548. This print shows the King at the end of his life, grossly fat and with an expression which hints at his growing paranoia and ill temper.

Portrait of a lady, thought to be Catherine Howard (c.1520-1542) by Hans Holbein. Henry VIII was infatuated with his fifth wife, who was about thirty years his junior. A recent theory suggests that this portrait might have been Cromwell's daughter in law, Elizabeth Seymour.

Charles Brandon, 1st Duke of Suffolk (c. 1484-1545), c.1540-45. Brandon was Henry VIII's closest friend and served him faithfully throughout his reign. A staunch conservative, he scorned low-born advisers such as Cromwell.

Stephen Gardiner, Bishop of Winchester (c.1495-1555). Although Gardiner, like Cromwell, had served his apprenticeship i Cardinal Wolsey's household, the two me became implacable enemies after the Cardinal's fall.

Thomas Howard, 3rd Duke of Norfolk (1473-1554) by Hans Holbein. As head of one of the oldest noble families in England, Norfolk despised Cromwell for his humble birth and reformist views. He too became a deadly enemy to the chief minister.

Thomas Cromwell, c.1537. The King elected Cromwell to the Order of the Garter, the highest and most ancient order of chivalry in England, in August 1537. This portrait, in which Cromwell wears the collar of the Order, was probably commissioned to mark his new status.

The Black Book of the Garter, recording the garter ceremonies of 1534. In the top left, Henry VIII is enthroned and surrounded by the Knights of the Garter. Upon receiving the Order, Cromwell was said to have given a speech of thanks 'with all the eloquence he was master of.'

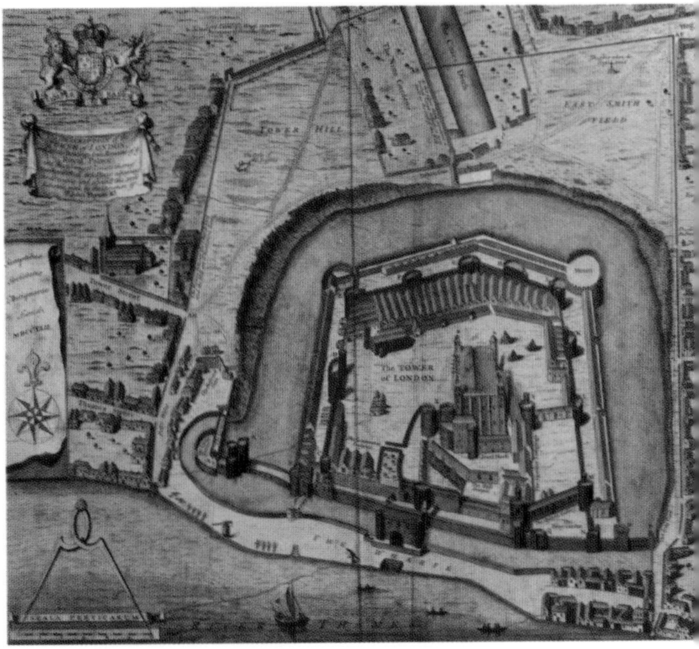

The Tower of London in 1597. The Lieutenant's Lodgings, where Cromwell may have been held, are shown at the bottom left. The Chapel of St Peter ad Vincula, where Cromwell's remains were buried, is towards the top left.

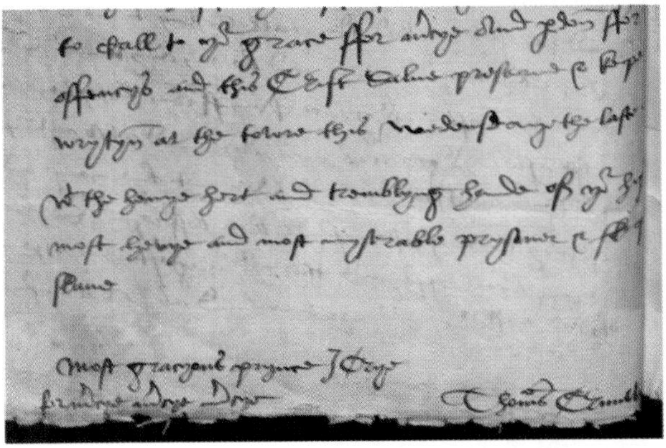

Cromwell's last letter to Henry VIII, 30 June 1540. Written from t Tower, this letter provided Henr with the evidence he needed to rid himself of Anne of Cleves. Cromwell added a desperate pos script for himself, pleading: 'Mos gracyous prynce I Crye for merc mercye mercye.'

London Bridge, 1616. The heads of traitors are displayed on the gateway at the bottom right of the picture, as Cromwell's would have been in 1540. The Tower of London can be seen on the opposite side of the river.

does nothing without first consulting the King, and also shows himself willing to do justice, especially to foreigners.'[1] This 'rough' style of government had served Cromwell very well during the past decade, winning him the admiration and trust of the king, to whom he had been careful to defer throughout. But it was this same style, derived no doubt from his humble origins, that now turned both king and council firmly against him. The blacksmith's son from Putney had ridden the wave of success for longer than anyone could have predicted. But now his noble enemies were closing ranks, eager to reclaim the business of government from this self-declared 'ruffian'.

The French ambassador's prediction was not as premature as it may have seemed. It is an indication of how embattled Cromwell felt that at the end of March he had attempted a reconciliation with Gardiner. Sir John Wallop, who was now the English ambassador in France, reported: 'This present hour, Wrisley [Wriothesley] showed me that yesterday my lord of Winchester dined at London with my lord Privy Seal, and were more than four hours, and opened their hearts, and so concluded that, and there be truth or honesty in them, not only all displeasures be forgotten, but also in their hearts be now perfect entire friends.'[2] That such a truce had been brought about was almost certainly as a result of a grovelling apology on Cromwell's part. Gardiner was secure in the knowledge that he had the king's favour, so it was up to his rival to make all the concessions. It must have been galling for the Lord Privy Seal, given that a short time ago he had enjoyed complete ascendancy over the bishop.

Even this humiliating performance was not enough to stave off his aggressors, however, for Cromwell was obliged to take more decisive action. Shortly afterwards, he resigned the secretaryship to his protégés, Ralph Sadler and Thomas Wriothesley, and the latter also joined the Privy Council. Quite why Cromwell chose this strategy is not clear: certainly, he could not have been forced into the resignation by his fellow councillors, no matter how aggressive their tactics might have been. Only the king could have taken the office away from him. It is possible that Cromwell, with a nod from

Henry, was making way for his forthcoming promotion, or wished to increase his influence within the council.

On 12 April a new session of parliament opened. Parliament had always been Cromwell's favourite arena, and he approached this one with as much outward confidence as he had the rest. Determined to align firmly with the king's more conservative stance, he made an opening speech in the House of Lords in which he emphasised Henry's wish for religious accord among his subjects. He proceeded to put in place measures for the appointment of a commission to correct all abuses and enforce respect for the scriptures. This was a blatant attempt to eradicate heresy, which would in turn lead to the unpicking of some of the reforms that Cromwell had held so dear. Two new committees were subsequently appointed with the specific objective of establishing the 'middle way' in religion that the king so desired.

But the minister did not entirely turn his back on reform. The only surviving stronghold of monasticism in England was the ancient military and religious order of the Knights of St John of Jerusalem. Cromwell had drawn up an Act to abolish them and divert their property to the crown. A lengthy debate followed, which culminated in triumph for the beleaguered minister when the Act was finally passed by both houses. He followed it up with a complex taxation bill, which would also swell the royal coffers considerably.

Parliament had once more – but for the final time – proved a triumph for Cromwell. It had enabled him to demonstrate more clearly than ever before the strength of his loyalty to the king. In paving the way for religious accord and bolstering the royal finances, he had performed a service that was at once valuable and self-sacrificing. It was probably in recognition of this that on 18 April Henry granted his minister the earldom of Essex, one of the most ancient and distinguished titles in the land, which had become vacant in March when Henry Bourchier, the second earl, had died after falling from his horse and breaking his neck. At the same time, Henry appointed him to the senior court office of lord great chamberlain, following the death of John de Vere, fifteenth Earl of Oxford. Meanwhile, Cromwell's son Gregory was given the honorary title of Lord Cromwell, and both he and Wriothesley were also knighted. This apparent volte-face on Henry's part prompted an astonished Marillac to remark that the new Earl of Essex 'was in as much credit with the King as ever he was, from which he was near being shaken by the Bishop of Winchester and others'.[3] Cromwell was immensely proud of his new title and thenceforth signed his letters 'Thomas Essex'. The fact that he had inherited the title and office of two of the most blue-blooded members of Henry's court was too much for Norfolk and his supporters to bear. Cromwell's very existence was now an insult. He must not be allowed to enjoy his newfound grandeur for much longer.

But more signs of royal favour were to follow. Henry granted Cromwell estates and income belonging to various disbanded monasteries in Essex, most notably St Osyth's. The substantial lands and rents were granted 'to the said Thomas lord Crumwell for life'.[4] Little did Cromwell know how short this life would be. He might have done well to reflect that, shortly before her downfall, Anne Boleyn had unexpectedly had great honours conferred upon her by the king. His favour could be terrifyingly fickle – even more so in recent years. Chapuys once wrote that he despaired of forming 'a judgment, considering the changeableness of this king'. The Spanish Chronicle agreed that 'when the King took a fancy to anyone he carried it to extremes' – but could withdraw it just as suddenly. Cromwell knew this better than anyone, although he had always praised his master's justice and steadfastness, 'being a prince most honorable obseruatour of his worde'. This formerly athletic and slender king was now 'very stout and marvellously excessive in drinking and eating'. His increasing girth put pressure on his ulcerated leg, and the pain made him even more prone to unpredictable bursts of temper. As a result, Marillac observed, 'people worth credit say he is often of a different opinion in the morning than after dinner.'[5]

Nevertheless, Cromwell's luck seemed to have turned and things continued to go his way. In mid-April a rumour reached the court in London that vindicated the new earl's foreign policy. It was reported that the French were fortifying Ardres, which lay close to

Calais. Cromwell instructed Wallop to demand an explanation for this apparently aggressive act from the French king. Henry's suspicions were aroused still further when his rival calmly retorted: 'He knewe not but that He myght aswell buyld there or fortefye uppon his borders as the Kinges Highnes dothe at Callais, Guysnes, and other his fortresses.'[6] Suddenly, the English king's blossoming hopes for an Anglo-French alliance appeared woefully optimistic, which in turn put Cromwell's alliance with Cleves in a more positive light.

But even as the king and his ministers were reacting to the news from France, there came tidings from the Netherlands of an even graver nature. Having successfully quashed a revolt in Ghent, Charles V had demanded that the Duke of Cleves surrender Gelderland. As the ally of Cleves, England would be called upon to go to the duke's aid, which in turn would bring them into direct conflict with the emperor – something that Henry had been at such pains to avoid. To make matters worse, affairs in Scotland and Ireland had also become unsettled, and the blame for these could be placed squarely on Cromwell's shoulders. Once more, the political tide had turned against the new Earl of Essex, and his enemies were quick to seize the initiative.

Events now gathered pace. Lord Lisle, the man who had been a thorn in Cromwell's side for so long, had arrived in London the day before his ennoblement. Norfolk had invited him, eager to swell the ranks of his supporters at court. But the duke had an even greater ace up his sleeve in the form of his niece, Katherine. The king probably first met Katherine Howard the previous December, when he had travelled to Rochester to meet his new wife. Daughter of Thomas Howard, the younger son of the second Duke of Norfolk, she had been appointed one of Anne's maids of honour. Her age is not certain, but she could have been only fifteen when Henry first set his lustful eyes on her. Although young, Katherine was no innocent. She had been raised by her father's stepmother, the Dowager Duchess of Norfolk, whose household was not known for its strict moral standards. An inappropriate liaison with her music teacher in 1536, when she may have been as young as twelve, was soon followed by a sexual relationship with her kinsman, Francis

Dereham, who used her 'in such sort as a man doth use his wife many and sundry times'.[7] That they were lovers was beyond doubt: Dereham even referred to Katherine as his wife. Virginity was a prerequisite for noble brides, so the affair was hushed up by the dowager duchess, who secured her a position in the new queen's household soon after discovering the affair.

Norfolk was quick to spot the king's obvious attraction to his young niece. Alluring and vivacious, Katherine provided a perfect foil to the wife whom Henry found so distasteful. He therefore began to arrange meetings between the pair. He was assisted in this by his ally Gardiner, who was reported to have provided feasts and entertainments at his Southwark palace in order to advance the courtship. By April 1540, the king's new love interest was known throughout the court. On the 24th of that month, Henry had granted Katherine the possessions of two murderers (the goods and property of convicted felons being forfeit to the crown), and on 18 May he bought her twenty-three sarcenet quilts. One observer noted that he 'crept too near another lady'.[8] The queen herself was aware of it, and on 20 June complained to the Duke of Cleves's ambassador in London, Karl Harst. Interestingly, in his subsequent report to the duke, Harst claimed that the affair had been going on for months, although there is no evidence to corroborate this. Meanwhile, tutored by her uncle, Katherine was careful to play the maid with her royal suitor. With the prospect of an annulment from Anne of Cleves tantalisingly close, she held out for the main prize.

Although Cromwell had been working towards the same annulment, the idea that the niece of his most deadly enemy should become the next queen was anathema to him. He was now placed in an impossible predicament: if he carried out the king's orders, then he would pave the way for Katherine Howard's accession; if he defied them, he would earn the censure of his royal master. Both scenarios spelled disaster. For the first time in his political career, Cromwell was cornered – and with little prospect of escape.

Nevertheless, for the next two weeks, Cromwell maintained business as usual. The fact that he continued to involve himself in the minutiae of legal and religious affairs is testament as much to his relentless energy and hard work as to his apparent confidence that his favour with the king was secure. Thus, he spent many hours examining the complaints against William Hargill of Kilmington in Somerset, who together with his sons had allegedly tried to murder a local man for demanding the return of a sow stolen by Hargill's servants. Likewise, he settled a petty dispute relating to the parsonage of Whitford in north Wales, and proceeded to secure a curacy for a clerk in Wiltshire.[9] If Cromwell had believed himself to be in danger, he would have focused all his efforts on safeguarding his position.

The traditional May Day jousts, held at Westminster Palace, seemed to confirm the Earl of Essex's return to favour. They began on Saturday, 1 May and lasted a full week. Among the challengers, all 'rytchlie apparayled' in white velvet and silk, was Cromwell's nephew, Richard. His son Gregory, meanwhile, was among the opponents.[10] Richard evidently relished the opportunity to show off his natural sporting prowess and went on to distinguish himself in the jousts, defeating, among other challengers, the soon to be notorious Thomas Culpeper. The king, who had been in constant attendance with his new wife, was so impressed that he declared: '"Formerly thou wast my Dick, but hereafter thou shalt be my diamond", and thereupon dropped a diamond ring from his finger, which Sir Richard taking up, his majesty presented it to him, bidding him ever afterwards bear such a one in the fore gamb of the demy lion in his crest.' Henry proceeded to bestow a knighthood upon the young man, much to his uncle's satisfaction, no doubt. Richard and his fellow challengers were also granted an annual fee of 100 marks, together with a house for them and their heirs, from the proceeds of the Friary of St Francis in Stamford, which had been dissolved in October 1538.[11]

If Cromwell had been heartened by these signs of favour, he would soon realise how foolhardy this was. On 9 May his royal master summoned him to a council. Although the records of the meeting have not survived, it had almost certainly been convened to discuss ways of extricating the king from the Cleves alliance.

Two days later, Cromwell was forced to write a letter to Richard Pate, the new ambassador to Charles V, instructing him to make conciliatory moves to the emperor by hinting that England's alliance with Cleves would soon be at an end. Henry's stance was confirmed when, towards the end of the month, he received Duke William's ambassadors at court with studied coldness, giving only the most non-committal of answers to their pleas for assistance against the emperor.

Rather than being cowed by these ominous developments, Cromwell lashed out at his opponents with renewed vigour. He set up the Court of Wards to administer the system of feudal dues, and this was confirmed by Act of parliament in June 1540. Meanwhile Lisle, far from receiving the promotions that Norfolk had assured him would be his, was taken to the Tower on suspicion of treason on 19 May. He would never leave it. By the end of May, he had been joined by two other prominent conservatives, the Catholic bishop Richard Sampson and Dr Nicholas Wilson.

Such decisive action had an air of desperation about it. Cromwell knew that the time for diplomacy had passed: in striking out so viciously against his conservative adversaries, he was forcing his royal master to choose between the two competing factions at court. It was a strategy that was as brave as it was dangerous. Henry might seem to have swung back towards Cromwell, but his goodwill could never be relied upon for long.

As well as taking the offensive against his religious opponents, Cromwell also attempted to capitalise on the more positive developments in the king's new marriage. Anne's attendance, with Henry, at the traditional May Day tournaments fuelled rumours that she would soon be crowned, this ceremony often following several weeks or even months after the wedding. She instructed Karl Harst, the Cleves ambassador and her close confidant, to discuss the possibility with her husband's councillors. Cromwell was almost certainly among the men with whom he consulted. When, late in May, the Earl of Rutland made moves to enable Anne's ladies to return to Cleves, Cromwell again urged him to advise Anne to act more pleasantly to the king.

But if Cromwell had staked his success on the survival of his royal master's marriage, he had backed the wrong horse. Henry might have been anxious to keep up appearances, but he had no intention of staying married to a woman whom he found repugnant – particularly when he had such a beguiling alternative in the Duke of Norfolk's niece. Moreover, Cromwell's aggressive action against his adversaries at court had only served to intensify their efforts to get rid of him once and for all. The Spanish Chronicle claims that Norfolk and Edward Seymour started a rumour that Cromwell had received a substantial fee from the Duke of Cleves for arranging the marriage. They sought an audience with the king and repeated their suspicions, telling him: 'All the nobles of the realm are surprised that your Majesty should give so much power to the Secretary, who, doubtless, received a large sum from the Duke of Cleves for bringing about your marriage as he did.'

At the same time, they were said to have planted the seed of doubt in the king's mind as to why Cromwell retained so many servants. The Spanish Chronicle describes how Norfolk told him: 'It appears to us that Cromwell's intentions are not good . . . None of us, however high we may be in the State, have so many servants as he has, and I can prove that in all parts of the kingdom people are wearing his livery and calling themselves his servants, under shelter of which they are committing a thousand offences.' Another councillor who was present agreed: 'I know that he has arms in his house for more than seven thousand men, and we do not like the look of it . . . We cannot help noticing that he has put into your Majesty's guard fully forty men who have been his servants, and in your Majesty's chamber there are five devoted servants of his, and many things have been seen and spoken about which convince me that, as things are going, he could do just as he liked, and carry it out successfully.' According to this source, Cromwell kept more than 300 servants at his house and a further 1,500 men throughout the country wore his livery. The first figure was something of an underestimate, but the second was almost certainly exaggerated. Henry was said to be greatly perturbed when he heard all this, and assured the lords: 'I promise you I will find a way to take his power away from him.'[12]

Although this meeting is not mentioned by any other source, Cromwell's enemies did whip up suspicion about the number of servants and retainers in his pay. Their underlying theme was that the new Earl of Essex had treacherous intentions. As the rumours got increasingly out of hand, it started to be whispered that he aimed at nothing less than becoming king. An unnamed 'gentleman' reported that he had dined with Ambassador Chapuys and Cromwell when the latter had declared: 'I hope to be a king myself one day.' The Spanish Chronicle claims that, armed with this information, Norfolk and Seymour returned at once to their royal master. Upon hearing the report, Henry was shocked but apparently not surprised. 'I may inform you that I greatly suspect him of a design to raise the kingdom and murder me,' he told his two councillors, 'for only a few days ago he had the effrontery to ask me for my daughter Mary for his wife.'[13] This charge, like the suspicion about Cromwell's retainers, would form part of the case against him. The Spanish Chronicle may have imagined these conversations restrospectively, but they were based on rumours that were circulating at the time.

By the beginning of June, tensions were running so high that Marillac reported: 'Things are brought to such a pass that either Cromwell's party or that of the bishop of Winchester [Gardiner] must succumb.'[14] Nevertheless, the ambassador had changed his mind about the outcome and was confident that Cromwell would triumph. He opined: 'Although both are in great authority and favour of the King their master, still the course of things seems to incline to Cromwell's side.' He cited as evidence the rumour that Barnes would shortly be released while a cleric with known 'Popish leanings' had recently been arrested, but could not resist adding: 'so great is the inconstancy of the English'. He went on: 'Meanwhile the state of religion remains in this unhappiness, the bishops in envy and irreconcileable division and the people in doubt what to believe, some of those who are Lutherans being periodically taken for heretics, the others more often as Popish traitors. A conclusion ought to be taken at this Parliament and a middle way found; but to all appearances it will result like the diets in Germany, of which one engenders several others, and the doubts, instead of ending, will increase.'[15]

untied the Garter [from Cromwell's knee].'[2] The beleaguered minister was then escorted through a side door that opened on to the river, and taken by boat on the ominously short journey from Westminster to the Tower. There, he was placed in the charge of the constable, Sir William Kingston, who had been dispatched to arrest Wolsey a decade before. It was a final, uncomfortable parallel with the life of his former master.

Later that afternoon, Audley was given the task of announcing Cromwell's arrest to the House of Lords. The news was met with a shocked silence. It was less than two months since Cromwell had been created Earl of Essex, and barely three weeks since Lisle's arrest had seemed to signal a revival of the chief minister's fortunes. That he should now find himself in the Tower on charges of treason was a salutary lesson for the ambitious courtiers left in his wake. Shrewd and pragmatic though he was, the greatest shock must have been felt by Cromwell himself. 'Who in this land commanded more than Cromwell? / Except the king, who greater than myself?' his dramatic persona mused in the play dedicated to his life.[3] Certainly, he had been fully aware of the danger of his situation, and of how finely balanced was his favour with the king. But his recent promotions, coupled with his victories over Norfolk and Gardiner, must have buoyed his confidence. His reaction to his sudden arrest was one of utter bewilderment as much as fear and fury.

Gregory Cromwell was nearby in the House of Commons as the announcement of his father's arrest was made. He would therefore have learned of it very soon afterwards. Shock and distress for his father no doubt combined with fear for his own welfare. The experience of Anne Boleyn's arrest four years earlier proved that the king did not flinch from rounding up anyone connected with the prisoner. Gregory's courtesy title of Lord Cromwell was immediately forfeited, as were all his father's houses, lands and goods. Although this technically rendered Gregory and his wife homeless, they were hardly destitute. Gregory had been granted some quite extensive property in his own right in November 1538, and he continued to receive the profits from this.[4] For now, no further action was taken. It may have been his marriage to the late queen's sister that saved Gregory from arrest. Edward Seymour may also have interceded with the king on the couple's behalf. Either way, Gregory was soon assured of his sovereign's favour. Some months later, the merchant Richard Hilles reported that Henry had conferred Cromwell's title 'and many of his domains while he was yet in prison upon his son Gregory . . . in order that he might the more readily confess his offences at execution'.[5]

While the announcement in the House of Lords was being made, the king had already dispatched a group of men to seize Cromwell's house at Austin Friars. Until now, news of Cromwell's arrest had not spread beyond the confines of the court, but when his neighbours saw the king's men searching Cromwell's house, the news spread like wildfire across the capital and beyond. Marillac had heard of it within an hour. He wrote at once to Francis I: 'Thomas Cramvel, keeper of the Privy Seal and Vicar-General of the Spiritualty, who, since the Cardinal's death, had the principal management of the affairs of this kingdom, and had been newly made Grand Chamberlain, was, an hour ago, led prisoner to the Tower and all his goods attached.'[6]

Cromwell's dismayed servants looked on as the king's men made an inventory of Cromwell's goods, which were reported to be 'not of such value as people thought', although 'too much for a man of his sort'. But they were not inconsiderable. A total of 7,000 pounds sterling (equivalent to more than £2 million today) was seized, along with silver plates, chalices, crucifixes and 'other spoils of the Church'. This was nearly an eightfold increase in the disposable cash he had held when his will had been drawn up in 1529. Marillac rightly observed that the fact that all these were taken straight to the king's treasury 'was a sign that they will not be restored'.[7]

As well as confiscating Cromwell's valuables, Henry's officers trawled his house for evidence that could help to condemn him. It did not take them long. 'Next day were found several letters he wrote to or received from the Lutheran lords of Germany,' Marillac reported. He had not been able to find out what they contained, 'except that this King was thereby so exasperated against him [Cromwell] that he would no longer hear him spoken of, but rather desired to abolish all memory of him as the greatest wretch ever born in England.' Francesco Contarini, the Venetian ambassador to the Imperial court in The Hague, claimed that the king's officers had also found letters 'showing that this Princess [Anne of Cleves] had [been] promised previously to another Prince of Germany.' The contemporary chronicler Charles Wriothesley agreed: 'She [Anne] was contracted to a Duke in her countrey before she came to England, and Sir Thomas Crumwell, Earle of Essex, had kept it secrett from the Kinge.'[8] If Cromwell really had withheld evidence of Anne's betrothal, it would have been enough to condemn him immediately. But given that this charge was never subsequently levied against him, it is likely to have been no more than gossip. The Venetian ambassador was writing at some distance from the English court and had little but rumour to go on – as proved by the fact that he then went on to report that Katherine Howard was already pregnant by Henry.[9]

The king was now as determined as Norfolk had been to reduce Cromwell to the obscurity under which he had laboured before entering royal service. All the property that he had held since 31 March 1538 was made forfeit to the crown. As it included the lands he had acquired from the dissolution of the monasteries, this comprised the bulk of his estate. Worse was to come. According to Marillac: 'To commence, this King distributed all his offices and proclaimed that none should call him lord Privy Seal or by any other title of estate, but only Thomas Cromwell, shearman, depriving him of all his privileges and prerogatives, and distributing his less valuable moveables among his [Cromwell's] servants, who were enjoined no longer to wear their master's livery.'[10] This may have been hearsay, but it is typical of the way that Cromwell's downfall was closely bound up with his lowly birth in the contemporary reports.

That Cromwell's ruin had been the result of a class war was a theme common throughout such dispatches. John Foxe regretfully observed that he had fallen victim to 'the hatred and enuie of certaine sedicious Noble men' who had conspired against him 'some for hatred, & some for Religions sake'.[11] Others were less sympathetic.

The disdain with which the dignitaries not just of England but of Europe had regarded this low-born heretic now became all too obvious. Marillac even apologised for bringing to his royal master's attention the fate of a commoner: 'Although this might be thought a private matter and of little importance, inasmuch as they have only reduced thus a personage to the state from which they raised him and treated him as hitherto everyone said he deserved, yet, considering that public affairs thereby entirely change their course, especially as regards the innovations in religion of which Cromwell was principal author, the news seems of such importance that it ought to be written forthwith.'[12] Marillac echoed what Cromwell's adversaries had long believed but had been unable to express while he was in power: his real crime was in aspiring to greatness when he was just a commoner. Now he had got his just desserts. Only the Venetian ambassador reported the matter without vitriol. His criticism was reserved for the fickleness of the English king. 'It is thought that he [Cromwell] likewise will make the same end as all the others most in favour with the King,' he wryly observed.[13]

Marillac did not have long to wait before being officially informed of Cromwell's arrest. He had almost finished his dispatch when a messenger arrived from the king himself. Henry was clearly eager to let the Catholic powers of Europe know that he had finally disassociated himself with the architect of his controversial and increasingly unpopular Reformation. The ambassador hastily reported that Henry had urged him not to be astonished that Cromwell had been sent to the Tower, and that 'as the common, ignorant, people spoke of it variously, he [the King] wished Marillac to know the truth.' He claimed that Henry wished 'by all possible means to lead back religion to the way of truth', and that 'Cromwell, as attached to the German Lutherans, had always favoured the doctors who preached such erroneous opinions and hindered those who preached the contrary.' The minister had recently been warned by some of his 'principal servants to reflect that he was working against the intention of the King and of the Acts of Parliament'. Unrelenting, Cromwell insisted 'that the affair would soon be brought to such a pass that the King with all his power could not prevent it, but rather acter assassination of his despised rival, the duke seized with bewildering speed the opportunity to destroy everything he had stood for and drag England back to religious conservatism. Realising that the king had long been ambivalent towards both Cromwell and his reforms, but that his current antipathy might not last – particularly if the beleaguered minister used his famed powers of persuasion to win Henry's sympathy – Norfolk wasted no time in constructing a watertight case against him. There must be no room for doubt, and no room for the king's notorious tendency to change his mind. The duke no doubt relished the news that his royal master had furiously rejected a set of letters received from 'Lutheran Lords' in Germany the day after Cromwell's arrest.

That Norfolk and his faction were instrumental in Cromwell's arrest is beyond doubt. Cromwell had long been their most dangerous and despised enemy, and his recent aggressive actions had only served to heighten their antipathy. The Spanish Chronicle claims that this had been his fatal error: 'If his pride had not betrayed him, and he had kept friendly with the lords [i.e. council], he would not have come to the end he did.'[16] But the nature of Henrician politics was such that Cromwell could not have secured the level of power he did without making enemies. A courtier's adversaries increased in direct proportion to the amount of influence he gained. If Cromwell had been content to work quietly behind the scenes, eschewing all promotion and favour, then he could hardly have wrought the ground-breaking changes he did. The stakes were high for anyone who wished to make his mark at the centre of royal power, but then so were the rewards. Cromwell had enjoyed the latter for the best part of a decade: now he faced the consequences.

The speed with which Henry abandoned the man who had been his mainstay for more than a decade suggests that their relationship had been fundamentally fragile. Admittedly, no courtier enjoyed the guaranteed and unchanging favour of an increasingly paranoid king, but there was an inequality in his relationship with Cromwell that stretched beyond the gulf in their status. Although the motivation behind some at least of his policies can be called into question, there can be little doubt that Cromwell's guiding force during the past eleven years had been his unswerving loyalty towards his royal master.

The king, for his part, had rewarded this loyalty with titles, privileges and riches – but with no corresponding fidelity. It is tempting to speculate that, had Cromwell been of noble birth, Henry might have felt more affinity, and therefore loyalty, towards him. But status was no guarantee of security, as the likes of Buckingham, Carew and Kildare had found to their cost. Even (or especially) being married to this ageing and increasingly volatile king offered no protection. His favour could change with the wind – and, once changed, it rarely reverted back to its original course.

But Henry's relationship with Cromwell was nothing if not complex. The Spanish Chronicle noted that the king had been 'very kind' to Cromwell's servants on his arrest, 'for he not only ordered them to be given what belonged to them, but commanded the gentlemen to choose servants from amongst them; and he himself took many of them into his own service to save them from want.'[17] Henry was also said to have ordered that his former minister should not be tortured, as was both permissible and expected for suspected traitors – especially those who proved reluctant to confess their crimes. In addition, he sent Cromwell some money, perhaps to buy him more comfort or food. A grateful Cromwell later wrote to 'humblye thanke your magestye For Suche money'.[18] A letter written just two days after Cromwell's arrest makes it clear how solicitious the king was for his former minister's welfare. He had told Sir William Kingston that Cromwell should write and tell him 'such thinges as I thought mete to be wryttyn Consernyng my most myserable State and Condicyon'. Cromwell thanked his master for his 'most haboundaunt goodnes benignyte and lycens', and must have seized upon this as a sign of hope that all was not lost. If Henry had altogether abandoned him, then surely he would not have cared how miserable were the conditions in which he was kept. No such clemency had been shown towards Cromwell's fallen rival, Anne Boleyn.

That Henry still displayed some favour towards Cromwell might suggest that he had ordered his arrest almost against his will, in order to placate Norfolk, Gardiner and the rest of their party. But this was an increasingly suspicious, dictatorial king. He might be influenced by his advisers, but there was no question of his being manipulated by them. If anything, Cromwell's ascendancy had motivated Henry to take a greater control over affairs of state than ever before.

Cromwell made the most of the opportunity that Henry's invitation to write had presented. His long and impassioned letter, dated 12 June and running to four closely written pages, was full of anguish at his arrest, as well as utter bemusement as to his supposed crimes. 'Moste gracyous King and most mercyfull souerayng', he began, describing himself as: 'your most humble and most obbeysand and most bounden subiett and most lamentable seruant and prysoner prostrate at the Feate of your most excellent magestye'. With all his lawyer's reason, he proceeded to chart the perilous course between insisting on his innocence while avoiding any implication that the king's justice was at fault. 'I haue beane accusyed to your Maiestye of Treason to that I saye I neuer in all my lyffe thought willinglye to doo that thing that myght or Sholde displease your Magestye and moche lesse to doo or saye that thing which of hit Selff is so highe and abhomynable offence as god knowyth who I dowt not Shall reueale the trewthe to your Highnes.' Careful to distinguish between the king and his 'accusers', he insisted: 'For as I ever have hade love to your Honour and person lyffe prosperyte helthe welthe Joye and Comforte and also your most dere and most entyerly belovyd Son the Prynce his grace and your procedinges god so helpe me in this myne adversyte, and Conffound me yf ever I thought the Contrarye.'

Realising that his only chance of survival was to convince the king of his absolute fidelity and dedication to his cause, Cromwell went on to remind him of everything he had done in his service during the past decade:

> What labours paynes and travayles I have taken according to my most bounden deutye god also knowyth, for yf it were in my power as yt is goddes to make your Magestye to lyve ever yong

> and prosperous god knoweth I woolde yf it hadde bene or were in my power to make you so riche as yet myght enryche allmen god helpe me as I wold do hit yf it hade bene or were in my power to make your Magestye so pusaunt as all the woorlde sholde be compellyd to obey you Crist he knowyth I woolde For so am I of all other most bounde For your Maiestye hathe bene the most bountyffull prynce to me that ever was kyng to his Subiect ye and more lyke a dere Father your Magestye not offended then a maister.

So confident was he that he could be guilty of none of the charges that were being prepared against him that he assured Henry: 'Sholde I now for Suche exceding goodnes benygnyte liberalyte and bountye be your traytor nay then the gretest paynes wer to lityll For me. Sholde any Faccyon or Any affeccyon to Any point make me a traytor to your Mageste then all the devylles in Hell Conffounde me and the vengeaunce of god light appon me.'

Having been kept in the dark about what he stood accused of, Cromwell evidently judged it better to defend himself to Henry against what he believed might be the charges, than to resign himself to speculating silently while his enemies convinced the king of his wrongdoings. Knowing that his work with the Court of Augmentations had sparked widespread criticism and resentment, and that it was believed that he had lined his own pockets from the sequestered monastic properties, he conjectured that this was one of the charges. He also supposed that Audley had been instrumental in his downfall, and reminded Henry that he had often warned Cromwell of his intrigues: 'What Maister Chauncelor hathe bene towardes me god and he best knowyth I will ne Can accuse hym. What I have been towardes hym your Magestye right well knowyth I woolde to Crist I hadde obbeyed your often most gracyous grave Counsayles and advertysmenttes then it hadde not bene with me as now it ys.'

Cromwell had also heard that another charge to be levied against him concerned the unlawful keeping of retainers. He swore that he had never retained anyone other than household servants, and that the only other people within his keeping were a number of his friends' children and acquaintances – men like Ralph Sadler. That

Cromwell's loyalty to his friends should be twisted into something altogether more sinister is an indication both of the malevolence of his enemies and of their desperation to grasp at anything that might help condemn him. Cromwell's denial was emphatic: 'This will I saye if ever I retaynyd any man but suche onlye as were my Howsholde servaunttes but ageynst my will god Conffound me.' He added that he had looked after his friends' children 'to my great Charge and For none evyll'.

Of one 'crime', though, Cromwell could be sure: his arranging the marriage between Henry and Anne of Cleves – and his failure to secure a swift annulment. He had heard that the king had complained to Kingston of 'A mattyer of gret Secresye which I dyde Reaveale contrarye to your expectacyon'. Although he knew that the king was referring to 'the thinges whiche your Highnes myslyked in the Quene', Cromwell denied that he had betrayed the secret (such as it was). The only people he had discussed it with were William FitzWilliam and the Earl of Rutland, but that had been at the king's behest.

Having thus defended himself against every accusation he could think of, Cromwell begged the king not to allow such a miscarriage of justice. 'Our Lorde yf it be his wille Can do with me as he dyde with Susan[19] who was Falslye accusyd . . . For other hope then in god and your Magestye I have not.' He ended with a profuse apology for any wrong he had unwittingly done, begging the king to be merciful:

> Sir I doo knowlage myself to have bene A most myserable and wrechyd Synner and that I have not towardes god and your Highnes behavyd my self as I owght and Sholde have done. For the which myne offences to god whyles I lyve I shall contynwallye kall for his mercye and For myne offencys to your grace which god knowyth wer never malycyous nor willfull, and that I never thought treson to your Highnes your Realme or posteryte So god helpe me ayther in woorde or dede nevertheles prostrate at your magestes [feet] in what thing soever I have offendyd I appell to your Highnes For mercye grace & pardon.

He signed the letter 'your most Sorowffull Subiect and most humble servant and prysoner this satyrday at your [Tower] of London, Thomas Crumwell'.[20]

Henry did not trouble himself to reply. He was too concerned to capitalise on Cromwell's downfall by currying favour with the French king. When he heard of the arrest, Francis I wrote at once to Marillac, declaring that the news

> has been to me not only agreeable, but such as, for the Perfect amity I have always borne towards my good brother, I have thanked God for; praying you to present him the letters of credence I have written you, and tell him from me that he has an occasion to thank God for having let him know the faults and malversations of such an unhappy person as Cromwell, who alone has been the cause of all the suspicions conceived against not only his friends, but his best servants. He shall know how much the getting rid of this wicked and unhappy instrument will tranquillise his Kingdom, to the common welfare of Church, nobles, and people.

He also instructed Marillac to encourage the English king in his prosecution of the disgraced minister, lest he have a change of heart. Marillac assured him that he had persuaded Henry 'of the harm done by such a minister, and the expediency of taking him away before he had completed his unhappy designs'.[21]

Francis also wrote to Henry himself, in order to hammer a final nail into Cromwell's coffin. He told his English rival that he had discussed (and no doubt condemned) the extent of Cromwell's influence with the latter's adversary: 'Norfolk will be able to remember what I said of it to him when he was last in France; to whom you shall first communicate this.' The French king's letter makes it clear just how far the tendrils of Norfolk's plotting had reached. Not content with swelling the ranks of Cromwell's enemies in England, he had garnered support from the Catholic potentates of Europe, using his various diplomatic missions as a means to do so directly – as well as his influence with England's ambassadors. On the very day of Cromwell's arrest, the duke had written to Richard Pate, English ambassador in the court of Charles V, instructing him to inform the emperor of all the details. Pate had done so with telling alacrity. But he had found Charles more reticent in his response than might have been expected. Clearly shocked, he cried: 'What! Is he in the Tower of London and by the King's commandment?' When Pate confirmed that this was so, the emperor declined to comment further.[22]

Norfolk and his envoys wasted no time in unpicking Cromwell's foreign policy with the same brutal efficiency as had been shown towards his religious reforms in England. On 27 July Pate reported that thanks to this reversal, the English king had 'lost the hartes of the Electors of thEmpire' but had 'contravailed thEmprour or the Frenche King in there places'.[23] The alliance with Cleves was brought to an abrupt end, the only obstacle being the small matter of the king still being married to Anne. It may have been in recognition of this fact that Henry made a rather half-hearted attempt to find the duchy another ally. He therefore let Francis I know that if he were to lend his support to Cleves, it would further improve Anglo-French relations. The Duke of Cleves had already dispatched ambassadors to the French court. In early July, Wallop and Sir Edward Carne reported that the French king had lent a sympathetic ear to their pleas, saying 'he would gladly make alliance with the duke of Cleves, as Henry approves of it, and was glad that Henry was sending another ambassador [Carne] to conclude the affair.'[24]

The aftershocks of Cromwell's dramatic fall from grace reverberated for several weeks. Not since Wolsey's fall a decade earlier had there been such shock, dismay and (for some) rejoicing at court. In his next dispatch to the French king, Marillac described 'the division among this King's ministers, who are trying to destroy each other'. The ambassador, who had only a few days before predicted Cromwell's triumph over his adversaries, was clearly taken aback by the turn of events. 'Cromwell's party seemed the strongest lately,' he observed. 'The thing is the more marvellous as it was unexpected by everyone.' That Cromwell had been forced to fend off the likes of Norfolk and Gardiner virtually single-handed was now all too obvious. Marillac reported that his party at court 'seems quite overthrown by the taking of the said lord Cromwell, who was chief of his band, and there remain only on his side the archbishop of Canterbury, who dare not open his mouth, and the lord Admiral [William FitzWilliam, Earl of Southampton], who has long learnt to bend to all winds, and they have for open enemies the duke of Norfolk and the others.'[25]

The said archbishop made the same heartfelt but inadequate plea on Cromwell's behalf as he had on Anne Boleyn's. He wrote to his sovereign, expressing his 'amazement and grief that he should be a traitor who was so advanced by the King and cared for no man's displeasure to serve him, and was so vigilant to detect treason that King John, Henry II, and Richard II, had they had such a councillor, would never have been so overthrown as they were'. Cranmer added that he had 'loved him [Cromwell] as a friend, and the more for the love he seemed to bear the King', but his next sentence gives the lie to that. He told Henry that he was 'glad' that Cromwell's 'treason' had been discovered, but also 'very sorrowful; for whom shall the King trust hereafter?' The archbishop ended by praying God 'to send the King a councillor he can trust, and who, for all his qualities, can serve like him'.[26]

Perhaps not surprisingly, Cranmer's letter produced no positive effect on the king. Even if Henry's conscience had been pricked by the archbishop's reference to Cromwell's service and fidelity, it would soon have been salved by Cranmer's apparently ready acceptance of the former minister's guilt. This in itself may have been a form of self-defence: it was rumoured that the archbishop would soon be following his ally to the Tower.

Inadequate it may have been, but Cranmer's letter stands alone as a lamentation on Cromwell's arrest. There is no evidence that his other close associates spoke up in his defence. Perhaps they were working quietly behind the scenes to try to rehabilitate him. But they were in an undeniably invidious position and risked being tainted, or even condemned, by association. Gregory's position was particularly difficult. He was the son of a suspected traitor but was married to the king's sister-in-law. When the king had shown his favour in the immediate aftermath of Cromwell's arrest, Gregory might have been tempted to petition him on his father's behalf. But his wife no doubt put pressure on him to protect their interests by remaining silent. She would soon prove just how eager she had been to distance herself from her father-in-law. By contrast, Richard Cromwell and Ralph Sadler, who had also recently enjoyed royal favour and were rising stars at court, still cherished a fierce loyalty for their master. This had been consistently proved throughout the previous decade, and even when it was clear that he was 'tottering', they had both remained firmly by his side. Having acted as Cromwell's secretaries and messengers for years, they had built up an excellent network of contacts at court and were no doubt working hard to secure his release. It may have been thanks to their persuasions that Cranmer had written to the king in their master's defence.

As the tidings of Cromwell's arrest spread across Europe, there was widespread celebration. The constable of Calais 'rejoiced at those newes, saying he was gladder of the same then to have had 1 million crownes'. The French king, meanwhile, declared it 'a very miracle of God'. Wallop gleefully reported that he had been besieged by French courtiers desperate for news that Cromwell had already been put to death. As he made his way through court one day, 'many asking him, by the way, if Cromwell were dead or not, they not a little rejoicing at his fate'. It was not long before the rumours started, all aimed at blackening Cromwell's character even more than it had been by his arrest. John Wallop, who was almost certainly an ally of Norfolk, wasted no time in declaring 'Cromwell's naughtiness at more length'. Meanwhile, the French cardinal and diplomat Jean du Bellay claimed that he had been reliably informed 'that the said late Privy Seal intended to make himselfe k[ing of] England when his tyme might serve him'. He had urged Wallop to let the English king know of this immediately.

An ambassador in Portugal had heard the same report, and added the embellishment that Cromwell 'shulde have the ladie Marie in mariage' – a tale that had apparently been well known among the ambassadors of Europe for the previous two years. Wallop needed no persuasion. He reported these rumours to his royal master the very same day: 'As to Cromwell, the Cardinal of Belly at once sent a man to Cattyllion, telling Wallop that three quarters of a year past he and the French king debated the matter and concluded that Cromwell would be made an earl or duke, and that Henry would then give him lady Mary, as, before, he gave the French queen to the duke of Suffolk.' It was for this reason, he said, that Cromwell had always done his best to break any marriage proposed for the king's elder daughter. Henry seized upon these rumours as much needed evidence in the undeniably flimsy case against his former chief minister, and ordered Wallop to validate the reports by finding hard evidence for them.[27]

Meanwhile, Cromwell himself was kept under close scrutiny in the Tower. Although the very name of the fortress was enough to strike terror into any English subject, Cromwell was well acquainted with it. As Master of the Jewels, he had overseen the rebuilding of the jewel houses on the south side of the White Tower. He had also introduced his friend Stephen Vaughan to the Royal Mint there. In 1536 he had instituted a major programme of repairs to other parts of the Tower, and shortly before his arrest he had ordered the building of the Queen's House, an elegant timber-framed building overlooking the scaffold site. As the king's chief enforcer, Cromwell had visited various high-profile prisoners in the Tower, most notably Thomas More and Anne Boleyn.

There is no record of where Cromwell himself was held, but the commonly held view is that it was in the Queen's Apartments (or lieutenant's lodgings), which were originally built for Catherine of Aragon and then refurbished for the coronation of Anne Boleyn. The building no longer exists, but it would have stood on the east side of the inner ward, between the Lanthorn Tower and Wardrobe Tower. If Cromwell had been kept here, then it was an irony that would not have been lost on him, for this is where his old adversary, Anne Boleyn, had been housed prior to her trial and execution. He knew the apartments well because he had arranged their refurbishment in 1532–3 on the king's orders. The lodgings were comfortable and well-appointed, and comprised a presence chamber, closet (which Anne had used as a private oratory), dining chamber and a bedchamber with a privy. If the furnishings were starting to show signs of neglect because they had lain unused for several years, they at least offered a good deal more comfort than most prisoners in the Tower could expect.

Not long after his arrest, Cromwell was subjected to intensive questioning. Among his interrogators was his arch-enemy, the Duke of Norfolk, who no doubt relished the task. The Spanish Chronicle provides an account of the vitriol that he and his colleagues unleashed now that they finally had their despised rival at their mercy. 'Cromwell, thou mayst well blame thyself and thy pride for bringing thee to this pass,' Seymour began with relish. 'Say, Cromwell, was it not enough for thee, a blacksmith's son, to have risen to lord it over the whole realm, and to have all of us to do thy bidding?'[28] For all his terror, Cromwell refused to give in without a fight. He demanded to know what he was accused of so that he could answer each charge in turn. He, more than anyone, knew how weak the case must be against him. True, he had orchestrated a revolution in government and religion, causing widespread discontent and rebellion along the way. But his every act had been authorised by the king, and he had never broken any laws or contravened any statutes or proclamations. Norfolk later recounted that Cromwell had 'desired, if he might not see his accusers, that he might at least know what the matters were; and if he did not answer truly every point, he desired not to live an hour longer.' Cromwell added the telling lament that he 'had always been pursued by great enemies about the king; so that his fidelity was tried like gold'. Perhaps this was a veiled threat to Norfolk and his fellow interrogators. They may have sensed that Cromwell intended to prove that they, not he, were guilty of treason. If so, then it worked. Cromwell was duly told of the charges against him, as well as the names of his accusers. This was an extraordinary privilege and had been granted to few before him.[29]

According to the Spanish Chronicle, the principal charge levied against Cromwell at this stage was the sheer scale of his ambition, which aimed at nothing less than marriage to the king's daughter and becoming a king himself. Declared Seymour:

> The devil must needs put it into thy head and furnish thee with such impudence as to presume to ask the King for the hand of his daughter. High, indeed, didst thou aspire, and nothing else can be believed but thou didst aim at usurpation of the realm, and to make thyself king, for so didst thou say one day at the Ambassador's [Chapuys's residence]. Oh, ignorant ingrate, dost thou not know that if the Emperor won kingdoms he has vassals far more worthy than thou; and besides, what service hast thou rendered to the Emperor that he should make a king of thee? By my faith! it is easier to believe, as we have said, that, if thou couldst have got Madam Mary, thou couldst easily have dispatched the King, for which purpose thou hadst surrounded him with thy creatures, the better to ensure thy fell design.[30]

This general condemnation done, the ministers turned to more specific lines of enquiry. One of the other most prominent themes was the marriage that Cromwell had arranged between his royal master and Anne of Cleves. That this was the issue in which the king had the closest interest is suggested by the fact that he himself drafted the questions that Cromwell should be asked on this matter. These ranged from what Henry had said to his minister on first meeting Anne at Rochester to the evidence that his new wife had been formerly betrothed. Seymour and his fellow interrogators pursued these questions with gusto: 'All the gentlemen began to talk, and everyone said to him what he liked – very abusive words.'[31]

Cromwell's response was no less scathing, according to the same source. 'If I had carried into effect what I intended once, you would not be ill-treating me now,' he told his interrogators. 'Do not take the trouble, my lords, to find out any more. It is my own fault for not revenging myself upon some of you. Let the King do as he likes with me, for I deserve to die; my only sorrow is that I did not see the death of some of you first.'[32] As ever, the chronicler had no doubt employed a degree of poetic licence because he would not have been present at the interrogation. But he was always well-informed about events at the heart of the court, and the verbal exchanges he imagined were consistent with the characters involved.

Cromwell remained defiant, stoutly defending himself against all the trumped-up charges. His royal master was growing impatient. In a letter written several months after the event, the merchant Richard Hilles claimed that the king had brought a range of psychological pressures to bear upon his former minister. He reported the rumour 'that he was threatened with burning at the stake instead of death by the axe if he did not confess his crimes at execution, and that he then said he was a miserable sinner against God and the King, but that what he said of having offended the King he said carelessly and coldly.' To support his claim that the king was using underhand tactics, Hilles recalled Henry's conferring of the earldom of Essex on Cromwell shortly before his arrest, 'just as he endowed queen Anne before he beheaded her', adding: 'some think this was an artifice to make people think he had been guilty of the most heinous treason.'[33] There is no reliable evidence to suggest that Cromwell was threatened with burning. This tale no doubt derived from wishful thinking on the part of the many traditional Catholics in England who viewed the disgraced minister as a heretic.

Although the rumours continued to fly, a full week passed before there was any further news. A bill of attainder was then introduced into the Lords. It was read for a second time two days later, on 19 June.[34] The list of indictments against this prisoner of 'very base and low degree . . . the most detestable traitor that has been seen during the King's reign' was staggeringly long: there were eleven in total and their detail ran to several pages. Principal among them was what can best be described as religious treason: Cromwell was a 'detestable herytike' who had conspired to bring Lutheranism into the country against the king's wishes. He had circulated heretical books that directly contravened articles enacted by parliament, especially those against the sacrament. This latter charge would later be strengthened so that Cromwell was directly accused of being a sacramentary – which, according to the first of the Six Articles, was a crime punishable by death, with no hope of pardon.

The wording of the document made it clear that this base-born minister had plotted to make himself more powerful than the king in all matters – political as well as religious – and had thus committed high treason, for which he was condemned to die. It accused Cromwell of 'usurpinge uppon your kingly estate power and authoritie and office, without your graces commandement or assent', and went on to relate the treacherous words that the minister was alleged to have spoken. 'Being a person of as poor and low degree as few be,' he had said publicly, 'that he was sure of you [i.e. the King], and it is detestable that any subject should speak so of his sovereign.' In his arrogance, he had become careless in his talk, uttering words that constituted treason. According to the charges, when the previous year certain 'heretical' preachers, including Robert Barnes, had been reported to Cromwell, he had openly supported them, vowing: 'If the King would turn from it, yet I would not turn; and if the King did turn and all his people I would fight in the field in mine own person with my sword in my hand against him and all other.' He had then held up his dagger saying, 'Or else this dagger thrust me to the heart if I would not die in that quarrel against them all; and I trust if I live one year or two it shall not lie in the King's power to resist or let it if he would.' Why it had taken a year for this conversation to be reported and acted on is not explained.

The charges went on. Cromwell had set at liberty persons guilty or suspected of treason, sold export licences, granted passports and drawn up commissions without the king's knowledge. He had also incited Anne of Cleves to act in a way that might win her husband's affection. This was intended to stoke Henry's fury because it implied that Cromwell had called his virility into question: why else would he struggle to consummate the union? The outlandish charge that Cromwell had plotted to marry the king's elder daughter, Mary, was added later. This can have been based on nothing more than the rumour put about by the Portuguese ambassador because Wallop had been able to find no corroborating evidence. Its inclusion in the charges was an indication of just how much of a witch hunt Cromwell's arrest had become. But nobody cared for that.

The indictment concluded with one final side-swipe at Cromwell's lack of pedigree: 'By bribery and extortion he obtained innumerable sums of money, and being so enriched, has held the nobles of the Realm in great disdain.'[35] The nature of the charges, and the phrasing of the bill, suggests that Norfolk had been instrumental in their drafting. He was determined to make the case against his old adversary so compelling that there would be no means of escape.

That Cromwell was now a step closer to the block caused intense excitement at court. Marillac gleefully reported: 'Nothing else is spoken of here, and in a week at latest the said prisoner is expected to be executed and treated as he deserves.' Now that Cromwell had been stripped of his offices and titles, it was anticipated that he would be treated as a common traitor. On 23 June Marillac reported to Anne de Montmorency, the highest ranking nobleman and official in France: 'From this it is inferred that he will not be judged with the solemnity accustomed to be used to the lords of this country, nor beheaded; but will be dragged up as an ignoble person, and afterwards hanged and quartered. A few days will show; especially as they have determined to empty the Tower at this Parliament, which finishes with this month.'[36] Norfolk encouraged Marillac in this view, assuring him that 'Cromwell's execution will take place immediately after Parliament closes, and his end will be the most ignominious in use in this country.'[37]

The bill of attainder was passed, with some amendments from the House of Commons, on 29 June. This terrifying instrument of royal jurisdiction, whereby noblemen could be stripped of their lands and their lives without recourse to the normal processes of the law, had been employed by Cromwell to eliminate many a political enemy in the past. Most attainders had been used to supplement a court's decision, but in 1537 Cromwell had arranged for Margaret Pole, Countess of Salisbury, to be convicted and executed on attainder alone, denying her the opportunity to put her case in court.[38] Now Cromwell was to be hoist by his own petard, as Cavendish observed:

> [I] Devised a law ayenst the accused,
> Condempnyng without answere, or he could understand
> The ground of his offence, it myght not be refused;
> Thus straytly the lawes my subtill wytt abused:
> Therfor, oon of the first, I ame tastying on the payn.[39]

Doubtless Cromwell appreciated the supremely ironic twist of fate whereby the world's most notorious lawyer had been condemned without trial.

But Henry had not quite done with Cromwell yet. By now desperate to escape his marriage to Anne of Cleves so that he could wed Katherine Howard, he was busy gathering evidence to prove that the union had not been consummated. Among those called to testify was Cromwell's former servant Thomas Wriothesley, who confirmed that the king had been so revolted by his new bride that he had been unable to perform the usual act of a husband. But Henry would not be satisfied until the man who had brought about the marriage in the first place swore to its invalidity. He therefore demanded that Cromwell give evidence, and was clear about what it should contain:

> As he [Cromwell] is condemned to die he will not damn [his soul, but declare what the King said, not only at the time but continually till] the day of mar[riage] and many times after, whereby his lack of consent will appear; and also lack of the will and power to consummate the same; wherein both he, my physicians, the lord Privy Seal that now is, Hennage and Denny can, and I doubt not will, testify according to truth; which is, that I never for love to the woman consented to marry; nor yet, if she brought maidenhead with her, took any from her by true carnal copulation.[40]

Seizing any opportunity for clemency, Cromwell did not hesitate to give his royal master what he wanted. The letter he composed the day after his attainder was more than just an avowal that no consummation had ever taken place between Henry and Anne, however. It was Cromwell's opportunity – probably his last – to persuade the king to pardon him. In short, he was writing for his life. The extreme desperation with which he composed it, carefully crafting each word so that it might produce the desired effect on his sovereign, is suggested not only by the numerous crossings out and redrafting, but by the fact that it ran to eight full pages. The original is now much decayed, but a copy that was taken of it soon after has ensured that Cromwell's words have been preserved for posterity.

The letter begins in the most humble and deferential way, with Cromwell expressing his desperate wish to serve the king in all things, even though circumstances prevent him: 'That it hath pleased your most royal and most merciful Majesty to send to me such honourable personages at two several times, at the one time sued for and at the other time declaring unto me my state and condition, in most honourable, prudent and sage fashion, my gracious and most benign sovereign lord . . . that I cannot condignly do my duty to your Majesty, but I will continually during my life pray to almighty God that He of his goodness may reward your graciousness and princely dealing towards me.' He went on to assure his sovereign:

> And where gracious prince they at their coming and repair towards me heard me in everything whatsoever I said without any interruption with such gentleness and patience that I could not more desire, so they pressed me by all means to do all that I could to detect and accuse any other person . . . who should in any wise not be true unto your Highness. Unto whom I answered as I now do, that if I knew any persons in your Realm that were not your true liegemen . . . I would as my duty is detect them, for gracious Prince, there is nothing earthly that I more covet than the security of your Royal person and the wealth of your Realm.

Referring to the bill of attainder being passed by the 'Upper' and 'Nether House' the day before, Cromwell attempted a show of humble acceptance that justice had been done: 'When I heard them I said as now I say that I am a Subject and born to obey laws, and knowing that the trial of all laws only consisteth in honest and probable witness, and considering that the state of your whole Realme had heard and received them and that they have proceeded, as I am sure they have done, without malice, I submitted me to their sentence.' His reference to the lack of malice in the proceedings reveals his insincerity: he must have been deeply embittered at the triumph of his enemy, Norfolk, in bringing him to such a pass.

Although Cromwell professed himself to be 'moche grieved' at being accused of treachery, he realised the futility of complaining about his rivals and instead chose to assure the king of his unfailing loyalty and devotion: 'God is god and knoweth both my faithfulness towards your Majesty, and your Realm . . . how dear your person was, is and ever hath been . . . I had your laws in my breast.' This would later be twisted by his enemies into an admission by Cromwell that he 'was punished by the just judgement of God, because he had loved the King more than God'.[41] Referring to himself as a 'ffull Crysten [Christian] man', Cromwell couched everything in terms of deference to God and the king, declaring: 'Most gracious prince, I humbly submit me to your Grace and ask of God mercy for my sins and of your Highness mercy and pardon for my offences, as to your high wisdom shall seem most convenient. And Sir that ever I have deceived you in any of your treasure, surely I have not, and that God almighty best knoweth, and so that I may be helped at my most need I beseech Christ.'

Thus far, Cromwell's letter conformed to the usual pleas for clemency that were written in desperation to the king by a prisoner awaiting execution. His protestations of loyalty and acceptance were both necessary and expected. However, the subject to which he now turned his attention was altogether closer to his heart. Fearing that Gregory's fate would be inextricably tied to his own, he begged Henry to look favourably upon him: 'Sir upon my knees I most humbly beseech your gracious majesty to be a good and gracious lord to my poor Son, the good and virtuous lady his wife and their poor Children . . . and this I desire of your grace for Christ's sake,' adding: 'I shall daily pray for your highness.' Making an explicit reference to Gregory's wife was probably intended to remind the king that he was related by marriage to his former minister, as well as to soften his heart by calling to mind Elizabeth's late sister, the beloved Queen Jane. That Cromwell should plead for his son before responding to the king's demand for evidence to support his divorce from Anne of Cleves is an indication of how desperate he was to safeguard Gregory's future.

Cromwell now turned to the main purpose of his letter – at least from his royal master's perspective – that of the Cleves marriage. He was in an extremely invidious position. If he testified that the marriage had been unlawful, he would pour scorn on himself as the architect of the union and thus give the king even more reason to put him to death. But if he defended the validity of the marriage, he would increase the king's displeasure against him. He therefore crafted his testimony with as much caution and balance as might be expected of such a skilful and experienced lawyer.

Cromwell began by describing how a delegation from the council (Norfolk, Audley and FitzWilliam) had 'movyd and [stirred me upon my] sowlle and conscyens to declare what [I knew in the] maryage betwene your magest[y and the Queen]'. He went on to describe the conversation he had had with Henry after the latter had first set eyes on his new bride at Rochester.

> I spoke with your grace and demanded of you how you liked the lady Anne, your grace being somewhat heavy as I took it answered and said she was no such manner of woman as she had been declared to you, with many other things which surely much grieved me, for I perceived your grace to be nothing content, nevertheless your highness determined for the meeting the next day to be had as it was before appointed . . . and after which meeting and your entry made . . . your grace called me unto you asking me whether your Grace had told me truth or no, to the which I said little, for I was very sorrowful to consider that your grace was no better content.

Knowing how valuable his evidence would be to Henry in extricating himself from his marriage, and what he was required to say in order to help achieve this, Cromwell then referred to the matter of Anne's previous betrothal to the Duke of Lorraine's son. Although he could not question the sincerity of the Cleves ambassadors in avowing that the betrothal had been formally dissolved, he hinted that they had deliberately withheld the necessary documentation to support it. He also repeated Henry's conviction that Anne's body had showed signs of previous sexual intercourse, and that as a result 'your hert Coulde never consentt to medyll with her Carnallye.' This was a tactful was of explaining his inability to consummate the union, and avoided any implication of impotence.

In case this deliberately ambiguous testimony should not fulfil the contradictory requirements of satisfying the king and defending Cromwell's actions, the prisoner ended with a protestation of his inability to give evidence in such a weighty business:

> I am a right simple man to be a witness in this matter, but yet I think next to your grace I know as much as any one man living in this Realm doth, and that this is true God shall be my witness who best knoweth the truth, and I trust my lord admiral will bear me witness what I said to him at your Grace's return from Rochester, and also at diverse other times. I doubt not all my lord's beforenamed might right well perceive both before the day of your gracious marriage and after that your highness was not well pleased, and before God I never thought your grace content after you had seen her.

Judging that he had thus fulfilled the king's request to help him escape his marriage to Anne, Cromwell assured his master: 'Making an end I shall whilst I continually pray for the long prosperity and wealth of your higness send your Majesty.' He ended the letter with a final plea for mercy. Perhaps it was the realisation that he may have just performed his last ever service to Henry that drove him to set aside his usual composure. The sheer terror with which he was now engulfed is painfully obvious. Referring to the 'shedding of my blood', he begged the king 'uppon my knees prostrate' to pardon him, and ended: 'Written at the Tower this Wednesday the last of June with the heavy heart and trembling hand of your higness' most heavy and most miserable prisoner and poor slave Thomas Cromwell.' Fearing that even this was not enough, he added a desperate postscript: 'Most gracyous prynce I Crye for mercye mercye mercye.'[42]

Despite his near-hysterical state, having lived at the heart of royal power for almost twenty years, Cromwell must have known all too well how unlikely it was that words alone could save him. Nevertheless, Henry was said to have asked for his letter to be read to him three times. Although Foxe implies that this was because he was so moved by its contents, it is at least as likely that the king wanted to be sure that it contained the requisite evidence to free him from his marriage to Anne of Cleves. The fact that Cromwell received no reply to his heartfelt pleas gives weight to the latter theory.

The king's silence was answer enough.

CHAPTER 19

'Many lamented but more rejoiced'

As Cromwell languished in the Tower anxiously awaiting news from court, the woman whom he had put on the throne was in the process of being ousted. On 24 June Anne had received orders from the council to remove herself from court and go to Richmond Palace. She confided to the Cleves ambassador that she feared she would meet the same fate as Catherine of Aragon. But Anne was no martyr. For all her sadness that the king did not want her, she was a pragmatist at heart and was prepared to submit with grace to what had become inevitable.

Henry's lawyers continued to use Anne's earlier betrothal to the Duke of Lorraine as the basis for the annulment. They claimed that this was why the king had been unable to consummate the marriage: it was 'relative' impotence, limited to one woman, they were careful to argue. No matter how urgently Henry might wish to be free of Anne, he was not about to have his manliness called into question. An ecclesiastical enquiry was duly commissioned, and a delegation of councillors, including the Duke of Suffolk, William FitzWilliam and Thomas Wriothesley, arrived at Richmond on 6 July to seek Anne's consent to the enquiry. Apparently shocked by this sudden turn of events, Anne fainted. When she had sufficiently recovered herself, she refused to cooperate. This rather unconvincing show of defiance was perhaps derived more from a wish to preserve a vestige of pride than a genuine desire to save her marriage.

Three days later, that marriage was declared illegal. Anne consented to the decree and wrote a formal letter of submission to the king, saying that 'though this case must needs be most hard and sorrowful unto me, for the great love which I bear your most noble person, yet, having more regard to God and his truth than to any worldly affection . . . I knowledge myself hereby to accept and approve the same.' Confirming that the marriage had not been consummated, she referred to 'your Majesty's clean and pure living with me', and offered herself up as his 'most humble servant'.[1] She reiterated the same in a letter to her brother later that month, declaring: 'My body remaineth in the integrity which I brought into this realm.'[2] Her capitulation enabled parliament to confirm that the marriage was invalid on 12 July.

Henry could now proceed with plans to marry Norfolk's niece. These plans proceeded in direct parallel to those for Cromwell's execution. This was scheduled for the morning of 28 July at Tower Hill. That Cromwell should be denied a private execution on Tower Green, away from the jeering crowds, was significant. On being condemned for treason, he had been stripped of all his honours. No longer the Earl of Essex, Lord Privy Seal or any of the many other titles he had enjoyed, he was to meet his death as a commoner.

Neither was Cromwell to be the only prisoner to die that day. Lord Hungerford, whose wife had appealed to him for assistance four years previously, was a former protégé of Cromwell, who had arranged his appointment as Sheriff of Wiltshire and rewarded him richly for his loyal service. But Hungerford had proved a good deal less loyal to the king, and was accused of harbouring a clergyman with known sympathy for the Pilgrimage of Grace. Moreover, he was said to have enlisted the services of a cunning man to predict the king's death. This was treason, and Hungerford was swiftly indicted. The charge of 'buggery' was also added to the growing list.

There is no record of Gregory Cromwell's activities during the run-up to his father's execution. He had apparently resigned himself to keeping a low profile, even if he had been working behind the scenes with Ralph Sadler, Richard Cromwell and others. His wife Elizabeth, meanwhile, had written a series of letters to the king, pleading for his forgiveness and clemency towards herself and her husband. Only one of them survives. It was written in July 1540, shortly before the date scheduled for Cromwell's execution. Elizabeth began by thanking Henry for his favour.

> After the bounden duty of my most humble submission unto your excellent majesty, whereas it hath pleased the same, of your mere mercy and infinite goodness, notwithstanding the heinous trespasses and most grievous offences of my father-in-law, yet so graciously to extend your benign pity towards my poor husband and me, as the extreme indigence and poverty wherewith my said father-in-law's most detestable offences hath oppressed us, is thereby right much holpen and relieved, like as I have of long time been right desirous presently as well to render most humble thanks, as also to desire continuance of the same your highness' most benign goodness.

She went on to assure the King that:

> considering your grace's most high and weighty affairs at this present, fear of molesting or being troublesome unto your highness hath disuaded me as yet otherwise to sue unto your grace than alonely by these my most humble letters, until your grace's said affairs shall be partly overpast. Most humbly beseeching your majesty in the mean season mercifully to accept this my most obedient suit, and to extend your accustomed pity and gracious goodness towards my said poor husband and me, who never hath, nor, God willing, never shall offend your majesty, but continually pray for the prosperous estate of the same long time to remain and continue.

This letter makes a lie of the affection that Elizabeth had formerly expressed towards Cromwell. No longer her 'good lord and father', he was now the perpetrator of 'heinous trespasses', 'grievous offences' and 'detestable' crimes.[3] She may have been persuaded to write it by her brother, Edward Seymour, or Henry himself may have demanded it. Gregory can hardly have approved of his wife's apparent disloyalty, but Cromwell himself might have been more understanding. His daughter-in-law had, after all, merely demonstrated the same pragmatism that had sustained him throughout his career.

On 24 July, four days before his execution was due to take place, Cromwell penned his last surviving letter. It was not a poignant farewell to his family or friends, but a justification to the Privy Council of his actions with regard to the seizure of booty from the governor of Picardy's ships. It was thanks to Francis I that this useful additional charge had been added at the last minute. He had written to Henry VIII after Cromwell's arrest, claiming that the minister had diverted the booty to his own profit. Cromwell emphatically denied any wrongdoing: 'I answer to god I never barre Favour in the matyer otherwise thenne to Justyce,' and called upon Norfolk, Gardiner and others who had been involved in the matter to testify to his actions. 'That ever I hade any partte of that pryse or that I wer promyssyd Any part theroff my lordes assure yoursellfes I was not as god shall and may helpe me.'[4] That the council had raised this petty dispute at such a time was probably intended to blacken Cromwell's character still further, so that the king's subjects and his international allies should be left in no doubt as to the fallen minister's guilt. It was a callous, final blow to what little morale he had left.

The Spanish Chronicle claims that on 27 July Cranmer and Seymour were ordered to visit Cromwell in the Tower and inform him that he was to die the next day. With typical brutality, Seymour pronounced: 'I am sure it is God's will that you should live no longer. It seems you have learnt well from the Cardinal.' But the prisoner was not to be provoked. Having lived under the shadow of the axe for seven long weeks, Cromwell's terror had given way to a calm acceptance. He was observed to have 'remained very pensive all that night'. Perhaps he had been told, at the last, that his sentence had been commuted from the horrors of the traitor's death to the swifter beheading. Marillac reported: 'Grace was made to him upon the method of his death, for his condemnation was to a more painful and ignominious penalty.' But this was hardly likely to have brought him much comfort. More likely is that Cromwell had at last relinquished any hopes of persuading his royal master to relent. With the loss of hope often comes a strange sort of relief. Not so for his fellow prisoner, Lord Hungerford, who 'seemed so unquiet that many judged him rather in a frenzy than otherwise'.[5]

When at last the hour appointed for Cromwell's execution on 28 July came, the sheriffs of London were ordered to escort him from his lodgings to the scaffold. It was recorded that 'he was brought forth with a thousand halberdiers, as a revolt was feared; and if all those who formerly wore his livery and called themselves his servants had been there, they might easily have raised the city, so beloved was he by the common people.' In the event, no such catastrophe occurred. It was with great composure that Cromwell mounted the scaffold and prepared to deliver a short speech to the assembled crowds. Among them was the seasoned courtier Thomas Wyatt, who was in great distress. According to the Spanish Chronicle, Cromwell addressed his long-standing protégé with these words of comfort: 'Oh, Wyatt, do not weep, for if I were no more guilty than thou wert when they took thee, I should not be in this pass.'[6]

If this was an acceptance of his guilt, Cromwell was apparently referring only to his political activities. In the speech he now gave to the onlookers, and which was subsequently printed and widely circulated, he began: 'Good people, I beseech you pray to God for me.' Then, seeing 'a great many courtiers' present, he addressed them:

> Gentlemen, you should all take warning from me, who was, as you know, from a poor man made by the King into a great gentleman, and I, not contented with that, nor with having the kingdom at my orders, presumed to a still higher state, and my pride has brought its punishment. I confess I am justly condemned, and I urge you, gentlemen, study to preserve the good you possess, and never let greed or pride prevail in you. Serve your King, who is one of the best in the world, and one who knows best how to reward his vassals.[7]

No matter how greatly his former colleagues and rivals triumphed to see his downfall, they must have shuddered at this salutary warning. The fickle favour of their king meant that they might one day find themselves surveying the crowds from Cromwell's vantage point, not their own.

Cromwell continued his speech in the traditional fashion, accepting the justice of his fate: 'I am come hether to dye, and not to purge my self, as maie happen, some thynke that I will, for if I should so do, I wer a very wretche and miser: I am by the Lawe condempned to die, and thanke my lorde God that hath appointed me this deathe, for myne offence: For sithence the tyme that I haue had yeres of discrecion, I have liued a synner, and offended my Lorde God, for the whiche I ask hym hartely forgeuenes.' It was entirely customary for condemned traitors to accept the justice of their fate in order to save those whom they left behind. The fact that Cromwell had been at such pains to persuade Henry to look benevolently on his son makes it likely that this was his intention. Moreover, later in the speech he declared: 'I hartely desire you to praie for the Kynges grace, that he maie long liue with you, in healthe and prosperitie. And after him that his sonne prince Edward, that goodly ympe, maie long reigne ouer you.' This reference to the prince may have been intended by Cromwell as another reminder to Henry that his son was the nephew by marriage of Gregory Cromwell.

The prisoner went on to reflect upon his life, and the great fortune to which he had risen: 'And it is not unknowne to many of you, that I haue been a great traueler in this worlde, and beyng but of a base degree, was called to high estate, and sithens the tyme I came thereunto, I haue offended my prince, for the whiche I aske hym hartely forgeuenes, and beseche you all to praie to God with me, that he will forgeue me. O father forgeue me.' This reference to his humble origins was a masterstroke: he knew that it had sparked much of the resentment against him, both among his fellow councillors and ordinary subjects alike. Yet it had not, of course, been something that could be included in the myriad charges against him: low birth was not a crime. By making such open reference to it, and pretending to share his adversaries' disgust that someone so lowly could have risen so high, Cromwell sought to win sympathy from the assembled crowds, many of whom would have been drawn from the lower classes.

The condemned man then turned to the matter of religion.

> I praie you that be here, to beare me record, I die in the Catholicke faithe, not doubtyng in any article of my faith, no nor doubting in any Sacrament of the Churche. Many hath sclaundered me, and reported that I haue been a bearer, of suche as hath mainteigned euill opinions, whiche is vntrue, but I confesse that like as God by his holy spirite, doth instructe vs in the truthe, so the deuill is redy to seduce vs, and I haue been seduced: but beare me witnes that I dye in the Catholicke faithe of the holy Churche . . . And once again I desire you to pray for me, that so long as life remaigneth in this fleshe, I wauer nothyng in my faithe.'[8]

Cromwell's avowal that he died in the 'Catholicke faith' has been taken as an utter denial of his religious reforms. Indeed, it has been speculated that it had been written by others and 'forced upon Cromwell's dying lips'.[9] Another possibility is that the printed version of the speech, contained within Hall's *Chronicle*, did not faithfully record what Cromwell said. On 11 September Cardinal Pole confided to an Italian associate that he feared he was 'wrong in writing of Cromwell's coming to his senses, for his last words as printed do not give the same impression as the narrative of those who told of his end and last words.' Pole concluded: 'The judgment of men belongs to Christ, who knows the hidden things of the heart.'[10] In fact, the speech that was recorded by Holinshed, Hall and Foxe, with a high degree of correlation between them, has all the hallmarks of Cromwell's powers of reason and oration, and there is little reason to doubt its accuracy. It was a brilliantly ambiguous statement that enabled Cromwell apparently to conform to the traditional Catholic faith that his royal master now espoused, while upholding his personal reformist stance. It must be remembered that Cromwell had not aimed at supplanting Catholicism, but Roman Catholicism. Ridding England of papal authority had been necessary in order to secure Henry VIII's divorce from Catherine of Aragon, and thereby further Cromwell's own political career. Dissolving the monasteries, meanwhile, had aimed at least as much to swell the royal coffers as to root out corruption and restore the purity of the religious orders.

Cromwell may have personally harboured reformist views and planned to introduce evangelical ideas into England, but by the time of his arrest he had done nothing more than prepare the groundwork. In his final speech, he was reiterating the fact that he had remained a good Catholic, like his sovereign. He also denied the accusation that his enemies had tried to pin on him at the last, namely that he had joined the sacramentaries – a sect reviled by Catholics and reformists alike. By insisting that he did not doubt 'in any sacrament of the Church', he was facing this charge head-on. Meanwhile, the inclusion of phrases such as 'not doubting in any Article of my Faith' and, most tellingly, 'I waver nothing in my Faith', demonstrate that Cromwell had far from relinquished his personal beliefs as he faced his final moments. In all, it was a speech worthy of England's most successful lawyer. He had said nothing that could bring down on him the censure of his king, but neither had he made himself a hypocrite by undermining everything he had spent the past decade striving for.

In acknowledging the justice of his fate and thus paying one final compliment to his royal master, Cromwell had completed the same performance as his late adversary, Anne Boleyn, four years earlier. Did he spare a thought for her, for Thomas More, and the others whom he had helped send to the block, as he now faced the same fate? When he knelt in prayer, though, it was more for his own soul than for theirs.

The chronicler Edward Hall describes how Cromwell 'made his praier, which was long, but not so long as both Godly and learned, and after committed his soule into the handes of God'.[11] The martyrologist John Foxe provides a full transcript of it. If this is accurate, then the condemned reformer's final words were full of remorse at a life filled with sin and wickedness. However, it is suspiciously devout, and the turn of phrase does not tally with that of Cromwell's final speech. The fact that it is only recorded in Foxe's work gives further room to doubt its authenticity. It may have been a convenient way for the author to convince his readers that Cromwell died a true martyr.

'I wretched sinner do submit my self wholly unto thy most blessed will,' Foxe's account began. 'Willingly now I leave this frail and wicked flesh, in sure hope that thou wilt in better wise restore it to me again at the last day in the resurrection of the just . . . I have no merits nor good works which I may alledge before thee. Of sins and evil works (alas) I see a great heap . . . Let thy Blood cleanse and wash away the spots and fullness of my sins. Let thy righteousness hide and cover my unrighteousness.' According to Foxe, the last words that Cromwell spoke in prayer – and in life – were thus: 'Finally, that the weakness of my flesh be not overcome with the fear of death. Grant me, merciful Saviour, that when death hath shut up the eyes of my Body, yet the eyes of my Soul may still behold and look upon thee, and when death hath taken away the use of my Tongue, yet my heart may cry and say unto thee, Lord into thy hands I commend my Soul, Lord Jesus receive my spirit, Amen.'[12]

'And thus,' says Foxe, 'his Prayer made, after he had godly and lovingly exorted them that were about him on the Scaffold, he quietly committed his Soul into the hands of God.' Turning to the headsman, whom he saw standing ready, he said: 'Pray, if possible, cut off the head with one blow, so that I may not suffer much.'[13] Cromwell then placed his head on the block. He might have wished that his royal master had extended the same privilege to him as to Anne Boleyn. His executioner, a man named Gurrea, was no skilled swordsman from France, but 'a ragged and boocherly myser, whiche very ungoodly perfourmed the Office'. The crowds looked on in horror as the king's former chief minister 'so paciently suffered the stroke of the axe'.[14] One account makes the unlikely claim that two executioners hacked away at Cromwell's neck and head 'for nearly half an hour'.[15] Had Norfolk, in a final act of cruelty, arranged for an inexperienced axeman to behead his old rival, or made sure that someone got him drunk first? Given the number of high-profile traitors who were executed on the king's orders, there would have been a host of expert axemen well trained for the task. That Cromwell's execution should be so botched was surely more than just bad luck.

After at least three blows of the axe, Cromwell's head was at last severed from his body and held aloft to those who still had the stomach to look. What was left of it was then set on a spike on London Bridge, in a traditional warning to any would-be traitors. After it had been displayed there for the requisite period of time, it was buried with Cromwell's body beneath the floor of St Peter ad Vincula in the Tower of London. In his will of 1529, Cromwell had meekly stated: 'Whan so ever I shall departe this present lif, I bequethe my bodie to be buryed where it shall please god to ordeyn me to die,' adding that his funeral should be performed 'without any erthelye pompe'. Ironically, both these wishes were carried out – but surely not in the way that Cromwell had envisaged more than a decade before.[16]

If they had been shocked at the manner of his dispatch, few regretted Cromwell's passing. As the Spanish Chronicle observed: 'And so ended this Cromwell, who had better never have been born.' The Roman Catholic powers of Europe rejoiced at his demise. Charles V's chief secretary in Madrid reported just two days after the execution that he had heard 'from England the news is that the King of that country has caused Cremuel, his great favourite, to be beheaded; the reason being, as it is understood, that he tried to persuade him to become a Lutheran. May this be the means of recalling the King to a sense of duty.' Francesco Contarini added his voice to the chorus of derision, observing that Cromwell had 'made a better end than the evil, of which he had been in great part the cause, deserved'.[17]

The contemporary chronicler Edward Hall, Cromwell's old friend, provides what is perhaps the most balanced account of the popular reaction to his death:

> Many lamented, but mo[re] reioysed, and specially suche, as either had been religious men, or fauored religious persones, for thei banqueted, and triumphed together that night, many

> wisshyng that that daie had been seuen yere before . . . Other who knewe nothyng but truth by hym, bothe lamented hym, and hartely praied for hym: But this is true that of certain of the Clergie he was detestably hated, & specialy of suche as had borne swynge, and by his meanes was put from it, for in dede he was a man, that in all of his doynges, semed not to fauor any kynde of Popery, nor could not abide the snoffyng pride of some prelates, whiche undoubtedly whatsoeuer els was the cause of his death, did shorten his life, and procured the ende that he was brought unto.[18]

A 'Ballad on Thomas Cromwell' was published shortly after his death, heralding the death of 'that false traitor'. But this was swiftly followed by several rebuttals, such as 'A Ballad Against Malicious Slanderers', all of which were generally sympathetic to the fallen minister. The original ballad may have been penned or sponsored by the authorities, but the rest were the work of ordinary citizens. It was said that only the 'common people' of London, who had held Cromwell so 'beloved', were grieved by his death.[19] Certainly he had been a great friend to the poor throughout his career, and had always taken care to listen to the grievances of the king's ordinary subjects.

But there were others who felt a genuine and abiding grief at Cromwell's passing. The records do not reveal whether Gregory Cromwell was present at his father's execution, or whether he petitioned the king for permission to bury him under the floor of the Chapel of St Peter ad Vincula in the Tower, as the family of Sir Thomas More had. Although no doubt deeply distraught at the loss of his beloved father, Gregory maintained his silence in the days after the execution. By contrast, his cousin Richard was so grief-stricken that he went about in open mourning. To show such respect to a convicted traitor was not just a sign of how much Richard had loved and revered his uncle, but of how courageous he was. Henry VIII had a dangerously low tolerance for even so much as hearing the name of a former favourite whispered at court after they had fallen from grace. He had not even been able to bear the sight of his younger daughter, Elizabeth, in the wake of Anne Boleyn's fall because she had reminded him too much of her mother.

Cromwell's former secretary Ralph Sadler also remained loyal to him. He had been a member of Cromwell's household since he was a boy, and had served him faithfully ever since. Among the various signs of how high Sadler had esteemed his master was that he had invited Cromwell to be godfather to his first two sons. After Cromwell's death, Sadler acquired Holbein's famous portrait of his former master and kept it hidden away safely during the remaining years of Henry's reign. If it had not been for his quick thinking, the painting would almost certainly have been destroyed and we would have had no accurate portrayal of the man who had once been the most powerful in England.

Cromwell was also mourned by those men – admittedly few in number by the time of his death – with whom he had struck up a friendship during his years at court. Principal among them was the poet Sir Thomas Wyatt, who had narrowly escaped conviction and execution during the scandal of Anne Boleyn's fall, thanks to Cromwell's intervention. Wyatt wrote a poem lamenting the loss of his patron and friend:

> The pillar perish'd is whereto I leant,
> The strongest stay of my unquiet mind;
> The like of it no man again can find,
> From east to west still seeking though he went,
> To mine unhap. For hap away hath rent
> Of all my joy the very bark and rind:
> And I, alas, by chance am thus assign'd
> Daily to mourn, till death do it relent.
> But since that thus it is by destiny,
> What can I more but have a woful heart;
> My pen in plaint, my voice in careful cry,
> My mind in woe, my body full of smart;
> And I myself, myself always to hate,
> Till dreadful death do ease my doleful state.

By contrast, nobody seemed less troubled by Cromwell's death than the man who had raised him to greatness. Far from keeping a respectfully low profile to mark the passing of his former minister and confidant, King Henry chose the very same day of Cromwell's execution for his wedding to Katherine Howard. His eyes were now firmly set on the future, not the past.

EPILOGUE

'A man of mean birth but noble qualities'

CROMWELL HIMSELF ONCE declared 'that there was nothing he desired so much in this world as to leave a good name behind him'. In this, he would be at least partly disappointed. Even before his death, Cromwell had divided opinion among contemporary commentators. Cardinal Reginald Pole denounced him as 'an agent of Satan sent by the devil to lure King Henry to damnation'. According to his assessment, the king's chief minister did not harbour an ounce of genuine evangelical sympathy, but was motivated solely by greed and Machiavellian statecraft. His views influenced two other Roman Catholics, Nicholas Sander and Robert Persons, who were writing in the second half of the sixteenth century. Although they grudgingly accepted that Cromwell's evangelical beliefs were genuine, they joined Pole in attacking his political ruthlessness and hypocrisy. Meanwhile, in his assessment of English affairs written in 1551, the Venetian ambassador Daniel Barbaro laid all the blame for Henry's divorce and the religious turmoil that followed on 'the evil persuasions of Lord Cromwell then in very great favour'.[1]

By contrast, John Foxe – whose *Acts and Monuments* first appeared twenty-three years after Cromwell's death – credits the minister with spearheading the English Reformation and claims that his whole life was 'nothing else but a continual care and travail how to advance and further the right knowledge of the gospel and reform of the house of God'. Foxe's portrayal may have influenced the play, *The True Chronicle Historie of the Whole Life and Death of Thomas Cromwell*, which was first published in 1602. The author was cited as 'W.S.' and some scholars have claimed that it was William Shakespeare. This interpretation charts the rise to fortune of an ambitious young

Cromwell who stays loyal to the benefactors who help him along the way, before being destroyed by Gardiner in revenge for the dissolution of the monasteries. The ecclesiastical historian John Strype also took a positive view of the fallen minister. 'He was a man whose merits raised him from a very low degree,' he observed. 'He was very zealous and very honest in doing the King his master's work, and sometimes his drudgery . . . which begat him many enemies, by whom he was overwhelmed at last.' Meanwhile, the late sixteenth-century chronicler Holinshed mused: 'If we shall consider his comming vp to such high degree of honor as he atteined vnto, we maie doubt whether there be cause more to maruell at his good fortune, or at his woorthie and industrious demeanor.' [2]

This positive view of Cromwell endured for a further two centuries. The idea of a principled, self-made man who laid the foundations of Protestant England but was brought down by the conservative, aristocratic establishment was one that appealed to historians of the Puritan and Enlightenment eras. As the seventeenth-century historian and theologian Gilbert Burnet neatly put it, Cromwell was 'a man of mean birth but noble qualities'.[3] But all that changed in the nineteenth century, when an altogether more negative portrayal of Cromwell was conceived. A campaign for greater freedom for Catholics combined with the emerging Romantic movement to inspire a harking back to England's pre-Reformation religion. As part of this, monasticism was also seen in a positive, nostalgic light. Little wonder, then, that the architect of its destruction now came under fierce criticism. One of the most outspoken – and influential – critics was William Cobbett, who denounced Henry VIII as a 'tyrant' king and his chief minister as 'the brutal blacksmith'. Readers of his *History of the Protestant Reformation in England and Ireland* were left in no doubt that Cromwell had been one of the greatest villains in history. 'Perhaps of all the mean and dastardly wretches that ever died, this was the most mean and dastardly,' Cobbett concluded.[4] Even Roger Merriman, who took the trouble to catalogue Cromwell's voluminous correspondence, portrayed him as a Machiavellian schemer and referred to his 'sinister genius'.[5]

There was some rehabilitation of Cromwell in the twentieth century, most notably by Geoffrey Elton, who described him as 'one of the most remarkable English statesmen of the sixteenth century', and claimed that he 'instigated and in part accomplished a major and enduring transformation in virtually every aspect of the nation's public life'.[6] But the notion of Henry's chief minister as a corrupt and unprincipled villain proved difficult to dispel. It was propounded in popular culture by films such as *A Man For All Seasons*, in which the saintly Thomas More is brought down by the evil machinations of Cromwell. That portrayal was turned on its head by Hilary Mantel's *Wolf Hall* – a fictionalised account of Cromwell that took the publishing world by storm in 2009. Together with its sequel, *Bring up the Bodies*, it presents an altogether more human, sympathetic – even heroic – Cromwell. It is a portrayal that, though fictional, is based on meticulous historical research and is all the more compelling as a result.

Among these many and varied portrayals of Henry's chief minister, where does the truth lie? Cromwell was undoubtedly a man of immense energy, ability and ambition. The same determination with which he dragged himself out of obscurity also propelled him to the very height of Tudor politics. Holbein's portrait of a stern, hard-working minister was accurate, if somewhat one-dimensional. Cromwell was capable of intense loyalty, and his service first to Wolsey then the king took precedence over even his most cherished personal ambitions. His evangelical beliefs grew from a convenient stance into a strong conviction, and the passion with which he drove home the later reforms, when reason might have dictated a more cautious policy, suggests a genuine personal piety. Although unquestionably highly focused and driven in his political career, Cromwell was also known for his wit, generosity and love of the arts. The few references to his personal life within contemporary sources hint at a loving husband, father and friend.

But the ruthlessness, corruption and Machiavellian tendencies that earned Cromwell widespread censure, both in his lifetime and during the following 500 years, cannot be apologised away entirely. The dissolution of the monasteries was inspired (initially at least) as much by a desire to swell the king's coffers as by a genuine concern for the religious welfare of his subjects. Likewise, the devious and underhand tactics that he employed to rid himself of opponents such as Anne Boleyn reveal a calculating and ruthless side to his character. But nobody could have risen so far in the court of Henry VIII without displaying a degree of ruthlessness and brutality. It was an arena ridden with intrigue, betrayal, treachery and deceit. Attack was not just the best, but the only means of defence. Moreover, in enforcing his new order, Cromwell was always careful to follow the letter of the law, and only when he deemed it a political necessity would he send men and women to their deaths. The claims that he was a tyrant are therefore unfounded. The same could not be said of his increasingly volatile royal master.

Whether Cromwell's personal traits made him more a hero or a villain is, in a sense, eclipsed by the undeniable scale of his achievement. One of the most brilliant legal minds of the age, he turned his hand to a host of businesses – all with dazzling success. These private concerns continued to thrive even when his public career became so demanding that he had barely a moment in a day to himself. During his meteoric rise to power, he masterminded some of the most seismic developments of the Tudor age: from the king's 'Great Matter' to the royal supremacy, and from the 'revolution' in government to the transformation of religious life. In so doing, he changed the face of England for ever. The demise of the monasteries was rapidly superseded by a new, more vibrant reformist faith, which advocated a personal relationship with God and brought his word to the masses by ensuring that every church held a copy of the English Bible – arguably one of Cromwell's greatest achievements. Cromwell's social reforms had improved the standards of living for many of Henry's poorest subjects. By the end of his tenure, he had created a more united and easily governable kingdom for his royal master, as well as a considerably healthier treasury, thanks to the riches of the monasteries. As Foxe concluded: 'thus through the industry of Cromwel . . . there was some reformation had throughout all Englande.'[7]

Parliament had also been transformed into a more permanent

and powerful institution. Under Wolsey, it had met only infrequently and its efficacy had been limited as a result. But his protégé had established it as a regular fixture in order to push through his reforms. Although Cromwell had ensured it remained tractable to the crown, in the absence of his controlling force it gradually became an instrument of constitutional power – and thus a threat to the crown. It is no small irony that it was Cromwell's own descendant, Oliver, who realised its ultimate potential as a means of ridding the country of monarchical rule. He and his followers became known as 'Parliamentarians' during the English Civil War of the mid-seventeenth century because they believed that parliament, not the king, should have supreme authority.

A true polymath, Cromwell had quickly become indispensable to his royal master. He was arguably the most effective, and certainly the most industrious, minister that Henry had ever had. But he was also a victim of his own success. The pace of change he orchestrated had eventually overtaken the king's own ambitions – with fatal consequences. Henry had been more than content to lavish favour on his chief minister for as long as he had carried out Henry's will, but as soon as he became uneasy about Cromwell's more radical ideas, the writing was on the wall. Quite when the delicate power balance between royal master and chief minister had begun to shift is difficult to determine. Certainly, by 1538 the king had been growing uneasy about Cromwell. But they might still have restored the delicate balance of their relationship if the conservative faction at court had not forced Cromwell's hand. In lashing out at them and urging Henry on to reforms that were clearly too radical for him, he had effectively signed his own death warrant. Henry might have enabled this blacksmith's son to rise to greatness, but he also – ultimately – destroyed him.

The king hoped that Cromwell's death would pave the way to the religious unity he sought in his kingdom. Henry had increasingly come to realise that for as long as Cromwell was his chief minister such unity would be impossible. The Lord Privy Seal had been too much of an evangelical, and had grown ever more uncompromising in the face of opposition from Norfolk, Gardiner and the other conservatives at court. As if to signal that he would favour neither party but a middle way from now on, two days after Cromwell's execution the king ordered that Robert Barnes and the two fellow evangelicals who had been arrested with him in March should be burned at the stake, along with three conservatives known to be loyal to Rome. That it was a symbolic gesture rather than a genuine conviction is hinted at by the fact that as Barnes prepared to meet his death, he asked the sheriff if he had 'any articles against me for the which I am condemned'. The sheriff could provide none.[8]

Although they had been counteracted by the execution of the three papists, the deaths of Barnes and his evangelical companions so soon after Cromwell's own suggests that he had been instrumental in keeping them alive. Foxe was certainly in no doubt that had it not been for Cromwell's influence, many more supposed 'heretics' would have gone to the flames. 'It were to long and tedious a declaration here to declare howe many good men through this mans helpe and defence, haue bene relieued and delyuered out of daunger, of whome a great nomber after his fall beyng (as it were) depryued of their patrone, dyd shortly after peryshe.'[9]

Most of Cromwell's so-called allies had hastily distanced themselves from him in the wake of his fall, and some of them now benefited from the sudden vacancy of his former property and offices. They included Thomas Wriothesley, who had been hauled in for questioning after Cromwell's arrest but had talked his way out of trouble. He was sufficiently restored to royal favour by the end of 1540 to be granted Cromwell's newly built 'great mansion' at Austin Friars. If he felt any unease at so readily stepping into a dead man's shoes, then he did not show it. As well as taking over Cromwell's property, he also revived his former alliance with the latter's adversary, Stephen Gardiner. Within months of Cromwell's fall, it was said that Wriothesley had 'obtained considerable power'. Meanwhile, a substantial collection of Cromwell's furniture was removed from Austin Friars and given to Anne of Cleves as part of her annulment settlement – a gesture that her estranged husband no doubt found satisfyingly appropriate.[10]

Marillac reported on the division of the spoils that had followed Cromwell's execution with unseemly haste. 'The Privy Seal has been given to the admiral FitzWilliam, whilst Master Russel has become Lord High Admiral of England in his room. The bishop of Durham [Cuthbert Tunstall] has been appointed first secretary, or viceregent in ecclesiastical causes . . . For the affairs of justice, the Chancellor [Audley] has been deputed.' He admitted, though, that 'in spiritual matters nothing has yet been decided.'[11]

The atmosphere at court had remained tense during the weeks and months that followed. Still convinced of his late minister's treasonous guilt, Henry took every opportunity to blacken his name even further. Legend has it that whenever he was dealt a knave at cards, he exclaimed: 'I have got Cromwell.' The king now regarded with suspicion anyone who had been closely associated with him, and had a number of them watched. Matters came to a head in January 1541 when Ralph Sadler, Sir Thomas Wyatt and several other men believed to have been connected with Cromwell were suddenly arrested. They were taken from Hampton Court to the Tower with their hands bound, accompanied by no fewer than twenty-four archers to prevent their escape. Marillac was quick to report this dramatic event to Montmorency, telling him that Wyatt 'was led to the Tower so bound and fettered that one must think ill, for the custom is to lead them to prison free'. He added: 'It is the third time Hoyet [Wyatt] has been there, and apparently it will be the last, for this must be some great matter and he has for enemies all who leagued against Cromwell, whose minion he was.' Marillac scornfully remarked that 'there could be no worse war than the English carry on against each other; for after Cromwell had brought down the greatest of the realm, from the Marquis to the Grand Esquire Caraud [Carew], now others have arisen who will never rest till they have done as much to all Cromwell's adherents, and God knows whether after them others will not recommence the feast. [I] never saw them look more troubled. As long as they are making war on each other they will innovate nothing against France.'[12]

Wyatt languished in the Tower until March, when he was released at the request of Queen Katherine Howard, who had apparently been beguiled by the poet's famous charm. Sadler could rely on no such favour, but he had learned much from his late master for he argued so effectively against the accusations of his interrogators that they had been obliged to release him after just a few days. Moreover, his testimony was so compelling that it apparently caused the king to question the justice of Cromwell's conviction and execution.

By then, though, Henry was already beginning to regret Cromwell's death. Nothing had seemed to go right for him since. His marriage to Katherine Howard, which had begun in a blaze of hope and passion, had soon been discovered to be a sham. The new queen – 'the handsomest of his wives, and also the most giddy' – was found guilty of adultery and beheaded a little over eighteen months after the wedding.[13] Unlike Anne Boleyn, the charges were justified: the flighty and flirtatious young queen, more than thirty years the king's junior, had been carrying on an illicit liaison with Thomas Culpeper, a gentleman of the privy chamber. Lady Rochford, whose evidence had sealed Anne Boleyn's doom, confessed that she had facilitated secret meetings between the couple. A letter in the young queen's own hand provided incontrovertible proof of their relationship. She wrote that she 'longed' to see Culpeper, who had been absent from court with an illness, and assured him of her affection, ending the letter with 'Yours as long as life endures, Katherine'. Her indiscretions came to the attention of Archbishop Cranmer, who conducted a discreet investigation. He found Katherine's letter, and much more besides. The queen's adolescent affair with her music master came to light, as did her liaison with Francis Dereham. In an act as audacious as it was foolhardy, she had appointed Dereham her personal secretary after becoming queen.

For as long as the king had remained in ignorance, his household and council had been dominated by Katherine's family – the Duke of Norfolk principal among them. But all that changed when Henry discovered the truth. Cromwell's faithful servant, Ralph Sadler, was instrumental in sealing the young queen's fate. When her infidelities were discovered by Cranmer in late 1541, Sadler worked assiduously to gather enough evidence to make certain of her conviction as a traitor. But he went further than that, realising that here lay an opportunity to secure the downfall not only of the queen, but of all those who had orchestrated Cromwell's downfall – Norfolk and Gardiner in particular. Together with his allies, most prominent among whom was Cranmer, he worked tirelessly to avenge his former master, but was not immediately successful. With war looming against France and Scotland, Henry could ill afford to lose the diplomatic and military skills of Norfolk and Gardiner. Nevertheless, their influence at court was diminished by the scandal of Katherine's downfall, and Sadler's star continued to rise for the remainder of the reign. He went on to serve each of Henry's children when they came to the throne. By the time of his death in 1587, he was one of the richest men in England: an achievement that would surely have impressed his original and most influential patron.

As early as December 1540, the king had shown favour towards Cromwell's son Gregory by creating him Baron Cromwell of Oakham and summoning him to parliament as a peer of the realm. The following February, Henry had granted him some lands in Leicestershire that had been owned by his late father. These centred on Launde Abbey, a lavish manor house that the elder Cromwell had started building on the site of an Augustinian priory. Gregory would live there with his family for the rest of his days, during which time he was made a Knight of the Order of the Bath and became a highly respected member of the court. That he cherished his father's memory is suggested by the fact that when his last-born child arrived in 1540, he chose to call him Thomas. Like his mother and sisters, Gregory died of the sweating sickness, on 4 July 1551. His widow Elizabeth married John Paulet, later second Marquis of Winchester, a mere three days later.

Cromwell's nephew Richard also prospered in the aftermath of his uncle's fall. In 1541 he was appointed High Sheriff of Cambridgeshire and Huntingdonshire and was returned as a member of parliament for the latter county the following year. It was also in 1542 that the king granted him the monasteries of St Mary's in

Huntingdon and St Neots. These earned him 488 pounds (£150,000) per year, and combined with the profits he received from various other grants and offices, he became a rich man as the decade progressed. Richard had learned the business of property and land acquisition from his uncle, and by the time of his death he had amassed such a fortune from his many estates that he was one of the wealthiest peers in the realm. Henry's favour towards Richard was further demonstrated when he appointed him a gentleman of the privy chamber in 1543. The king had long admired Richard's prowess in the tournament field, and when war broke out with France later that year, he had no hesitation in sending him there as general of the infantry. Richard died in 1546 leaving two sons. The elder of these, Henry Cromwell, followed in his father's footsteps as High Sheriff of Cambridgeshire and Huntingdonshire, and won great favour with Elizabeth I. By his first wife, Joan Warren, daughter of the Lord Mayor of London, Henry had two sons and five daughters. The younger of the boys, Robert, was the father of Oliver Cromwell, the Parliamentarian commander during the English Civil War who defeated and executed King Charles I, and became Lord Protector of England, Scotland and Ireland.

If Cromwell's allies had prospered in the wake of his fall, the same could not be said of his chief adversaries. The Duke of Norfolk had suffered a loss of favour after the disgrace of his niece, Katherine Howard. He joined the French campaign in 1543, but earned a stinging rebuke from the king for withdrawing his forces without having won any significant victories. During the last years of Henry's reign, he lost further ground to Edward Seymour and the new queen, Katherine Parr, Henry's sixth and final wife, both of whom espoused the reformist faith. Together with Gardiner, he hatched a plot to have Archbishop Cranmer arrested, but it failed. He and his fellow religious conservatives were now firmly on the back foot. Worse was to come. The increasingly arrogant and erratic behaviour of his son and heir, Henry Howard, Earl of Surrey, landed them both in trouble. When Surrey displayed the royal arms on his coat of arms it was interpreted as a sign that he had his sights set on the throne. In December 1546 he and his father were arrested and sent to the Tower. Norfolk pleaded his innocence to the king but it fell on deaf ears. Members of his own family, including the estranged wife who had sought Cromwell's help some years before, gave evidence against him and he was found guilty of having 'concealed high treason, in keeping secret the false acts of my son'. Like Cromwell, he was attainted by statute, without trial, and sentenced to death. Henry's own death won him a stay of execution, but he remained in the Tower throughout the reign of the late king's son, Edward VI. He was eventually pardoned by Henry's daughter Mary when she became queen in 1553 and was re-sworn as a privy councillor. He died at Kenninghall the following year.

Norfolk's old ally Stephen Gardiner had suffered a similar loss of favour in the last years of Henry's reign. He had taken Cromwell's execution as a signal to step up his campaign to reassert the conservative faith, and had presided over the high-profile trial of Anne Askew, who was subsequently executed for heresy. He was also rumoured to have conspired against Queen Katherine Parr and tried to have her arrested as a heretic. His increasingly extreme religious stance rapidly alienated the king, who at the end of his life ordered that Gardiner's name be removed from the list of executors and councillors who were to rule during his son's minority. When Gardiner's allies tried to persuade the dying king to reconsider, Henry refused, insisting that the bishop was 'too wilful in his opinion, and much bent to the popish party', and 'not meet to be about his son'. Gardiner was never destined to prosper in the new reign, which was dominated by a Protestant king and councillors, and he was imprisoned twice for preaching against the reformist faith. Like Norfolk, he was released when the Roman Catholic Mary came to the throne, and was re-appointed to the Privy Council. He was made Lord Chancellor a few days later and retained the office until his death in 1555.

Although Norfolk and Gardiner ultimately survived their loss of favour during the closing years of Henry VIII's reign, the fact that they had fallen foul of the king is indicative of the latter's feelings towards Cromwell. Henry soon made it painfully clear that he lamented his chief minister's demise. Cromwell had not been replaced after his fall. Perhaps this ageing and increasingly paranoid king was determined never to invest so much power in an individual courtier again. Or perhaps he had come to realise that Cromwell had been a man of such exceptional skill and ability that he could never be replaced. It is telling that, the year after Cromwell's execution, the king ordered that a fine be levied on parishes that failed to buy a copy of Coverdale's Great Bible. As Foxe observed: 'This is moste certayne, that the kyng dyd afterwarde greatly and earnestly repente hys death, but alas to late, who was heard oftentymes to saye, that nowe he lacked his Cromwell.'[14]

Rather than shouldering the blame for the loss himself, Henry lashed out at his council. On 3 March 1541, a little over seven months after the former chief minister's execution, Marillac reported that the king 'sometimes even reproaches [his ministers] with Cromwell's death, saying that, upon light pretexts, by false accusations, they made him put to death the most faithful servant he had ever had'.[15]

ACKNOWLEDGEMENTS

This is my first book with Hodder & Stoughton, and the biggest thanks go to them. I have been overwhelmed by the warmth, enthusiasm and commitment that they have shown towards me from the beginning. I am particularly indebted to my editor, Maddy Price, for her insights, encouragement and attention to detail, and for conceiving the idea for the biography in the first place. Likewise, to Rupert Lancaster for having faith in me as an author, and for his unfailing wisdom and good humour. Emilie Ferguson, Emma Daley and Bea Long have been fantastic to work with on publicity, marketing and events, and Juliet Brightmore has been the most assiduous and inspired picture researcher I have ever known.

As well as the wonderful new team at Hodder, I have been very fortunate to have had the support of more familiar faces once more. My agent, Julian Alexander, has been at his gloriously understated best throughout, keeping a calm head when excitement or anxiety have got the better of me. Alison Weir was kind enough to take time out of a relentlessly busy schedule to read a draft of the book and to provide extremely positive feedback. Jean MacIntyre, my friend and colleague at Bishop Grosseteste University in Lincoln, has been unfailingly supportive and irreverent in equal measure, and I am also indebted to my colleagues at Historic Royal Palaces, not least Ella Sullivan, Sam Cousens, Lucy Worsley and the chief executive, Michael Day.

I have been privileged to strike up a lively and enlightening email correspondence with Hilary Mantel, who has been kind enough to share her insights into Cromwell's life and character, and whose books have – of course – been an inspiration. Dr Nick Holder,

Lecturer in English History at Regent's University London, has been extremely generous in sharing his research on Cromwell's house at Austin Friars, and in allowing me to reproduce plans and sketches from his thesis. The Duke of Buccleuch very kindly waived the reproduction fee for the stunning portrait of Catherine of Aragon, and I am grateful to Gareth Fitzpatrick at Boughton House for arranging this. The picture section has also been greatly enhanced by the addition of complimentary images from The National Archives, thanks to Hester Vaizey and Paul Johnson, and Historic Royal Palaces, thanks to Annie Heron and Clare Murphy.

As ever, I have been incredibly lucky in having the encouragement of my wonderful family and friends. My parents have continued to support me in every way possible, and my Mum has been particularly kind in providing so much help with childcare. Jayne, Rick, Livvie and Neve Ellis have continued to take an interest in my writing career, and have kept my daughter Eleanor brilliantly entertained. Stephen Kuhrt has been a dedicated and enthusiastic follower of this book from its very inception, and I am deeply grateful for his advice on everything from evangelicals to screen portrayals of Cromwell. I am also indebted to Julian Humphrys for his insights into Cromwell's military career, to Nicola Tallis for sharing her research on his career as Master of the Jewels, and to Steve Earles for his expertise on Ireland (not to mention for the regular gifts of chocolate). Other friends, such as Sophie Grant and Georgie Wilkins, have provided practical help at key moments, and I hope that this book will convince my loyal friend and critic, Honor Gay, that Cromwell wasn't all bad.

My final thanks are to Tom Ashworth for his unstinting support, for bearing with my frequent absences at the British Library and for ensuring that, as Merriman said of Cromwell, I kept my 'eyes steadily fixed upon the goal'.

BIBLIOGRAPHY

Selected Archival Sources

BL Additional MS 25114 fos.160–1 Cromwell to Gardiner and Wallop regarding Anne Boleyn's fall, 14 May [1536]

BL Additional MS 25114 fos.175–7 Cromwell to Gardiner, upbraiding him for accusing him of acting against his interests, July [1536]

BL Additional MS 48028 fos.160–5 Act of Attainder of Thomas Cromwell, 29 June 1540

BL Cotton MS Otho C x fo.241 Questions written in Henry VIII's own hand to be put to Cromwell, June 1540

BL Cotton MS Otho C x fo.242 Cromwell's last letter to Henry VIII, regarding Anne of Cleves marriage

BL Cotton MS Titus B i fos.257–69 Cromwell's letters to Henry VIII

BL Harley MS 282 fos.211–12 Cromwell to Wyatt, 12 October 1537, announcing Edward VI's birth

BL Harley MS 3362 fo.17 Cromwell's last words on scaffold

TNA SP1/57 fos.92–3 and 294–7 Cromwell to Wolsey, 5 May and 18 August [1530]

TNA SP1/78 fos.26–7, SP1/80 fos.51–2 and SP1/82 fo.98 Cromwell to Henry VIII

TNA SP1/83 fos.98–9 Cromwell to Cranmer regarding Fisher and More's refusal to swear to the Act of Succession, April 1534

TNA SP1/120 fos.165–6 Cromwell to Norfolk regarding the suppression of the Pilgrimage of Grace, 22 May [1537]

TNA SP1/161 fos.173–4 Cromwell to the Privy Council, 24 July [1540]

Printed Primary Sources

Amyot, T., 'Transcript of an Original Manuscript, Containing a Memorial from George Constantyne to Thomas, Lord Cromwell', *Archaeologia*, 23 (London, 1830), pp.50–78

Anon., 'The Life and Death of Thomas Lord Cromwell', in *The Ancient British Drama*, Vol. I (London, 1810)

Baker, J.H. (ed.), *Reports of Sir John Spelman*, Vols. I and II (London, 1977)

Bray, G. (ed.), *Documents of the English Reformation* (Cambridge, 1994)

Brown, R. (trans. and ed.), *Four Years at the Court of Henry VIII: Selection of despatches written by the Venetian Ambassador, Sebastian Giustinian, and addressed to the Signory of Venice, January 12th 1515, to July 26th 1519*, 2 vols. (London, 1854)

Bruce, J. and Perowne, T. (eds.), *Correspondence of Matthew Parker* (Cambridge, 1853)

Byrne, M.S.C. (ed.), *The Lisle Letters*, 6 vols. (Chicago and London, 1981)

Calendar of the Carew Manuscripts, Preserved in the Archiepiscopal Library at Lambeth, 1515–1574 (London, 1867)

Calendar of the Close Rolls Preserved in the Public Record Office ... Henry VII, Vol. II, 1500–1509 (London, 1963)

Calendar of Letters, Despatches, and State Papers, relating to the negotiations between England and Spain, preserved in the archives at Simancas and elsewhere, Vols. II–VI, Part I (London, 1866–90)

Calendar of State Papers, Foreign Series, of the Reign of Elizabeth, Vol. I 1558–9 (London, 1863)

Calendar of State Papers, Venice, Vols. I-V (London, 1864-1873)

Cavendish, G., *Metrical Visions*, in Singer, S.W. (ed.), *The Life of Cardinal Wolsey*, 2 vols. (London, 1825)

Cavendish, G., *The Life and Death of Cardinal Wolsey*, ed. Sylvester, R.S., Early English Text Society, orig. l ser., 243 (London and New York, 1959)

Cox, J.E. (ed.), *Miscellaneous Writings and Letters of Thomas Cranmer* (Cambridge, 1846)

Cranmer, T., *Works of Archbishop Cranmer*, ed. Cox, J.E. (Cambridge, 1844)

Dickens, A.G., *Clifford Letters of the Sixteenth Century*, Publications of the Surtees Society, Vol. 172 (Durham and London, 1962)

Dowling, M. (ed.), *William Latymer's Chronicle of Anne Boleyn*, Camden Miscellany XXX, Camden Society, 4th ser. Vol. 39 (London, 1990), pp.23–66

Drayton, M., *The Legend of Great Cromwell* (London, 1607)

Drayton, M., *The Historie of the Life and Death of the Lord Cromwell, sometime Earl of Essex and Lord Chancellor of England* (London, 1609)

Ellis, H. (ed.), *Original Letters Illustrative of English History*, 2nd and 3rd series (London, 1827, 1846)

Fisher, J., *The English Works of John Fisher. Bishop of Rochester, 1469–1535*, ed. Hatt, C.A. (Oxford, 2002)

Foxe, J., *Actes and Monuments* (London, 1563)

Froude, J.A. (ed.), *The Pilgrim: A Dialogue of the Life and Actions of King Henry VIII, by William Thomas, Clerk of the Council to Edward VI* (London, 1861)

Hall, E., *A Chronicle; Containing The History of England, During the Reign of Henry the Fourth, and the Succeeding Monarchs, to the End of the Reign of Henry the Eighth* (London, 1809)

Harpsfield, N., *The Life and Death of Sr Thomas Moore, Knight*, ed. Hitchcock, E.V., Early English Text Society, orig. ser., Vol. 186 (Oxford, 1932)

Historical Manuscripts Commission, *The Manuscripts of His Grace The Duke of Rutland, KG, Preserved at Belvoir Castle*, Vols. I and IV (London, 1905)

Holinshed, R., *Chronicles of England, Scotland and Ireland*, Vol. VI (London, 1587)

Hughes, P.L. and Larkin, J.F. (eds.), *Tudor Royal Proclamations*, Vol.1 (New Haven and London, 1964)

Hume, M.A. (ed. and trans.), *Chronicle of King Henry VIII of England ... written in Spanish by an unknown hand* (London, 1889)

Kaulek, J. (ed.), *Correspondance Politique de MM. de Castillon et de Marillac, Ambassadeurs de France en Angleterre (1537–1542)* (Paris, 1885)

Letters and Papers, Foreign and Domestic, of the Reign of Henry VIII, 1509–47, ed. Brewer, J.S., et al., 21 vols. and 2 vols. addenda (London, 1862–1932)

Loades, D.M. (ed.), *The Papers of George Wyatt Esquire ... son and heir of Sir Thomas Wyatt the Younger*, Camden Society, 4th ser., Vol. V (London, 1968)

Machiavelli, N., *The Prince*, trans. Bull, G. (London, 1999)

Mayer, T. (ed.), *Correspondence of Reginald Pole, Volume 1: A Calendar, 1518–1546* (Aldershot, 2002)

Merriman, R.B. (ed.), *Life and Letters of Thomas Cromwell*, 2 vols. (London, 1902)

More, T., *A Dyaloge of Syr Thomas More* (London, 1529)

Muir, K., *Life and Letters of Sir Thomas Wyatt* (Liverpool, 1963)

Muller, J.A. (ed.), *The Letters of Stephen Gardiner* (Cambridge, 1933)

Nichols, J.G., *Narratives of the Reformation*, Camden Society, 1st ser., Vol. LXXVII (London, 1859)

Norton, E., *The Anne Boleyn Papers* (Stroud, 2013)

Payne, J. (ed. and trans.), *The Novels of Matteo Bandello Bishop of Agen*, Vol. IV (London, 1890)

Pocock, N. (ed.), *Records of the Reformation: The Divorce, 1527–1533* (Oxford, 1870)

Pole, Cardinal R., *De Unitate* (1536)
Pratt, J. (ed.), *Actes and Monuments of John Foxe*, 8 vols. (London, 1877)
Robinson, H. (ed.), *Zürich Letters*, 2 vols. (Cambridge, 1842, 1845)
Robinson, H. (ed.), *Original Letters Relative to the English Reformation*, 2 vols. (Cambridge, 1846–7)
Rogers, E.F., *Correspondence of Sir Thomas More* (Princeton, 1947)
Roper, W., *The Lyfe of Sir Thomas Moore, Knighte*, ed. Hitchcock, E.V., Early English Text Society, 197 (Oxford, 1935)
Sampson, G. (ed.), *The Utopia of Sir Thomas More ... with Roper's Life of More and some of his letters* (London, 1910)
Shakespeare, W., *Henry VIII* (London, 1623)
State Papers of the Reign of Henry VIII, Record Commission, 11 vols. (London, 1830–52)
Statutes of the Realm, 11 vols. (London, 1963)
Stow, J., *A Survey of London Written in the Year 1598*, ed. Morley, H. (Stroud, 1994)
Strype, J., *Ecclesiastical Memorials, Relating Chiefly to Religion, and the Reformation of it ... under King Henry VIII, King Edward VI and Queen Mary I*, 3 vols. (Oxford, 1822)
Strype, J., *Memorials of Thomas Cranmer*, 3 vols. (London, 1840)
Turnbull, W.B., *Calendar of State Papers, Foreign Series, of the Reign of Edward VI*, (London, 1861)
Tyndale, W., *The Practice of Prelates* (London, 1530)
Vergil, Polydore, *Anglica Historia* (London, 1534)
Williams, C.H. (ed.), *English Historical Documents*, Vol. V, 1485–1558 (London, 1967)
Wood, M.A.E., *Letters of Royal and Illustrious Ladies of Great Britain*, 3 vols. (London, 1846)
Wright, T. (ed.), *Three Chapters of Letters relating to the Suppression of the Monasteries*, Camden Society, Vol. 26 (London, 1843)
Wriothesley, C., *A Chronicle of England During the Reigns of the Tudors, From A.D.1485 to 1559*, ed. Hamilton, W.D., 2 vols., Camden Society, 2nd ser. (London, 1875)
Wyatt, T., *Collected Poems*, ed. Daalder, J. (Oxford, 1975)

Secondary Sources

Ackroyd, P., *The Life of Thomas More* (London, 1998)
Anglo, S., *Spectacle and Pageantry and Early Tudor Policy* (Oxford, 1997)

Anon., *The Life of Thomas Lord Cromwell, A Black-Smith's Son, born at Putney in Surry* (London, 1715)

Bean, J.M.W., *The Decline of English Feudalism, 1215–1540* (Manchester, 1968)

Beckingsale, B.W., *Thomas Cromwell: Tudor Minister* (London and Basingstoke, 1978)

Bernard, G.W., 'The Fall of Anne Boleyn', *English Historical Review*, 106 (1991), pp.584–610

Bernard, G.W., 'The Making of Religious Policy, 1533–1546: Henry VIII and the Search for the Middle Way', *Historical Journal*, 41 (1998), pp.321–49

Bernard, G.W., *Power and Politics in Tudor England* (Aldershot, 2000)

Bernard, G.W., *The King's Reformation: Henry VIII and the Re-making of the English Church* (New Haven and London, 2005)

Bevan, A.S., 'The Role of the Judiciary in Tudor Government, 1509–1547', Ph.D. diss., University of Cambridge, 1985

Bindoff, S.T., *The History of Parliament: The House of Commons 1509–58*, Vols. I and III (London, 1982)

Black, M. et al., *A Taste of History: 10,000 Years of Food in Britain* (London, 1993)

Bobbitt, P., *The Garments of Court and Palace: Machiavelli and the World that he Made* (London, 2013)

Bowker, M., 'The Supremacy and the Episcopate: The Struggle for Control, 1534–40', *Historical Journal*, 18 (1975), pp.227–43

Bradshaw, B., 'Cromwellian Reform and the Origins of the Kildare Rebellion, 1533–34', *Transactions of the Royal Historical Society*, 5th ser., 27 (1977), pp.69–94

Brecht, M., *Martin Luther*, trans. Schaff, J.L., 3 vols. (Philadelphia and Minneapolis, 1985, 1990, 1993)

Brigden, S., 'Thomas Cromwell and the Brethren', in *Law and Government under the Tudors: Essays presented to Sir Geoffrey Elton*, ed. Cross, C., Loades, D. and Scarisbrick, J.J. (Cambridge, 1988), pp.31–49

Brigden, S., *London and the Reformation* (Oxford, 1989)

Brigden, S., *New Worlds, Lost Worlds* (London, 2001)

Burnet, G., *History of the Reformation of the Church of England*, 4 vols. (London, 1865)

Cameron, E., *The European Reformation* (Oxford, 1991)

Cobbett, W., *History of the Protestant Reformation in England and Ireland* (New York, 1824–7)

Coby, J.P., *Thomas Cromwell: Henry VIII's Henchman* (Stroud, 2012)

Coleman, C. and Starkey, D. (eds.), *Revolution Reassessed: Revisions in the History of Tudor Government and Administration* (Oxford, 1986)

Cross, C., Loades, D. and Scarisbrick, J.J. (eds.), *Law and Government under the Tudors: Essays presented to Sir Geoffrey Elton* (Cambridge, 1988)

D'Alton, C., 'William Warham and English Heresy Policy after the Fall of Wolsey', *Historical Review*, 77/197 (2004), pp.337–57

Daniell, D., *William Tyndale: A Biography* (New Haven and London, 1994)

Davies, C.S.L., 'A New Life of Henry VIII', *History*, LVII (1969)

Dickens, A.G., *Thomas Cromwell and the English Reformation* (London, 1959)

Dickens, A.G., *The English Reformation* (London, 1989)

Dowling, M., 'Anne Boleyn and Reform', *Journal of Ecclesiastical History*, Vol. 35 (Cambridge, 1984), pp.30–45

Duffy, E., *The Stripping of the Altars: Traditional Religion in England, c.1400–c.1580* (New Haven and London, 1992)

Ellis, J.J., *Thomas Cromwell* (London, 1891)

Ellis, S., *Tudor Frontiers and Noble Power* (Oxford, 1995)

Ellis, S.G., *Ireland in the Age of the Tudors* (London, 1998)

Elton, G.R., 'Thomas Cromwell's Decline and Fall', *Cambridge Historical Journal*, 10 (1951), pp.150–85

Elton, G.R., *The Tudor Revolution in Government* (Cambridge, 1953)

Elton, G.R., *Star Chamber Stories* (Cambridge, 1958)

Elton, G.R., *Policy and Police: The Enforcement of the Reformation in the Age of Thomas Cromwell* (Cambridge, 1972)

Elton, G.R., *Reform and Renewal: Thomas Cromwell and the Common Weal* (Cambridge, 1973)

Elton, G.R., *Studies in Tudor and Stuart Politics and Government*, 4 vols. (Cambridge, 1974–92)

Elton, G.R., 'Tudor Government: The Points of Contact: I. Parliament', *Transactions of the Royal Historical Society*, 5th ser., XXIV (1974)

Elton, G.R., 'Tudor Government: The Points of Contact: II. The Council', *Transactions of the Royal Historical Society*, 5th ser., XXV (1975)

Elton, G.R., 'Tudor Government: The Points of Contact: III. The Court', *Transactions of the Royal Historical Society*, 5th ser., XXVI (1976)

Elton, G.R., *Reform and Reformation: England, 1509–1558* (London, 1981)

Elton, G.R., *The Tudor Constitution: Documents and Commentary*, 2nd edn (Cambridge, 1982)

Elton, G.R., 'A New Age of Reform?', *Historical Journal*, 30 (1987), pp.709–16

Elton, G.R., *Thomas Cromwell: Secretary, Minister and Lord Privy Seal* (Cambridge, 1991)

Elton, G.R., 'How Corrupt was Thomas Cromwell?', *Historical Journal*, 36 (1993), pp.905–8

Elton, G.R., *England under the Tudors* (London and New York, 2005)

Eppley, D., *Defending Royal Supremacy and Discerning God's Will in Tudor England* (Aldershot, 2007)

Erler, M.C., *Reading and Writing during the Dissolution: Monks, Friars, and Nuns 1530–1558* (Cambridge, 2013)

Foister, S., *Holbein and England* (New Haven and London, 2004)

Fox, A.G. and Guy, J.A. (eds.), *Reassessing the Henrician Age: Humanism, Politics and Reform 1500–1550* (Oxford, 1986)

Fraser, A., *The Six Wives of Henry VIII* (London, 1993)

Friedmann, P., *Anne Boleyn: A Chapter of English History*, 2 vols. (London, 1884)

Fuller, T., *Church History of Britain* (London, 1655)

Galton, A., *The Character and Times of Thomas Cromwell* (Birmingham, 1887)

GEC, *The Complete Peerage of England Scotland Ireland Great Britain and the United Kingdom*, Vol. III (London, 1913)

Grummitt, D., 'Calais 1485–1547: A Study in Early Tudor Government and Politics', Ph.D. diss., University of London (1997)

Gunn, S.J. (ed.), *Early Tudor Government* (1995)

Gunn, S.J. and Lindley, P. (eds.), *Cardinal Wolsey: Church, State and Art* (Cambridge, 1991)

Guy, J.A., 'Communications – The Tudor Commonwealth: Revising Thomas Cromwell', *Historical Journal*, 23/3 (1980), pp.681–7

Guy, J.A., 'Henry VIII and the Praemunire Manoeuvres of 1530–1', *English Historical Review*, 97 (1982), pp.481–501

Guy, J.A., *Tudor England* (Oxford, 1988)

Guy, J.A. (ed.), *The Tudor Monarchy* (London, 1997)

Guy, J.A., *Thomas More* (London, 2000)

Gwyn, P., *The King's Cardinal: The Rise and Fall of Thomas Wolsey* (London, 1990)

Haigh, C., *English Reformations: Religion, Politics and Society under the Tudors* (Oxford, 1993)

Head, D., *Ebbs and Flows of Fortune: Life of Thomas Howard, Third Duke of Norfolk* (Athens, 1995)

Holder, N., 'The Medieval Friaries of London', Ph.D. diss., University of London (2011)

Hornsey, I., *A History of Beer and Brewing* (Cambridge, *c.*2003)

Hoyle, R.W., *The Pilgrimage of Grace and the Politics of the 1530s* (Oxford, 2001)

Hurstfield, J., 'Was There a Tudor Despotism After All?', *Transactions of the Royal Historical Society*, 5th ser., LII (1967)

Hutchinson, R., *Thomas Cromwell: The Rise and Fall of Henry VIII's Most Notorious Minister* (London, 2008)

Hutchinson, R., *Young Henry: The Rise to Power of Henry VIII* (London, 2011)

Ives, E.W., 'Faction at the Court of Henry VIII: The Fall of Anne Boleyn', *History*, LVII (1972), pp.169–88

Ives, E.W., *Anne Boleyn* (1986)

Ives, E.W., 'The Fall of Anne Boleyn Re-considered', *English Historical Review*, 107 (1992), pp.651–64

Ives, E.W., 'Anne Boleyn and the Early Reformation in England: The Contemporary Evidence', *Historical Journal*, 37 (1994), pp.389–400

Ives, E.W., *The Life and Death of Anne Boleyn* (Oxford, 2004)

Jones, J.G., *Early Modern Wales, c.1512–1640* (1994)

Lehmberg, S.E., *The Reformation Parliament, 1529–1536* (Cambridge, 1970)

Lehmberg, S.E., 'Sir Thomas Audley: A Soul as Black as Marble?', in Slavin, A.J. (ed.), *Tudor Men and Institutions* (Louisiana, 1972)

Lehmberg, S.E., *The Later Parliaments of Henry VIII 1536–1547* (Cambridge, 1977)

Lehmberg, S.E., 'The Religious Beliefs of Thomas Cromwell', in *Leaders of the Reformation*, DeMolen, R.L. (ed.) (London and Toronto, 1984)

Loades, D., *Power in Tudor England* (London, 1997)

Loades, D., *Tudor Government: Structures of Authority in the Sixteenth Century* (Oxford, 1997)

Loades, D., *Henry VIII: Court, Church and Conflict* (Kew, 2007)

Loades, D., *Thomas Cromwell: Servant to Henry VIII* (Stroud, 2013)

MacCulloch, D. (ed.), *The Reign of Henry VIII: Politics, Policy and Piety* (Basingstoke, 1995)

MacCulloch, D., *Thomas Cranmer: A Life* (New Haven and London, 1996)

MacCulloch, D., *Reformation: Europe's House Divided* (London, 2003)

McEntegart, R., *Henry VIII, The League of Schmalkalden, and the English Reformation* (Woodbridge, 2002)

Mantel, H., *Wolf Hall* (London, 2009)

Mantel, H., *Bring up the Bodies* (London, 2012)

Marius, R., *Thomas More* (New York, 1984)

Mathew, D., *The Courtiers of Henry VIII* (London, 1970)

Mattingly, G., *Catherine of Aragon* (London, 1942)

Neame, A.,*The Holy Maid of Kent* (London, 1971)

Noble, M., *Memoirs of the Protectorate House of Cromwell*, 2 vols. (Birmingham, 1784)

O'Day, R., *The Debate on the English Reformation* (Cambridge, 1986)

O'Day, R., *The Longman Companion to the Tudor Age* (Cambridge, 1995)

Ormerod, G., *History of the County Palatine and City of Chester*, 3 vols. (London, 1819)

Parmiter, G. de C., *The King's Great Matter: A Study of Anglo-Papal Relations 1527–1534* (London, 1967)

Pettegree, A. (ed.), *The Reformation World* (London, 2000)

Phillips, J., 'The Cromwells of Putney', *Antiquarian Magazine and Bibliographer*, Vol. II (London, 1882), pp.56–62

Plowden, A., *Tudor Women: Queens and Commoners* (Sutton, 2002)

Redworth, G., *In Defence of the Church Catholic: The Life of Stephen Gardiner* (Oxford, 1990)

Rex, R.A.W., *Henry VIII and the English Reformation* (Basingstoke, 1993)

Rex, R.A.W., *The Tudors* (Stroud, 2002)

Richardson, W.C., *Stephen Vaughan, Financial Agent of Henry VIII: A Study of Financial Relations with the Low Countries* (Louisiana, 1953)

Ridley, J.G., *Henry VIII* (London, 1984)

Ridley, J., *Thomas Cranmer* (Oxford, 1948)

Robertson, M.L., 'Thomas Cromwell's Servants: The Ministerial Household in Early Tudor Government and Society', Ph.D. diss., University of California, Los Angeles (1975)

Robertson, M.L., 'The Art of the Possible: Thomas Cromwell's Management of West Country Government', *Historical Journal*, 32/4 (1989), pp.793–816

Robertson, M.L., 'Profit and Purpose in the Development of Thomas Cromwell's Landed Estates', *The Journal of British Studies*, Vol. 29, no. 4 (Cambridge, 1990)

Robinson, J.M., *The Dukes of Norfolk* (Chichester, 1995)

Ryrie, A., *The Gospel and Henry VIII: Evangelicals in the Early English Reformation* (Cambridge, 2003)

Scarisbrick, J.J., *Henry VIII* (London, 1968)

Scarisbrick, J.J., *The Reformation and the English People* (Oxford, 1984)

Schofield, J., *The Rise and Fall of Thomas Cromwell: Henry VIII's Most Faithful Servant* (Stroud, 2011)

Slack, P., *The English Poor Law, 1531–1782* (Cambridge, 1990)

Slavin, A.J., *Politics and Profit* (Cambridge, 1966)

Slavin, A.J., *Thomas Cromwell on Church and Commonwealth: Selected Letters, 1523–1540* (New York, 1969)

Slavin, A.J., 'Thomas Cromwell and the Printers: The Boston Pardons',

Proceedings of the Center for the History of British Political Thought (Washington, 1984)

Starkey, D., 'A Reply: Tudor Government: The Facts?', *Historical Journal*, 31 (1988), pp.921–31

Starkey, D. (ed.), *A European Court in London* (London, 1991)

Starkey, D., *The Reign of Henry VIII: Personalities and Politics* (London, 2002)

Starkey, D., *Six Wives: The Queens of Henry VIII* (London, 2003)

Starkey, D., and others (eds.), *The English Court: From the Wars of the Roses to the Civil War* (London and New York, 1987)

Strong, R., *Holbein and Henry VIII* (London, 1967)

Strong, R., *Tudor and Jacobean Portraits*, 2 vols. (London, 1969)

Underwood, W., 'Thomas Cromwell and William Marshall's Protestant Books', *Historical Journal*, 47, (2004), pp.517–39

Walker, G., 'Rethinking the Fall of Anne Boleyn', *Historical Journal*, 45/1 (2000), pp.1-29

Ward, P.J., 'The Origins of Thomas Cromwell's Public Career: Service under Cardinal Wolsey and Henry VIII, 1524–30', Ph.D. diss., London School of Economics and Political Science (1999)

Warnicke, R.M., *The Rise and Fall of Anne Boleyn* (Cambridge, 1989)

Warnicke, R.M., *The Marrying of Anne of Cleves: Royal Protocol in Early Modern England* (Cambridge, 2000)

Weir, A., *Henry VIII: King and Court* (London, 2001)

Weir, A., *The Six Wives of Henry VIII* (London, 2007)

Weir, A., *The Lady in the Tower* (London, 2009)

Weir, A., *Mary Boleyn* (London, 2011)

Wilding, P., *Thomas Cromwell* (London and Toronto, 1935)

Williams, G., *Renewal and Reformation: Wales, c.1415–1642* (Oxford, 1993)

Williams, N., *The Cardinal and the Secretary* (London, 1975)

Williams, P. and Harriss, G.L., 'A Revolution in Tudor History?', *Past and Present*, XXV (1963), pp.3–58

Wilson, D., *In the Lion's Court: Power, Ambition and Sudden Death in the Reign of Henry VIII* (London, 2002)

Youings, J., *The Dissolution of the Monasteries* (London, 1971)

NOTES

AUTHOR'S NOTE

I have retained the original spelling and punctuation of quotations when these are short and easily understood. For longer quotes, and those where the original spelling and punctuation makes them less comprehensible, I have modernised them.

A NOTE ON CROMWELL'S COAT OF ARMS, DISPLAYED ON PAGE III

The lions of England surround a Tudor rose, which is flanked by two Cornish choughs – distinctive birds with black plumage and brightly coloured legs, feet and bills. This central strip was taken from the arms of Cromwell's first patron, Cardinal Wolsey.

INTRODUCTION

1. Foxe, Book III, p.645.
2. Merriman, Vol. I, pp.313–14.
3. *Letters and Papers*, Vol. XIV, no. 399.
4. Merriman, Vol. I, p.87.

CHAPTER 1: *'A great traveller in the world'*

1. Foxe, Book III, p.645.
2. Ibid., pp.645ff.
3. A survey of Wimbledon Manor taken in 1617 supports this notion because it describes on that spot 'an ancient cottage called the smith's shop, lying west of the highway from Richmond to Wandsworth'. Walford, E., 'Putney', *Old and New London*, Vol. 6 (1878), pp.489–503.
4. Fulling is the cleansing of cloth or wool to remove oils, dirt and other impurities, and to make it thicker. The process involved soaking wool in vats of human urine.

5. This was according to the Imperial ambassador Chapuys. How he knew this is not clear, as there is no other reference to it in contemporary sources. *Letters and Papers*, Vol. IX, no. 862.
6. *Calendar of Letters, Despatches, and State Papers, Spain*, Vol. V, Part I, p.468. He made the remark during the debate about Henry VIII's 'Great Matter' and whether Catherine of Aragon was still capable of bearing a living son.
7. *Calendar of the Close Rolls ... Henry VII*, p.18.
8. Williams, C.H., pp.188–90.
9. In order to prevent the sale of bad beer, an ale-taster was appointed to pass or condemn as unfit all the brewing in a parish.
10. Hornsey, pp.321–2.
11. Merriman, Vol. I, pp.3–4.
12. Ibid., pp.2–4.
13. Foxe, Book III, pp.645ff.
14. *Letters and Papers*, Vol. IX, no. 862.
15. Anon., *Life of Thomas Lord Cromwell*, p.3; Williams, C.H. pp.190, 196; Holinshed, p.951.
16. Payne, p.107.
17. Foxe, Book III, pp.645ff; Merriman, Vol. I, p.23.
18. Anon., 'Life and Death of Thomas Lord Cromwell' p.351.
19. Williams, C.H., p.189.
20. Foxe, Book III, pp.645ff; Merriman, Vol. I, p.23.
21. Payne, pp.106–7.
22. Foxe, *Actes and Monuments*, Book II, pp.419–34. This is repeated in Holinshed, p.951.
23. Payne, p.107.
24. Merriman, Vol. I, pp.18–19.
25. *Letters and Papers*, Vol. X, no. 1218; Merriman, Vol. I, p.11. The Syngsson Mart was one of the foremost markets in the Netherlands.
26. *Letters and Papers*, Vol. I, Part i, no. 1473.
27. Ibid., Vol. IX, no. 862.
28. Muller, p.399.
29. *Letters and Papers*,Vol. I, no. 3195.
30. Merriman, Vol. I, p.303.
31. Foxe, Book III, pp.645ff; Merriman, Vol. I, p.23.
32. Holinshed, p.951.
33. *Letters and Papers*,Vol. IV, no. 6346.
34. The account, recorded by Pole in 1538, recalled a conversation that

had taken place during the 1520s. The timing has prompted doubt about its authenticity because *Il Principe* was not published until 1532. But given Cromwell's connections, the theory that he obtained an early manuscript edition is plausible. Indeed, Pole claims that Cromwell had offered to lend it to him, provided he promised to read it.

35. Williams, C.H., p.190.
36. Ibid., p.196.
37. Holinshed, p.951.
38. Anne is also referred to as Alice in the contemporary sources.
39. It has been incorrectly asserted that Gregory entered Pembroke College, Cambridge, in 1528. This has led some historians to assert that his date of birth could have been as early as 1514. In fact, Gregory was appointed a Tutor from Pembroke College in 1528, but did not go there himself. See below, p.73.
40. Pratt, Vol. V, pp.363–5.
41. There is some evidence to suggest that Cromwell undertook two visits to Rome on behalf of the Boston guild: one in 1510 and the other in 1517/18. There were two sets of payments in the Boston account books. However, the date of 1510 is cited only by Foxe, and it is at least equally possible that the confusion over dates in Cromwell's early career led to an assumption that he made two visits, rather than one.
42. Pratt, Vol. V, p.364.
43. Hall, pp.838–9.
44. Pratt, Vol. V, p.365.

CHAPTER 2: *The Cardinal*

1. Cavendish, *Life and Death of Cardinal Wolsey*, p.7.
2. Tyndale, p.307.
3. Weir, *Henry VIII*, pp.1–2, 19.
4. Ibid., p.2.
5. Williams, C.H., p.389; Weir, *Henry VIII*, p.3.
6. Hall, p.712.
7. Starkey, *Reign of Henry VIII*, p.3.
8. Cavendish, *Life and Death of Cardinal Wolsey*, pp.11–12.
9. Strype, *Ecclesiastical Memorials*, Vol. I, Part i, p.6.
10. Hume, p.1.
11. Cavendish, *Life and Death of Cardinal Wolsey*, pp.11–12; Tyndale, p.307.

12. Brown, Vol. I, pp.139, 155; *Letters and Papers*, Vol. II, Part ii, Appendix, no. 12.
13. Williams, C.H., p.402.
14. *Letters and Papers*, Vol. II, Part i, no. 1959.
15. Cavendish, *Life and Death of Cardinal Wolsey*, p.12.
16. A useful summary of this debate is provided in Ward, pp.23–4.
17. *Letters and Papers*, Vol. IX, no. 862.
18. Foxe, Book III, p.648.
19. Merriman, Vol. I, pp.14–15.
20. Williams, C.H. pp.388–9.
21. Payne, p.108.
22. *Letters and Papers*, Vol. III, no. 2441.
23. See for example *Letters and Papers,* Vol. III, no. 2624.
24. *Calendar of Letters, Despatches, and State Papers, Spain*, Vol. V, Part II, p.145.
25. His constituency has not been identified.
26. Merriman, Vol. I, pp.30–44.
27. Ibid., pp.313–14.
28. *Letters and Papers*, Vol. IV, no. 6262.
29. *Calendar of Letters, Despatches, and State Papers, Spain*, Vol. IV, Part II.ii, p.752.
30. *Letters and Papers*, Vol. III, no. 2394. Creke (also spelled Creak) may have been a clerk of the hanaper. This was an office (now abolished) in the department of the chancery. The clerk, also known as warden of the hanaper, was paid fees and other moneys for the sealing of charters, patents, writs, etc.
31. Merriman, Vol. I, pp.313–14.
32. Ibid., p.314.
33. BL Cotton MS Galba B x fo.9r.
34. *Letters and Papers*, Vol. V, no. 247.
35. See for example *Letters and Papers*, Vol. IV, no. 6429.
36. *Letters and Papers*, Vol. V, no. 247.
37. Richardson, p.18.
38. See for example *Letters and Papers*, Vol. IV, no. 6429.
39. *Letters and Papers*, Vol. IV, no. 6429.
40. Ibid., no. 6744.
41. Ibid., no. 4107.
42. Ibid., Vol. V, no. 247.
43. *Calendar of State Papers, Venice*, Vol. V, p.93.
44. Foxe, Book III, p.650.
45. Sampson, p.203.

46. Roper, pp.11–12.
47. Foxe, Book III, p.648.
48. Stow, p.190.
49. I am indebted to Dr Nick Holder for sharing his fascinating and detailed research on Austin Friars, which is encapsulated in his thesis: 'The Medieval Friaries of London'.
50. *Letters and Papers*, Vol. V, no. 1509.
51. Ellis, H. p.125; Merriman, Vol. I, p.314; *Letters and Papers*, Vol. IV, Appendix, no. 57.
52. *Letters and Papers*, Vol. IV, no. 1768.
53. Knox, J., *First Blast of the Trumpet Against the Monstrous Regiment of Women*, first published 1558 (New York, 1972), pp.9–10.
54. Merriman, Vol. I, pp.56–63.
55. See below, pp.284–7.
56. Black, p.140.
57. Ibid., p.156.
58. *Calendar of Letters, Despatches, and State Papers, Spain*, Vol. V, Part I, p.590; Vol. VI, Part I, p.17.
59. *Letters and Papers*, Vol. V, no. 1509; Vol. IX, no. 862; Weir, *Henry VIII*, p.307.
60. *Letters and Papers*, Vol. IV, no. 3197. See also Holder.
61. Holder, p.161.
62. Ibid.
63. *Letters and Papers*, Vol. X, nos. 819, 840, 855; Vol. XIV, Part ii, no. 782.
64. Robertson, 'Thomas Cromwell's Servants',pp.101–2.
65. *Calendar of Letters, Despatches, and State Papers, Spain*, Vol. V, Part I, p.569.
66. *Letters and Papers*, Vol. IV, no. 1732.

CHAPTER 3: *'Not without sorow'*

1. Ashdown, D.M., *Ladies in Waiting* (London, 1976), pp.23–4.
2. Strickland, A., *Lives of the Queens of England* (London, 1851), Vol. II, p.572.
3. Turnbull, no. 491.
4. Hume, p.105.
5. Cardinal's College was later re-founded by Henry VIII as Christ Church.
6. Hume, p.25.
7. Merriman, Vol. I, p.318.
8. Ibid., pp.323–4.

9. Foxe, Book III, p.585.
10. Williams, C.H., p.422.
11. Ibid., p.423.
12. Ibid., p.422.
13. Merriman, Vol. I, p.319.
14. Foxe, Book III, pp.645ff.
15. *Letters and Papers*, Vol. IV, no. 3334.
16. Merriman, Vol. I, p.19.
17. Hume, pp.25–6.
18. Cavendish, *Life and Death of Cardinal Wolsey*, p.126.
19. Merriman, Vol. I, p.47.
20. The date of Anne's birth was not recorded, but it is estimated at around 1500 or 1501. Elizabeth I's seventeenth-century biographer, William Camden, claimed that Anne was born in 1507, as did other sources of that time. But this would have made her no more than six years old when she entered Margaret of Austria's service in 1513, an impossibly young age.
21. *Calendar of State Papers, Venice*, Vol. IV, p.365.
22. In reality, this was little more than a second nail growing on the side of one of her fingers. Anne was so self-conscious about it that she took to wearing long-hanging oversleeves, which instantly became fashionable among court ladies.
23. Wyatt, in Cavendish, *Life and Death of Cardinal Wolsey*, pp.424, 441.
24. Foxe, J., *Actes and Monuments*, edited by Clarke, A (London, 1888), p.209.
25. *Letters and Papers*, Vol. IV, Part II i, no.1467.
26. Ibid., p.1468.
27. Henry VIII sought to end his marriage to Catherine through an annulment, not a divorce. However, I have mostly referred to it as the latter, partly for ease of comprehension but partly also because that is how many contemporaries and subsequent historians have termed it.
28. *State Papers*, Vol. I, p.194.
29. Leviticus, chapter 20, verse 21.
30. *Letters and Papers*, Vol. II, p.ccvii.
31. Norton, pp.105–6.
32. Ibid., p.106.
33. *Letters and Papers*, Vol. IV, Part ii, no. 4468.
34. A number of more recent sources cite her death as occurring at Stepney, although there is no corroborating evidence for this in the contemporary sources.
35. *Letters and Papers*, Vol. IV, no. 5772; Merriman, Vol. I, pp.56–63. Joan

later married John Williamson, an old friend of Cromwell, who became prominent in his service.

36. *Letters and Papers*, Vol. XII, Part ii, nos. 35, 100–1.
37. Foxe, Book III, p.648.
38. *Letters and Papers*, Vol. V, no. 19.
39. Ibid., no. 17. For Margaret's correspondence with Cromwell, see Erler, pp.88–106.
40. Ibid., Vol. IV, no. 4560. Gregory had been temporarily moved from Cambridge to the countryside because of the onset of plague in the city.
41. Ibid., no. 4561.
42. Ibid., no. 6457.
43. Ibid., nos. 4916, 6219, 6722.
44. Ibid., Vol. VI, no. 696.
45. Ibid., Vol.IV, no. 6722.
46. Ibid., no. 4916.
47. Ibid., nos. 4433, 5757, 6219.
48. Norton, p.65.
49. A full transcript of this is provided in Merriman, Vol .I, pp.56–63.
50. They were living with him by November 1532, when Thomas Alvard reported to an absent Cromwell after a visit to Austin Friars that they were both well. *Letters and Papers*, Vol. V, no. 1509; Vol. VI, no. 696.
51. Merriman, Vol. I, p.61.
52. Ibid., p.325.
53. Hall, p.772; *Calendar of Letters, Despatches, and State Papers, Spain*, Vol. IV, Part I, p.189.
54. Hall, p.759.
55. *Letters and Papers*, Vol. IV, no. 6019.
56. Cavendish, *Life and Death of Cardinal Wolsey*, p.102.
57. *Letters and Papers*, Vol. IV, no. 6030.

CHAPTER 4: *'Make or marre'*

1. Shakespeare, W., *Henry VIII*, Act III, scene ii.
2. Cavendish, *Life and Death of Cardinal Wolsey*, pp.169, 170.
3. Ibid., p.105.
4. Ibid., p.112.
5. Norton, p.277.
6. Mathew, p.70.

7. Hall, p.764.
8. *Letters and Papers*, Vol. IV, no. 6112.
9. Ibid., no. 6447.
10. Cavendish, *Life and Death of Cardinal Wolsey*, p.119.
11. *Letters and Papers*, Vol. IV, no. 6036.
12. Ibid., no. 6058.
13. Ibid., nos. 6080, 6098.
14. Ibid., nos. 6114, 6076.
15. Ibid., no. 6114.
16. Although he had made the most of his illness, it was genuine. Less than a month later, his physician, Dr Augustine, wrote in panic to Cromwell, urging him to secure leeches and a 'vomitive electuary' from the king's doctors. Ibid., no. 6151.
17. Ibid., nos. 6115, 6181.
18. Ibid., nos. 6076, 6199.
19. Ibid., Vol. X, no. 601.
20. *Calendar of Letters, Despatches, and State Papers, Spain*, Vol. IV, Part II.ii, p.819.
21. Cavendish, *Life and Death of Cardinal Wolsey*, p.126.
22. *Letters and Papers*, Vol. IV, no. 6112.
23. Elton, *Tudor Revolution in Government*, p.88.
24. *Calendar of Letters, Despatches, and State Papers, Spain*, Vol. V, Part II, p.56.
25. Ibid., Part I, p.298.
26. Merriman, Vol. I, p.373.
27. *Calendar of Letters, Despatches, and State Papers, Spain*, Vol. IV, Part II.ii, p.759.
28. *Letters and Papers*, Vol. IV, no. 6554.
29. Ibid., no. 6196.
30. Ibid., nos. 66, 5034.
31. Wood, Vol. II, p.66.
32. *Letters and Papers*, Vol. IV, no. 6420; Elton, *Tudor Revolution*, p.85.

CHAPTER 5: *'The frailty of human affairs'*

1. Weir, *Henry VIII*, p.27; Starkey, *Reign of Henry VIII*, p.17.
2. *Letters and Papers*, Vol. X, no. 601; *Calendar of Letters, Despatches, and State Papers, Spain*, Vol. V, Part II, pp.81–2.
3. *Letters and Papers*, Vol. IV, nos. 6076, 6181, 6203.

4. Ibid., no. 6203.
5. Ibid., nos. 6213, 6214.
6. Ibid., no. 6076.
7. Ibid., no. 6226.
8. Ibid., no. 6076.
9. Ibid., nos. 6199, 6344, 6335.
10. See for example ibid., no. 6262.
11. Ibid., nos. 6076, 6571.
12. Ibid., no. 6076; Merriman, Vol. I, p.327.
13. Cavendish, *Life and Death of Cardinal Wolsey*, p.126.
14. *State Papers*, Vol. I, no. 362; *Letters and Papers*, Vol. IV, nos. 6076, 6524.
15. *Letters and Papers*, Vol. IV, no. 6076.
16. Ibid., nos. 6076, 6554.
17. Ibid., nos. 6076, 6571; Merriman, Vol. I, p.331.
18. *Letters and Papers*, Vol. IV, no. 6110.
19. Ibid., nos. 6100, 6699.
20. Ibid., no. 6720; Cavendish, *Life and Death of Cardinal Wolsey*, pp. 174, 178–9; Holinshed, p.951.
21. *State Papers*, Vol. VII, no. 213; Norton, p.149.
22. Foxe, Book III, pp.645–55.
23. Merriman, Vol. I, pp.17–18; Hume, pp.31, 87.
24. Foxe, Book III, p.645.
25. Hume, p.95; *Calendar of Letters, Despatches, and State Papers, Spain*, Vol. V, Part II, pp.207, 239.
26. Cavendish, *Metrical Visions*, Vol. II, p.52.
27. Holinshed, p.951.
28. *Calendar of State Papers, Venice*, Vol.IV, pp.294–5.
29. Merriman, Vol. II, pp.20, 23.
30. *Letters and Papers*, Vol. IV, no. 2387.
31. Merriman, Vol. I, pp.357–8.
32. The so-called 'Reformation Parliament' was first summoned in 1529 and was finally dissolved in 1536. It had several breaks in between.
33. *Letters and Papers*, Vol. V, no. 628.
34. Merriman, Vol. I, p.92.
35. Ibid., pp.90–1.
36. Strype, *Ecclesiastical Memorials*, Vol. I, Part i, p.316.
37. *Letters and Papers*, Vol. V, nos. 15, 18.
38. Ibid., no. 17.
39. *State Papers*, Vol. I, p.380.

CHAPTER 6: *The King's 'Great Matter'*

1. *Calendar of State Papers, Venice*, Vol. IV, p.287.
2. *Letters and Papers*, Vol. V, Part i, no. 24.
3. *Calendar of State Papers, Venice*, Vol. IV, p.288.
4. Ibid., pp.57, 288.
5. *Letters and Papers*, Vol. IX, no. 861.
6. Ibid., Vol. VI, Part i, no. 324.
7. Ibid., no. 805.
8. *Calendar of Letters, Despatches, and State Papers, Spain*, Vol. V, Part I, p.484.
9. Merriman, Vol. I, p.343.
10. Ibid., pp.134–5; *Letters and Papers*, Vol. IX, no. 725(1).
11. Merriman, Vol. I, p.135; *Letters and Papers*, Vol. VII, no. 1554; *Calendar of State Papers, Venice*, Vol. V, p.26.
12. Merriman, Vol. I, p.135.
13. Ibid.; *Letters and Papers*, Vol. VII, no. 1554.
14. Bray, p.59.
15. Ibid.
16. Lehmberg, *Reformation Parliament*, p.146.
17. Hall, p.788.
18. Sampson, p.240.
19. *Calendar of Letters, Despatches, and State Papers, Spain*, Vol. V, Part II, p.257.
20. Merriman, Vol. I, p.62.
21. *Letters and Papers*, Vol. IV, nos. 6076, 6391.
22. Ibid., no. 3197.
23. Cavendish, *Life and Death of Cardinal Wolsey*, p.106.
24. *State Papers*, Vol. I, p.384.
25. Brigden, 'Thomas Cromwell and the Brethren', p.41.
26. Foxe, Book III, p.654.
27. *Letters and Papers*, Vol. V, no. 153.
28. Merriman, Vol. I, pp.335–9; *Letters and Papers*, Vol. V, no. 248.
29. *Letters and Papers*, Vol. V, no. 533.

CHAPTER 7: *'The suddaine rising of some men'*

1. *Letters and Papers*, Vol. V, no. 1452.
2. Ibid., Vol. IV, no. 6146; Vol. XIV, Part ii, no. 782.

3. Chapuys estimated that the new residences were 'half a league' away. Ibid., Vol. X, no. 351. Although it is difficult to translate a league into modern measurements accurately, it equated to around three miles.
4. Holder, p.162.
5. Stow, pp.191–2.
6. *Letters and Papers*, Vol. IX, no. 340.
7. The slow progress can partly be explained by the fact that in October 1536 Cromwell's nephew Richard took eighty of the workers to Yorkshire to help suppress the Pilgrimage of Grace. Holder, pp.163–4.
8. *Letters and Papers*, Vol. X, no. 351.
9. Stow, p.191.
10. SP 1/85, fo.56.
11. *Letters and Papers*, Vol. VII, no. 1135.
12. Ellis, Vol. I, pp.343–5.
13. *Letters and Papers*, Vol. VII, no. 1135.
14. Ibid., Vol. VIII, no. 618.
15. Merriman, Vol. I, p.343; Vol. II, p.137.
16. *Letters and Papers*, Vol. XIV, Part ii, no. 290; Ellis, H., Vol. I, p.340; Noble, Vol. I, p.18.
17. Bindoff, Vol. III, p.251.
18. Ibid., Vol. I, p.369.
19. Strype, *Ecclesiastical Memorials*, Vol. I, Part i, pp.561–2; Norton, pp.260–1; *Letters and Papers*, Vol. IX, no. 964.
20. An excellent appraisal of Cromwell's household is provided by Robertson: 'Thomas Cromwell's Servants'.
21. Stow, p.34
22. Merriman, Vol. II, p.267.
23. Stow, p.34, and Foxe, Book III, p.645; *Letters and Papers*, Vol. IX, no. 651; Robertson, 'Thomas Cromwell's Servants',p.375. The boy does not appear in the records of Cromwell's household thereafter, so his audacity does not seem to have been rewarded.
24. *Letters and Papers*, Vol. VI, nos. 696, 698.
25. Strype, *Ecclesiastical Memorials*, Vol. I, Part I, p.221.
26. Merriman, Vol. I, p.348.
27. Ibid., pp.353–4.
28. Fuller, p.231.
29. Nichols, pp.244–5.
30. Stow, p.34.

31. *Letters and Papers*, Vol. VI, no. 1365; Vol. XII, Part ii, no. 952.
32. Elton, *England under the Tudors*, p.133.
33. *Letters and Papers*, Vol. VI, Part i, no. 653.
34. Ibid., Vol. VI, no. 465; *Calendar of Letters, Despatches, and State Papers, Spain*, Vol. IV, Part II.ii, pp.669, 677.
35. Norton, p.325.
36. *Letters and Papers*, Vol. VI, no. 1510.

CHAPTER 8: *'Hevy wordes and terrible thretes'*

1. *Letters and Papers*, Vol. VI, Part ii, no. 1089.
2. Ibid., Vol. VII, Part i, no. 1112; Weir, *Six Wives of Henry VIII*, p.258.
3. *Letters and Papers*, Vol. VII, Part i, no. 809; Vol. VI, Part ii, no. 1125.
4. *Calendar of Letters, Despatches, and State Papers, Spain*, Vol. V, Part I, p.295.
5. Wyatt, *Collected Poems*.
6. *Calendar of Letters, Despatches, and State Papers, Spain*, Vol. V, Part I, p.438.
7. Ibid., Vol. II, p.451.
8. Ibid., Vol. V, Part I, pp.219–20; Part II, p.95.
9. Ibid., Vol. IV, Part II.ii, p.752.
10. Ibid., p.760.
11. Ibid., Vol. V, Part I, p.126.
12. Merriman, Vol. I, pp.360–1, 371.
13. Ibid., p.374.
14. Ibid., pp.373–9.
15. *Letters and Papers*, Vol. VII, no. 287.
16. Ibid., no. 575.
17. Merriman, Vol. I, p.381.
18. *Letters and Papers*, Vol. VII, nos. 1149, 496.
19. Ibid., no.1025.
20. Bray, pp.113–14.
21. Merriman, Vol. I, p.389.
22. *Letters and Papers*, Vol. VIII, no. 196.
23. Merriman, Vol. I, p.154.
24. See for example Merriman, Vol. II, pp.80–2.
25. *State Papers*, Vol. II, p.553n.

26. Ibid., p.551n.
27. Merriman, Vol. I, pp.155–6; *Letters and Papers*, Vol. VII, no. 1554.
28. Elton, *Reform and Renewal*, p.45.
29. Merriman, Vol. II, pp.43–4.

CHAPTER 9: *'Good master secretary'*

1. *Calendar of Letters, Despatches, and State Papers, Spain*, Vol. V, Part I, p.294.
2. Ibid., Vol. IV, Part II.ii, p.841; Vol. V, Part I, pp.465–6.
3. Stow, p.34; *Calendar of Letters, Despatches, and State Papers, Spain*, Vol. V, Part I, p.569; Wood, Vol. II, p.268.
4. Elton, *Studies in Tudor and Stuart Politics and Government*, Vol. II, p.225.
5. Norton, pp.203–5.
6. Mary was eventually forgiven by her sister and attended Anne during her final, ill-fated pregnancy in 1536.
7. Anon., *Life of Thomas Lord Cromwell*, p.18. A similar account is provided by Bandello: Payne, p.111.
8. Payne, pp.113–14.
9. *Calendar of State Papers, Venice*, Vol. V, p.82.
10. Payne, p.114.
11. Merriman, Vol. I, p.362.
12. *Letters and Papers*, Vol. VIII, no. 108. NB The date of the letter is incorrectly cited as 26 January 1535, but has been proven to be 1 July 1536. Erler, p.99n.
13. Cavendish, *Metrical Visions*, Vol. II, p.52.
14. Some of them would remain there even after Cromwell had been replaced as Master of the Rolls by Christopher Hales in July 1536. Robertson, 'Thomas Cromwell's Servants'.
15. *Letters and Papers*, Vol. IX, nos. 272, 339, 340.
16. Ibid., no. 340.
17. An excellent analysis of Cromwell's land and property holdings is provided by Robertson, 'Profit and Purpose in the Development of Thomas Cromwell's Landed Estates', pp.317–46.
18. In August 1538, for example, he helped arrange a large grant of land at Wimbledon, Putney and Roehampton to Walter Williams, who is cited as Cromwell's nephew but may have been the brother-in-law of

his sister, Katherine. *History of Parliament* online.

19. Foxe, Book III, p.654.
20. Williams, N., p.150.
21. *Letters and Papers*, Vol. XIV, Part ii, no. 782.
22. Ibid.,Vol. XIII, Part i, no. 1450; Vol. XIV, Part ii, nos. 85, 782; Robertson, 'Thomas Cromwell's Servants',pp.102–3.
23. *Letters and Papers*, Vol. XIV, Part ii, no. 782.
24. Ibid.
25. Ibid.
26. Ibid., Vol. VII, no. 1554.
27. Merriman, Vol. I, pp.402–5.

CHAPTER 10: *Dissolution*

1. The high rate of infant mortality was largely responsible for life expectancy being so low. Those who survived infancy could expect to live to their fifties or early sixties.
2. Payne, p.107.
3. *Calendar of Letters, Despatches, and State Papers, Spain*, Vol. V, Part I, pp.411, 428, 436, 452.
4. *Letters and Papers*, Vol. VIII, no. 121.
5. Norton, p.288. Cromwell was later obliged to surrender one of these rooms to Jane Seymour in order to facilitate her courtship with his master.
6. Muller, pp.60–1.
7. Foxe, Book III, p.646.
8. Muller, p.399.
9. *Letters and Papers*, Vol. XI, no. 29; BL Add MS 25114 fos.175–7.
10. Foxe, Book III, p.646.
11. Elton, *England under the Tudors*, p.141.
12. Foxe, Book III, p.649.
13. *Letters and Papers*, Vol. X, no. 45.
14. *Calendar of State Papers, Venice*, Vol. V, p.26. A later ambassador, Giovanni Soranzo, concurred that Cromwell was the 'supreme ruler in England'. Ibid., p.550; Cavendish, *Metrical Visions*, Vol. II, p.51.
15. *Letters and Papers*, Vol. VIII, nos. 609, 661.
16. Merriman ,Vol. I, p.410; Pratt, Vol. V, pp.391, 394–6; Anon., *Life of Thomas Lord Cromwell*, pp.23–4.
17. Sampson, p.258.

18. Rogers, p.533.
19. Ibid.
20. Harpsfield, p.185.
21. Ibid., pp.193, 196.
22. Ibid., p.103.
23. Ibid., p.104.
24. Merriman, Vol. I, pp.417–19.
25. More and Fisher were both canonised by Pope Pius XI in May 1935, 400 years after their deaths.
26. *Letters and Papers*, Vol. VIII, no. 475.
27. Hume, p.27.
28. *Calendar of Letters, Despatches, and State Papers, Spain*, Vol. V, Part I, p.542.
29. Bodleian Library MS Don.C42 fos.21–33.
30. *Letters and Papers*, Vol. VII, Part ii, p.251.
31. Norton, pp.197–8.
32. *Letters and Papers*, Vol. X, no. 901.
33. Ibid.
34. Starkey, *Six Wives*, p.584.
35. *Letters and Papers*, Vol. VII, Part ii, no. 1257.
36. Norton, p.297.
37. Weir, *Six Wives*, p.345; *Letters and Papers*, Vol. X, no. 1069.
38. SP 3/7, fo. 28*r*.
39. Wright, p.156; Merriman, Vol. I, pp.167, 169; *Letters and Papers*, Vol. IX, nos. 509, 632.
40. Wright, p.156.
41. Foxe, Book III, pp.646, 649.
42. *Letters and Papers*, Vol.10, no. 254.
43. *Statutes of the Realm*, Vol. III, pp.575–8.
44. Hume, p.26.
45. Wright, pp.180–1.
46. Ellis, Vol. III, pp.33, 34; Merriman, Vol. I, p.172.
47. Hume, p.26.
48. *Calendar of State Papers, Venice*, Vol. V, p.543.

CHAPTER 11: *'A more gracious mistress'*

1. Merriman, Vol. I, p.439.
2. Ibid., Vol. II, p.1; *Letters and Papers*, Vol. VII, no. 1095.

3. *Calendar of Letters, Despatches, and State Papers, Spain*, Vol. V, Part II, p.59; *Letters and Papers*, Vol. X, nos. 59, 351.
4. *Letters and Papers*, Vol. X, no. 141.
5. Merriman, Vol. I, pp.228–9.
6. Ibid., Vol. II, pp.1–2; *Letters and Papers*, Vol. X, no. 141.
7. *Letters and Papers*, Vol. X, no. 141.
8. Merriman, Vol. II, p.3; *Letters and Papers*, Vol. X, no. 141.
9. *Letters and Papers*, Vol. X, p.102.
10. Ibid., no. 351; Weir, *Six Wives*, p.293.
11. Norton, p.286.
12. *Calendar of Letters, Despatches, and State Papers, Spain*, Vol. V, Part II, p.81.
13. *Letters and Papers*, Vol. X, no. 601.
14. *Calendar of Letters, Despatches, and State Papers, Spain*, Vol. V, Part I, p.484; Part II, p.81.
15. *Letters and Papers*, Vol. X, no. 601; *Calendar of Letters, Despatches, and State Papers, Spain*, Vol. V, Part II, p.81.
16. *Calendar of Letters, Despatches, and State Papers, Spain*, Vol. V, Part I, p.484.
17. Norton, p.325.
18. *Calendar of Letters, Despatches, and State Papers, Spain*, Vol. V, Part I, p.484.
19. *Letters and Papers*, Vol. X, no. 699.
20. *Calendar of Letters, Despatches, and State Papers, Spain*, Vol.V, Part I, p.573.
21. *Letters and Papers*, Vol. X, no. 752.
22. Merriman, Vol. I, p.414.
23. See for example BL Cotton MS Titus B i fos.261r, 264.
24. *Calendar of State Papers, Venice*, Vol. V, p.47.
25. Starkey, *Reign of Henry VIII*, p.101.
26. Merriman, Vol. II, p.36.
27. Ibid., pp.5–6.
28. *Letters and Papers*, Vol. X, no. 351.
29. Ibid.
30. Ibid.
31. *Calendar of Letters, Despatches, and State Papers, Spain*, Vol. V, Part 1, p.125.
32. *Letters and Papers*, Vol. VIII, no. 1105.
33. Ibid., Vol. X, no. 699; *Calendar of Letters, Despatches, and State Papers,*

Spain, Vol. V, Part II, pp.91–3.
34. *Letters and Papers*, Vol. X, no. 699.
35. Ibid., no. 700.
36. Elton, *Reform and Reformation*, p.172.
37. *Letters and Papers*, Vol. X, no. 699.
38. Merriman, Vol. II, p.196.
39. *Calendar of Letters, Despatches, and State Papers, Spain*, Vol. V, Part I, p.466.
40. *State Papers*, Vol. II, pp.551–3n.
41. Ibid., p.552n.
42. *Calendar of Letters, Despatches, and State Papers, Spain*, Vol. II, pp.453–4.
43. *Letters and Papers*, Vol. VIII, no. 938.
44. Cavendish, *Metrical Visions*, Vol. II, p.51.
45. Starkey, *Reign of Henry VIII*, p.83.
46. *Letters and Papers*, Vol. X, no. 351.
47. *Calendar of Letters, Despatches, and State Papers, Spain*, Vol. V, Part II, p.84.

CHAPTER 12: *'The Lady in the Tower'*

1. *Calendar of Letters, Despatches, and State Papers, Spain*, Vol.V, Part II, p.137.
2. *Letters and Papers*, Vol. X, no. 575.
3. *Calendar of Letters, Despatches, and State Papers, Spain*, Vol. V, Part II, p.137.
4. *Letters and Papers*, Vol. X ,no. 700.
5. Cavendish, *Life and Death of Cardinal Wolsey*, p.30.
6. Ibid., p.452.
7. Hume, p.66.
8. Weir, *Lady in the Tower*, p.63.
9. Ibid., p.89.
10. *Calendar of State Papers, Foreign Series, of the Reign of Elizabeth*; Weir, *Lady in the Tower*, p.99.
11. Weir, *Six Wives of Henry VIII*, p.312.
12. BL, Cotton MS Otho C x fo.225.
13. Hume, p.61.
14. Ibid., p.62.
15. Weir, *Lady in the Tower*, p.5.
16. Byrne, Vol. III, no. 648; *Letters and Papers*, Vol. X, no. 909.

17. Wriothesley, Vol. I, p.36.
18. Hume, p.65.
19. Wyatt, *Collected Poems*, p.cxlix.
20. Hume, p.66.
21. Muir, p.201.
22. Hume, pp.63–4.
23. According to the French ambassador, Cromwell remained Wyatt's protector during the years that followed, quelling his royal master's irritation against the courtier on at least one occasion. Kaulek, p.157.
24. Merriman, Vol.II, pp.12, 21.
25. Norton, p.333.
26. Ibid., p.346.
27. *Calendar of Letters, Despatches, and State Papers, Spain*, Vol. V, Part II, p.137.
28. Ibid., p.196.
29. Merriman, Vol. II, p.12.
30. Ibid., pp.12, 21.
31. Amyot, p.65.
32. Merriman, Vol. II, p.12.
33. Ibid.
34. *Letters and Papers*, Vol. X, pp.361–2.
35. Wriothesley, Vol. I, pp.37–8.
36. *Letters and Papers*, Vol. X, p.330.
37. Ibid., nos. 910, 1070.
38. Ibid., no. 792.

CHAPTER 13: *Rebellion*

1. They were not as thorough as the king might have wished. Some of the old 'HA' emblems can still be spotted in the great hall at Hampton Court Palace.
2. Merriman, Vol. II, p.21; *Letters and Papers*, Vol. XI, no. 29.
3. Norton, p.329.
4. *Calendar of Letters, Despatches, and State Papers, Spain*, Vol. V, Part I, p.420.
5. *Letters and Papers*,Vol. X, no. 973.
6. Wood, Vol. II, pp.246–7; Vol. III, p.13.
7. *Letters and Papers*,Vol. X, no. 1110; Merriman, Vol. II, pp.17–18.

8. *Letters and Papers*,Vol. X, no. 24.
9. Ibid., no. 1186; Wood, Vol. II, pp.250–9.
10. Merriman, Vol. II, p.21.
11. *Calendar of Letters, Despatches, and State Papers, Spain*, Vol. V, Part II, p.198.
12. *Letters and Papers*,Vol. XI, no. 148.
13. Wood, Vol. II, p.261.
14. Perry, M., *The Word of a Prince* (London, 1990), p.23.
15. *Letters and Papers*, Vol. X, no. 351.
16. *Calendar of Letters, Despatches, and State Papers, Spain*, Vol. V, Part II, pp.183–6.
17. *Letters and Papers*, Vol. XIV, Part ii, no. 782.
18. Merriman, Vol. II, p.21.
19. Historical Manuscripts Commission, *Rutland* I, p.310.
20. *Letters and Papers*, Vol. XI, p.190, no. 479.
21. Ibid.
22. BL Cotton MS Nero B vi, fo.135r.
23. Starkey, *Reign of Henry VIII*, pp.97–8.
24. Mayer, p.98.
25. This is referred to in a letter from Chapuys to Charles V, 21 April 1536. *Letters and Papers*, Vol. X, no. 699.
26. Ibid.; *Calendar of Letters, Despatches, and State Papers, Spain*, Vol. V, Part II, p.198.
27. *Letters and Papers*, Vol. XI, no. 147.
28. Hume, p.36.
29. Anon., 'Life and Death of Thomas Lord Cromwell', p.368.
30. The three sacraments promoted by the articles were baptism, the eucharist and penance.
31. Merriman, Vol. I, p.142.
32. Ibid., Vol. II, pp.25–9.
33. *Calendar of Letters, Despatches, and State Papers, Spain*, Vol. V, Part I, p.500.
34. Ibid., p.427.
35. Merriman, Vol. II, p.30.
36. Ibid., p.35.
37. *Letters and Papers*,Vol. XI, no. 42.
38. Merriman, Vol. II, pp.31–2, 49.
39. Ibid., pp.131–2.
40. *Letters and Papers*, Vol. XI, no. 786 (3).

41. Ibid., Vol. XII, Part i, no. 163.
42. Ibid., Vol. XI, no. 576.
43. Ibid., no. 576; *Calendar of Letters, Despatches, and State Papers, Spain*, Vol. V, Part II, p.268.
44. *Letters and Papers*, Vol. XI, no. 601.
45. *LP Henry VIII* Vol.XI no.714.
46. Merriman, Vol. II, pp.36, 40–1.
47. Hume, p.35.
48. Ibid., Vol. I, p.137; *Letters and Papers*, Vol. VIII, no. 892.
49. *Letters and Papers*, Vol. XII, Part i, no. 976.
50. *Calendar of Letters, Despatches, and State Papers, Spain*, Vol. V, Part II, no. 268.
51. Hume, p.36; *Calendar of Letters, Despatches, and State Papers, Spain*, Vol. V, Part II, p.313.

CHAPTER 14: *'Some convenyent punishment'*

1. Merriman, Vol. II, p.60.
2. Ibid., p.57.
3. *Letters and Papers*, Vol. XIV, Part ii, no. 782.
4. Ibid., Vol. XII, Part i, nos. 594, 636.
5. Ibid., no. 118.
6. This may have been in order to give greater authority to the king's newborn son, Edward, Prince of Wales.
7. Lord Grey was eventually recalled to London and attainted for treason. He was executed in July 1541.
8. *Letters and Papers*, Vol. XII, Part ii, no. 870.
9. Merriman, Vol. II, p.58.
10. Jane came to share her husband's Catholic beliefs. Together with their daughter Alice, her husband William Whitmore and their children, the family all came to the attention of the authorities as recusant Catholics in the reign of Elizabeth I. Wark, K.R., *Elizabethan Recusansy in Cheshire* (Manchester, 1971), pp.153, 168.
11. *Letters and Papers*, Vol. X, no. 129.
12. Ibid., Vol. XI, no. 233.
13. Ibid., Vol. XVI, no. 578.
14. Merriman, Vol. II, p.53.

15. Starkey, *Reign of Henry VIII*, p.83.
16. *Letters and Papers*, Vol. XII, Part i, no. 678.
17. Merriman, Vol. II, p.60.
18. *Letters and Papers*, Vol. XII, Part ii, no. 97.
19. There is no confirmed portrait of Elizabeth Cromwell. However, it has recently been claimed (with some justification) that the *Portrait of an Unknown Woman* by Holbein, previously thought to have been Katherine Howard, was in fact the wife of Gregory Cromwell. Wilson, D., *Hans Holbein: Portrait of an Unknown Man* (London, 2006), p.215.
20. *Letters and Papers*, Vol. XII, Part ii, no. 629.
21. Wood, Vol. II, pp.355–6.
22. Schofield, pp.277–9; *Letters and Papers*, Vol. XIV, Part ii, no. 556; Wood, Vol. II, pp.267–71.
23. Erler, pp.99–105.
24. Wood, Vol. II, pp.271–5.
25. *Letters and Papers*, Vol. XII, Part ii, nos. 143, 1049; Wood, Vol. II, pp.218–26; Vol. III, pp.96–100.
26. Wood, Vol. II, pp.373–8.
27. Marshall, R.K., *Queen Mary's Women* (Edinburgh, 2006), p.108.
28. *Letters and Papers*, Vol. VII, p.7.
29. Wood, Vol. II, pp.292–3.
30. See Wood, Vols. II and III.
31. Hume, p.73.
32. BL Harley MS 282 fos.211–12; Merriman, Vol. II, p.94.
33. Merriman, Vol. II, p.96.
34. *Letters and Papers*, Vol. XII, Part ii, no. 972.
35. Merriman, Vol. II, pp.96–7.
36. See for example Merriman, Vol. II, p.122.

CHAPTER 15: *'These knaves which rule abowte the kyng'*

1. Merriman, Vol. II, p.98; Hume, p.95.
2. Froude, p.11.
3. *Calendar of Letters, Despatches, and State Papers, Spain*, Vol. II, p.457.
4. Merriman, Vol. I, pp.235–6; *Calendar of State Papers, France,* Vol. XIII, Part I (London, 1899), pp.995, 1147, 1355.
5. Merriman, Vol. II, p.193.

6. Mayer, p.78.
7. Merriman, Vol. II, pp.84–6.
8. Ibid., p.88.
9. Ibid., pp.86–90; Mayer, p.136.
10. Ellis, H., Vol. III, pp.192–4.
11. *Letters and Papers*, Vol. XIII, Part i, no. 1059.
12. Ibid., no. 1281; Ellis, H., Vol. III, pp.208–9.
13. Wood, Vol. II, p.358; *Letters and Papers*, Vol. XIV, Part ii, no. 782.
14. *Letters and Papers*, Vol. XIII, Part i, no. 231; Wriothesley, Vol. I, p.83.
15. *State Papers*, Vol. II, p.551n.
16. Merriman, Vol. II, pp.151–4.
17. Ibid., p.145.
18. Ibid., pp.146–7.
19. Williams, pp.811–14.
20. Strype, *Memorials of Thomas Cranmer*, Vol. I, p.83.
21. *State Papers*, Vol. I, p.540.
22. Wriothesley, Vol. I, p.31.
23. *Letters and Papers*, Vol. XIV, Part ii, no. 399.
24. Norton, p.278.
25. Elton, *Thomas Cromwell*, p.19.
26. *Calendar of Letters, Despatches, and State Papers, Spain*, Vol. VI, Part I, pp.40, 53.
27. Strype, *Ecclesiastical Memorials*, Vol. I, Part i, p.530.
28. Merriman, Vol. II, p.162.
29. Ibid., p.214.
30. TNA KB 8/11/2.
31. Hall, p.827.
32. Wood, Vol. III, pp.67–9; Vol. III, p.112.
33. Ibid., Vol. III, p.112.
34. *Letters and Papers*, Vol.IV, Part i, no. 655.
35. *Calendar of Letters, Despatches, and State Papers, Spain*, Vol. V, Part I, p.442.
36. Merriman, Vol. II, p.167.
37. Elton, *Tudor Revolution in Government*, p.312.
38. Foxe, Book III, p.589.
39. MacCulloch, *Reign of Henry VIII*, p.43.
40. Merriman, Vol. II, p.307.
41. Ibid., pp.216–19.
42. Ibid., pp.216–22.

43. Ibid., p.65.
44. One of the most bitter arguments had arisen in September 1533 when Lord Lisle had attempted to introduce new measures regarding corn. Cromwell had upbraided him for angering the king and for being swayed by the advice of others, in particular his wife: 'For although my lady be right honourable and wise yet yn soche causes as longithe to your auctoritie her advise and discresion can litle prevayle.' The following year, he had chastised the governor for what he termed his 'excesse in living'. Merriman, Vol. I, pp.364, 391.
45. Bray, pp.222–3.
46. Merriman, Vol. II, pp.128–31.
47. Shaxton remained in custody for the rest of the year, and when he and Latimer were pardoned in spring 1540, it was only on condition that they refrain from preaching or coming near London or any of the universities.
48. *Letters and Papers*, Vol. XIV, Part ii, no. 782.
49. Ibid., Vol. XIV, Part i, no. 1260.

CHAPTER 16: *The Flanders Mare*

1. A matrimonial alliance between England and Cleves had been proposed as early as 1530, when the duke had written to Henry VIII promising military assistance if such an alliance was forged. Eager to prove the pedigree of his house, he had assured Henry that he was 'descended from the same stock as the kings of England'. The proposal had come to nothing. *Letters and Papers*, Vol. IV, no. 6364.
2. Merriman, Vol. I, p.244n.
3. Ibid., Vol. II, pp.174–5.
4. Ibid.
5. Froude, p.12.
6. Merriman, Vol. I, p.253.
7. Ibid., Vol. II, pp.175, 200.
8. Ibid., Vol. I, p.262; Hume, p.88.
9. Hume, p.89.
10. Merriman, Vol. II, p.238; Hume, p.90.
11. Merriman, Vol. II, p.241.
12. *Letters and Papers*, Vol. XIV, Part ii, nos. 622, 630.
13. Ibid., Vol. XV, no. 14.

14. Ibid., Vol. XIV, Part ii, no. 707.
15. Merriman, Vol. II, pp.268–76; *Letters and Papers,* Vol. XV, nos. 823, 824.
16. Merriman, Vol. II, pp.268–9.
17. Hume, p.108.
18. Merriman, Vol. II, p.270.
19. Ibid.; *Letters and Papers,* Vol. XV, no. 823.
20. Hume, pp.92–3.
21. Ibid., p.94.
22. Ibid., pp.91–2.
23. Merriman, Vol. II, pp.269–70.
24. Ibid., pp.270–1.
25. Ibid., p.271; Strype, *Ecclesiastical Memorials*,Vol.I, pp.555–6.
26. Strype, *Ecclesiastical Memorials*, Vol. I, Part ii, p.462.
27. Starkey, *Reign of Henry VIII*, pp.101–2.
28. BL Cotton MS Titus B i.
29. Starkey, *Reign of Henry VIII*, pp.98–9.
30. Hall, p.837.
31. Merriman, Vol. I, pp.261–2.
32. Hume, pp.94–5.
33. Merriman, Vol. I, p.284.
34. Hume, pp.100–1.
35. *Letters and Papers,* Vol. XIV, no. 414; Ellis, H., Vol. III, pp.258–65.
36. *Letters and Papers,* Vol. XV, no. 737.

CHAPTER 17: *'Cromwell is tottering'*

1. *Letters and Papers,* Vol. XV, no. 486.
2. Ibid., no. 429.
3. Merriman, Vol. I, p.290.
4. *Letters and Papers,* Vol. XV, no. 611.
5. Ibid., Vol. VII, no. 1554; Vol. XVI, no. 590; Hume, p.105; Merriman, Vol. II, p.60.
6. Merriman, Vol. I, p.290.
7. Plowden, p.101.
8. Weir, *Six Wives*, p.413.
9. Merriman, Vol. II, pp.256–9, 260–1.
10. Wriothesley, Vol. I, p.117.
11. Noble, Vol. I, p.11.

12. Hume, pp.96–7, 99.
13. Ibid., p.97.
14. *Letters and Papers,* Vol. XV, no. 737.
15. Ibid.
16. Merriman, Vol. II, pp.263–4.
17. Strype, *Ecclesiastical Memorials*, Vol. I, Part II, pp.459–60.

CHAPTER 18: *'Mercye mercye mercye'*

1. *Letters and Papers,* Vol. XV, no. 804. By 'laws' they presumably meant the Treasons Act of 1534. The Spanish Chronicle gives a different account of the controversy, claiming that Cromwell's bonnet had blown off as he and his fellow councillors were walking to dinner before the fatal meeting. It was customary if a gentleman lost his cap for any other gentlemen present to doff theirs, but on this occasion nobody did, which aroused Cromwell's suspicions. Hume, p.98.
2. *Letters and Papers,* Vol. XV, no. 804.
3. Anon., 'The Life and Death of Thomas Lord Cromwell' p.368.
4. It included the manors and lordships of Oakham and Langham in Rutland, Clapthorne, Haculton and Pedyngton in Northamptonshire, Blayston in Leicestershire, and the manors of Northelmeham and Beteley in Norfolk. *Letters and Papers,* Vol. XIII, Part i, no. 1519 (2); Part ii, no. 967 (54); Vol. XVI, no. 744.
5. Ibid., Vol. XVI, no. 578.
6. Ibid., Vol. XV, no. 804.
7. Ibid.
8. Wriothesley, Vol. I, p.119.
9. *Letters and Papers,* Vol. XV, no. 804; *Calendar of State Papers, Venice*, Vol. V, pp.86–7.
10. *Letters and Papers,* Vol. XV, no. 804.
11. Foxe, Book III, pp.645, 654.
12. *Letters and Papers,* Vol. XV, no. 766.
13. *Calendar of State Papers, Venice*, Vol. V, p.84.
14. *Letters and Papers,* Vol. XV, no. 766; *Calendar of Letters, Despatches, and State Papers, Spain*, Vol. VI, Part I, pp. 537–9.
15. Merriman, Vol. I, p.294n.
16. Hume, p.36.
17. Ibid., p.99. The varying fortunes of Cromwell's servants after his

fall are described by Robertson: 'Thomas Cromwell's Servants' pp.400–8.

18. BL Cotton MS Otho C x fo.242.
19. This story, from the apocryphal section of the Book of Daniel, tells how a fair Hebrew wife named Susanna was wrongly accused by two lecherous elders who had spied her bathing in her garden. They threatened to call her virtue into question unless she agreed to have sex with them. She refused to be blackmailed and was arrested and condemned to death for promiscuity. But Daniel prevented the sentence from being carried out by demanding that the two men be interrogated. When their stories were found to be inconsistent, they were put to death and Susanna was freed.
20. BL Cotton MS Titus B i fos.267–9.
21. *Letters and Papers,* Vol. XV, no. 803.
22. Ibid., nos. 785, 786, 794.
23. Merriman, Vol. I, p.300.
24. *Letters and Papers,* Vol. XV, no. 842.
25. Ibid., no. 767.
26. Ibid., no. 770.
27. Ibid., nos. 792, 801, 842.
28. Hume, pp.99–100.
29. Burnet, Vol. III, p.296. On his own arrest six years later, Norfolk demanded the same privilege. He 'prayed the lords to intercede with the King, that his accusers might be brought face to face, to say what they had against him; and he did not doubt but it should appear he was falsely accused.' Ibid.
30. Hume, p.100.
31. BL Cotton MS Otho C x fo.241; Hume, p.100.
32. Hume, pp.100–1.
33. *Letters and Papers,* Vol. XVI, no. 578. The Venetian ambassador at Charles V's court in Bruges also reported that 'Cromwell will be burnt, together with two other heretics.' *Calendar of State Papers, Venice*, Vol. V, p.85.
34. BL Additional MS 48028 fos.160–5; *Letters and Papers,* Vol. XV, no. 498. A transcript of the indictment is printed in Burnet, Vol. IV, pp.416–21.
35. BL Additional MS 48028 fos.160–5; *Letters and Papers,* Vol. XV, no. 498.
36. *Letters and Papers,* Vol. XV, no. 804.
37. Ibid., no.847.
38. Foxe claims that Cromwell's intention with this 'violent lawe' had been

'for a certayne secret purpose, to haue entangled the byshop of Wynchester [Gardiner]', but this is pure conjecture. The timing of the Act suggests that it had been an expedient to deal with Lady Margaret Pole.

39. Cavendish, *Metrical Visions*, Vol. II, p.54.
40. *Letters and Papers,* Vol. XV, no. 825.
41. Norton, p.332.
42. BL Cotton MS Otho C x fo.242; Merriman, Vol. II, pp.268–76; *Letters and Papers,* Vol. XV, no. 824. Another (edited) version is provided at no. 823.

CHAPTER 19: *'Many lamented but more rejoiced'*

1. Wood, Vol. III, p.161. Anne was to be richly rewarded for her compliance. She was given possession of Richmond Palace and Bletchingly Manor for life, together with a considerable annual income. She was later awarded some additional manors, including Hever Castle, which became her principal residence. Anne was allowed to keep all her royal jewels, plate and goods in order to furnish her new properties. She was also to be known as the king's 'sister', and as such to take precedence over all his subjects, with the exception of his children and any future wife he might take.
2. *Letters and Papers,* Vol. XV, no. 898.
3. Wood, Vol. III, p.159.
4. Merriman, Vol. II, pp.277–8.
5. Hume, p.103; *Letters and Papers,* Vol. XV, no. 926; Harrison, W.J., 'Hungerford, Walter (1503–1540)' *Dictionary of National Biography,* Vol. XXVIII (Oxford, 1891), pp.259–61.
6. Hume, pp.103–4.
7. Ibid.
8. Hall, p.839; Foxe, Book III, p.654.
9. Merriman, Vol. I, p.301.
10. *Letters and Papers,* Vol. XVI, no. 40; Mayer, p.254.
11. Hall, p.839.
12. Merriman, Vol. I, pp.303–4.
13. Hume, p.104.
14. Foxe, Book III, p.654; Hall, p.839. The Spanish Chronicle gives a different account, and claims that 'the headsman succeeded in striking off the head with a single stroke of the axe.' Hume, p.104.

15. Galton, p.156.
16. Merriman, Vol. I, p.56. Cromwell's remains were excavated in the 1870s and reburied in the vaults of the chapel.
17. *Calendar of Letters, Despatches, and State Papers, Spain*, Vol. VI, Part I, p.243; *Calendar of State Papers, Venice*, Vol. V, p.87.
18. Hall, pp.838–9.
19. Hume, pp.103–4.

EPILOGUE: *'A man of mean birth but noble qualities'*

1. *Calendar of Letters, Despatches, and State Papers, Spain*, Vol. V, Part I, p.436; *Calendar of State Papers, Venice*, Vol. V, p.346.
2. Foxe, Book III, pp.363–5; Strype, *Ecclesiastical Memorials*, Vol. I, Part i, p.561; Holinshed, p.951.
3. Burnet, G. and Burnet, T., *Bishop Burnet's History of his Own Time*, 2 vols. (London, 1724–34), Vol. I, pp.281–2, 454.
4. Cobbett, Vol. I, pp.157, 189.
5. Merriman, Vol. I, p.165.
6. Elton, *Studies in Tudor and Stuart Politics*, Vol. III, p.373.
7. Foxe, Book III, p.654.
8. Ibid., pp.363–5.
9. Ibid., p.646.
10. Hume, p.105; Holder, p.169.
11. *Calendar of Letters, Despatches, and State Papers, Spain*, Vol. VI, Part I, p.541.
12. *Letters and Papers*, Vol. XVI, no. 467.
13. Hume, p.77.
14. Foxe, Book III, p.654.
15. *Letters and Papers*, Vol. XVI, no. 590; Kaulek, p.274.

Picture Acknowledgements

© Alamy: 2 above left/Colin Palmer Photography, 5 below/Skyscan Photolibrary, 8 below/Darryl Gill, 16 below/The Art Gallery Collection. © The British Library Board: 10 below (C.18.d.10). By kind permission of the Duke of Buccleuch & Queensberry KBE: 4 above right. The Dean and Canons of Windsor: 15 below. Frick Collection New York/ Henry Clay Frick Bequest (accession number 1915.1.76)/photo Alamy: 1. © Hatfield House Archives, by courtesy of the Marquess of Salisbury: 16 above left (The Cecil Papers CP1/24). Crown Copyright: Historic Royal Palaces: 16 above left. Houses of Parliament Westminster London: 7 below/photo Bridgeman Art Library. Kunsthistorisches Museum Vienna: 9 above right/photo Bridgeman Art Library. Louvre Paris: 12 above right, 13 above left/photos Bridgeman Art Library. Magdalen College Oxford: 3 above/photo Bridgeman Art Library. Metropolitan Museum of Art New York: 11 above right/The Jules Bache Collection 1949 (accession number 40.7.28). © The National Archives London: 8 above left (E344/22 f2). National Gallery of Art Washington DC: 9 above left/photo Bridgeman Art Library. © National Portrait Gallery London: 8 above right, 14 above right, 15 above. National Portrait Gallery London: 4 below, 7 above left, 10 above, 13 above right /photos Bridgeman Art Library. © National Trust Images: 11 below/photo Dennis Gilbert, 14 left/photo J. Whitaker. His Grace the Duke of Norfolk, Arundel Castle: 14 below right/photo Bridgeman Art Library. Pinacoteca Nazionale Siena: 12 above left/photo Bridgeman Art Library. Private collections: 2 above right and below, 5 above, 6 above, 7 above right, 13 below/photos Bridgeman Art Library. Royal Collection Trust © Her Majesty Queen Elizabeth II, 2014: 3 below, 4 above left, 6 below, 9 below, 11 above left/photos Bridgeman Art Library. Villa Farnese Italy: 12 below/photo Bridgeman Art Library.

INDEX

INDEX